ONT • RICHARD DUMONTIER • BENOIT DUMOULIN • MARC DUMOULIN • YVES DUMOULIN • ROBERT DUNCAN • PAUL DUNFORD • MATHEW DUNSKI • NHAN THI DUONG • THIEN HUONG DUONG • RICHARD DUPERCHE • CLAUDE DUPERRE • REAL DUPLESSIS • CLAUDE DUPLESSIS • SYLVAIN DUPLESSIS • PATRICE DUPONT • NORMAND DUPONT •
ONT • DANIEL DUPONT • DENIS DUPONT • PATRICK DUPONT • MARIE JOSEE DUPRAS • SERGE DUPRE • JEAN FRANCOI DUPRE • PIERRE DUPUIS • STEPHANE DUPUIS • LYETTE DUPUIS • STEPHANE DUPUIS • FRANCINE DUPUIS • MARIO DUPUIS • FR … QUETTE
ETTE • MARC ANDRE DURANCEAU • DAVID DURAND • ISABELLE DURAND • JEAN YVES DURANLEAU • GAETAN DUREAU • ALAIN DUROCHER • JOHANNE DUROCHER • ROBERT DUROCHER • SYLVAIN DUSSAULT • MICHEL DUSSAULT • JOHANNE DU … DUTTA •
• JIRI DVORAK • ROSANNAH DWARKA • JESS DZIEGIELEWSKI • GERRY DZIUB • MARC DZUMEDZEY • LINDA EAMES BUCHE • GORDON EASEY • ROGER GRANT EATOCK • LINDA ECKERLIN • SERGE EDE • MARK EDER • JOSEPH EDERHY • RICHARD … UESSY •
AZ • MICHEL ELBAZ • FEISAL ELDARDIRY • ALINE ELHAGE • SYLVAIN ELIE • STEPHANE ELISSON ANTOINE • AMER ELJAM • JAMES ELLIOT • BRUCE ELLIOTT • MARTIN ELSENER • JEAN CLAUDE ELYSEE • ALICE EMILI • DENIS EMOND • PAUL EMOND • JEAN … ERNESTI
COBAR • ROBERT ESCRIVA • NOORALI ESMAIL • ANTONIO ESPOSITO • FRANCOIS ESTRADE • ALAIN ETHIER • JEAN LUC ETHIER • MARTIN ETHIER • FIDELIO EUGENIO • HOWARD EVA • NEKTARIA EVANGELIDIS • ROBERT EVANS • KATHLEEN EVE … FABRE •
FARD • MARC FAILLE • GARY FAILLER • ALAIN FALARDEAU • GIUSEPPE FALCICCHIO • ITALO FALCONE • GIUSEPPE FALDUTO • CAMERON FALLOW • GEORGES FAMERY • FILIP FARAG • HANI FARAG • PIERRE FARAH LAJOIE • PAUL FARANT • ANA … RRANT •
RRELL • MARK FARRELL • SAM FARRUGGIA • JEAN FATTAL • CHRISTIANE FATTER • SERGE FAUBERT • ROBERT FAUCHER • CLAUDE FAUCHER • JEAN-PAUL FAUCHER • ERIC FAUTEUX • DANIEL FAUVELLE • BENOIT FAVREAU • RICHARD FEATHERSTONI … FEDELE
O FEITO • JEAN DENIS FELX • YVAN FELX • HENRY FENCHEL • MICHEL FERLAND • FRANCOIS FERLAND • ALAIN FERLAND • CLAUDE FERLAND • PATRICE FERLAND • GILLES FERLAND • SUZIE FERLAND • NORMAND FERLAND • JULES FERLAND • F … NANDES •
NANDES • BAUTISTA FERNANDEZ • PAOLO FERRANTE • CLAUDE FERRARI • ELIZABETH FERREIRA • PAULO FERREIRA • BERNARD FERRIER • EMMANUEL FETICHANOPOULOS • GERALD FEX • YVON FEX • CLAUDETTE FEX • CHARLES FICHET • ROBERT … HEL FIL
COI FIL • YVES FILIATRAULT • MICHEL FILIATREAULT • SERGE FILIATREAULT • RICHARD FILION • GAETAN FILION • GILBERT FILION • BERNARD FILLION • DENIS FILLION • ROBERT FILTEAU • JONATHAN FINDLAY • BENJAMIN FINKELSTEIN • IRINA … IORINI •
ENZE • ALLEN FIRTH • GUSTAVO FISCINA • MICHEL FISET • MICHAEL FISETTE • ROBERT FISHER • DOUGLAS FISHER • SELWYN FISHER • EDITH FITOUSSI • RICHARD FITZMAURICE • JAMES FITZPATRICK • GORDON FLETCHER • DAVID JOHN FLET … LEURY •
URY • ERIC FLORENT • ARTURO FLORES • GEORGES FLUET • MARIO JORGE FONSECA • SERGE FONTAINE • COLLEEN FONTAINE • ALAIN FONTAINE • DANIEL FONTAINE • DANIEL FONTAINE • BERNARD FONTAINE • SOO GUEK FOO • RICHARD FORAND • … ORCIER
ORD • MARGARET FORDE • BOB FORDHAM • TERESA FOREST • PIERRE FOREST • RICHARD FOREST • LUCIE FOREST • JACQUES FORGET • MICHEL FORGET • FRANCOIS FORGET • NORMAND FORGET • NICOLAS FORGET • HUGUETTE FORGET • A … FORGET • PIERRE FORGET • GHISLAIN FORGET •
RGUES • EMIDIA FORLINI • DOMENIC FORTE • RICHARD FORTIER • RICHARD FORTIER • MARTHA FORTIER • YVAN FORTIER • JEAN YVES FORTIER • CLAUDE FORTIER • PATRICE FORTIER • FERNAND FORTIER • GERALDINE FORTIN • YVES FORTIN • PIERRE FORTIN • CHRISTIAN FORTIN • SONIA FORTIN • GASTON MARC FORTIN • FRANCE FORTIN
IN • YVAN FORTIN • ROBERT FORTIN • CLAUDE FORTIN • STEVE FORTIN • JEANOT FORTIN • MICHEL FORTIN • DOMINIQUE FORTIN • DANY FORTIN • CARL FORTIN • MARC ANDRE FORTIN • CARMINE CARL FORTUNATO • GARY FOSTER • PIERRE FOSTER • LISA FOSTER • MARC FOUCAULT • DANIEL FOUGERE • JOCELYNE FOULIDIS • LUC FOUQUETTE
OURNELLE • BENOIT FOURNELLE • PIERRETTE FOURNIER • JEAN FOURNIER • ISABELLE FOURNIER • LUC FOURNIER • CAROLE FOURNIER • RICHARD FOURNIER • MARIE JOSEE FOURNIER • PATRICE FOURNIER • PIERRE FOURNIER • ANNE FOX • SYLVAIN FRADETTE • ORAZIO FRANCH • ROBERT JAMES FRANCIS • ALAIN FRANCOEUR •
ANCOEUR • CLAUDE FRANCOEUR • GASTON FRANCOEUR • JOCELYNE FRANCOEUR • JEAN FRANCOEUR • GERALD FRANCOEUR • ALAIN FRANCOEUR • LUCIE FRANCOEUR • YVAN FRANCOEUR • JEAN MARIE FRANCOIS • PIETRO FRANCOLINI • MARIO FRAPPIER • PIERRE FRAPPIER • STEPHANE FRAPPIER • BERTRAND FRASER • MARTIN FRASER
FRASER PICHE • YVES FRECHETTE • JOANNE FRECHETTE • GILBERT FRECHETTE • ANNIE FRECHETTE • GERMAIN FRECHETTE • ALAIN FRECHETTE • GUY FRECHETTE • MICHEL FRECHETTE • JACQUES FRECHETTE • DENIS FRECHETTE • SERGE FRECHETTE • DENIS FRECHETTE • STEPHANE FRECHETTE • MICHEL FRECHETTE • ALAIN FRECHETTE
ECHETTE • ERIC FRECHETTE • ROBERT FREEMAN • DOUGLAS FREEMAN • PHILIP FRENCH • STEPHANE FRENETTE • SERGE FRENETTE • MARCEL FRENETTE • MARTIN FRENETTE • ROBERT FRENETTE • ROGER FRIGON • ERNEST LOUIS FRITZ • MICHAEL DESM FROST • MARIO FUENTES • GILLES FUGERE • PETER FULGINITI • MICHAEL FULGINITI
INO • GEORGE WILLI FULLER • GRAEME FULTON • GLENN FUNAMOTO • SUSAN FUNNELL • VINCENZO FURGIUELE • MICHAEL FURLONG • GIOVANNI FUSCO • RODRIGUE GABAUD • ODILE GADOUA • DANIEL GADOURY • CAROLE GAGNE • THERESE GAGNE • DANIEL GAGNE • PASCAL GAGNE • STEPHANE GAGNE • JULIEN GAGNE • PIERRE GAGNE
IE • DANIEL GAGNE • GHISLAIN GAGNE • NORMAND GAGNE • GAETAN GAGNE • PAUL GAGNE • REJEAN GAGNE • RONALD GAGNE • ANDRE JR GAGNE • DANIEL GAGNE • CLAUDE GAGNE • RICHARD GAGNE • REJEAN GAGNE • GERALD GAGNIERE • LUC GAGNIERE • ROLAND GAGNON • STEPHANE GAGNON • LYNE GAGNON • LUC GAGNON •
ON • JACQUES GAGNON • PIERRE GAGNON • ANDRE GAGNON • ANDRE GAGNON • ANNIE GAGNON • MARTIN GAGNON • SERGE GAGNON • SYLVAIN GAGNON • MICHEL GAGNON • PAUL GAGNON • YVES GAGNON • GUY GAGNON • LINDA GAGNON • RENE GAGNON • ROGER GAGNON • BERNARD GAGNON • JACQUES GAGNON • ROSE MARIE GAGNON
GAGNON • CLAUDINE GAGNON • BERNARD GAGNON • ROBERT GAGNON • PATRICK GAGNON • JACQUES GAGNON • MICHEL GAGNON • ROCH GAGNON • PAULA GAGNON • REJEAN GAGNON • CAROLE GAGNON • DANIEL GAGNON • BENOIT GAGNON • DENIS GAGNON • PATRICK GAGNON • TONY GAGNON • JEAN GAGNON • PAULINE GAGNON •
ON • GERMAIN GAGNON • WALTER GAGNON • SERGE GAILLOUX • NORMAND GALARNEAU • ERIC GALARNEAU • JORGE GALEGO • OTTORINO GALESSO • MARTIN GALIC • MARC GALIN • DOMINIC GALIPEAU • DAVID GALLAGHER • FRANCIS GALLAGHER • THOMAS GALLAGHER • RENAUD GALLANT • MARC ANDRE GALLANT • PATRICK GALLANT •
E GALLANT • MARIO GALLE • RENE GALLIEN • RICHARD GALLIVAN • SHARON GALLOTI • LISE GALLOU • BRIAN GALT • GERARD GAMACHE • MICHELE GAMACHE • JACQUES GAMACHE • BERTRAND GAMACHE • SERGIO GAMMIERI • HASUMATI GANDHI • DINO GANGAI • ROBERT GAOUETTE • SYLVAIN GARAND • CHRISTIANE GARANT • JEANNIE GARBE
MARC GARCEAU • MANUEL DIAS GARCIA • JESUS GARCIA • ARTURO GARCIA COCINA • ANDRE GAREAU • MARIE CLAUDE GAREAU • JOVETTE GAREAU • JEAN GAREAU • DANIEL GAREAU • NEIL GARGUL • ERIC GARIEPY • CHARLES GARNEAU • DIANE GARNEAU • ANTONIO GAROFALO • DAVID GARVIN • DAVID GARZON • LUCIE GASCON •
SPAR • ANDRE GASSE • PIERRE GATIEN • ANDRE GATINEAU • CLAUDE GAUDET • PIERRE GAUDET • RAYMOND GAUDETTE • JACQUES GAUDETTE • JOSEE GAUDREAU • MICHEL GAUDREAU • LEON GAUDREAU • GERALD GAUDREAULT • ERIC GAUDRON • YVES GAULIN • ALAIN GAULIN • DANIEL GAULIN • LINDA GAULT • DANIEL GAUMOND •
AUTHIER • GAETAN GAUTHIER • DANIEL GAUTHIER • MARYSE GAUTHIER • DORIS GAUTHIER • DENIS GAUTHIER • RICHARD GAUTHIER • GILLES GAUTHIER • LIN GAUTHIER • SYLVAIN GAUTHIER • LISE GAUTHIER • PIERRE GAUTHIER • ROCH GAUTHIER • STEPHANE GAUTHIER • ANDRE GAUTHIER • SYLVAIN GAUTHIER • JEAN-YVES GAUTHIER •
THIER • ANDRE GAUTHIER • DENIS GAUTHIER • GILLES GAUTHIER • PHILIPPE GAUTHIER • SYLVIE GAUTHIER • RENE GAUTHIER • JEANNINE GAUTHIER • CAROL GAUTHIER • YVES GAUTHIER • PIERRE GAUTHIER • LAURAINE GAUTHIER-MOROSO • CLAUDE GAUVIN • RICHARD GAUVIN • GILBERT GAUVIN • JEAN FRANCOI GAUVIN •
UVREAU • HELENE GAUVREAU FONTAINE • HUSSAIN GAYA • RAYMOND GAZAILLE • JOSEPH GAZALE • MANNY GDALEVITCH • IHOR GEGAR • ALAIN GELINAS • SERGE GELINAS • GERALD GELINAS • SYLVAIN GELINAS • MANON GELINAS • ROSAIRE GELINAS • JEAN PIERRE GELINAS • MARIO GEMME • GILBERT GENDREAU • JEAN LUC GENDRON
DRON • PIERRE PAUL GENDRON • MARCEL GENDRON • RICHARD GENDRON • ANDRE GENDRON • NICOLE GENDRON • SYLVAIN GENDRON • REAL GENDRON • MARTIN GENEREUX • SYLVAIN GENEREUX • DANIEL GENEST • LISE GENEST • LUC GENEST • ROBERT GENEST • ANGELO GENNARO • MARINO GENTILE • DOMINIC GENTILO • ROY GENTRY
EOFFRAY • DOMINIQUE GEOFFRION • COSTAS GEORGAKLIS • PETER GEORGAKOPOULOS • LUC GEORGE • DAVID LLOYD GEORGE • LUC GERBER • DANIEL GERMAIN • PAUL GERMAIN • PATRICK GERMAIN • MICHELINE GERMAIN • ROGER GERMAIN • LOUIS GERMAIN • CELINE GERMAIN • SYLVAIN GERMAIN • MARTIN GERMAIN • MARTIN GERMAIN
RMAIN • ANDRE GERMAIN • PAUL GERVAIS • REAL GERVAIS • DANIEL GERVAIS • RENE GERVAIS • ANDRE GERVAIS • HELENE GERVAIS • MICHEL GERVAIS • SERGE GERVAIS • NATHALIE GERVAIS HOWELL • JOHN GETTY • ELIAS GHADBAN • NORMA GHANTY • ZIA-UL-HASSA GHAZNAVI • ALFREDO GIACOMIN • PATRICK GIARD • CHRISTIAN GIARD
IN • ROSS GIBSON • DIANA GIGOUX • ROBERT GIGUERE • ROCH GIGUERE • JEAN CLAUDE GIGUERE • MARCO GIGUERE • MARGO GIGUERE • YVON GIGUERE • ANDRE GIGUERE • ERIC GIGUERE • GILLES GIGUERE • JACQUES GILBERT • CLAUDE GILBERT • MAURICE GILBERT • ROBERTO GILBERT • SERGE GILBERT • MARCEL GILBERT •
T • OLIVIER GILBERT • DENIS GILBERT • KENNETH GILBERT • MAURICE GILCHRIST • MICHAEL GILFILLAN • IGOR-DAVID GILKA • LOUISE GILL • RUDOLPH GILL • ROBERT GILLESPIE • DONALD GILLIS • GLENN GILMORE • DEREK GILMOUR • LUIGI GILUNI • DANNY GINGRAS • MICHEL ANDRE GINGRAS • JEAN GINGRAS • DARIO GINGRAS •
GRAS • FERNAND GINGRAS • ANDRE GINGRAS • LOUISE GINGRAS • ROBERT GINGRAS • DENISE GIOCONDESE • ARISTIDE FRA GIOFFRE • GINO GIORGI • ALAIN GIRARD • GARY GIRARD • DENIS GIRARD • MONIQUE GIRARD • JEAN GIRARD • PAUL GIRARD • NATHALIE GIRARD • MARLENE GIRARD • SYLVAIN GIRARD • GAETAN GIRARD • REAL GIRARD
IRARD • PHILIPPE GIRARD • ANDRE GIRARD • PATRICK GIRARD • GASTON GIRARD • LUC GIRARD • ISABELLE GIRARD • CLAUDE GIRARD • BRIAN GIRARD • JEAN-FRANCOI GIRAUD • JEAN PIERRE GIRAUDOU • LOUIS MARTIN GIROUARD • CHARLOTTE GIROUX • MAURICE GIROUX • NEIL GIROUX • YOLANDE GIROUX • GILLES GIROUX • JUDITH GIROUX
ROUX • JAIME GISBERT • DANIEL GIUGLEA • ELIO GIULIONE • EUGENIO GIUNTI • MICHAEL GIVERIN • RICHARD GLADU • MICHAEL GLADU • WAYNE GLASGOW • JACQUES GLOBENSKY • CLIVE GLOCKLING • MICHAEL GLOWACKI • SUZIE GOBEIL • STEPHANE GOBEIL • SYLVAIN GODARD • JOANNE GODARD • CHRISTIAN GODARD •
ODCHARLES • DAVID GODIN • JEAN PIERRE GODIN • FRANCOIS GODIN • SYLVAIN GODIN • JEAN MARC GODIN • STEPHANE GODIN • MICHEL GODIN • RICHARD GODIN • GUY GODIN • LORNA GODLINGTON • RAYNALD GODON • MICHEL GODON • STUART GOGARTY • MAURICE GOHIER • LESLIE GOLDSTEIN • JOSEE GOLLAIN • ROBERT GOMOLA •
NCALVES • BERNARD GONON • GUY GONTHIER • ANTONIO GONZALES • LINDA GOODFELLOW • BILL GOODWIN • DEBBIE GOODWIN • SAMUEL GOPAUL • CRAIG GORDON • RICHARD GORDON • LEIB GORDON • MICHEL GORDON • GUENTHER GORITSCHNIG • DAVID GORMLEY • BERNARD GOSSELIN • LINDA GOSSELIN • JOSEE GOSSELIN •
ELIN • MICHEL GOSSELIN • ROGER GOSSELIN • GILLES GOSSELIN • GERALD GOSSELIN • FRANCE GOSSELIN • OLIVIER GOUDARD • ATHANASIA GOUDAS • YVON GOUDREAU • WILLIAM ERNE GOUDREAU • ROGER GOUDREAU • FERNAND GOUDREAU • BERNARD GOUDREAULT • VINCENT GOUDREAULT • CHRISTIAN GOUGEON • JEAN
UGEON • CHRISTIAN GOULET • ROBERT GOULET • JEAN PIERRE GOULET • DIANE GOULET • NICOLE GOUPIL • MICHEL GOUPIL • ALAIN GOUR • DANIEL GOUR • CLAUDE GOURAUD • GERMAIN GOYER • GEORGES GOYER • DANIEL GOYER • JULIE GOYER • LUC GOYETTE • CONRAD GOYETTE • ROBERT GOYETTE • MICHEL GOYETTE •
BOSKY • KURT GRABOWSKI • GEORGE GRAHAM • ROBERT GRAHAM • PIERRE GRAND'MAISON • JEANNE D'ARC GRAND'MAISON • GHISLAIN GRANDCHAMP • GEOFF GRANICH • CICERO GRANJA • PIERRE GRANO • HORST GRANZ • BEN GRASS • FRANK GRASSO • YVES GRATTON • LAURENT GRATTON • RICHARD GRAVEL • GHISLAIN GRAVEL •
AVEL • JEAN-MARC GRAVEL • GILLES GRAVEL • YVAN GRAVEL • LUC GRAVEL • BENOIT GRAVEL • DENIS GRAVEL • DEBBIE GRAVEL • NICOLE GRAVEL • LOUIS GRAVEL • LOUIS GRAVEL • MARIO GRAVEL • NEIL GRECHUK • LESLIE GREEN • GARY GREEN • WILLIAM GREENING • MICHEL GREFFARD • RONALD GREGOIRE • JOSEF GREGOR •
ER • DANIEL GRENIER • REJEAN GRENIER • JEAN CLAUDE GRENIER • PIERRE GRENIER • FRANCINE GRENIER • MARCEL GRENIER • JEAN-GUY GRENIER • YVES GRENIER • GILBERT GRENIER • SERGE GRENIER • GUYLAINE GRENIER • CHARLES GRENIER • NORMAND GRENIER • GUY GRENIER • ALAIN GRENIER • RALPH GRIFFIN • THOMAS GRIFFIN
FFIS • GREG GRIFFITH • MARIUS L GRIGORE • JEAN BERNARD GRIMARD • GAETAN GRIMARD • FRANCINE GRIMARD • PIERRE GRIMARD • FRANCOIS GRIMARD • BRUNO GRISE • MARTIN GRISE • CSABA GROF • JEAN GROLEAU • PIERRE GRONDIN • THIERRY GRONDIN • VICTOR GRONKOWSKI • PETER GRONKOWSKI • GUY GROTHE • MICHEL GROULX
A GUARINO • MICHEL GUAY • MICHEL GUAY • DENIS GUAY • FRANCOIS GUAY • MARC GUAY • STEPHANE GUAY • ALAIN GUAY • PETER GUAY • MARTIN GUAY • GERARD GUAY • ANDRE GUENET • LUC GUENETTE • CARLE GUENETTE • ROBERT GUERARD • DENIS GUERARD • MARCEL GUERETTE • JEANNE GUERIN • RICHARD GUERIN • ANDRE GUERIN
RIN • LUC GUERIN • DANIEL GUERNON • ROGER GUERTIN • ROLLAND GUERTIN • JEAN GUEVREMONT • JOSEPH GUGLIELMI • CIRO GUIDA • DANIEL GUIDI • NORMAND GUILBAULT • LUCIE M GUILBAULT • RAYMOND GUILBAULT • FRANCE GUILBAULT • MICHEL GUILBERT • PAUL GUILLEMENOT • HUGUETTE GUILLEMETTE • REAL GUILLEMETTE •
LLEMETTE • DENIS GUILLEMETTE • BERNADETTE S GUILLO • CLAUDE GUILLOT • REJEAN GUILLOTTE • JOHN GUIMOND • MARK GUIMOND • RONALD GUIMOND • SYLVIE GUIMOND • REJEAN GUIMONT • GILLES GUINARD • JOCELYN GUINDON • CLAUDE GUINDON • VITAL GUINDON • LYNE GUINDON • NORMAND GUINDON • SYLVAIN GUITE •
TE • LUC GUITE • VINOD GULATI • MOHINDER GULATI • KEVIN GUMBLEY • KIRK RICHARD GUMBLEY • MARTHA GUTIERREZ • MICHEL GUY • MARIE GUYON • MARK GUZEVICIUS • BERNARDO GUZMAN • MICHEL GUZZI • TRA HA • REMI HABAK • MICHEL HABEL • ROBERT HABJANIC • LOUIS PHILIP HACHE • JOSEPH WILLI HACHEY • ROGER HACHEY
HADE • SHEILA HADWIN • MOHAMMED HAFEEZ • MARGARET HAFNER • JEREMY HAINES • JAMES HAINES • ABDULRAZAK HAJIBRAHIM • MOKTAR HALFI • SANDRA HALL • PHILIPPE HALL • MARIO HALLE • ALFRED HAMACHER • SYLVAIN HAMANN • ROBERT HAMBSCH • MICHEL HAMEL • CLEMENT HAMEL • NICOLE HAMEL • DENIS HAMEL • ALAIN HAMEL
MEL • BENOIT HAMELIN • ROBERT HAMELIN • JOCELYN HAMELIN • MAURICE HAMELIN • DANIEL HAMELIN • HELENE HAMELIN • PIERRE HAMELIN • JEAN MARC HAMELIN • MICHAEL HAMER • MICHEL HAMEURY • MIKE HAMILTON • MOUNIR HANNA • RICHARD HANON • LOUISE HANSELL • RALPH HANSEN • AMAN HAQUE • SALAMON HARAVAN •
DING • RICHARD HARDING • MICHEL HARDOUIN • GHISLAIN HARDY • PIERRE HARDY • YVES HAREL • ROBERT HARGRAVE • PETER JOHN HARGROVE • EDWARD JOHN HARING • PATRICK HARKANS • DANNY HARKIN • DANNY HARNOIS • LILIAN HARPER • THOMAS HARPER • JAMES HARPER • RODRIGUE HARRISON • PETER HARRISON •
SON • DENNIS HARVEY • DANY HARVEY • GUY HARVEY • GONTRAN HARVEY • PAULINE HARVEY • DANIEL HARVEY • CLAIRE HARVEY • MICHEL HARVEY • MARINA HARVEY • ANDRE HARVEY • HENRY HARWOOD • ULRICH HASS • GABRIEL HASSAN • PHIL HATCHELL • GEORGE HATZIPETROS • RONALD BENSO HAUGHTON • CLIFFORD HAUGHTON
SLER • MARTIAL HAVARD • JACQUELINE HAYES • FRANCE HAYES • DAVID HAYES • JOHN HAYES • ALLAN HAYES • LORNE HEALEY • PATRICK HEALY • JOHN HEATH • THOMAS HEATHER • LAURA HEATHFIELD CAPALDI • PHILIPPE HEBERT • RONALD HEBERT • MICHEL HEBERT • JAMES HEBERT • GUY HEBERT • MARC HEBERT • MICHEL HEBERT
EBERT • YVES HEBERT • MAURICE HEBERT • JEAN PAUL HEBERT • JULES HEBERT • MARIO HEBERT • ROLAND HEBERT • PETER HEIBL • SYLVAIN HELIE • SUZANNE HEMMINGSEN • JEAN PIERRE HENAFF • SYLVAIN HENAULT • SYLVAIN HENAULT • WAYNE HENDERSON • RONALD HENDERSON • BRUCE HENDERSON • ROY HENNEMANN •
RY • GLENN HENZELL • RICHARD HEPPELL • ROLLANDE HERARD • GARRY HERBERS • JOSE HERNANDEZ • ANA DELMY HERNANDEZ • JOSE HERNANDEZ • YVES HEROUX • CLAUDE HEROUX • YVAN HEROUX • DANIEL HEROUX • LUC HEROUX • JOHN HERRON • PIA HERZELE • DAVE HETHRINGTON • CHRISTIAN HETU • GILLES HETU • ERIC HEUSER
WITT • LINDSAY HICKMAN • STUART HILL • PAMELA HILLIER • KAREN HILLSDON • ZOE HINDLE • VINCENT S HINDS • HAROLD HINTON • TERRY HINTON • DENIS HINTON • KHOA VAN HOANG • LUC HOANG VAN • PHUOC HOANG-VAN • LAWRENCE HOBBS • JOHN HOBBS • MICHAEL HOBBS • MICHAEL HODGE • JOHN HODGKINSON • JANET HOGAN
GUE • ANDRE HOGUE • BENOIT HOGUE • MURL HOLDER • JOHN HOLDING • WAYNE HOLLINGSWORTH • LYNDA HOLLYLEE • JOANNE HOLOWCHAK • WILSON HOLT • CHRISTIAN HOLZL • ESTHER HOLZMULLER • FRANCOIS HOPKINS • HUBERT HOPPER • IGOR HORIL • DANIEL HORMAN • JOHN HORNYAK • MARIANNA HORVATH • JOSEPH HORVATH
LES HOSMANS • ADEL HOSNY • AMER HOSNY • DANIEL HOSSON • MICHEL-BERNA HOUDE • GUY HOUDE • RONALD HOUDE • MICHEL HOUDE • STEPHANE HOUDE • JACQUES HOUDE • ALAIN HOUDE • SUSAN HOUGHTEN • CAMILLE HOULE • RENE HOULE • JACQUES HOULE • RENE HOULE • ALAIN HOULE • BERTRAND HOULE • WILLIAM HOUSTON
VINGTON • GERALD HOWARD • MICHAEL HOWARD • RICHARD HOWARTH • ANGIE HOWELL • LEONARD HOWELL • URBAN HOWLETT • JOHN GILBERT HOYLAND • MIROSLAV HROMY • ZENON HRYCHOWIAN • THANH TUNG HUA • JOSEPH HUANG • EDOUARD HUARD • MICHEL HUARD • BERTRAND HUARD • DOMINIQUE HUBERT • LOUIS HUBERT •
RT • DAVID HUDDLESTON • LINE HUDON • EDWARD HUDSON • LESLIE HUGHES • TREVOR HUGHES • DAVID JOHN HUGHES • DAVID HUGHES • YVES HUGRON • BARRY HUM • PAUL HUNT • RON HUNT • GRAHAM HUNTER • PIERRE HUOT • RICHARD HUOT • MICHEL HUOT • LAURENT HUOT • MICHAEL HUOT • LORRAINE HUOT • BERNARD HUOT •
PPERETZ • MICHAEL HURLBERT • SERGE HURTUBISE • JACQUES HURTUBISE • SUSAN HURYN • VERMONT HUSSETT • HERBERT HUSSON • DOMINIC HUSSON • ERIC HUSSON • DONALD HUSTON • DANIEL HUTTON • LISA HUUMO • AAMER HYJAZIE • DANIEL HYNES • ROBERTO IACOBACCI • GIOVANNI IACOBO • GUY IANNUZZI • SANDRO IAROCCI
CI • TANIL IDINIAN • ARTHUR IKNEJIAN • VLAD ILIESCU • DINO INFANTINO • KENNETH INGRAM • IGINO IOANNONI • BURT IRVING • MAURICE ISCONTE • JOHN ISHERWOOD • CARMINE IULIANO • OANA RUXANDR IVANOV • LARRY IVKOVIC • BRENT JACKLE • ROBERT JACKSON • MARTIN JACKSON • MIRIAM JACKSON LAWRENCE • ROGER JACOB •
• SEBASTIEN JACQUES • ALAIN JACQUES • CLAUDE JACQUES • SYLVAIN JACQUES • JOCELYN JACQUES • ROBERT JACQUES • GAETAN JACQUES • ANAAM ABOOD JAFAR • RENE JALBERT • GAETAN JALBERT • BERTRAND JALBERT • SYLVAIN JALBERT • JOSEPH JAMES • KEITH JAMES • JOHN JANISZEWSKI • ROBERT JANKOVICS •
ROSINSKI • LEON JARRABET • ELZBIETA JAZWINSKA • MARIO JEAN • ALAIN JEAN • LYNDA JEAN • GAETAN JEAN • MARIO JEAN • LUCIEN JEAN • EMMANUEL JEAN DENIS • EVEILLARD JEAN LOUIS • CLAUDEL JEAN PAUL • DENIS JEAN-LOUIS • ALAIN JEANNOTTE • HANS JEHLE • MALDWYN JENKINS • KAREL JERABEK • DENIS JEROME •
RONIMO • MOHAMEDAL JETHA • JEAN CLAUDE JETTE • CHRISTIAN JETTE • PATRICK JETTE • MICHEL JETTE • WILLIAM JEWER • MARYLIN JEWER • DIANA LYNN JEWER • ALEXANDRE JIPA • DENIS JOANNETTE • GUY JOANNETTE • DORIS JOBIN • PIERRE JOBIN • YVON JOBIN • CHRISTIAN JOBIN • RICHARD JOBIN • MARCEL JODOIN • GUY JODOIN
N • ALLAN JOHNSON • DAVID JOHNSON • PEARL JOHNSON • ERROL BRENTF JOHNSON • PAUL AUSTIN JOHNSON • MICHEL JOHNSON • DANIEL JOHNSON • DEAN JOHNSON • LARS JOHAN JOHNSSON • ROBERT JOHNSTON • PIERRE JOLICOEUR • MARC JOLICOEUR • DANIEL JOLY • JACQUES JOLY • JEAN JOLY • JOANNE JOLY • MICHELINE JOLY
LY CARLE • ALAIN JONCAS • JOSEPH WILLI JONES • GLYN JONES • KEVIN JONES • LINDA JOOSEN • SHAWN JORDAN • WAYNE JOTKUS • MARCEL JOUVE • BRUNO JOYAL • MARIO JOYAL • MICHEL JOYAL • MARC JUBINVILLE • SUZIE JUBINVILLE • SYLVAIN JUILLET • PAUL JULIEN • GEORGE JUNDZIS • DENIS JUNEAU • REJEAN JUNEAU •
NEAU • FERNANDO JUNIO • ESPINO JURADO • MICHEL JUTEAU • RONALD JUTRAS • MOHAMED KACEM • DESMOND KACK • DANIEL KAESER • AHMAD KAFAEI • FASSI KAFYEKE • THOMAS KAGAWA • BEDROS KAHWAJIAN • TARJINDER KAINTH • TANIA KALANDJIAN • MARIE KALAS • NASIM KALIM • CONSTANTINA KALIMERIS • JOHN KALIOTZAKIS •
LIO • EVAN KALOXILOS • AUGUSTINE KAM-THONG • SARKIS KAMANJIAN • DIMITRA KAMPER • KENNETH KAN • ROGER KANASH • GEORGE KANIEWSKI • BRANKO KAPUSTA • GEORGE KARAMINAS • MARIE KARAOGLANIAN • CAROLYN KATORSKY • GEORGE KATSILAKIS • JIMMY KATSOUROS • PAUL KAVANAGH • DIKRAN KAZAROSSIAN • DAVID KEARN
EENE • JOHN KELERIS • HANS KELLER • JOHN KELLY • CYNTHIA KELLY • JOHN KELLY • RUSSELL KENNARD • JACQUES KENNEDY • LYETTE KENNEY • LEO KENNY • MICHAEL KERNER • STEWART KERNOHAN • ISTVAN KERTESZ • ERIC KERUB • STANLEY KERWIN • RANGACHARI KESAVAN • ARA KESSERIAN • WASIL KHAN • MINAWAR KHAN •
B • AHAROUN KHOBASARIAN • PIERRE KHOKAZ • PHALIKA KHONG • KHAMTOUN KHOUNSOMBATH • MAURICE KHOURY • HEDILI KILANI • JASON KILGER • CHHENG LEANG KIM • JACKIE KING • BRYANT KING • FERNANDO KING • JAMES KINGSLEY • GUILLAUME KINGSLEY • KEVIN KINLOUGH • JEFF KIRDEIKIS • JOHN KIRK • MICHEL KIROUAC •
JAC • CLAUDE KIROUAC • FRANK KISA • HYMAN KLEIN • ROBERT KLESSENS • ROBERT KLINE • FRANK KLOSS • LEO KNAAPEN • TERRY WADE KNEE • BRUNO KNEZ • PAVEL KNOTEK • ANDRIUS KNYSTAUTAS • PETER KOCH • SACHIO KOHARA • FARROKH KOHIYAR • MARTTI KOIVUNEN • MICHAEL KONICKI • CHRISTOPHER KONINGS •
ONUK • DOMINIK KOPCZYNSKI • VICTOR KORCZ • JURGEN KOSAMURNIG • VIJAY KOTECHA • ANNETTE KOURI • LESLIE KOVACS • KALMAN KOVACS • WILLIAM KOWAL • RICHARD KRAUSS • DAVID KREDL • ZAHARIAS KRIPOTOS • KENNETH KROEGER • GERRIT JAN KROON • KORNELIS KROON • WOJCIECH KRUCZEK • WILLI KRUMMEN • REINE
AN • JOSEPH KUCZMARSKI • STANISLAW KUKLINSKI • PETER KUKULSKY • WOJCIECH KULCZYK • MICHAEL KULIS • JOHANNE KULZER • SIME KUMANOVIC • OMAR KUNZLE • ANTHONY KURBEL • MYRON KURYLYSZYN • KIM HUNG KWOK • GUY L'ALLIER • MARIO L'ECUYER • GINETTE L'ECUYER • SYLVAIN L'HERAULT • MICHEL L'HEUREUX •
EUX • ALEXANDRE L'HEUREUX • ROBERT L'HEUREUX • RONALD L'HEUREUX • SERGE L'HOSTIE • PHILIPPE LA BERGE • MAJDI LABBAT • YOLANDE LABELLE • PATRICE LABELLE • MARCUS LABELLE • ROBERT LABELLE • ROBERT LABELLE • JEAN-GUY LABELLE • ROBERT LABELLE • PIERRE LABELLE • BENOIT LABELLE • ALAIN LABELLE •
LLE • MARCEL LABELLE • JEAN LABELLE • LUCIE LABELLE • MICHELLE LABELLE • FRANCOIS LABELLE • CHANTAL LABERGE • BERNARD LABERGE • JOHANNE LABERGE • YVES LABERGE • MARIO LABERGE • DIANE LABERGE MILLS • CAROLINE LABONNE • RAYMOND LABONTE • RICHARD LABONTE • GHISLAIN LABONTE • RAYNALD LABOSSIERE
LABRANCHE • RICHARD LABRECHE • ANDRE LABRECQUE • PATRICK LABREQUE • CONRAD LABRIE • SYLVAIN LABRIE • SUZANNE LABRIE • GAETAN LABROSSE • MARTIN LABROSSE • SERGE LACAILLE • MICHEL LACASSE • JACQUES LACASSE • PIERRE LACELLE • ROBERT LACHAMBRE • SYLVIE LACHAMBRE • MICHEL LACHANCE •
CHANCE • MARTIN LACHANCE • MURIELLE LACHANCE • JEAN LACHANCE • DOMINIQUE LACHANCE • ROBERT LACHANCE • MARIO LACHANCE • ALAIN LACHANCE • JEAN-RENE LACHANCE • YVON LACHAPELLE • ALAIN LACHAPELLE • MICHEL LACHAPELLE • RICHARD LACHAPELLE • LUC LACHAPELLE • GILLES LACHAPELLE • JACQUES LACHAPELLE
ACHAPELLE • ALAIN LACHARITE • MARCEL LACOMBE • RONALD LACOMBE • JEAN LACOMBE • JACK ROSS LACOMBE • JEAN LACOMBE • RICHARD LACOMBE • PIERRE LACOSTE • JEAN DENIS LACOURSE • CLEMENT LACOURSE • MICHEL LACOURSE • SUZIE LACOURSIERE • VINCENZO LACROCE • MICHAEL LACROIX • HELENE LACROIX • JEAN
OIX • DANIEL LACROIX • REAL LACROIX • GILLES LACROIX • DANIEL LACROIX • BERNARD LACROIX • ANTOINE LACROIX • PIERRE LACROIX • JOSEE LACROIX • ALAN LADD • ALAIN LADOUCEUR • ANNA LADOUCEUR • SERGE LADOUCEUR • MARTINE LADOUCEUR • CARMEN LADOUCEUR PEPIN • PHILIPPE LADRIERE • GEORGES LADRIERE •
RANTAYE • NORMAN LAFAILLE • ERIK LAFERRIERE • DENIS LAFERRIERE • SERGE LAFETIERE • ANDRE LAFETIERE • KIM LAFFIN • CLAUDE LAFLAMME • MARIO LAFLAMME • SEAN LAFLAMME • GILLES LAFLECHE • DENIS LAFLEUR • JEAN MARC LAFLEUR • SYLVAIN LAFLEUR • JACQUES LAFLEUR • JOSEE LAFOND • PIERRE LAFONTAINE •
FONTAINE • GILLES LAFONTAINE • DANIELLE LAFONTAINE • REAL LAFOREST • RICHARD LAFOREST • GEORGE R LAFORME • FRANCOIS LAFORTUNE • ROGER LAFORTUNE • DENISE LAFORTUNE • NICOLE LAFRAMBOISE • ROLAND LAFRANCE • SERGE LAFRANCE • JEAN PIERRE LAFRANCE • STEPHANE LAFRANCE • MARC LAFRANCE •
RANCE • LOUISE LAFRANCE • ALAIN LAFRANCE • PAULINE LAFRENIERE • ROLAND LAFRENIERE • FRANCIS LAGACE • JEANNOT LAGACE • FRANCOIS LAGACE • MARCO LAGACE • ORAZIO LAGALANTE • FRANCO LAGALANTE • CAROLE LAGARDE • PIERRE LAGIMONIERE • COLETTE LAGRANGE • PATRICK LAGUERRE • MICHEL LAGUEUX •
EUX • GILBERT LAHAISE • MARIO LAJEUNESSE • RAY LAJEUNESSE • GUY LAJEUNESSE • JEAN YVES LAJEUNESSE • BOBBY LAJEUNESSE • CHRISTIAN LAJOIE • YVAN LAJOIE • BERNADETTE LAJOIE • CHRISTINA LAKE • CASIMIR LAKOTA • EUGENE LAKOTA • PIERRE G LALANCETTE • DENIS LALANCETTE • MAURICE LALANDE • MICHELINE LALANNE
BERTE • GISELE LALIBERTE • ALAIN LALIBERTE • YVAN LALIBERTE • ROLAND LALIBERTE • ANNIE LALIBERTE • PASCAL LALIBERTE • LUC LALLIER • ROBERTO LALLITTO • STEPHANE LALONDE • JOHANNE LALONDE • MICHEL LALONDE • DANIEL LALONDE • JEAN PIERRE LALONDE • JEAN LALONDE • ROBERT LALONDE • ROBERT LALONDE •
ONDE • RICHARD LALONDE • CHRISTIAN LALONDE • MARCEL LALONDE • NORMAND LALONDE • MICHEL LALONDE • SERGE LALONDE • GINETTE LALONDE • RAYNALD LALONDE • JULIE LAMAIRE • PATRICK LAMANNA • CLAUDE LAMARCHE • MARCEL LAMARCHE • CLAUDE LAMARCHE • RENE LAMARCHE • MICHEL LAMARCHE • SERGE LAMARRE •
AMARRE • GASTON LAMARRE • DAVID LAMB • GILLES LAMBERT • RENE LAMBERT • GERARD LAMBERT • ERIC LAMBERT • LUC LAMBERT • JONATHAN LAMEY • YVES LAMOND • KERRY LAMONT • PATRICIA LAMONT • SERGE LAMONT • ALAIN LAMONTAGNE • ALAIN LAMONTAGNE • RONALD LAMONTAGNE • MICHEL LAMONTAGNE •
ONTAGNE • MICHEL LAMONTAGNE • GUYLAINE LAMOTHE • RICHARD LAMOTHE • DONAT LAMOTHE • JEAN PIERRE LAMOTHE • JACQUES LAMOTHE • MICHEL LAMOTHE • MICHEL LAMOTHE • NOEL LAMOTHE • GUY LAMOTHE • DANIEL LAMOUREUX • JOCELYN LAMOUREUX • ERIC LAMOUREUX • DANIEL LAMOUREUX • RICHARD LAMOUREUX •
UREUX • ROBERT LAMOUREUX • DANIEL LAMOUREUX • NOEL LAMOUREUX • JEAN LAMOUREUX • CLAUDE LAMPRON • MARIO LAMPRON • BERNARD LAMY • SERGE LAMY • MARIO LANCI • RALPH LANDOLFI • PIERRE LANDREVILLE • PATRICK LANDREVILLE • ANDRE LANDRIAU • YVON LANDRIAU • FRANCE LANDRY • GERMAIN LANDRY •
NDRY • HERVE LANDRY • CLAUDE LANDRY • ALAIN LANDRY • GEORGES LANDRY • ALAIN LANDRY • YVON LANDRY • PATRICE LANDRY • DANIEL LANDRY • MICHEL LANDRY • GUY LANDRY • MARIUS LANDRY • GILLES LANDRY • PIERRE LANDRY • MICHEL LANDRY • YVES LANDRY • ALAIN LANDRY • CLAUDIO LANDUCCI • GEORGE LANE •
NE • RAOUL LANERO • LE TIEN LANG • CAROLINE LANGEVIN • BERNARD LANGEVIN • ROBERT LANGEVIN • JEAN LANGEVIN • JACYNTE LANGLAIS • PATRICK LANGLAIS • DIANE LANGLAIS • SUZANNE LANGLOIS • CLAUDE LANGLOIS • MICHEL LANGLOIS • CAROLINE LANGLOIS • BERNARD LANGLOIS • MARTIN LANGLOIS • DANIEL LANGLOIS •
OIS • MARIO LANGLOIS • DANIEL LANGLOIS • DENIS LANGLOIS • MARIO LANGLOIS • BRUNO LANGLOIS • FRANCE LANGLOIS • RENALD LANGLOIS • RONALD LANGLOIS • DENIS LANGLOIS • JEAN CLAUDE LANGOVISTH • GILLES LANIEL • SYLVAIN LANIEL • BEATRICE LANNI • REAL LANOIE • LUC LANOUE • ROBIN LANOUE • FERNAND LANTEIGNE
DE LANTEIGNE • ROBERT LANTHIER • HELENE LANTIN • DIANE LAPARE • DANIEL LAPERRIERE • YVES LAPERRIERE • REJEAN LAPERRIERE • MARC LAPERRIERE • YVAN LAPERRIERE • STEPHANE LAPIERRE • BARBARA LAPIERRE • ROBERT LAPIERRE • MAURICE LAPIERRE • ANDRE LAPIERRE • PATRICE LAPIERRE • ROLLAND LAPIERRE •
RRE • SERGE LAPIERRE • YVES LAPIERRE • MICHEL LAPIERRE • MICHEL LAPIERRE • MANON LAPLANTE • DIANE LAPLANTE • JULIETTE LAPLANTE • CHRISTIANE LAPLANTE • PIERRE LAPLANTE • MARIO LAPLANTE • PIERRE LAPOINTE • SERGE LAPOINTE • MARIO LAPOINTE • SYLVAIN LAPOINTE • FRANCE LAPOINTE • LANGIS LAPOINTE •
POINTE • CHRISTIAN LAPOINTE • GERALD LAPOINTE • DONALD LAPOINTE • MARC LAPOINTE • REAL LAPOINTE • JEAN PIERRE LAPOINTE • ROBERT LAPOINTE • JEAN LAPOINTE • MARTIN LAPOINTE • PATRICK LAPOINTE • HUGHES LAPOINTE • SUZANNE LAPOINTE • GILBERT LAPOINTE • MICHAEL LAPOINTE • MARCEL LAPOINTE • SYLVAIN LAPORTE
ORTE • PAULINE LAPORTE • BERNARD LAPORTE • ROBERT LAQUERRE • GERALD LARABIE • LOUIS LARAMEE • RICHARD LARCHER • ROBERT LARCHER • ALAIN LARCHER • DANIEL LAREAU • GILLES LAREAULT • DENIS LAREAULT • MICHEL LARIN • GILLES LARIVEE • BRIGITTE LARIVIERE • MICHEL LARIVIERE • ANDRE LAROCHE • YVAN LAROCHE
HE • PATRICK LAROCHE • ANDRE LAROCHE • JEAN-GUY LAROCHE • PATRIC LAROCHELLE • JOHANNE LAROCHELLE • BRUNO LAROCHELLE • ANDRE LAROCQUE • MANON LAROCQUE • STEPHANE LAROCQUE • DENIS LAROCQUE • CAMIL LAROCQUE • BENOIT LAROCQUE • BERNARD LAROCQUE • FRANCOIS LAROCQUE • SERGE LAROCQUE •
UE • DANIEL LAROSE • ANDRE LAROSE • MARC LAROSE • MARK LAROSE • MICHEL LAROSE • PIERRE LAROUCHE • MONIA LAROUCHE • STEPHANE LAROUCHE • YVON LAROUCHE • RUSSELL LARSEN • MARCEL LARUE • JACQUES LASANTE • DANIEL LASANTE • ANDRE LASCELLES • WENDY LASHLEY • DIANE LATERREUR • STEPHANE LATERREUR
ATOUR • DANIEL LATOUR • MICHEL LATOUR • RENAUD LATOUR • STEPHANE LATOUR • MONIQUE LATOUR • DEBRA LYNN LATOUR-BELANGER • STEPHANE LATOURELLE • DANIEL LATREILLE • ANDRE LATREILLE • MICHEL LATREILLE • DENIS LATULIPE • DENIS LATULIPPE • PAUL EMILE LATULIPPE • BRIAN LAUBER • DOMINIQUE LAUNOIS •
URENCE • LOUISE LAURENDEAU • ERIC LAURENT • MICHEL LAURENT • MICHEL LAURIER • JOE LAURIERI • GINETTE LAURIN • STEPHANE LAURIN • CLAUDE LAURIN • BERNARD LAURIN • GUY LAURIN • LUC LAURIN • STEPHANE LAURIN • DENIS LAURIN • ALAIN LAURIN • LUCIE LAURIN GAMACHE • PIERRE LAUZE • MARIO LAUZE • JOHANNE LAUZIER
LAUZIER • PIERRE LAUZIERE • ROBERT LAUZON • CHRISTIAN LAUZON • MICHEL LAUZON • YVAN LAUZON • RICHARD LAUZON • MICHEL LAUZON • MARTIN LAUZON • ANDRE STANLE LAUZON • LINDA LAUZON • MONIQUE LAVALLEE • MICHEL LAVALLEE • LOUIS LAVALLEE • CLAUDE LAVALLEE • SIMON LAVALLEE • NORMAND LAVALLEE •
EE • MICHEL LAVALLEE • GUY LAVALLEE • CHRISTIAN LAVALLIERE • SYLVAIN LAVALLIERE • JEAN-MARIE LAVERDIERE • DOMINIQUE LAVERDIERE • ALAIN LAVERDIERE • RICHARD LAVERDURE • DENIS LAVERGNE • ALAIN LAVICTOIRE • ROBERT LAVICTOIRE • MARLENE LAVIGNE • ANDRE LAVIGNE • RICHARD LAVIGNE • JONATHAN LAVIGNE •
GNE • DANIS LAVIGNE • ROBERT LAVIGNE • NORMAND LAVIGNE • RONALD LAVIGNE • DANIEL LAVIGNE • DANIEL LAVIGNE • SYLVAIN LAVIGNE • RAYMOND LAVIOLETTE • DOROTHY LAVIOLETTE • JACQUES LAVIOLETTE • FERNAND LAVOIE • CHRISTIAN LAVOIE • JEAN PIERRE LAVOIE • RENE LAVOIE • SYLVAIN LAVOIE • GILLES LAVOIE •
OIE • JO ANN LAVOIE • YVON LAVOIE • SERGE LAVOIE • DIANE LAVOIE • JEAN-PIERRE LAVOIE • CHRISTINE LAVOIE • CLAUDE LAVOIE • LOUIS LAVOIE • DANIEL LAVOIE • RUSSEL LAVOIE • JEAN LAVOIE • CLAUDE LAVOIE • JOHN LAWSON • ALAIN LAZURE • ANH DUNG LE • TUAN SINH LE • ROBERT LE BLANC • RONALD BRIAN LE BLANC • FRANCOIS LE
LE CLAIR • PATRICK FRAN LE GAC • MICHAEL LE NIR • JEFFREY LE NOBLE • JOHN LE ROSSIGNOL • TRIEN LE THANH • NGUYEN LE TRAN • LUC LEBEAU • YVAN LEBEAU • SERGE LEBEAU • REAL LEBEAU • NOELLA LEBEAULT • THOMMY-ETIEN LEBEL • PHILIPPE LEBEL • LANGIS LEBEL • DANIEL LEBEUF • SYLVAIN LEBLANC • ALAIN LEBLANC •
C • CLAUDE LEBLANC • YVON LEBLANC • STEPHANE LEBLANC • SANDRA LEBLANC • SONIA LEBLANC • HARRY LEBLANC • STEVEN LEBLANC • NATHALIE LEBLANC • ANDRE LEBLANC • DANNY LEBLANC • BENOIT LEBLANC • GUY LEBLANC • PIERRE LEBLANC • MARALYN LEBLANC • GUYLAIN LEBLANC • ALAIN LEBLANC • LUC LEBLANC •
NC • REAL LEBLANC • YVES LEBLANC • MICHEL LEBLANC • MARIE LEBLANC • RICHARD LEBLANC • SUZANNE LEBLANC • RICHARD LEBLANC • PIERRE LEBLANC • CLAUDE LEBLANC • ANDRE LEBLANC • ROBERTO LEBLOND • SYLVAIN LEBOEUF • PIERRE LEBOEUF • MARC LEBRUN • NORMAND LEBRUN • JACQUES LEBRUN • LORNE LEBRUN •
N • GUY LECAVALIER • ANDRE LECERF • JEAN FRANCOI LECHASSEUR • LOUISE LECLAIR • SYLVAIN LECLAIR • REAL LECLAIR • JEAN-YVES LECLAIR • FRANCOIS LECLERC • YVAN LECLERC • GUY LECLERC • GREGOIRE LECLERC • DANIEL LECLERC • DAVID LECLERC • GINETTE LECLERC • JOHANNE LECLERC • STEPHANE LECLERC •
LERC • MARTINE LECLERC • BENOIT LECLERC • SYLVAIN LECLERC • REAL LECLERC • DENIS LECLERC • ROBERT LECLERC • MARIO LECLERC • CHRISTIAN LECOMTE • FREDERIC LECORRE • OVILA LECOURS • FRANCINE LECOURS • JEAN MARIE LECOURS • ALAIN LECOURS • STEPHANE LECUYER • ROBERT LEDOUX • PHILIPPE LEDOUX •
• PATRICK LEDUC • SERGE LEDUC • JEAN PIERRE LEDUC • SYLVAIN LEDUC • RAYMOND LEDUC • ANDRE LEDUC • JULES LEDUC • SYLVAIN LEDUC • DENIS LEDUC • ANDRE LEDUC • ALLAN-MOW LEE • ERIC LEE • MICHAEL LEE • MICHEL LEE • GARY LEEF • ANDREW LEEMING • KATHLEEN LEEMING • ROBERT LEFCORT • SERGES LEFEBVRE •
RE • LUC LEFEBVRE • SERGE LEFEBVRE • LUCIE LEFEBVRE • YVES LEFEBVRE • ISABELLE LEFEBVRE • ROBERT LEFEBVRE • GILLES LEFEBVRE • GUYLAINE LEFEBVRE • BERNARD LEFEBVRE • PAUL LEFEBVRE • DENIS LEFEBVRE • MANON LEFEBVRE • MARGUERITE LEFEBVRE • RENE LEFEBVRE • RAYMOND LEFEBVRE • ALPHONSE LEFEBVRE
FEBVRE • PAUL LEFEBVRE • GILLES LEFEBVRE • RENE LEFEBVRE • JACQUES LEFEBVRE • ANDRE LEFEBVRE • CLARENCE O LEFORT • DANIEL LEFRANCOIS • SYLVAIN LEFRANCOIS • ALAIN LEGARE • GUY ROGER LEGAULT • RICHARD LEGAULT • CHRISTIAN LEGAULT • MARC LEGAULT • JEAN LEGAULT • PIERRE LEGAULT • JEANNETTE LEGAULT
GAULT • BERNARD LEGAULT • LUC LEGAULT • BERTRAND LEGAULT • MARCEL LEGAULT • IVAN LEGAULT • YVES LEGAULT • GILLES LEGAULT • LUC LEGAULT • CHRISTIAN LEGAULT • LINDA LEGAULT • DANIEL LEGER • SYLVAIN LEGER • ROBERT LEGER • LOUIS LEGER • JEAN PIERRE LEGER • LLOYD LEGGO • STEPHAN LEGIN • JEAN
OUTE • ALICE LEGROS • LOUIS LEGROS • MARTIN LEI • CHRISTOPHER LEIGH • BELINDA LEIGHTON • MARIE LELIEVRE • PIERRE LELIEVRE • ALAIN LELIEVRE • BRUNO LELIEVRE • LEONARD LELIEVRE • GERALD LELIEVRE • HAROLD LELIEVRE • PIERRE LEMAIRE • SYLVAIN LEMAIRE • HAROLD LEMAY • PAUL LEMAY • GUY LEMAY • MARIE LEMAY
LEMAY • PAUL LEMAY • RENE LEMAY • MARIO LEMELIN • REAL LEMELIN • DANIEL LEMERISE • FRANCOIS LEMIEUX • MARTIN LEMIEUX • GILLES LEMIEUX • MICHEL LEMIEUX • MARC LEMIEUX • BRIGITTE LEMIEUX • GERALD LEMIEUX • CHANTAL LEMIEUX • MARTIN LEMIEUX • MARTIN LEMIRE • FREDERIC LEMIRE • DENIS LEMIRE • YVES LEMIRE
IRE • JOSEPH LEMME • JACQUES LEMOINE • GISELE LEMOINE • TANYA LENAR • HERMAN LENZ • JACQUELINE LEONARD • LEON LEONARD • ALLAN GEORGE LEONARD • MICHEL LEPAGE • ROBERT LEPAGE • ANDRE LEPAGE • ROBERT LEPAGE • LOUISE LEPAGE • BRUNO LEPAGE • CYRIL LEPAGE • RENE LEPAGE • MICHELINE LEPAGE •
EPAGE • MARIO LEPAGE • MICHEL LEPAGE • MICHEL LEPINE • SYLVAIN LEPINE • SERGE LEPINE • JEAN GUY LEPINE • PATRICK LEPROHON • CLAUDE LEPROHON • JUDY LEROUX • PIERRE LEROUX • NANCY LEROUX • ROBERT LEROUX • ANDRE LEROUX • ALAIN LEROUX • DANIEL LEROUX • SYLVAIN LESAGE • MARC LESAGE • PATRICK LESAGE
CARBEAU • MARTIN LESCARBEAULT • LUC LESLEY • LINDA LESLIE • FRANCOISE LESSARD • PAUL LESSARD • JEAN LESSARD • MARCEL LESSARD • HUGUES LESSARD • YVES LESSARD • GHISLAINE LESSARD • ISABELLE LESSARD • ROBERT LESSARD • DANIEL LESSARD • DIANE LESSARD • SIMON LESSARD • SERGE LESSARD • SYLVAIN LESSARD
SSARD • MONIQUE LESSARD LEDUC • MICHEL LESTAGE • ANDRE LETARTE • ROBERT LETARTE • SUZANNE LETENDRE • GUY LETENDRE • MARC LETOURNEAU • CLAUDE LETOURNEAU • RICHARD LETOURNEAU • CHRISTAIN LETOURNEAU • RICHARD LETOURNEAU • SERGE LEVAC • ERICK LEVAC • FRANCE LEVASSEUR • JEAN PIERRE LEVASSEUR
SSEUR • PIERRE LEVASSEUR • CLAUDE LEVASSEUR • MARTIN LEVEILLE • JEAN-GUY LEVEILLEE • DANIEL LEVEILLEE • ANDRE LEVERT • LYNE LEVESQUE • SUSAN LEVESQUE • SYLVAIN LEVESQUE • JEAN CLAUDE LEVESQUE • ANDRE LEVESQUE • NANCY LEVESQUE • LEOPOLD LEVESQUE • RONALD LEVESQUE • MICHEL LEVESQUE •
EVESQUE • MARGARET LEVESQUE • MARC LEVESQUE • GILLES LEVESQUE • RICHARD LEVESQUE • JEAN GUY LEVESQUE • DENIS LEVESQUE • AMIR LEVIN • VICTOR LEVIN • PIERRE LEVINE • RICHARD LEVINGSTONE • JEAN LEVIS • NEAL LEVITT • MARCOS LEVY • DARLENE LEWIS • STEVEN LEWIS • WILLIAM LEWIS • YAJIE LI • STEVE LIAKAKOS
BURSKI • PETER LICHNOFSKY • PETER R LIKORAY • JAMES LIKORAY • EROTOCRETOS LIKOUDIS • PETER LILLIS • VUTHY LIM • REJEAN LIMOGES • SYLVAIN LIMOGES • JASON LIN • JEFF LINDEGAARD • NICOLAS LINDEMAN • PIERRE LINGUENHELD • ANTHONY LINSDELL • ROLAND LIPARI • ROBERT LISCUM • GERALD LISK • JANET LISSEMORE •
• SYLVIE LITTNER • JUI LUN LIU • ANTHONY LIVELY • JOSEPH LIVNI • ROSS LIZEE • YVON LIZEE • MARIO LIZEE • MALCOLM LLOYD • TRACY LLOYD • YVON LOCAS • RICHARD LOCAT • JULES LOCKE • RANDY LOCKHART • MICHAEL LOHMANN • MICHEL LOIGNON • JEAN LOISELLE • CHRISTIAN LOISELLE • STEPHANE LOISELLE • FRANCINE LOISELLE
LE • ALAIN LOMBART • PAUL LONDEI • STEPHANE LONG • FRANCESCO LONGO • JEAN MARC LONGPRE • JACQUES LONGTIN • LUC LONGTIN • EDUARDA LOPES • CARLOS LOPES • JUAN RAMON LOPEZ • GUY LORANGER • ANDRE LORANGER • ALAIN LORANGER • FRANCOIS LORD • JEAN MARC LORD • CLAUDE LORD • ALLEN LORD •
ENSON • DAVID B LORETTO • CHANTAL LORION • JOHN LORKOVIC • PIERRE LORTIE • BRUNO LORTIE • PASCAL LORTIE • DIANE LORTIE • ALAIN LORTIE • LOUIS LORTIE • VALERI LOSIER • PIERRE LOUERGLI • GREGORY LOUGHRAN • GABRIEL YVES LOUIS • YVON LOYER • PERRY LUCHIA • MICHAEL LUCK • TONY LUDOVICO • RON LUI • IAN LULHAM
UNARDINI • HENRIK LUND • DENIS LUNEAU • ROBERT LUNNEY • CHARLES LUNNY • DANNY LUNNY • HOAN LUONG • ROBERT LUSIGNAN • CLAUDE LUSIGNAN • WILLIAM LUSK • JACQUES LUSSIER • PIERRE LUSSIER • JOCELYN LUSSIER • JACQUES LUSSIER • ALAIN LUSSIER • MARIE FRANCE LUSSIER • SHMUEL LUSTGARTEN • DAVID LUTCHMAN
N LY • ANTHONY LYCZKO • PETER LYNCH • ROBERT LYNCH • PIERRE LYONNAIS • RENE LYONNAIS • STEVE LYONS • BERNARD LYONS • RICHARD LYTWYNUK • PETER LYVER • VAN DE MA • WILLIAM MABEY • ERNEST MAC DONALD • PAMELA JEAN MAC GIBBON • JUDE MAC WILLIAMS • JAMES BRYAN MACCORMACK • WENDY MACDONALD •
DONALD • KAREN MACDONALD • MALCOLM MACDONALD • ROBERT MACFARLANE • JOSE MACHADO • COLIN L MACKAY • DAVID MACKENZIE • SYLVAIN MACKENZIE • ERIC JAMES MACLEAN • MALCOLM MACLEOD • BARRY WAYNE MACLEOD • GORDON MACMILLAN • GARY MACMILLAN • KATHERINE MACNEIL • GUIDO MADDALENA •
DEN • DWAIN MADDEX • SARANTOS MADIMENOS • MIGUEL MAEZO • RENAUD MAFFREN • ROBERT MAFFREN • YVETTE MAGEE • GILLES MAGNAN • ROGER MAGNAN • PAUL MAGWOOD • YVES JEAN MAHAUT • MICHEL MAHEU • MARCELLE MAHEUX • GILLES MAHEUX • BARBARA ANN MAHONEY • DAVID MAILHOT • CLAUDE MAILHOT • MICHEL MAILLE
ILLET • JOSEE MAILLETTE • MELANIE MAILLOUX • MARCEL MAILLOUX • GINA MAILLOUX • YVES MAINVILLE • GUY MAINVILLE • GILLES MAINVILLE • ERIC MAINVILLE • FERNAND MAINVILLE • DENIS MAISONNEUVE • GILLES MAISONNEUVE • PIERRE MAISONNEUVE • MAURICE MAJCHER • RUDY MAJNIK • GAETAN MAJOR • YVAN MAJOR •
AJOR • DANIEL MAJOR • DENIS MAJOR • NOELLA MAJOR • STEPHANE MAJOR • STEPHEN MAJOR • BRAHIM MAJOUJI • SULEIMAN MAKHLOUF • EDWIN MAKI • JOSEPH MAKOUKJI • MICHEL MALABORZA • ANTONIO MALASPINA • MICHEL MALBOEUF • ALBERT MALCOLM • VICTOR MALCOLM • JUNE MALCOLM • RICHARD MALE • JACQUELINE MALETTE
LETTE • MICHEL MALETTE • CRAIG MALLA • THOMAS P MALLON • GAETAN MALO • MICHEL MALO • RENE MALO • LUC MALO • MARJOLAINE MALOIS • SHAWN MALONEY • NICK MALORNI • NICK MALORNI • ANTONIO MALORNI • MICHEL MALOUIN • PIERRE MALTAIS • JAMAL MAMMAH • GINO MAMMOLITI • ERNESTO MANCINI • PETER MANCO •
DATO • ITZHAK MANDEL • PAUL MANELLI • GINO MANISCALCO • HARBHAJAN MANKU • PEGGY MANN • PETER MANNI • ANTONIOS MANOUSAKOS • PETROS MANOUSAKOS • FRANCISCO MANRIQUE • RICHARD MANSEAU • ANTOINETTE MANSI • ROBERT MANTHA • LUC MANTION • FRANCOIS MARANDA • BENOIT MARCHAND • MADELEINE MARCHAND
HAND • FRANCOIS MARCHAND • PATRICIA MARCHAND • CLAUDE MARCHAND • PETER MARCHETTI • NATHALIE MARCHILDON • ALAIN MARCHILDON • LISE MARCIL • GHISLAINE MARCIL • CLAUDE MARCOTTE • BENOIT MARCOTTE • MICHEL MARCOTTE • BRUNO MARCOTTE • PIERRE MARCOTTE • ERIC MARCOTTE • CHRISTIAN MARCOUX •
OUX • PIERRE MARCOUX • NICOLAIE MARCU • PAUL MARCUS • PAUL MARETTE • DONALD MARGRETT • CLAUDE MARIER • ALAIN MARINEAU • DANIEL MARINEAU • ANGELO MARINELLI • FRANCOIS MARION • SYLVAIN MARION • ANDRE MARION • FELICE MARIOTTI • SERGE MARIOTTI • KEVIN MARKS • SYLVAIN MARLEAU • ANDRE MARLEAU •
RLEAU • CHRISTINE MAROIS • JACQUES MAROIS • ANDRE MAROTTE • MARIO MAROTTE • MARIO MAROTTE • BRIAN F MARQUES • LIDIMO MARQUES • HECTOR MARQUEZ • LUCIE MARQUIS • RICHARD MARQUIS • MARCEL MARQUIS • JEAN CLAUDE MARQUIS • GILBERT MARQUIS • HELENE MARQUIS • CARL MARQUIS • ERIC MARQUIS •

Canadair

THE FIRST 50 YEARS

Canadair

THE FIRST 50 YEARS

RON PICKLER
LARRY MILBERRY

CANAV Books

(Title page) Bombardier Global Express

(Endpapers) A listing of current and retired Canadair employees.

Canadian Cataloguing in Publication Data

Pickler, Ronald A. (Ronald Arthur), 1921–
    Canadair : the first 50 years

Issued also in French under title: Canadair : cinquante ans d'histoire
Includes index.
ISBN 0-921022-07-7

1.Canadair Limited – History. 2. Aircraft industry – Canada – History.
I. Milberry, Larry, 1943– . II. Title

HD9711.C34C357 1995   338.7'62913334'0971   C95-930506-8

COPY EDITING: Jane Werniuk, Toronto

TRANSLATION: Johanne Duchesne Daoust, Montreal

ADDITIONAL RESEARCH: Wayne Saunders, Montreal

PHOTO RETOUCHING: Stephen Ng, Toronto

DESIGN: Robin Brass Studio, Toronto

Printed and bound in Canada by Friesen Printers Ltd., Altona, Man.

Published by
CANAV Books
Larry Milberry, Publisher
51 Balsam Avenue
Toronto, Ont. M4E 3B6
Canada

Thousands of Canadair's family and friends on the tarmac at Plant 3 in 1994, enjoying the display of company products at Canadair's 50th anniversary. (CL C71331-23)

CONTENTS

A CL-215T water bomber attacks a fire near Alcoy, Spain on August 21, 1994. Cliff Symons of Canadair's photography department took second place (Editor's Choice category) in *Aviation Week* magazine's 1994 photo contest. (CL)

FOREWORD

In an industry where change is constant, Canadair is recognized worldwide for advancing the development of superior quality aircraft.

Canadair: The First 50 Years chronicles in vivid detail the determination, ingenuity and pride of a company eager to tackle new technological challenges. The story richly documents Canadair's evolution, from building mostly military aircraft according to other manufacturers' designs in the early days to designing, manufacturing and supporting its own growing family of civil aircraft today.

It is also the story of the people who contributed to Canadair's success since its creation in 1944; it is to these people, more than 80,000 in all, that the book is dedicated. Their collective efforts serve as important symbols of commitment, perseverance and leadership as Canadair, now working closely with other members of the Bombardier Aerospace Group, prepares to meet the challenges of the 21st century.

I know you will find this story both interesting and informative

ROBERT E. BROWN
PRESIDENT
BOMBARDIER AEROSPACE GROUP–NORTH AMERICA

In less than a decade Canadair went from manufacturing lumbering Canso patrol planes for the war effort to sleek F-86 jet fighters. Here the Canso line is in full swing at Cartierville, while the Sabres of the RCAF Golden Hawks demonstration team are shown peeling away for the photographer. While it built such designs under licence, Canadair gradually moved into original projects, its first complete in-house project being the CL-41 Tutor jet trainer. (CL, DND)

ACKNOWLEDGEMENTS

"Never a dull moment" might have been a good title for this book, for it sums up the feelings of most of the nearly 200 present and former Canadair employees Larry Milberry and I talked with about their years at Canadair. Most of them belong to that happy breed who lived the roller-coaster existence that was Canadair during the 1950s and '60s, survived the layoffs of the early '70s and experienced the excitement and frustration of the early Challenger years. A few were still around in 1995, enjoying the new spirit of Bombardier ownership.

That same comment describes my last 18 months. When, in May 1993, Catherine Chase first asked Larry to produce the book and me to write it, I had misgivings about accepting. I wasn't sure I was capable of doing it, that it could be done in the time allotted, or that I wanted to be tied down for such a long period. I thought too that not living in the Montreal area would be a handicap. Four factors made the job possible, however. First, Larry, Canada's foremost aviation publisher, assumed responsibility for the vital tasks of selecting the photos, writing the captions, organizing the layout, preparing the index and handling the publishing arrangements. Next, Canadair public relations still had the research material I used to prepare "The First Forty Years". Efficient communications compensated for distance, and I was blessed with a wife, Nan, who supported me with patience and understanding and seldom complained about the lonely times she endured while I fought with the word processor.

It turned out to be a rewarding experience, despite occasional periods of frustration (I spent at least a week trying to establish how the CL-89 got started and an entire day unearthing "Slim" Harte's full name, Bernard N. Harte). The project gave me an opportunity to meet old friends, make new contacts and learn much about the company, its products and its people that I didn't know before.

The credit for creating this history belongs, however, not to Larry and me, but to many of the more than 80,000 people who worked at Canadair over the past 50 years. Some worked only a day or two while others, like Frank Reynolds and Joey Wilkinson, spent their entire working careers at Canadian Vickers and Cartierville. Regardless of the length of time they worked, however, all contributed to the company's history for it was these people who created and developed Canadair. While many may say they would have had an easier life working somewhere else, most will admit privately they wouldn't have missed it for the world. These people wrote the book; we just put it together.

We have tried to create a personal history by including the names of the key individuals involved with each program. Despite our efforts to list everyone, however, we will inevitably have missed some, and to them we offer sincere apologies.

First and foremost, we acknowledge our debt to Catherine Chase, Canadair's director of public relations, for choosing us to do the book and supporting us along the way. She kept a firm hand on the reins and didn't hesitate to haul me in when I let my personal feelings influence my commentary.

A special vote of thanks goes to the "Brains Trust" of Len Box, Dick Faucher, Ben Locke, Ross Richardson, Dick Richmond and Harry Whiteman. They not only gave us the benefit of their collective 200-plus years with Canadair, but took the time to wade through many drafts, patiently correcting, modifying and amplifying the contents, answering a stream of questions, identifying photographs and offering advice.

We are grateful to other individuals who made special

contributions. People like Bob Agar, Gerry Barabé, Gerry Coleman, Tom Harvie, Gerry LaGrave, Al Lilly, Ed Norsworthy, Bob Raven, Bob Stapells and Jack Waller, who contributed much of the early history. Peter Aird, Gil Bennett, Harry Halton, John MacKenzie, Bryan Moss, Jim Taylor and Bob Wohl helped us get the Challenger story straight. Pat Campbell reviewed text and allowed us to use portions of "The End of the Line", his description of the development of manufacturing techniques and practises at Canadair.

Brian Darling wrote the history of the air cadet squadrons. Doug Follett loaned us the original of Duncan Macpherson's brilliant cartoon. Jean-Paul Fréreault loaned us the complete sets of *Actualité Canadair* and *Info Canadair* he collected during his 43 years with the company (this inveterate collector still has all his Canadair payslips as well as what is reputed to be the largest privately-owned collection of Bing Crosby recordings). Jack Greeniaus contributed 165 minutes of taped memories and his photo album of the early Challenger days. Bob Lefcort reviewed every word of the text and steered us clear of potential legal problems. George Parker, though long deceased, left a legacy in the form of a remarkably detailed record of many Canadair products, and Wayne Saunders researched much of the material for the appendix, reviewed text, and uncovered a seemingly endless supply of rare data.

Also much appreciated were the contributions of others who reviewed portions of the drafts and provided valuable information and advice. They were Gary Bingham, Ron Broad, Peter Candfield, Peter Clignett, Hélène Crevier, Philippe Crevier, Peter Hargrove, John Holding, Ray Mathieu, Matt Milnes, Walter Niemy, Nick Perkins, John Reid and Bill Upton.

We are grateful for the patience of others we interviewed, either in person or by phone. They were Doug Adkins, Walter Allatt, Vince Ambrico, Glen Baxter, Marion (Baker) Gall, Saul Bernstein, Bob Brown, Ray Campbell, Cherry Cherrington, Barry Coleman, Bob Deans, Paul Del Rizzo, Joe Ederhy, Jack Forbes, Frank Francis, Roland Gagnon, Réal Gervais, Barry Gilmore, Hugh Gosnell, Eric Haines, Dave Hanchet, Ralph Hayward, Trevor Hughes, Ethel Jones, Bob Lording, Don Lowe, Yves Mahaut, Eric McConachie, Ken McDonald, Don McVicar, Walter Meacher, Lou Mehl, Tony Natlacen, Bill Palmer, Fred Phillips, Bob Ross,

Lawrence Rowley, Bud Sager, Gordon Stringer, Andy Throner, Kostas Velegrinis, Moe White and Alec Wright.

And those who filled in the gaps by sending letters, supplying or identifying photos and answering queries. They were Barry Allen, Guy Baribeau, Hélène Beauchamp, Herbie Brehn, Bernie Campbell, Jim Carnwarth, Bill Carr, John Chisnall, Dave Clark, Hedley Everard, Wes Ewanchyna, Jim Fitzpatrick, Ron Foran, John Gilmore, Dave Godfrey, Ed Grose, Ken Hale, Jack Heine, Jim Henry, Maurice Holloway, Rex Hynes, Derek Jones, Don Kennard, John Kerr, Joe Knap, Guy Lapointe, Tony Lebrun, Ron Ledwidge, Harold Leflock, Leo Lejeune, Gordie Lloyd, Guy Lortie, Dr. H.J. Luckert, Joe MacBrien, Charlie Massé, Fotis Mavriplis, Bob McCall, Bob McIntyre, Scotty McLean, George Moffatt, Jim Moffatt, Mike Panasiuk, Arthur & Nora Pennance, Al Rankin, Chuck Rathgeb, Wally Remington, Elfriede and Jim Rollo, Stan Rose, Lorraine Ross, Brian Smith, John Smith, Jorge Sobolewski, Jim Steel, Al Stone, Malcolm Stride, Roy Swanson, Kenneth I Swartz, Henry Szot, W.M. "Turbo" Tarling, Gerry Verreault, Hank Volker and Ernie Walford.

We couldn't have wished for better cooperation than that we got from Garth Dingman, Lucio Anodal, Paul Sagala, Cliff Symons and John Wulfraat of the photographic department; from Bob Dallabona and the graphic design group; Margaret Levesque and the library staff, and Ron Paquet and Kath Weaver of public relations.

For all their efforts, however, the book would never have been produced without the enthusiasm and professional expertise of editor Jane Werniuk, translator Johanne Duchesne Daoust and book designer Robin Brass.

RON PICKLER

Sources

The following documents provided source material: Ashworth, R.C.B (Chris): "Canada's All-Seeing Monster", Canadian Aviation Historical Society *Journal*, Fall 1992 issue; *Bombardier: A Dream with International Reach*; Campbell, Patrick: "The End of the Line"; Fricker, John: "The Canadair Company", *The Aeroplane*, April 17, 1953; Godfrey, David: "Score Sheet on the Half Century", *Canadian Aviation*, June 1978; Hornick, James: Articles in

The Regional Jet airliner typifies the advanced designs produced by Canadair in the 1990s. (CL)

the *Globe and Mail*, Toronto, February 4 and 5, 1953; Irbitis, Karl: *Of Struggle and Flight;* Logie, Stuart: *Winging It – The Making of the Canadair Challenger;* Lovegrove, CMR Officer Cadet Dwayne: "Canadair and Canadian Aviation" (thesis); Main, J.R.K.: *Voyageurs of the Air;* McVicar, Don: *Mosquito Racer;* Milberry, Larry: *Aircom: Canada's Air Force;* Milberry: *Aviation in Canada;* Milberry: *Sixty Years: The RCAF and CF Air Command 1924-1984;* Milberry: *The Canadair North Star;* Milberry: *The Canadair Sabre;* Molson, K.M. and Taylor, H.A.: *Canadian Aircraft since 1909;* Molson, K.M.: "Cartierville: Canada's Oldest Airport", CAHS *Journal*, Winter 1990 issue;

Phillips, Fred: "A History of Aerospace Research and Development in Canadair Ltd." Canadian Aeronautics and Space Institute *Journal*, Vol. 25, No. 2, 1979; Pickler, Ron: *The First Forty Years – A Record of Canadair Operations 1944-1984;* Whiteman, Harry: "A Well Bred Family", CAHS *Journal*, Fall 1992 issue.

Note

The names Canadair, de Havilland, Learjet and Shorts, and the names of those companies' products, are trademarks of Bombardier Inc.

A 1930 view towards the northwest of the Canadian Vickers complex on the St. Lawrence River showing the plant, dry-docks and air harbor. Stranraers and PBYs were built in the extensions near the river adjacent to the main plant. Shop 5 (north side of the inner harbor, far right) was for Hampden bomber production. By 1995 this area was an industrial wasteland awaiting redevelopment. (CL)

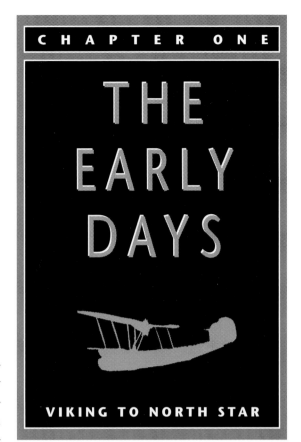

CHAPTER ONE

THE EARLY DAYS

VIKING TO NORTH STAR

There is a legend that the islands of Japan sprang, fully formed, from the eye of a goddess. That may have been so in Japan, but it just doesn't happen that way in business. Trace any aerospace company to its origin and chances are you will find a handful of people and a dream. If the company prospers, its success will have been due largely to people, for prosperity depends on the strength of people, not only finances, modern buildings, or state-of-the-art equipment.

So it has been with Canadair. It began in 1944 as the aircraft department of Canadian Vickers which once had a mere eight employees and was practically unknown outside Canada. Today the name Canadair is known and respected around the world as a major component of Bombardier Inc., an international business empire of some 37,000 employees, and annual sales close to $6 billion. Most of the credit for that success belongs to the more than 80,000 people who have worked for Canadair over the years. Some of those stayed only briefly, but a surprising number stayed for their working careers.

Canadair's people came from everywhere. The predominantly Canadian-born labor force of the 1940s was swamped by an influx of immigrants during the 1950s to the point where over 90 per cent in the engineering design office were British, or Europeans from Britain. As the world changed, so did Canadair. In the early 1970s, an informal survey revealed that 48 languages could be spoken and understood among the 250 or so personnel in the design office alone. In recent years the pattern has changed again: now almost all new employees are from the province of Quebec. Regardless of origin, people are the soul of the company.

Canadian Vickers

Canadair's origins date to the early part of the century and the formation of Canadian Vickers Limited. In June 1911, at the invitation of the government of Canada, the British ship builder Vickers Sons & Maxim established Canadian Vickers (CV). In 1912 it began construction of a shipyard in Montreal to produce vessels for the Royal Canadian Navy. The yard was at Viau and Notre Dame Streets in the east Montreal suburb of Maisonneuve where the Lachine Rapids of the St. Lawrence River end their swirling flow in the calmer waters of St. Mary's current. Here is the spot where Ethan Allan and his army of Vermont rangers were captured in 1775 and sent as prisoners to England. During the First World War, Canadian Vickers built nearly 300 ships of various types and a few submarines for the navies of Canada and the United States. The submarines were under contracts from the Electric Boat Co. of Groton, Connecticut.

Canadian Vickers's first encounter with aviation came in 1916 when it was asked to consider making Curtiss OX engines for aviation pioneer J.A.D. McCurdy of Curtiss

Aeroplanes & Motors Ltd. of Toronto. This never materialized. In 1920, however, two aircraft–a Felixstowe F.3 flying boat and a Fairey III Transatlantic–were assembled and tested at the shipyards for a flight across Canada. In 1922, Canadian Vickers obtained a contract from Laurentide Air Services Ltd. to repair and overhaul Curtiss HS-2L flying boats.

By the end of 1922, with war surplus aircraft like the HS-2L wearing out, the Canadian Air Force (CAF) called for tenders for replacements. Believing the time was ripe to establish an aircraft industry, Ottawa specified that the aircraft be built in Canada. Laurentide Air Services and Canadian Vickers submitted tenders, and on February 23, 1923, Canadian Vickers won a contract to supply eight Vickers Viking IV flying boats. Parts for the first two were manufactured in England while production facilities were being set up in Montreal. The parts were then shipped to Montreal for assembly by CV's newly formed aircraft department, with engines supplied by the CAF. The first Ca-

One of the large Viking flying boats assembled at Canadian Vickers in 1923 was photographed on forestry patrol over Alberta. (DND)

nadian Vickers Viking made its maiden flight on June 15, 1923, and the first of six Canadian-built Vikings flew on July 23.

British aircraft manufacturers now began to take an interest in Canada. A number of them crossed the Atlantic in 1924 to get a first-hand impression of the country and its aviation needs. They soon realized that airplanes designed in Europe were not necessarily suitable for Canada, and agreed that Canada should build its own aircraft where possible.

With the encouragement of its parent, Canadian Vickers set up an aircraft design staff in 1924, and began to work on a forestry patrol aircraft smaller than the Viking and more suited to Canadian conditions. The parent company had already done some initial design of a small flying boat which appeared to fit the bill, so preliminary drawings were shipped to Canada with a design engineer to oversee the program. This was W.T. Reid who had been hired away from Bristol Aircraft. The design Reid brought was for a three-seater with the improved takeoff and climb performance needed to operate from small lakes and rivers. It was called the Vedette.

The first Vedette, powered by a Rolls-Royce Falcon engine, flew on November 4, 1924. Between 1924 and 1930, Canadian Vickers built 60 Vedettes, mostly with Wright Whirlwind or Armstrong Siddeley Lynx engines. Of these, 42 were for the Royal Canadian Air Force (RCAF); 12 were for Canadian provincial governments and commercial operators; six amphibious Vedettes went to Chile. Vedettes served as the RCAF basic flying boat trainer until 1940.

In October 1927, corporate control passed to a group headed by James Playfair of Midland, Ontario, and thereafter the British parent held only a minority interest in Canadian Vickers. Between 1924 and 1941, Canadian Vickers produced such original designs as the Vancouver, Vanessa, Varuna, Velos, Vigil, and Vista. Other types were built under licence including the Avro 504N, Bellanca Pacemaker, Curtiss HS-3L, Fairchild FC-2 and Fokker Super Universal.

In 1936, with war in Europe a practical certainty, Ottawa gave Canadian Vickers a contract for Supermarine Stranraer flying boats for the RCAF. Forty were turned out by 1941. The coastal patrol Stranraer served on both

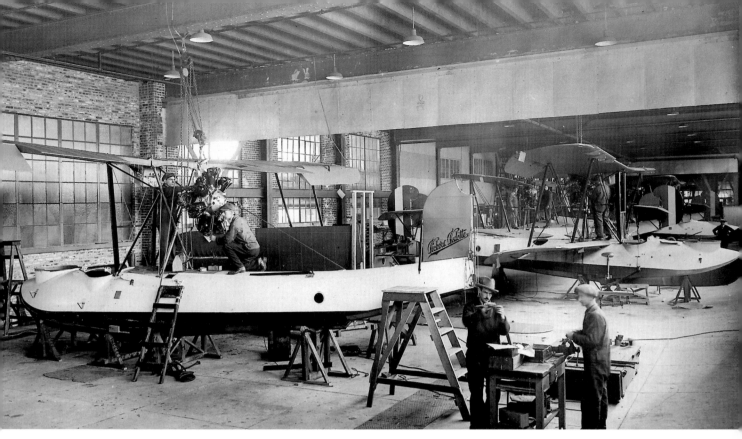

Canadian Vickers (CV) designed Canada's first indigenous production airplane, the Vedette. A small utility flying boat, it became popular with the RCAF and civil operators. Of 60 built, several went to Chile in the first export sale of a Canadian-designed production airplane. Except for nails and fittings, the Vedette was entirely of wood covered in fabric. The Vedettes above are nearing completion. Another is about to be launched beside the dry dock. (CL 28550, F4055)

Canada's east and west coasts until replaced by the PBY mid-way through the war.

The PBY Program

The start of the Second World War created an urgent need for a long-range amphibian for maritime patrol, anti-submarine warfare, and search and rescue. Ottawa signed a licence agreement with Consolidated Aircraft of San Diego, California, to build the rugged PBY-5A (the amphibious version of the PBY-5 flying boat). On July 25, 1941, Canadian Vickers won an initial contract for 39 PBY-5A Cansos (so named by the RCAF) from the Department of Munitions and Supply.

Because space at the Maisonneuve facility was limited, the first 25 Cansos were assembled in hangars at St-Hubert airport where Hampden bombers had been made. To speed production the Canadian government decided to build a new plant at Cartierville Airport in

Canadian Vickers introduced various types in the 1920s including the attractive Vigil, seen here on skis. (CL H150)

The Vista flying boat was another CV project. Both Vigil and Vista were for forestry work but only one of each was built. (H4)

Canadian Vickers also designed the twin-engine Varuna forestry flying boat for the RCAF. Experience in the design and manufacture of such types positioned CV for more modern projects as technology advanced. (CL)

Canadian Vickers' first modern projects were the Northrop Delta aerial photo plane and Supermarine Stranraer coastal patrol flying boat built for the RCAF. The first of 20 Deltas (No. 667, seen here) flew in August 1936. (CL F2565)

The CV Stranraer flew in October 1938. The Delta and Stranraer brought new materials, machinery and skills to Canadian Vickers. (F3734)

(Above) A new Stranraer is launched. (CL)

(Right) The Vancouver forestry/ fisheries flying boat was designed and built by CV for the RCAF. It served through the 1930s. (CL)

Saint-Laurent. Canadian Vickers was to supervise plant construction and manage its operation.

Cartierville Airport

Cartierville was first used as an airfield in June 1911 while still the site of the Montreal Polo Grounds. The polo club leased the property from Gervais Cousineau, a local farmer. Meanwhile Percy Hall Reid (not related to W.T. Reid) was building an airplane in a shop at Bishop and St.

Catherine streets in Montreal. In 1912 the polo club ceased operations; and Cousineau let Reid use the field, which was about 1.6 km (1 mi.) long and 300 m (1,000 ft.) wide. Reid soon built a hangar (the first in Canada) along what is today Marcel-Laurin Boulevard.

During the First World War, Cartierville was used by visiting military aircraft. The first Canadian air mail was flown from there to Toronto in a JN-4 Canuck on June 24, 1918. In early 1928, W.T. Reid left Canadian Vickers, founded the

Some of those who built the Cansos at Canadian Vickers. Gerry Barabé, who joined CV in 1940 as an eighteen-year-old, recalled in 1994 how the original PBY contour tooling control was done using the wreck of a US Navy aircraft. The first jigs were lined up using a wooden PBY profile. CV-built PBYs were trucked to St-Hubert for test flying. Shop-floor workers in 1940 were earning about 40 cents an hour. (CL M3576)

Reid Aircraft Co. at Cartierville to produce a two-seat light aircraft called the Rambler. His prototype flew in September 1928. The Rambler became a popular club and private plane.

The Curtiss Aeroplanes & Motors Co. of Garden City, New Jersey, guided by Canadian pioneer pilot J.A.D. McCurdy, became interested in the Rambler and its tubular metal construction. In December 1928, it acquired the rights to the aircraft and access to the Canadian market by buying Reid's company which became the Curtiss-Reid Aircraft Co. In 1929, it levelled and drained Cartierville

The company logo was updated to include three PBYs in flight. (CL)

airport, and erected a 3,300-m² (36,000-sq.-ft.) brick factory on its north side and a third hangar beside the two built by Reid. Curtiss-Reid failed in 1932. Its assets were taken over by Montreal Aircraft Industries Ltd. headed by McCurdy. Curtiss-Reid Flying Services survived the Depression, however, and operated the flying school at Cartierville until its hangars and seven aircraft were destroyed by fire in November 1959.

In the spring of 1935, Noorduyn Aircraft Ltd. rented 1,100 m² (12,000 sq. ft.) of the former Curtiss-Reid factory and began construction of the Norseman bushplane which first flew on November 12, 1935. In 1938, Noorduyn bought the entire Curtiss-Reid facility. By mid-1939, Cartierville had two 600-m (2000-ft.) landing strips. When Noorduyn moved out of Curtiss-Reid, Federal Aircraft Ltd. rented the building to administer production of the Avro Anson in Canada. In 1943, Federal gave up its lease, which was then taken up by Canadian Car & Foundry to build the prototype Burnelli CBY-3 Loadmaster transport which first flew July 17, 1945.

Cartierville airport in 1929. Montée St-Laurent (later Laurentian Blvd., now Marcel Laurin Blvd.) runs south from the bottom towards Montreal. Bois Franc Rd. (today's Henri Bourassa) goes across the bottom. The Curtiss-Reid Flying Service hangars sit along Montée St-Laurent with the field in front. The large building on Bois Franc is the Curtiss-Reid factory, later Canadair's B402. Aviation historian K.M. Molson wrote of Cartierville: "Usually there are several contenders for first place in competitions, but for the distinction of being Canada's oldest airport, Cartierville is an easy winner. No other airport is even close. The Cartierville site was used by an aircraft in June 1911, only about 7½ years after the Wright brothers first flew..." (CL PL2795)

PBY Production at Cartierville

In 1940, the Department of Munitions and Supply began to acquire land at Cartierville for the new PBY factory. It also took over the airfield and in late 1941 constructed a hard-surface northeast-southwest runway. Noorduyn was responsible for airfield maintenance. When Dorval Airport opened nearby in 1941, its circuit overlapped Cartierville's, so the Cartierville circuit was changed from the normal left-hand direction to a right-hand, or clockwise,

The Curtiss-Reid Rambler (43 built) was popular for training and pleasure flying. Pat Campbell of Canadair had his first plane ride in this example on June 22, 1938. (Campbell Col.)

First flown in 1935, the Noorduyn Norseman brought fame to Cartierville. During WWII hundreds were built for the US Army. The rugged type still served the Canadian northland 60 years later. (CANAV Col.)

The Burnelli CBY-3 being readied for first flight at Cartierville in 1945. The backdrop is the CCF plant, built originally for Ramblers and still part of Canadair Plant 4 in 1994. (CANAV Col.)

direction. Noorduyn meanwhile had moved into a large building on the west side of the airfield formerly owned by Quinlan Cut Stone Co. and constructed a complex for Norseman and Harvard production. (Noorduyn lost its financial backing in 1945 and ceased operation, selling the Norseman rights to Canadian Car & Foundry Ltd.)

On May 1, 1942, ground was broken at Cartierville for a 150,000-m² (1.6-million-sq.-ft.) government-owned PBY plant, to be managed by Canadian Vickers. In charge of construction was plant engineer Ralph G. Stopps. Because of wartime restrictions on the use of steel, the plant was built mainly of wood. Canadian Vickers began moving PBY component production into the plant as fast as buildings were erected.

Cartierville's first PBY part—a punch press item—was turned out less than three months after ground-breaking. Thereafter came the rush to turn out airplanes. The plant still had no walls, only immense tarpaulins to help keep

This empty field, seen above in May 1942, was the future site of CV's St. Laurent plant. The view is northeasterly across the site of today's Plant 1 (P1). Laurentian Blvd. runs across from left to right. Some temporary construction shacks have been put up along the road. (CL 54547)

(Right) Preliminary excavations along the west side of Laurentian Blvd. in May 1942 signaled a start for the new plant. The view is southward. As the subsequent photos show, a great deal of construction had been completed by early July, and six weeks later the plant already had that "sprawling" look. (CL 54544, '265, '549)

Sheet metal activity in the St. Laurent plant in November 1943. Many women had been hired to replace men serving in the military. At left, a candid shot of a riveter on the PBY line. For riveting, Canadair turned exclusively to women, some of whom were promoted—Millie Batley became the first female lead hand. In the photo below, workers pose with one of the Cansos they were building. (CL F2669, F2919, F2672)

(Left) The float of a CV Canso has been papered with Victory bonds in one of the endless war bond drives. (CL F2694)

Once a PBY hull was built it was removed from the jig, rolled right-side up (below) and moved down the line for completion. In the lower photo on the facing page, a completed fuselage is being slung along the line by an overhead crane. (CL D1366, F3092)

The facing illustration shows the use of floor space in the St-Laurent plant in 1944. (CL F3390)

(Overleaf) Wing and fuselage are mated in the last big step on the final line. (CL D1370)

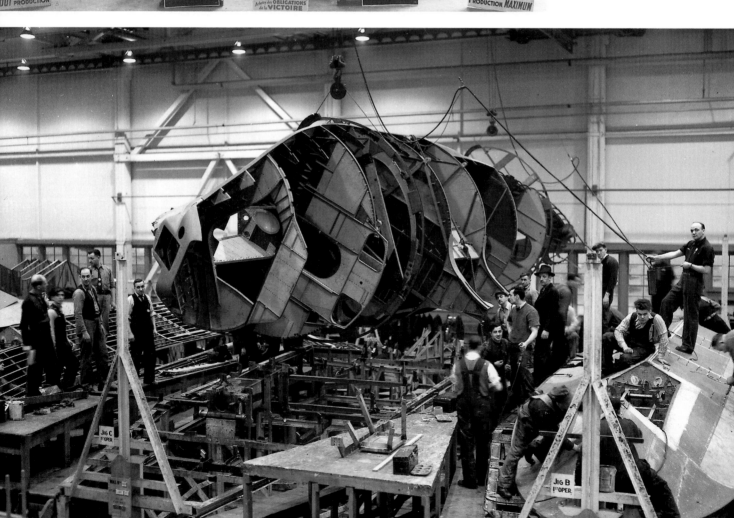

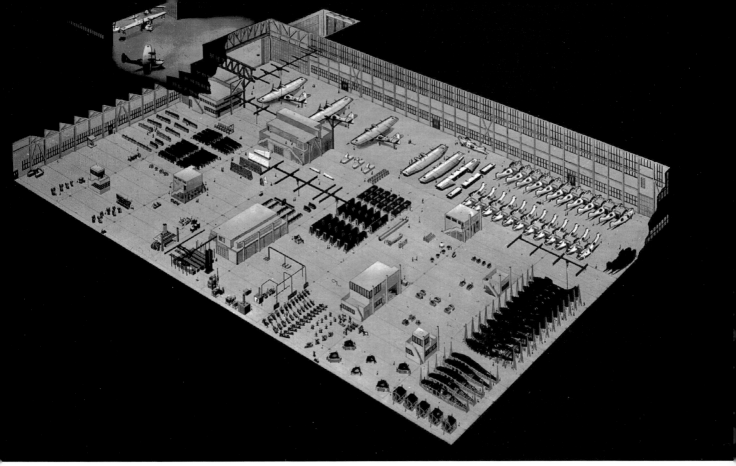

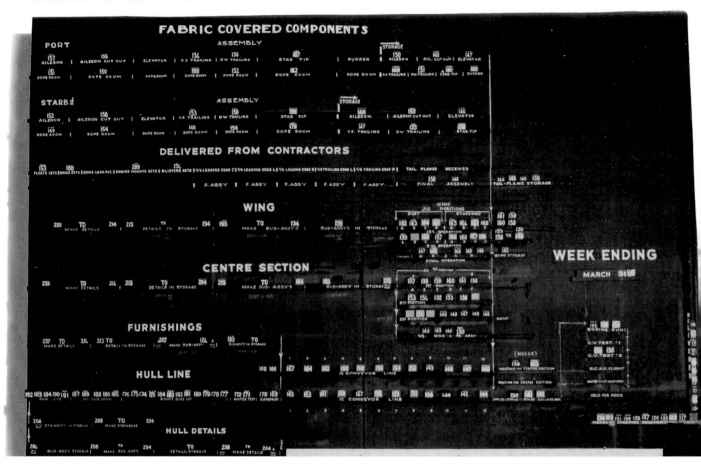

One of Ben Franklin's progress charts for tracking PBY production, then (facing page) a floor plan showing departments by number, and, below, a flow chart of the key engineering people at Canadian Vickers at this time. (CL F2952, F2903, F2890)

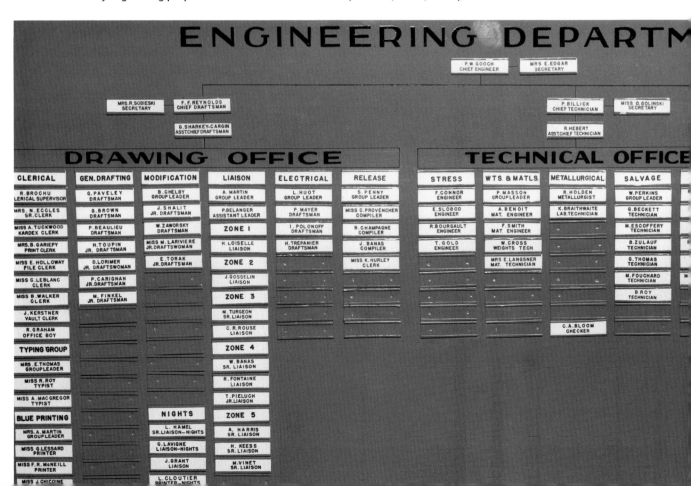

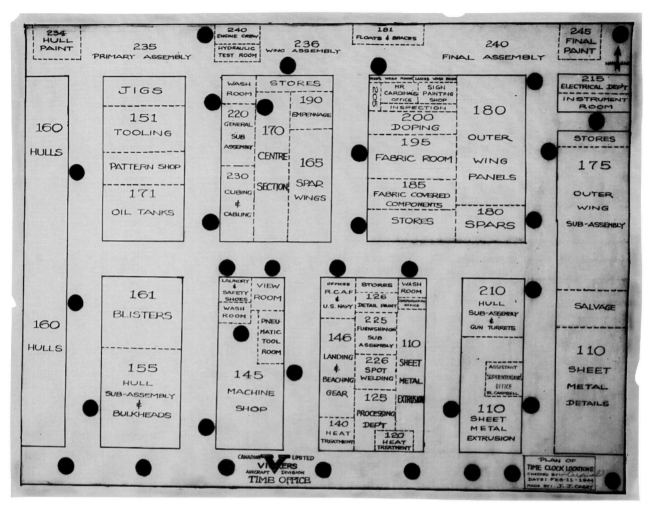

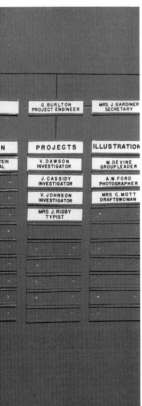

out the elements. Jean-Jacques Chartrand, who started in stores at Vickers in 1942, recalled how these kept out the wind, freezing rain and snow; and how people worked in winter boots, coats and gloves. Chartrand earned 43 cents an hour and worked shifts from 7 a.m. to midnight. Bill Palmer, preflight mechanic, had some 48-hour shifts broken only by short naps on the parachute racks. General manager, Benjamin (Benny) W. Franklin, would show up in the middle of the night to find out how things were going, exhorting the crew to "get them out fast!"

Joey Wilkinson was an assistant foreman in final assembly earning $60 for a 45-hour week. He recalled not only the cold at the plant but also the long streetcar ride from the city in the early morning hours. Cartierville could have been in Siberia as far as the city dwellers were concerned. The streetcars from the city converged at the Garland terminus at the junction of Van Horne and Décarie boulevards. There they changed to the No. 17 line for the five-mile grind which took them alongside Décarie and eventually along what is now Grenet Street, to Plants 1 and 4. Workers at Plant 2 then took the 17A along what was Bois Franc Road.

Final Canso assembly continued at St-Hubert until February 1943, by when everything had moved to Cartierville. The same month, Canadian Vickers received a contract for 230 OA-10As, a variant of the PBY-5, for the U.S. Army. The main assembly building was finally completed in June 1943 and the first Canso completed there (No. 9835) was delivered on September 13, 1943.

Canadair employees head for home, some on the No.17 street-car, others across the fields to neighboring streets east of the plant. (CL)

At war's end, Canadair employed 18,000. The day the PBY contract was cancelled, Ben Franklin called his workers together, told them they were laid off, but added that "no birds would ever fly in this building." This would have been the scene as the workers left the plant that day. (CL)

One of the Lancaster Mk. 10s built at Malton by Victory Aircraft for the CGTAS. By 1945 the "Lanc" was obsolete and Ottawa decided to buy a replacement. (CL 57358)

An April 1944 sketch of the new Canadian transport fitted with Merlin engines. (CL P3139)

The Search for a New Transport

Toward the end of 1943, the Canadian government decided to procure a four-engined, long-range transport for the RCAF, Trans-Canada Air Lines (TCA) and the general postwar commercial market. The original requirement was 50 for the RCAF and 25 for TCA.

TCA formed on April 10, 1937, with the passing of the Trans-Canada Air Line Act, the brainchild of Canada's minister of transport, Clarence Decatur Howe. Born in Waltham, Massachusetts in 1886, he had graduated from the Massachusetts Institute of Technology in 1908 with an engineering degree. He went straight to Dalhousie University in Halifax to teach engineering. In 1913, he took out Canadian citizenship and in 1935 entered politics, won a federal seat and became minister of transport, all in one year. Probably the wealthiest member of the cabinet, he was also certainly its only self-made entrepreneur.

TCA, owned and operated by the Canadian National Railways, began air mail and freight service between Montreal and Vancouver in 1938. Its existence might have been brief, for in 1939 the military attempted to absorb it into the Empire Air Training Plan. The Canadian government responded by passing an Order-in-Council under the War Measures Act exempting TCA personnel from military service. Nevertheless, some TCA crews were loaned to British Overseas Airways Corporation (BOAC) for transatlantic ferry operations. The advantage of this became clear when Ottawa launched the Canadian Government Trans-Atlantic Air Service in July 1943, using converted Lancaster bombers flown by TCA crews and operated mainly between Montreal and Prestwick (Scotland).

The search for TCA's new transport was necessarily concentrated in the United States because early in 1942 Britain and the United States agreed that Britain would build bombers and fighters. This left the Americans clear to develop and manufacture transports. Canada had a choice of the Douglas DC-4 (a civil version of the proven C-54) and the Lockheed C-69 Constellation. A TCA

An example of the DC-4 upon which CV based its new transport. The DC-4 first flew in June 1938; this one was still operating in 1995. Below, the first C-69 Constellation. It first flew in January 1943 and was the other type being considered for TCA in 1944. (Larry Milberry, Lockheed)

The two leading men in the search for a new transport for TCA—
C.D. Howe (right), sometimes referred to as "minister of everything",
and H.J. Symington, president of TCA. (CL DX8177)

Vickers Wins the Contract

Believing Canadian Vickers to be committed to building
Lincoln bombers for A.V. Roe of Britain, the Department
of Munitions and Supply under C.D. Howe had promised the contract to build the new transport to Boeing in
Vancouver. However, Howe had not reckoned on the per-
suasive ability of general manager Benny Franklin. The
story goes that Franklin struck a deal with Howe: if
Franklin could persuade Sir Roy Dobson of A.V. Roe that
the other plants designated as Lincoln manufacturers (Victory Aircraft, Fleet, and Canadian Car & Foundry) were capable of producing the required 40 Lincolns a month,
Howe would give the new transport to Canadian Vickers.

Howe agreed, Franklin convinced Dobson, and on
March 11, 1944, Howe agreed that he was prepared to accept Franklin's proposal to build the new transport under
the following terms:

- the contract would cover 50 DC-4s, including spare
  parts up to a dollar value of 25 per cent of the cost
  of the airframe;
- the 50 airplanes would be built on the basis of an
  average target cost of $350,000 each;
- the fee to Canadian Vickers would be $4,500 per air-
  craft plus a bonus 25 per cent of the savings on target cost;
- the first aircraft would be delivered within 13
  months of receiving the required drawings and engineering data from Douglas;
- the government would make the Cartierville factory
  available for the purpose of the contract "to the extent it is not required for the government's war
  work."

Shortly thereafter Canadian Vickers sent 18 engineers
to the Douglas plant at Santa Monica, California, to gain
design experience. Seven others including Bruce McCall,
Bob Stapells and Bob Agar went to the development department of Rolls-Royce at Hucknall, England, to study
Merlin engine performance and the changes required if
the Merlin was chosen to power the new transport. Another 20 assembly and planning people went to Douglas
to learn assembly methods, including the use of the
drivmatic machine which was to play an important part in
many later programs. Some of the engineers who went to

internal report from February 1945 opted for the DC-4:
"… it would be a more economical aircraft to operate
than the Constellation and would still have adequate performance, though it would not fly as fast. The airframe of
the DC-4, as a result of its worldwide use as the C-54 during the past two years, has been through its teething
troubles and is now in a state where little maintenance
trouble can be expected. The experience of TCA with previous Lockheed airplanes indicates that a considerable
period will elapse before all minor deficiencies are eliminated from the maintenance standpoint in the Constellation." On February 29, 1944, the government negotiated
a licence agreement whereby Douglas would furnish
plans for the DC-4 and the newer DC-6 (then in the design stage) and assist in the development and construction in Canada of a type based on these two designs.

Ben Franklin was the brains behind the founding of Canadair and was
its first president. (CL DX8163)

This photo from April 6, 1945 shows those sent to Douglas in California to study C-54 production. In the back row in this "happy times" snapshot are: Bob Raven, Johnny Walker, Maurice Finkel, Leo Audet, Bill Carter, Paul Belanger, Al Herschfield, Garth Parker, Les Wiebe, Harold Oatway, Jean Langevin and Jim Maclure. In front are Charlie Bloom, Johnny Orlando, Rod Irving, Ian Gordon, Jim Carnwath, Bob Aiken and Bert Edwards. (Pierre Masson via Jim Carnwath)

Douglas stayed for two years; several made lifelong careers in California industry.

Meanwhile TCA was doing some research of its own. It was discussing with Victory Aircraft of Toronto about producing an airliner version of the Avro York, a British military transport which used a Lancaster wing. However, in a memo to the operations manager of TCA of March 1944, J.T. (Jim) Bain, TCA's superintendent of engineering and maintenance, expressed doubts that Victory Aircraft could supply a suitable aircraft in the required time. This proved accurate and Victory built only one York.

Vickers Backs Out

While licensing negotiations with Douglas were going on, Canadian Vickers general manager, T.R. McLagan, told Ottawa that Vickers' obligations to build ships for the allied navies and the merchant service involved such heavy commitments that his company could no longer continue with both ships and aircraft; it was contemplating getting out of the aircraft business. Howe was disappointed because he had never wanted the government in the aviation industry. He had hoped to persuade Canadian Vickers to take over the Cartierville plant as a private concern. This was not to be.

In mid-1944, McLagan asked the government to relieve Vickers of its management responsibilities relating to the plant. Ottawa agreed and took the first step in establishing the plant as a private operation by entering into a management contract with, as Howe told the press: "... a new company which will devote itself exclusively to aircraft production. The new company, to be known as Canadair Limited, will be under the management of Benjamin W. Franklin, formerly in charge of aircraft production for Canadian Vickers Limited."

Canadair Limited

The founding of Canadair was not a spur-of-the-moment idea; Franklin had been working to this end for several

years. Alexander (Al) J. Lilly, then chief test pilot for Royal Air Force (RAF) Ferry Command, first met Franklin in 1942 when he

T. Rodgie McLagan of Canadian Vickers was one of the founders of Canadair. Such men brought knowledge, experience and wisdom to the new company. (CL D9747)

asked for a ride with a number of VIPs Lilly was flying from Montreal to Detroit. Lilly recalled Franklin sitting in the co-pilot's seat and talking for the entire trip about how he was building the company, and all the wonderful people he was going to get to run it. Franklin's plans bore fruit on October 3, 1944, when Canadair was

Lou Adamson (left) and Walter Meacher were key CV men who later worked at Canadair. (CL F3567)

incorporated with an authorized capital stock of 10,000 shares at $1.00 par value.

The first board of directors was made up of former Canadian Vickers personnel: Benjamin W. Franklin, president; John E.L. Duquet, vice-president; Clayton F. Elderkin, secretary/treasurer; Ralph G. Stopps, factory manager and Walter H. Meacher, chief accountant. Other members of senior management were engineers Peter Gooch, Clem Christie and Paul Billick, and manager of spare parts, Lou Adamson. Stopps recalled that it was Franklin who chose the name Canadair, after initially proposing Canada Air.

Benjamin W. Franklin

Canadian-born and, as far as can be determined, unrelated to his American namesake, Benny Franklin was a small, dapper man with shiny black hair and a voice that was clipped, rapid and incisive. A former farm machinery and insurance salesman, he had little aircraft experience prior to joining Canadian Vickers in 1940. He was an able organizer, manager and administrator and had good connections in aviation. He was a close friend of First World War ace Eddie Rickenbacker who would later become president of Eastern Airlines, and Donald Douglas, head of the company that bore his name. Bob Raven remembered Franklin as shrewd, a great negotiator and a dynamo–but not always in the right direction. He was one of those remarkable people who could party until 2 a.m. and still show up bright-eyed in the shop at 7 a.m.

Jim Bain, who was loaned by TCA to Canadair as Franklin's executive assistant, described him as

a remarkable man in many regards. "He will invariably come out on the top side of any negotiation," wrote Bain. "He possesses singular mental agility but is certainly closer to being a promoter in the worst sense of the word than he ever has been a manager of an aircraft company." Franklin's secretary, Marion (Baker) Gall, described him as a very clever and charismatic person who did a lot of good for many people at Canadair. Preflight mechanic Bill Palmer said he was a great guy who could show up in preflight in the middle of the night and have coffee and doughnuts brought out to the crew.

As he was often away at Douglas or Rolls-Royce for six months of the year, Franklin taught Gall to think like him so that when Howe or the government's director general of military production, Ralph Bell, called with questions, she could answer just as Franklin would have. Franklin also devised a color-coded status board which enabled him to see the status of each contract at a glance. Gall recalls that he would arrive in his office from a trip, take a quick glance at the board, and head down to the shop to tear a strip off anyone holding up production.

Canadair Assumes Control

At midnight on November 11, 1944, Canadian Vickers formally relinquished management of the Cartierville plant to the government, which then passed control to Canadair. Earlier that day, the government had granted Canadair a lease with an option to purchase the facilities.

Ralph G. Stopps started with Canadian Vickers in 1936. Under Ben Franklin he became plant manager at St. Laurent in 1943. In early Canadair days he corralled great amounts of valuable war surplus aircraft parts, tools and jigs in the US for a fraction of their value. His astute deals put Canadair in an enviable position—while similar firms were laying off and closing down, Canadair held its own and was soon growing. Stopps retired to Prescott, Ontario, in 1972 and passed away on September 12, 1991. (CL D9716)

It would become effective if Canadair could raise capital stock of not less than $2.5 million on or before May 1, 1945. That day arrived without Canadair having the money, although, according to Gall, Franklin approached every available source for funds. Ottawa agreed, however, to allow Canadair to carry on until other arrangements could be made.

As far as the 9,000 or so employees at Cartierville were concerned, life went on unchanged, except that they now worked for Canadair. Production of Cansos for the RCAF had finished but there was still much to be done on the remaining OA-10As for the U.S. Army and to fill an order for 119 PBY hulls and 172 centre sections for Consolidated Vultee at Biloxi, Louisiana. At this time, Ray Campbell was shop superintendent; Cy McNeil was in charge of production, aided by Albert Kemp, Leo Audet and Eddie Forest.

The PBY program ended with the delivery of the final OA-10A on May 17, 1945–nine days after the end of the war in Europe. In just 18 months, Cartierville had turned out 340 PBY-5As and OA-10As, 57 of which were produced by Canadair. A further 29 PBY-5As had been assembled earlier at St-Hubert.

Several employees held vivid memories of the day the PBY program ended. Jean-Jacques Chartrand remembered being in the crowd assembled below the catwalk at the north end of Plant 1 to hear Franklin announce that, now the war was over, PBY production would be terminated and many would be laid off. He assured everyone that Canadair was here to stay; that he had plans for the future. He thanked the workers for their loyal service, but for now he wanted them all to go home until recalled. He asked them to leave in an orderly way without doing any damage.

Chartrand, Palmer, Wilkinson and Dick Faucher were among the thousand or so employees not laid off. They recalled the long lines of workers patiently awaiting clearance–happy the war was over, sad their jobs had ended, but buoyed by Franklin's infectious charisma. They remembered, too, the three months of inactivity, the empty aisles, the silent machines and the idle workers hiding each time someone from management appeared on the shop floor. They found a little to do manufacturing PBY spares and Mosquito ailerons for de Havilland; repairing Mitchells, Liberators and Lancasters for Ferry Command; and cannibalizing and scrapping a number of Consolidated RY-3s that had been on their way to England when the war ended. All in all, though, it was scarcely enough to keep even a thousand people busy.

The C-47 Conversion Program

By good coincidence, Franklin chose this time to send factory manager Ralph Stopps to Douglas in Santa Monica, to study DC-4 production requirements. There Stopps discovered that the U.S. government had ordered Douglas to close its C-47 production plants within 24 hours of war's end. Douglas now wanted to concentrate on the DC-6 and it intended to dispose of all tooling and spares for the C-47/DC-3 at its Oklahoma City plant, as well as some C-54 fuselages in a Chicago plant. Stopps alerted Franklin who arranged with Donald Douglas for Canadair to have first call on all this material. When Douglas told Franklin that he could have the contents of a specific area of the Oklahoma City plant, Franklin sent Cy McNeil and Ray Campbell to scour the plant for desirable items and move them into the area designated for Canadair. Stopps and Hymie Crystal did a similar job at the Chicago plant.

Through this opportunism, Canadair obtained over 600 carloads of materials and cornered the market on conversion of military C-47s to civilian DC-3s as well as their modification, repair and overhaul. Stopps paid $40 a ton for tools and $200 a ton for parts. Included were more than 60 fuselages for the C-54 some of which would later play an important role in the long-range transport program. For weeks Douglas parts arrived at Cartierville by train, truck and air. With each shipment, workers from every department would be pressed into service unloading.

With airlines around the world clamoring for equipment, Canadair next went looking for surplus C-47s to convert to DC-3s. Many were bought from the RAF and ferried from Britain by pilots hired by Don McVicar's World Wide Aviation. Others came from Bush Field in Augusta, Georgia, and Walnut Ridge, Arkansas.

On January 1, 1946, Canadair leased the former Noorduyn plant at Cartierville for its Douglas-approved conversion centre. It was officially called the Canadair Conversion Plant, but was known to all employees simply as "Noorduyn." B. Wensley King was in charge of the program; Cy McNeil was plant superintendent, Jimmy Appleton his assistant, Ed Norsworthy, Kirwin Rollo and

Harry Whiteman the project engineers, Fred King chief pilot, Jan De Vries the chief inspector, Od Cleven and Bob Lording two of the crew chiefs, and Ernie Dionne in preflight.

Most of the aircraft still bore wartime camouflage, some had signs of tropical operations, and even battle damage. In each case, the damage had been covered with external patches with little effort to check inside for structural damage. At Cartierville, they were thoroughly washed with steam hoses. Various litter was discovered including M-1 rifles and dead snakes. One mechanic hastily exited the cabin of a newly arrived aircraft shouting that he had seen a tarantula! The aircraft was sealed and

filled with insecticide. Wensley King related that floor boards from the cockpit of one C-47 had "kist" printed on the underside–a sign that they had come from a Sunkist orange crate!

Conversion consisted mainly of changing the heavy military cargo floor and wide cargo door to a lighter basic weight, and installing a customized interior and avionics. Eastern Airlines was the first conversion customer. It supplied its own aircraft, but when they were returned to the United States, Eastern had to pay a 30 per cent duty on the value added by Canadair. Eastern, however, considered that the quality and cost of the work outweighed the duty.

Canadair supplied 21 DC-3s to TCA, several to

Aircraft components from one of Ralph Stopps' Douglas purchases arrive at a Montreal rail siding in 1945. (CL F3394)

The fuselage of the XC-54GM (brought up from the U.S. to become Canadair's prototype) is seen in Plant 1. (Below) A group of CV personnel is shown as the transport line takes shape. Fifth from the left in front is chief engineer Peter Gooch. (CL DX 8424-A, F3709)

A typical TCA DC-3 fresh from Canadair in May 1946. It served TCA until 1958 then was sold to the Department of Transport as CF-DTB. (CL)

Canadian Pacific Airlines and other Canadian carriers. The rest went to foreign customers like Aerolineas Argentinas, Aerovias Equatorianas, Air France, FAMA, Icelandair, LAN Chile, the Netherlands East Indies Air Force, Sabena and Zonda. Canadair bought one, a C-47 with only 16 hours flight time, for $15,000, for its private, 18-seat corporate plane. The Air France conversions were known for the fine gray gabardine material used on their seats. It was not long before the odd Canadair employee was spotted in downtown Montreal wearing a smart gray gabardine suit. At the peak of the conversion program in mid-1946, some 40 C-47s were being handled simultaneously.

In 1950, the RCAF bought some ex-RAF C-47s in Egypt and ferried them to Canadair for conversion to target tugs. Barry Gilmore, an electrician on the job, recalled

that these bore an unmistakable camel scent. Conversion included installing a large winch in the side door from which a drogue target was streamed, and an observation bubble to let the winch operator see the target. When Al Lilly and crew chief Art Childs flew the first tug, Gilmore was watching. The aircraft took off, made a slow, wide circuit and approached with its rudder leaning at an unusual angle. It fell off completely as Lilly touched down. It turned out that someone had reamed out a worn rudder pin hole, correctly inserted a bushing, but re-installed the old washer. It was too small and allowed the pin and bushing to fall out.

In addition to conversions, Canadair did a roaring trade in DC-3 spares. At Douglas' Oklahoma plant, one of the Canadair group had found a list showing which

This DC-3 landed at Canadair on March 18, 1945, the first of hundreds to undergo conversion. It was originally NC34979 of Trans World Airlines. In November 1942 it was impressed into the USAAF as a C-49K. Canadair picked it up from the Reconstruction Finance Corporation, the US agency disposing of war surplus material. It was converted for Eastern Airlines, and later flew with other US operators. W.H. Meacher (retired May 1970) of Canadair and Capt Davis, the ferry pilot, are beside the plane. (CL D1861)

Wensley King started at Canadair heading the DC-3 program. He later became president of the Sperry instrument company in Montreal. (CL D9722)

(Below) Ralph Stopps with company pilots Fred King and Bill Anglin in front of a TCA DC-3 in September 1945. (CL F3674)

C-47 parts were equivalent to DC-3 parts. Canadair was then able to supply spares from stock within 24 hours while Douglas was quoting six months for delivery.

Doubting Canadair's ability to meet its needs, the RAF ordered Dakota spares from Douglas, only to have its orders re-directed to Canadair. Stopps estimated Canadair made $13 million simply by taking parts out of one box and putting them into another. Some parts bought at five cents a pound, he sold back to Douglas at 15 cents. Eventually Douglas realized what was happening and sued Canadair for $6 million for selling spares to the U.S. Air Force. The matter was settled amicably when Canadair agreed to pay Douglas a five per cent royalty on all USAF sales.

Another source of revenue originated with a request from the U.S. State Department. It asked Canadair to se-

Canadair's DC-3 conversion plant in full swing in 1945. A few PBYs were still at the far end of the building. (CL)

Before and after. These cockpit photos show how some C-47s arrived at Cartierville, then how they came out of the conversion plant. (CL D3827, D5957)

Workers at Canadair strip a war-weary C-47. (D2071)

(Above and below) Shop and conversion line work in the DC-3 plant during April 1946. (CL D2777, '80)

CF-TED No. 1 was Canadair's corporate DC-3. TCA asked for the same registration, so Canadair's TED became CF-DXU. It did a hundred-and-one jobs until sold in 1968, after which it served various Canadian carriers until a 1981 accident. (CL D2757)

lect suitable aircraft from USAF stocks in the United Kingdom and ferry them home. This Canadair agreed for a ferry charge of $800 per aircraft, on condition that all aircraft came via Montreal so that it could inspect them before they went on their way. Canadair repaired any deficiencies and billed Washington.

Harry Whiteman recalled some conversion work on three Beechcrafts, one of which, destined for a major mining company, was fitted with a stainless steel toilet seat in deference to the owner's wife's fear of germs. The seat must have been quite stimulating on a cold morning.

On January 15, 1946, the Canadair board accepted the subscription of Benny Franklin for 9,000 shares (90 per cent) of the capital stock of the company at $1.00 a share, payable in cash. The first changes to Canadair's board of directors were made in mid-April 1946. Duquet resigned and was replaced as vice-president by D.H. Macfarlane. Marion Gall became company secretary. Meacher remained treasurer and comptroller, and Stopps plant manager. Gall wielded a great deal of authority. Many employees referred to her as "the Boss" and Franklin described her to Al Lilly as "the one who ran the show."

Ben Franklin's personal secretary Marion Gall (left) and Marion Lowe, another top Canadair secretary, pose with Franklin's Cadillac and the first North Star. (CL DX8164)

DETA's CR-ABK being readied for ferrying to Portuguese Mozambique. While Portugal's African empire was shrinking in 1972, ABK entered the Portuguese Air Force. It was last noted as derelict in Guinea-Bissau in 1979. (CL D2620)

(Right) This crew was at Canadair in July 1946 to ferry SE-BBO to Stockholm. It served until the mid-1960s, then was scrapped in Denmark. (CL D3149)

(Below) This conversion came from the USAAF in North Africa. From Cartierville it went to Mexico, where it flew till 1977. The story of its 1948 Transair color scheme is not known. (CL)

CF-TDJ runs up at Canadair in September 1945. This was TCA's first DC-3. Instead of the usual Pratt & Whitney R-1830 engines, it had Wright R-1820s. TCA sold TDJ to Goodyear Canada in 1948. (CL D2431)

(Right) A typical DC-3 long-range installation with fuel tanks bolted to the floor of DT976 (Netherlands East Indies Air Force). Its route was Cartierville-Indonesia in March 1946. (CL D2535)

(Below) A TCA DC-3 on approach to Cartierville in 1946. It has just passed Laurentian Boulevard, beyond which is some of the old wartime housing, and a well-known feature of the day—the huge billboard advertising Hygrade sausages. On the left is Curtiss-Reid Flying Service with some war-surplus Tiger Moths and a Cessna Crane out front. (CL D3222)

Two close-ups of colorful DC-3s fresh from Canadair: one for General Mills (NC50314), the other for Doris Yellowknife Gold Mines. (CL)

(Below) This DC-3 served in Australia during the war and is thought to have been the last Canadair conversion. It was handed over to the Department of Transport in February 1950. Here it flies over farmland on the south shore of the St. Lawrence with the Victoria and Jacques Cartier bridges in the background. (CL D5562)

An Argentine customer for Canadair was ZONDA. LV-ABX sports its new colors as it runs up. After a local flight in September 1946 ABX suffered a collapsed landing gear at Cartierville. (CL)

(Below) Goodyear's DC-3 served until December 1983 then was handed over to the National Aviation Museum in Ottawa. In this April 1971 photo it is at home base in Toronto. (Larry Milberry)

Another 1940s Canadair executive conversion was this ex-TCA Lock-heed Lodestar for British American Oil. Other Lodestars were done for the T. Eaton and Massey Harris companies of Toronto. Shown at right is the VIP interior of the Massey Harris plane. (CL)

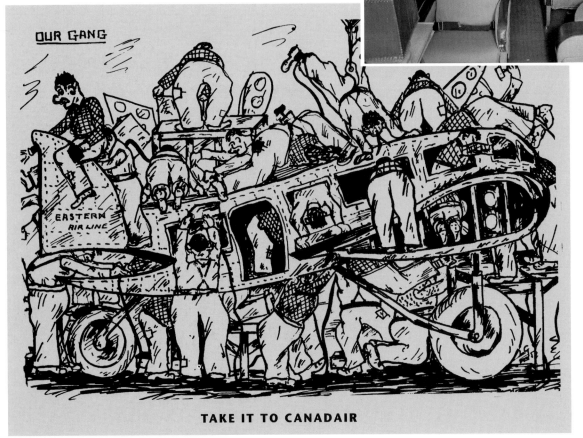

OUR GANG

EASTERN AIR LINE

TAKE IT TO CANADAIR

A conversion plant cartoon that surfaced in the company archives after 50 years. (CL)

The Merlin Engine Controversy

Meanwhile, the long-range transport program became the subject of controversy. The choice of engine created a political uproar. A TCA document of July 1944, entitled "Engine Selection for the Douglas DC-4", listed the following alternatives: Pratt & Whitney R-2000-9 and R-2800-C; Rolls-Royce RM-14-SM and RM-20-SM (Merlins) and Griffon; Bristol HE-10 Hercules; and Wright R-2600-22. An extensive evaluation eliminated all but the R-2800-C and RM-14-SM with the eventual choice being the latter.

According to the report the Merlin's rated power was higher than the others above 20,000 feet where maximum power was needed for safe transatlantic service. The cruising power used to obtain equal performance was therefore at a lower percentage of rated power with the RM-14-SM than any other engine giving payload-ton-miles per Imperial gallon of 3.32 with the Merlin versus 2.53 with the R-2800. Direct operating costs per ton-mile were $0.295 for the Merlin and $0.392 for the R-2800.

Also in the Merlin's favor was Rolls-Royce's promise to unconditionally guarantee a reasonable service for their

A.G. Mould and D.S. Burns of Rolls-Royce (Canada); Ted Emmert; Lord Hives of Rolls-Royce (England); then Kelly Smith and Roger Lewis in a photo from September 1949. The Rolls-Royce men were key in the supply/servicing of Merlins for the North Star program. (CL D9019)

New Merlins are inspected in Canadair's engine shop. (CL)

The first North Star shines in the sun at Cartierville in July 1946. (CL)

engines. The report stated: "Rolls-Royce has a very extensive development section where the entire power plant is designed and tested to give optimum performance of the engines. As yet, American engine manufacturers are unable to assume the responsibility for the design of the entire powerplant." Despite the report's conclusions, some regarded choosing the Merlin as a political decision—a friendly gesture to assist Britain in the lean postwar years. Whatever the reasons, it proved an advantage when the opportunity later arose to sell the aircraft in the UK.

The North Star

Shortly after the war, Canadian requirements were reduced to 24 transports for the RCAF and 20 for TCA. This increased unit cost but TCA still estimated it at below the cost of importing comparable planes from the United States. A major difference between TCA and RCAF requirements was in cabin pressurization. TCA regarded pressurization as essential for high altitude Atlantic operations while the RCAF felt that its operations did not merit the expense of a pressurization. The RCAF version, designated C-54GM, was unpressurized and built mainly of C-54 parts. TCA aircraft—designated DC-4M2—were pressurized, had a DC-4 empennage, rear fuselage, flaps, ailerons and wing tips; C-54G wing centre and

outer wing panel; DC-6 fuselage shortened by 2.0 m (80 in.), and DC-6 nose section and landing gear. To put Canadair to work as soon as possible and avoid impending layoffs, the first aircraft on the line were C-54GMs with fuselages from the 60 Chicago C-54s.

On March 31, 1946, TCA ordered 20 DC-4M2s. The contract stipulated that the first be ready for July 1947 with two per month in August, September and October, and at least two per month thereafter. The price of each would be $660,000. TCA agreed to use the aircraft only within the Dominion of Canada, or in international operations primarily originating in and based in the Dominion of Canada. Canadair, in turn, agreed to complete as quickly as possible, an investigation to increase permissible gross takeoff weight to 36,000 kg (80,000 lb.) from an initial 35,000 kg (78,000 lb.)

TCA wanted to get an early start on postwar civil operations. Feeling it could not wait for the pressurized M2s, it appealed to Ottawa which arranged for the RCAF's first six C-54GMs to be loaned until TCA's M2s were ready. TCA was not charged for this, but agreed to convert the "GMs" to RCAF configuration before returning them. With TCA, these six aircraft were DC-4M1s. They differed from the GMs in that their aft cargo doors were modified for passenger use, and a DC-6 landing gear was installed to permit a gross weight increase of 2,000 kg (5,000 lb.).

In mid-July 1946, the new airplane was ready to fly. At Benny Franklin's suggestion it was named "North Star." Franklin had intended the name to apply only to the first aircraft, CF-TEN-X, but TCA liked the name; on July 20, Mrs. C.D. Howe christened CF-TEN-X "North Star". The name was destined to be remembered in Canadian aviation, for different reasons by different people.

CF-TEN-X made its maiden flight in the late afternoon of July 15, 1946. At the controls were Robert P. Brush, chief pilot from Douglas Santa Monica, and Al Lilly, Canadair's chief test pilot. W.L. (Smokey) Harris was the flight engineer and Clayton H. Glenn of TCA was aboard with his knowledge of the propeller control unit (which had been giving problems). The 25-minute flight was routine. Brush noted that stall characteristics were not as good as for the DC-4 or DC-6; cruise speeds were slightly below estimates and fuel consumption was slightly high. After a month, Brush returned to Douglas and Lilly took over test flying.

Lilly had learned to fly at Moose Jaw, Saskatchewan in 1927. He joined the Royal Canadian Mounted Police in 1932 and, while on detachment in northern Saskatchewan, promoted greater use of bush planes in policing. When he transferred to Moncton, Lilly obtained his commercial pilot's licence.

Just before the war Lilly joined Imperial Airways and was busy as a co-pilot, route-proving the Armstrong Whitworth Ensign airliner in Europe, when the war brought him home. After a tour in the British Commonwealth Air Training Plan as chief flying instructor at Moncton, New Brunswick, he moved to Ferry Command headquarters at St-Hubert. He delivered aircraft to Europe and North Africa before becoming chief test pilot for Ferry Command. Toward the end of the war, he helped set up a freighting service from Florida to the

Two early advertisements that promoted the forthcoming North Star. (CL)

Word of North Star jobs drew hundreds of Montreal's unemployed, many idled from Canadair at war's end, out to Cartierville. These men wait to put in their applications. (CL)

(Right) Smokey Harris, on the left, and Al Lilly joined Canadair early and crewed on the first North Star flight. They are wearing their natty Canadair uniforms with monogrammed wing and buttons. The second photo shows Bob Brush and Ben Franklin the day the North Star first flew. (CL D9488, DX8115)

(Below) The first North Star is pushed out in June 1946. At this time, it was still referred to as the XC-54GM. It was mainly built from components bought from Douglas, then had Merlins fitted. (CL DX8046)

North Star wing spars are built up on the shop floor. The model below shows the production floor plan for B102. (D9366, D4772)

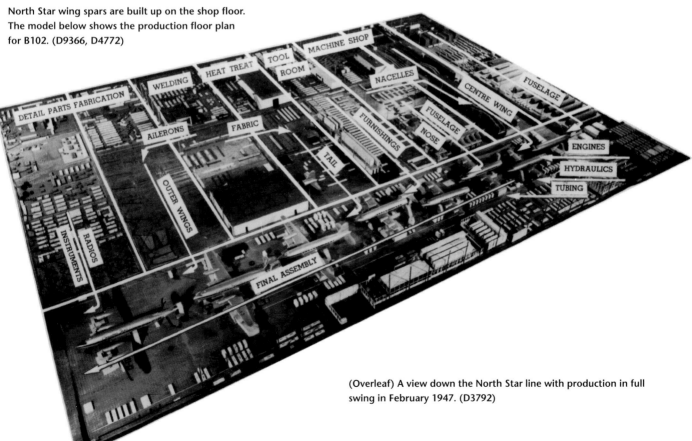

(Overleaf) A view down the North Star line with production in full swing in February 1947. (D3792)

Caribbean using Stranraers, then flew briefly for Maritime Central Airways. Lilly joined Canadair in June 1946 and was chief test pilot until 1953. Thereafter he became assistant to the president, director of sales, then director of customer relations, before retiring in 1970. His contributions to aviation in Canada were recognized officially in 1984 when he was inducted into Canada's Aviation Hall of Fame.

Electric Boat Buys Canadair

It cannot be established precisely when the Electric Boat Co. of Groton, Connecticut, first became interested in aviation, but on May 18, 1944, its board of directors authorized this amendment to the company's certificate of incorporation: "To manufacture, fabricate, assemble, and sell aircraft of whatsoever kind and description."

Electric Boat was founded in 1899 by entrepreneur Isaac Rice. He had made a reputation as a railroad lawyer before turning to a career in the electric storage-battery business—batteries were a major source of electrical power because early dynamos were unreliable. Rice combined Holland Torpedo Boat Co. of Bayonne, New Jersey, developers of the world's first practical submarine; Electro Dynamic Co. of Philadelphia, Pennsylvania, manufacturer of small electric motors; and Electric Launch Co. of Morris Heights, New York City to form Electric Boat with the intention of manufacturing and selling battery-operated submarines and launches. By 1946, Electric Boat was the largest private submarine manufacturer in the United States. During both world wars, it also built motor-torpedo boats and sub-chasers; in peacetime it manufactured pleasure craft, electric motors and generators.

Electric Boat had enjoyed a long association with Canadian Vickers, having been a Vickers customer throughout both wars. The first indication of interest in Canadair appears in Electric Boat's 1946 annual report: "In 1944, management commenced an investigation into the possibility of the Company's becoming interested in operating the most important aircraft manufacturing plant in Canada, located at Cartierville in the Parish of St. Laurent, near Montreal. A Canadian corporation, Canadair Limited, has been managing this plant during the war under a Government contract."

Benny Franklin was probably aware of this interest. When Howe charged him with finding a reputable firm to buy the Cartierville facility and operate it on a permanent basis, he struck a deal with John J. Hopkins, who was then vice-president of Electric Boat. Hopkins jumped at the chance. While Electric Boat was restricted in what it could earn from small-quantity submarine orders, a Canadian aircraft manufacturing operation could provide a higher percentage of profit than any equivalent U.S. aircraft concern because, at that time, Canada did not have an equivalent of the U.S. excess profits tax.

John J. Hopkins, who liked to be called "Jay", was born in Santa Ana, California. He served in the U.S. Navy in the First World War, earned a law degree from Harvard in 1921, and was special assistant to the Secretary of the Navy in 1932 and 1933. From 1936 until 1941, he had his own law and finance business. In 1937 he joined the board of Electric Boat, and in 1941 became its vice-president of legal and financial affairs. He was appointed president of Electric Boat and chairman of Canadair in 1947.

A stocky, handsome man, Hopkins looked much younger than his age. He was an ardent deep-sea fisherman, but his greatest sporting interest was golf. He sponsored International Professional Golf Association (PGA) team matches for the Hopkins Trophy and created the International Invitation Twosomes for the Canada Cup, an event which brought some of the world's top golfers to Canada. He was on the board of the U.S. PGA and used his golf affiliation to contact top businessmen in other countries who were members of their national golf associations.

Gordon J. Stringer, Canadair's manager of public relations in its early years, described Hopkins as a shrewd businessman and a showman who always seemed to be doing something that made you stop and notice. For example, when the *Nautilus*, Electric Boat's first nuclear submarine, was launched, President Truman and dignitaries from many nations attended the ceremony. All were dressed in dark suits, except Hopkins—he was right in the middle, in white.

John J. Hopkins came to Canadair in 1946. He had joined Electric Boat as a director in 1937 and became a top shareholder and chairman. In 1952 Electric Boat became the nucleus of General Dynamics with Hopkins as chairman of the board, and Canadair as a subsidiary. Hopkins passed away in 1957. (CL D9752)

One of the best air-to-air portraits of CF-TEN-X is this one taken July 26, 1946. (CL DX8141)

On April 26, 1946, Electric Boat's board authorized an agreement with Franklin to purchase 1,000 shares or 10 per cent of the capital stock of Canadair for $100,000 U.S. with an option to purchase an additional 6,500 shares for $400,000 up to December 1. Franklin must have been ecstatic for, just three months previously, he had paid only $9,000 Cdn for 9,000 shares.

When the agreement was signed on April 30, 1946, Franklin agreed to use all reasonable means to obtain the following:

- valid and effective licences for Canadair from Douglas regarding the North Star;
- valid and effective licences from Rolls-Royce granting Canadair exclusive North American rights for the Merlin and other products;

- long-term leases, with option to purchase from the Crown the two plants and the airport at Cartierville.

In return Electric Boat agreed to provide Canadair working capital of not more than $2 million.

When Howe found that the deal Franklin had made with Hopkins included the C-47 conversion program, he blew up. All the money the government had put into the program was now going to benefit only Franklin and Electric Boat. Howe tried to persuade Hopkins to deal directly with the government and exclude Franklin, but Hopkins refused saying that he wanted Franklin to be president of the new subsidiary. Howe countered by persuading Hopkins instead to hire H. Oliver West, executive vice-president of Boeing.

H. Oliver West began his career as an inspector of raw

materials for Boeing in Seattle, and worked his way up to be executive vice-president by 1937 when he came to Canada. In 1939 he returned to the U.S. and Boeing where he was a leading figure in the production of B-17 Flying Fortress and B-29 Superfortress bombers.

West was a short man who favored linen suits and ascots. A martinet with a quick temper, he was a driver and a perfectionist. He is best remembered for the good he did for the company. He got Canadair going by bringing in the right people and equipment, enabling it to win the Sabre and T-33 contracts and international industry recognition.

Howe had become involved with West and Boeing in 1935 when there had been accusations in the United States of conflict of interest in awarding airmail contracts. An investigation had revealed that Boeing was involved with United Airlines. This violated anti-trust laws which prohibited an aircraft manufacturer from being financially linked to an air carrier. In 1937, when it appeared the U.S. government might institute criminal proceedings against Boeing's president, Philip G. Johnson, and executive vice-president, Oliver West, it became convenient for them to come to Canada as consultants for TCA. With the outbreak of the Second World War, Washington dropped the charges, and Johnson and West returned to Boeing. West became available to take over Canadair when Johnson died and he lost out to William Allen in the battle for the Boeing presidency.

In 1947 H.O. West became Canadair's first president in the Electric Boat era. One retiree recalled that, besides his official job, West was Canadair's "chief decorator". Hunting through warehouses in Montreal he acquired its original collection of antiques. He had two huge loads delivered to Plant 2 for stripping and restoration by professionals. To suit his arthritis-wracked hands, West had Dick Faucher design special brass doorknobs for head office. (D9728)

West did not come alone to Canadair, but brought along some top American technical and management people. Hopkins could not refuse this opportunity to get a management team which knew not only how to build air-craft but how to market them. So West was hired and Franklin resigned.

On September 15, 1946, an agreement was signed between the Canadian government and a new Canadair for the lease of and option to purchase the land, buildings, machinery and equipment of the Cartierville plant. The term of the lease was 15 years at an annual rental of $200,000. The basic value of the plant was fixed at $4 million. This would depreciate annually until the option to purchase was exercised. The government also assigned to Canadair the Douglas licence and any and all rights with respect to the development of the North Star. The new Canadair assumed all obligations of the former company effective September 14, 1946. Total value of all production at Cartierville up to then had been:

U.S. government contracts and subcontracts	$54,780,000
RCAF contracts for PBYs	$27,340,000
TCA for DC-3 conversions	$2,730,000
Foreign customers for DC-3 conversions	$10,480,000
Inventory on hand	$9,750,000
Total	$105,080,000

The C-47 and North Star had enabled management to maintain a substantial labor force since the war, but when the C-47 program started to run down in late 1946 the labor force too began to diminish. On December 31, 1946, employment at Canadair stood at 7,383 but by the following July had fallen to 6,380 and to 5,062 in September.

On January 21, 1947, the Canadian Privy Council formally approved arrangements for the Electric Boat take-over, despite strong political opposition and unfavorable public reaction to the sale of an important Canadian company to a U.S. owner with no apparent knowledge of the aviation industry. The sale was to become a major issue in the lead-up to the federal election two years later.

On January 23, 1947, a joint statement to the press by C.D. Howe and John Hopkins, confirmed that Hopkins would become the new chairman of the board of Canadair and Oliver West would be president. Two days later, the board accepted the resignations of Benny Franklin and Marion Gall. Franklin, however, agreed to remain on the board and maintain an office in Montreal until December 15, 1947. He had done well financially from the sale, his 9,000 one-dollar shares having brought about half-a-million dollars in the three months he had held them. Bob Raven was present at a small party Franklin gave at the Mount Royal Hotel in Montreal, to celebrate the sale. Part way through the evening, Franklin went home, but phoned later to enquire if there was a white envelope on the piano. He had forgotten the large cheque he had received for his shares!

The minutes of the January 25, 1947 board meeting list the holders of Canadair shares as: Electric Boat 7,493; Franklin 2,500, and Hopkins, West, Lawrence Y. Spear, T. Rodgie McLagan, Otto Marx, Henry Marx and John E.L. Duquet, one share each. Spear and the Marx brothers were members of the board of Electric Boat; McLagan was general manager of Canadian Vickers, and Duquet, a Montreal lawyer, had been a founding member of the original Canadair board. The same meeting authorized capital to be increased by the creation of 1,990,000 shares, without nominal or par value, to two million shares. Of these, 990,000 were issued to Electric Boat at one dollar each.

The American "Invasion"

Though on his arrival at Canadair, West had told senior management members that they would get "all the plums" in the new organization, he soon began bringing in Americans. First came Robert A. (Bob) Neale, Dean P. Stowell, Theodore J. Emmert, Theron V. Chandler, James Egbert and Charles A. Ulsh, all from Boeing; Kelly G. Smith and Ivan Manley from Douglas; and Roger Lewis from Lockheed.

West appointed Neale, who had been director and operations manager of 11 Boeing plants on the Pacific Coast, first to assistant general manager and factory manager, then to vice-president, manufacturing. Stowell became manager, industrial engineering; Emmert, assistant to the president; Chandler, manager, procurement; Egbert, manager, plant engineering; Ulsh, assistant factory manager; Smith, manager, engineering; Manley, contract administrator; and Lewis, first as sales manager, then vice-president, sales.

The Americans were not welcomed by everyone. Shortly after Kelly Smith arrived, Emmert called in Peter Gooch, who had been chief engineer since Vickers days. "Peter, I want you to meet your replacement, Kelly Smith," said Emmert. Gooch was unimpressed—he resigned and moved to Canadian Vickers Industrial as president.

Not all the new faces were American. With the 1947 closing of Fairchild Aircraft at Longueuil, Edward H. (Ed) Higgins, Robert D. (Dick) Richmond and Jason J. (Jack) Waller joined other established Canadians like Lou Adamson, Jim Appleton, Saul Bernstein, Charlie Bloom, Ray Campbell, Issie Finkelstein, Hugh Gosnell, Ray Hebert, Tom Harvie, Gerry LaGrave, Walter Meacher, Cy McNeil, Ed Norsworthy, Bob Raven, Bob Stapells, Ralph Stopps, Jim Tooley, Henry Viger, Harry Whiteman and Tommy Whitton. All would have important careers at Canadair.

On May 8, 1947, Canadair changed from a public to a private company. The number of shareholders was limited to 50, excluding present or former employees already holding shares. The general public could not hold shares or debentures in the company.

North Star Development

While Canadair was being taken over by Electric Boat, North Star development ran into problems. TCA presi-

Bob Neale during the ceremonial "sod turning" for an addition to P1 in September 1949. He joined Canadair from Boeing in 1947, became vice-president of manufacturing in 1948 and remained till 1957. In 1961 he came out of retirement to join Convair's airline division. (CL D7934)

Roger Lewis was Canadair's vice-president of sales but left in 1950 to join Curtiss-Wright in New Jersey. There he signed various UK companies to licence agreements (e.g. for the Bristol Sapphire jet engine which Wright built as the J-65). Lewis was later in the U.S. Defense Department, a vice-president at Pan American World Airways, head of General Dynamics, then of Amtrak. (CL)

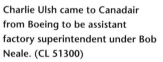

Kelly Smith wishes Ted Emmert well on his retirement in January 1950. Canadair's Americans mainly returned to the U.S. Smith went to Texas with Chance Vought Aircraft, Emmert eventually was president of Ford. (CL F3916)

Charlie Ulsh came to Canadair from Boeing to be assistant factory superintendent under Bob Neale. (CL 51300)

The North Star in Service

Canadair delivered the first 36-passenger DC-4M1 to TCA on November 19, 1946, and transatlantic service between Montreal, Prestwick and London was inaugurated on April 15, 1947. There were teething problems, but TCA established an unparalleled reputation for speed and dependability combined with high utilization. In the first 58 days of operation it completed 58 Atlantic round trips. Before the end of 1947, the six M1s were making 14 round trips a week on the route. Even though the sight of a North Star landing with a propeller feathered became common, its record for three-engine Atlantic crossings was no worse than contemporaries like the Constellation and the Stratocruiser.

TCA's first pressurized DC-4M2 flew on August 17, 1947, and was delivered on October 1. TCA had two versions: the M2-3 (domestic) with Merlin 622 or 722 engines, four-bladed propellers and a maximum gross weight of 36,000 kg (79,400 lb.); and the M2-4 (transatlantic) with Merlin 624 or 724 engines, three-bladed propellers and a maximum gross weight of 36,400 kg (80,200 lb.). Initially 40-seaters, the M2s later carried 48, 52 or 62 passengers.

During 1947, TCA North Stars set three world records: Montreal to London in 10 hours 30 minutes, Shannon to Montreal in 12 hours 57 minutes, and Vancouver to Montreal in 6 hours 52 minutes. The TCA inaugural flight to Chicago was not auspicious. The aircraft left Montreal with Montreal mayor Camilien Houde and

dent H.J. Symington eventually persuaded Franklin to allow Jim Bain to manage the program until problems could be solved. Franklin agreed, and for the next few months Bain found himself switching hats at meetings between Canadair production personnel and TCA.

Engine noise was critical—the unmuffled exhaust stacks vented straight against the fuselage. Symington ordered Bain to find a solution. After his first North Star flight, Oliver West gave his engineers two weeks to come up with an answer, but it would to take six long years. TCA eventually adopted a cross-over exhaust designed by one of its own engineers, Merlin "Mac" McLeod. BOAC developed a similar system, but neither solved the problem completely.

Some of Canadair's important Canadians, seen at a dinner at Ruby Foo's restaurant: Ed Norsworthy (service), Ernie Ledingham (aircraft interiors), Gord Stringer (PR), Dick Richmond (aerodynamics) and Issie Finkelstein (electrical). (CL F4015)

picked up the mayors of Toronto and its suburbs en route. Their short stay in Chicago featured so many toasts that when they re-boarded for the return flight, nobody was feeling any pain. It was a hot day and the pilot, unfamiliar with the air-conditioning/pressurization system, managed to close the fresh air inlets to the cabin. With the temperature around 120 degrees Fahrenheit, Mayor Houde was down to his undershorts before they reached Toronto. TCA vice-president Bill English later asked Canadair to have Bob Stapells and Ed Norsworthy check out every TCA North Star crew on how the system worked.

The last of TCA's 20 M2s was delivered on June 4, 1948, and the five remaining M1s were returned to the RCAF by year's end; the sixth (CF-TEL) burned following a crash at Sydney, Nova Scotia on August 12, 1948.

Air Force North Stars

The RCAF received 24 North Stars at a reported cost of $680,000 each. The first went to 426 Squadron at Dorval on September 12, 1947; the last flight by an RCAF North Star was on December 8, 1965, when aircraft 17506 flew from Downsview to Trenton. In the intervening 18 years, the North Star established a remarkable RCAF safety record by flying 310 million km (193 million mi.) without a fatality. This did not prevent passengers from criticizing the North Star at every opportunity solely on account of its noisy engines.

RCAF operations took North Stars to every part of the globe. In 1950, Canada was asked to assist United Nations (UN) Forces in the Korean War. On July 7, Air Vice-Marshal W.A. Curtis ordered 426 Squadron into action, and on July 25 six North Stars left Dorval for McCord

The first TCA DC-4M1 rolls off the final line. It was delivered November 19, 1946. Later it became a VIP North Star with 412 Squadron in Ottawa. (CL D4144)

(Below) Inside and outside views of one version of the cross-over exhaust installed on CF-TEN-X in August 1949. (CL DX8386, '88)

(Facing page) The standard interior in a TCA M1. Four-across seating made for a big airplane in 1946. TCA accepted its first M2 (lower photo) on October 1, 1947. "Champlain" was the name given to CF-TFC. Its fine Douglas lines combined with those of the Merlin engine made for one of the most attractive airliners. After TFC left TCA in 1962, it freighted between Toronto and Havana before being scrapped. (Above) CF-TFV, seen at Dorval in May 1955, was one of three TCA M2s converted to freighters. With only passenger doors loads were restricted, but at least TCA had a start in air cargo. (CL, CL D7048, F2784)

AFB near Tacoma, Washington, on the first stage of Operation Hawk.

The first three North Stars left Tacoma on July 27 for Tokyo via Alaska and the Aleutians. For nearly four years, North Stars plied this inhospitable route hundreds of times, and there are many stories of harrowing instrument landings, mainly on the grim Aleutian strip at Shemya with its ferocious crosswinds. By the time the airlift ended in 1954, 426 Squadron had flown 34,000 hours and made 599 round trips on the Pacific, safely carrying 13,000 personnel and 3 million kg (7 million lb.) of freight and mail.

In 1960, Canada again supported the UN, this time in the Congo. Belgium had granted its former colony independence, but on June 30, the province of Katanga separated, factions warred and army units mutinied. The UN appealed for help, and on July 18, a North Star left Trenton for Leopoldville with a cargo of food. For a year, until the Canadair Yukon took over, 426 Squadron North Stars made twice weekly, then daily flights from Trenton to the Congo, supporting the Canadian contingent which was providing internal communications, especially air traffic control. UN officials were loud in their praise for the work done by the Canadian contingent under Wing Commander W.K. (Bill) Carr. He later became the first commander of Air Command (1975), and following retirement from the Canadian Forces, was a vice-president at Canadair.

RCAF North Stars also served the UN in Cyprus, Indo-China, the Middle East and Yemen. They carried emergency supplies to Jamaica and Italy in 1951, and in 1956 flew medical supplies to Vienna to help victims of the Hungarian revolt. Following an earthquake in Chile in May 1960, North Star No. 17502 delivered an emergency load of flour to Victoria where the plane was besieged by a mob trying to escape the disaster zone. The crew boarded some 100 people, seating them on the floor as there were no seats, and flew them 560 km (350 mi.) to safety in Santiago. North Star No. 17513 was used for electrothermal ice research and the measurement of cloud properties. Dubbed the "Rockcliffe Ice Wagon," it sported an airfoil-shaped fin atop the fuselage. This was used to investigate the effectiveness of experimental de-icing and

A typical civil North Star flight deck and a look at the navigator's station. Navigators were not required on domestic or U.S. routes. (CL D6274, D7526)

North Star 510 with two props feathered during an airshow at Hamilton, Ontario, around 1960. (Jack Whorwood)

Four RCAF Sabres beat up the field as a 426 North Star awaits at Marville, France. (CF PL54316)

(Below) RCAF North Stars of 426 "Thunderbird" Squadron on the tarmac at Dorval. Top right are a Bristol Freighter and two Beech 18s. (CL H83)

(Above) The C-5 in June 1966, still looking magnificent after its retirement to the RCAF storage base at Mountain View, Ontario. (Right) A sample of the comfort provided aboard the C-5. (Larry Milberry, CL)

anti-icing equipment under natural conditions that entailed flying into icing conditions and observing the results.

The C-5

The crash of CF-TEL left the RCAF short one North Star, so the government, encouraged by an insurance settlement, ordered one more aircraft for about $1.5 million. Designated the C-5, it was a VIP transport equipped with Pratt & Whitney R-2800s instead of noisy Merlins. It made its maiden flight on May 15, 1950, piloted by Al Lilly and Bill Longhurst.

During its career, the C-5 flew C.D. Howe to South America in 1953; Prime Minister Louis St-Laurent around the world in 1954, and External Affairs Minister Lester B. Pearson to three continents and 12 countries in 1955. With such important passengers, the crew strove to make each trip a flawless one. Nonetheless, there were a few anxious moments. During the Duke of Edinburgh's 1955 Canadian tour, the C-5's hydraulic system failed on the approach to Vancouver. The co-pilot and flight engineer took turns madly hand-pumping the landing gear and flaps. Once the aircraft had stopped, they breathed a sigh of relief, confident that the Duke hadn't noticed anything out of the ordinary, but when they looked up, he was smiling in the doorway. "Nicely rowed, chaps!" he quipped.

Refurbished in 1966 for $343,000, the C-5 was sold almost immediately to a U.S. company for $49,000. After

Configured for 27 passengers and a crew of seven, the C-5 was Canada's premier VIP aircraft for 15 years. The RCAF had not officially accepted it when the C-5 had to carry Prime Minister Louis St-Laurent to Calgary to open the Stampede in July 1950. Under the circumstances, Canadair operated the plane. Shown here are the PM, F/O Bert Miller (pilot), Al Lilly, Tom Harvie, Bob Stapells and F/O N.E. Bohn. (CL 38594)

the new owner was denied U.S. certification, the once stately propliner was stripped of useful parts and scrapped.

The Argonaut

In the hope of selling aircraft overseas, Canadair supplied the airlines with comparisons showing the North Star to be superior to the Constellation. The Canadair-Douglas licence agreement, however, allowed Canadair to sell North Stars only in the United Kingdom and Canada. It also prohibited their resale by the original purchaser for a period of two years after the initial purchase, or until the aircraft had logged 5,000 hours.

BOAC needed a new long-range airliner but did not particularly want to buy Canadian. It took an intensive marketing effort by Oliver West, Roger Lewis and Ted Emmert, in the face of strong U.S. competition, to swing BOAC to the North Star, but the British Merlin was the final clincher. On September 30, 1948, BOAC ordered 22 North Stars (and spares) worth $16,633,000. The following month, Britain allowed its former colony, Newfoundland, to join Canada. This coincidence gave rise to joking comments that Britain had traded Newfoundland for Canadair airplanes!

Because of the differences between the BOAC and TCA aircraft, Canadair designated the BOAC version "C-4." While nearly identical to the M2-4, the C-4 had a heavier gross weight—37,000 kg (82,300 lb.)—and more powerful engines.

Al Lilly and Bill Longhurst flew the first C-4, G-ALHC, on March 6, 1949. The flight test and certification program which followed included some of those incidents that increase the pulse rate. Because of ice and snow at Cartierville, Lilly flew a team of engineers and maintenance technicians, under Dick Richmond, first to Florida, then to Texas to complete the program. While in Florida, just after takeoff in a one-engine-out climb, at maximum weight with sandbag ballast for a forward-centre-of-gravity, the aircraft filled with smoke. As Lilly prepared for an emergency landing, Richmond, Smokey Harris and others moved dozens of sandbags from front to rear in the cabin. The aircraft landed safely, but the crew's hands

Visitors pose with the first BOAC Argonaut in late November 1948. Bob Neale and Kelly Smith of Canadair are in the doorway. Ted Emmert is fourth from the right in front, Charlie Ulsh is on the far right. (CL D9062)

(Below) Argonaut G-ALHD runs up at Canadair. (CL C2028)

were raw from handling sandbags. A few months later at Dallas, in the same configuration, the three live engines quit simultaneously. Only Harris's quick switch of fuel tanks averted a disaster.

Aircraft G-ALHC was handed over to BOAC in Montreal on March 21. That night, a celebration was in full swing at Montreal's Queen's Hotel when Charlie Ulsh got a message that an explosion had damaged the aircraft. Everyone rushed out to the plant to see. Apparently a mechanic had tried to charge the aircraft's battery without first removing it from the aircraft. When he connected the ground charger the cabin lights went out. He had to jam a piece of two-by-four under a button in the nose wheel well to put the lights on again so others could continue work in the cabin. What he forgot was that charging the battery generated hydrogen—when he removed the two-by-four, the switch caused a spark and an explosion.

Repairs were completed in three days, but the plane's troubles were by no means over. A welcoming celebration had been arranged for its arrival in England. BOAC hierarchy and their guests were waiting when "HC" landed in pouring rain. No sooner had it turned off the runway than its brakes locked, and the crew had to be rescued by car. An inspection disclosed that whoever had painted the bulkhead after the explosion had seen two open ports in some pipes, capped them to protect them from the paint, then forgot to uncap them. The ports were exhausts for the brake system which, when capped, prevented brake release. When the pilot applied them, they stayed on!

BOAC had already chosen "Argosy" as the class name for the C-4. A later contest among employees suggested the name, "Argonaut," which was adopted. BOAC introduced the Argonaut on its London–Buenos Aires–Santiago route on February 19, 1950. It cut scheduled time en route by 18 hours compared to slower planes like the York.

At first, Argonauts carried 24 passengers in the forward

(Facing page) Cartierville at the height of the North Star program in August 1947. In the upper photo, P1 is lower centre with "Noorduyn" (DC-3 conversion plant) at the top, and the CNR's Val Royal yards across Bois Franc—they were important for shipping lumber and scrapping older rail equipment. Canadian Car and Foundry is top right at Laurentian and Bois Franc. Fourteen North Star "gliders" can be seen at P1, awaiting engines due to a backlog in shipping from the UK. The second view was taken the same day looking eastward with P2 closest on the left. (CL H186, D6093)

(Below) A closer view of "Noorduyn" showing PBYs and the Burnelli (left) in front, and DC-3s. The Marlborough Golf Course is beyond the Val Royal yards. John J. Hopkins had wanted to buy it for Canadair's employees, but this did not transpire. (CL D2094)

Flaps down and Merlins at idle, a BOAC Argonaut flares to land after an early shakedown flight. (CL)

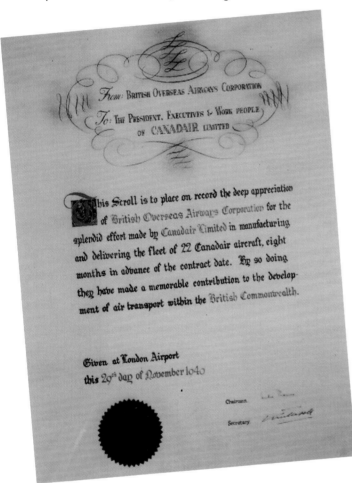

When BOAC desperately needed aircraft in the booming post-war years, Canadair was able to deliver. This scroll expressed BOAC's delight. (CL D9637)

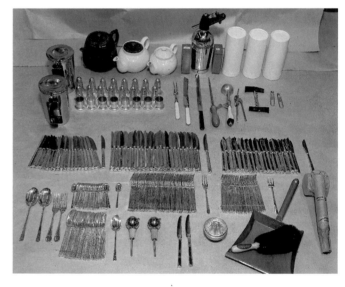

Silverware and miscellaneous accoutrements from the galley of a BOAC Argonaut. (CL D⁰016)

The famous Speedbird emblem adorned BOAC's Argonauts for 11 years. BOAC operated Argonauts in the Middle East, Far East, Southeast Asia, East Africa and South America. When the last one retired, the fleet had flown 520,000 hours and logged 190 million km (120 million mi.). (CL D9607)

cabin, and 16 in the rear but in 1954 they were modified as 54-seaters. The rear cabin was frequently converted for VIP accommodation. It was one of these Argonauts, *Atalanta*, that left London for East Africa and Australia on January 31, 1952, with Princess Elizabeth and the Duke of Edinburgh. Six days later, it returned *Queen* Elizabeth and her consort to London following the death of her father, King George VI.

BOAC's last new Argonaut left Montreal for London on November 10, 1949, carrying 1,800 kg (4,000 lb.) of Christmas food parcels from the people of Windsor, Ontario, to the people of Windsor, England. A month later, BOAC presented Canadair with a parchment scroll marking the delivery of the Argonaut fleet eight months ahead of schedule.

Adventures in the Far East

On June 30, 1952, Argonaut G-ALHH crashed at Tokyo. It needed a new wing centre section but adequate facilities were unavailable. Thus "HH" was barged to Hong Kong while a new centre section was ordered from Canadair to be shipped by sea. The unit measured 21 by 8 by 4 m (70 by 25 by 13 ft.) and getting it from Cartierville to the Montreal docks proved a challenge. It left Plant 1 under police escort at 2 a.m. on November 17, and after numerous problems with streetcar cables and other obstacles along the 19 km (12 mi.) route, arrived at the docks at 6 a.m. After it sailed, the ship narrowly missed an encounter with a typhoon en route, but the cargo was delivered safely. Waiting for it was the Canadair team of Len Cudney, Stan Daws-Knowles, Vic Fangor, Jack Forbes, Jack Heine, Ben Kaganov, Ed Pichey, Bill Sawka and John Speak.

Jack Forbes was a technical representative on the job (Canadair relied on its "tech reps" to uphold the reputation of its products in the field). Forbes got HH's fuselage onto a cradle of railroad ties in a big steel shed. When the crew tried to lift the fuselage to make room for the centre section, it would not move although the jacks appeared to

G-ALHH following its mishap at Tokyo. Then its new centre section on the truck that took it to the Montreal docks. Next, it's aboard the *City of Birkenhead*, ready to sail. The other views show it going ashore at Hong Kong, then being installed. HH flew on with BOAC until sold to Rhodesia in 1960. It returned to England for Air Links and Transglobe and finally was used as a training aid by the fire department at Stansted airport. They put it to the torch in 1971. (CL D9646, D9666, M20355, M24354, M20352)

BOAC Argonauts await delivery. It was a godsend for BOAC at a time when England's Hermes, Tudor and York airliners could not meet demand. The Argonaut plugged a hole and soldiered on for a decade until replaced by the DC-7C and Britannia. (CL D9604)

be functioning. Forbes realized that instead of the jacks lifting the aircraft, they were pulling down the shed! Later, when they tried to pressurize the cabin with jack hammer compressors, the carbon monoxide they gave off made everyone sick. It took several months to get the aircraft flying again, but it ended up serving BOAC a further seven years.

(Facing page) G-ALHG went to BOAC on July 5, 1949, and was christened *Aurora*. On April 8, 1960, it operated the final BOAC Argonaut service then went to Derby Aviation and British Midland Airways. On approach to Manchester on June 4, 1967, it crashed killing 72 of the 84 aboard. *Atalanta* often carried royalty in BOAC days. It finished its days with Flying Enterprise of Denmark and was scrapped at Kastrup in 1965. (CL D9386, Campbell Col.)

In Service with Canadian Pacific Airlines

When Canadian Pacific Airlines (CPA) applied to operate from Canada to the Pacific Rim countries and Australasia, C.D. Howe made it a condition that it do so with Canadair C-4s. On October 25, 1948, CPA placed an order for four C-4-1s at a price of over $800,000 each. The C-4-1 was similar to the M2-4 and C-4 except that its gross weight was 36,220 kg (79,850 lb.).

In April, 1949 CPA carried out a survey of its planned route to Japan and Hong Kong using a borrowed RCAF North Star. This was followed by a proving flight to Australia and New Zealand in a C-4-1 between May 28 and June 11. The official inaugural to Australia left Vancouver on July 13.

Business on the Pacific was slow at first, but it exploded

Ted Emmert describes the C-4 throttle mechanism to CPA president Grant McConachie during his visit to Canadair of January 19, 1949. Kelly Smith is immediately behind McConachie. (CL D8454)

thanks to two bonanzas. One was Chinese immigrant traffic from Hong Kong to Vancouver which began in 1949; the other the Korean airlift between Tacoma and Tokyo. It was not long before U.S. military chiefs realized that CPA's first class service was being wasted on the ordinary soldier. They remedied this by packing the flights with officers and letting the lower ranks find other, inevitably less enjoyable, means of going to war.

On the night of February 2, 1950, CPA lost CF-CPR when it overshot its landing at Tokyo and crashed into a sea wall. Nine aboard suffered minor injuries. Jack Heine, a customer service expert hired from Douglas in 1947, went to Tokyo to see if the aircraft could be salvaged. He found that sea water had been sucked into the engines, and prolonged immersion of the forward structure had corroded the thin aluminum and magnesium parts beyond repair.

Canadair test pilot Bruce Fleming was monitoring CPA president Grant McConachie's first takeoffs and landings in another C-4 when news of the accident came over the company radio. McConachie turned to him and said coolly, "Well, I guess I'd better accept this thing so we can get it over there as a

replacement." Seldom has a product been so readily accepted by a customer.

The C-4 established CPA as an important international airline. In 1948 it flew 6,461,927 revenue kilometres (4,015,365 mi.); in 1951–11,717,089 km (7,280,861 mi.). Passenger revenue rose from $4,561,803 (1950) to $10,765,746 (1951). Nonetheless, it was apparent, even to the optimistic McConachie, that the C-4-1 was not suitable on the Pacific. Its range was insufficient for long stages; payload restrictions limited passengers to 36 (making it a marginal revenue earner), and it was too noisy for comfortable travel over long hours. In 1951 CPA sold its C-4s to TCA which sorely needed the extra capacity at the time.

The North Star Era Ends

The compact galley aboard a CPA C-4. (CL D8428)

When North Star production ended with the delivery of the C-5, 71 aircraft had rolled off the line: 24 C-54GM/DC-4M1s; 20 DC-4M2s; 22 C-4s; four C-4-1s; and the C-5. Despite political and media suggestions that it was almost a deathtrap, the North Star finished with an excellent safety record, particularly compared with some of its contemporaries.

Fifteen aircraft failed to survive operations with their original owners and loss of life was low. Nine RCAF GMs were written off, but only one involved injuries. TCA lost three aircraft: a TCA M1 that crashed at Sydney, Nova Scotia, in August 1948; a TCA M2 that flew into a mountain in British Columbia in December 1956; and a TCA

Empress of Vancouver after its watery mishap at Tokyo. It ended up recycled into pots and pans. (CL D8441)

CF-CPP *Empress of Hong Kong* on June 16, 1949. Few aircraft of this era presented such a pretty picture. Once sold to TCA, this C-4 became CF-TFW. It was lost over Moose Jaw, Saskatchewan, on April 8, 1954, in a collision with an RCAF Harvard. (CL D8664)

The world's last flying North Star was CF-SVP-X. After a career as RCAF No. 17514 it went to the National Aeronautical Establishment in Ottawa. There its data-gathering tasks varied from research into anti-submarine warfare to studying the theory of continental drift. It is seen at Toronto on May 11, 1971, equipped with its 25-ft. (7.6-m) magnetic anomaly detector (MAD) boom used in measuring the earth's magnetic field. SVP left the NAE in1976 and was sold to a Texas company for $26,000. It ran drugs as N8022L but in 1978 landed for the last time on Great Inagua Island off Cuba. There it languished while some of those involved in it went to jail. Rumors floated around that N8022L would be resurrected again. One was that some New Orleans drug dealers were interested in it to run drugs—they liked the North Star's big payload, long range and high cruise speed. In the end "Twenty-two Lima" was cut up for scrap in the late 1980s, leaving Ottawa's 17508 the last North Star in the world. (Larry Milberry)

This North Star made a European sales tour in May/June 1947. Oliver West headed the delegation; Al Lilly led the flight crew and a total of 17 were along. They visited London, Hucknall (Rolls-Royce), Hurn and Dunsfold in the UK, then Paris, Geneva, Prague, Amsterdam and Copenhagen. There was great interest everywhere, and West's approach convinced BOAC to place an order. (CL)

M2 that collided with a Harvard over Saskatchewan, in April 1954. BOAC lost two Argonauts: one on takeoff from Kano, Nigeria, in June 1956; the other on landing at Tripoli in September 1955. CPA lost the C-4 at Tokyo.

In early 1961, TCA began retiring its North Stars, and by July the fleet was in storage at Dorval. A deal was struck with Overseas Aviation in the UK for 15 aircraft plus spares for $660,000. Eleven were delivered, but Overseas suddenly folded. TCA made a new deal with John Gaul in the UK. For $100,000 cash he took the 11 delivered North Stars, and for another $65,000 he got a large quantity of spares. Another five ex-TCA aircraft went to Lineas Aereas Unidas SA in Mexico, three to International Air Freighters of Toronto for operations to Cuba, and two to World Wide Airways of Dorval.

The RCAF North Stars were phased out by 1966. Seven went to Cavalier Aircraft in Florida. Of these, four were scrapped, one was sold to El Salvador; and two went to Air Caicos for Caribbean freighting. The latter machines were scrapped in 1976.

The prototype North Star eventually went to the RCAF as No. 17525. It was written off in June 1959 after a hard landing at Athens. North Star 17514, re-registered CF-SVP-X, was transferred to the National Aeronautical Establishment in Ottawa in September 1965. It was operated as an airborne geophysical laboratory until May 1976. Sold to Aircraft Salvage in Dallas, it was re-registered N8022L, and then went to a Miami concern. Several people associated with it were arrested when a U.S. Drug Enforcement Agency investigation revealed that N8022L had been used on "clandestine" operations. The aircraft was later scrapped on Greater Inagua Island off Cuba. TCA's old CF-TFG, the last M2, operated as the Wings Café at Mexico City Airport until June 1993, when it finally was broken up.

BOAC started selling Argonauts as early as 1957, with

the majority gone by 1960. Four went to the Rhodesian Air Force, the rest to various British operators. G-ALHJ was used for firefighting practice at London's Heathrow Airport till finally scrapped. The sole North Star in existence, RCAF No. 17515, belongs to Canada's National Aviation Museum in Ottawa. By 1994 it had spent about 30 years exposed to the elements, getting sadder looking with each passing winter.

"I warned you not to wait too long outside Canadair"

The North Star: The Final Verdict

Before the first North Star even left the ground the program had caused an uproar in Parliament and the press, but during the run-up to the 1949 federal election the mud really flew. The Liberals under Louis St-Laurent were seeking re-election. They were vigorously opposed by the Conservatives led by George Drew. At one point he described the North Star as "a haphazard combination ... a travesty of the laws of aerodynamics". Drew's mouthpiece was the Toronto *Globe and Mail* which ran such headlines as: "UK Secret Report Says North Star Wings Crack"; "Two Planes Lost Is Cost of Trying Out Merlins for Long Range Flying"; and "Failures of North Stars Cited in TCA Bulletin".

Drew was delighted when an internal TCA memo focusing on Merlin engine failures was leaked to the press, but the *Globe and Mail's* facts were largely incorrect or taken out of context. The effect of this was to deceive the

public about an airplane that was having fewer development problems than most of its contemporaries. While such attacks had some effect–TCA noted a few cancelled reservations on North Star flights–the issue blew over.

The 1949 election campaign also featured a bitter attack by Drew on the sale to Electric Boat. Drew called the sale a national scandal of the first magnitude and claimed that: "... by secret negotiation, Trade Minister C.D. Howe turned over the Canadian government-built Canadair plant and equipment to international arms racketeers who had discouraged peaceful solutions of international difficulties and dealt with Germany, Spain and Japan."

The *Globe and Mail* cried: "Canadair Sold to Arms Ring for Fifth of its Cost". It claimed that Electric Boat's chairman, Lawrence Y. Spear, was a close associate of "that famous international armament racketeer, Sir Basil Zaharoff." A review of media coverage of the period turned up only one other reference to Zaharoff, and that concerned a letter from him to Electric Boat in 1925, which could have been interpreted as an offer to use his influence to close a deal.

Whatever the facts, the public was not influenced. The Liberals won the largest majority in Canadian parliamentary history, taking 192 of 262 seats while the Conservatives could win only 42. On June 27, 1950, the Commons Public Accounts Committee announced that it had found no fault in the sale of Canadair to Electric Boat.

Gordon R. McGregor, TCA's president from 1948 to 1968, wrote in his book *Adolescence of an Airline*, that "... the Merlin was a great engine, manufactured by a great and completely

Seven of those involved with the North Star. Ron Baker (left) was TCA's test pilot. The rest were leading Canadair men: Tom Harvie, Al Lilly, Dick Richmond, Bob Raven, Peter Gooch and Ray Hébert. They were attending the book launching for *The Canadair North Star* in November 1982. Author Larry Milberry and his daughter Stephanie are in front. (Monty Montgomery)

To allay fears about the North Star raised by George Drew, Oliver West ran this letter in newspapers across Canada. (Fred Hotson Col.)

Canadair
LIMITED · MONTREAL

A STATEMENT TO THE PEOPLE OF CANADA:

In order that you may share with us the pride we have in our aircraft, I am quoting below, for your information, a statement by Captain Alfred Gilmer Lamplugh, C.B.E., F.R.Ae.S., M.I.A.E., F.R.G.S., Underwriter and Principal Surveyor of The British Aviation Insurance Co. Ltd. of London, England. Captain Lamplugh's firm, the leading company in the London aviation insurance market, directly or indirectly insures nearly all the airlines of the world including Trans-Canada Air Lines.

Captain Lamplugh's Statement:

"Canadair aircraft (Canadair Four and North Star) are regarded as among the soundest aircraft structurally. They have an excellent record with regard to safety. The insurance rates for these particular aircraft compare most favourably with any similar type. These rates are based on Trans-Canada Air Lines' operation which has been so excellent."

We consider Captain Lamplugh's statement to be a magnificent tribute to the management and personnel of Trans-Canada Air Lines and an authoritative appraisal of the quality and worth of Canadair's aircraft.

And we believe you will all agree.

May 19th, 1949

H.O. West
President

P.S.   Captain Lamplugh also holds the following positions: Convenor, Survey Panel, Air Registration Board (The British Government's Regulating and Licensing Agency, equivalent to the Canadian Department of Transport or the United States Civil Aeronautics Authority); Vice President, International Union of Aviation Insurers; Chairman, Air Transport Section, London Chamber of Commerce; Chairman, Joint Aircraft Committee; Warden, Guild of Air Pilots; Honourary Member, British Airline Pilots' Association; Learned to fly 1911; Holds "B" License #155; Served in R.F.C. and R.A.F. 1916 - 1919.

ethical company, but basically a racehorse called upon to pull a heavy cart, when it fell into the hands of the airlines." A 1950 TCA report found: "The aircraft power plants have proved exceptionally costly to maintain, with a high replacement parts consumption, relatively high prices for each replacement part, a short overhaul interval (450 hours for the cylinder blocks and heads) and fuel consumptions in excess of those originally forecast by the manufacturer." The saving grace, from TCA's standpoint was Rolls-Royce's agreement to compensate TCA with free spare parts, should the operational cost of the engine and power plants become excessive for any reason associated with design or manufacture.

Once the teething problems were solved, flight crews

In 1952 General Dynamics got Canadair the chance to bid on U.S. government contracts. One was for a trainer/transport. Roger Lewis, then Undersecretary of the Air Force, got Canadair to make a proposal. Although the U.S. could not award contracts for such a plane to a foreign country, it promised Canadair substantial work if it would collaborate with Beech on the concept. The plane was designated T-36 (CL 36-1002)

generally developed a favorable attitude toward the air-craft, as summed up by Capt. Frank A. Taylor, MVO, DFC, a senior BOAC pilot with many flying hours in the Argonaut: "May I say 'Thank you' to Canadair for what was undoubtedly, in its day, an efficient, safe and reliable aircraft." C.D. Howe, a politician not given to bombast, had earlier referred to George Drew's North Star bluster-ing as "perfect nonsense", and so it was.

The C-7

In 1950, Canadair offered 15 C-7 aircraft to TCA in ex-change for North Stars which it would then sell to Brazil. More like a DC-6, the C-7 was never built because the difference between its price ($850,000) and the resale value of the North Star ($500,000) was too great. Also, C-7s would have committed TCA to piston engines for years to come at a time turbojet and turboprop airliners were on the horizon. TCA later bought a number of Su-per Constellations to tide it over, but only after an unsuc-cessful attempt to buy some Argonauts from BOAC. (In 1956, BOAC, pressed by busy times, tried unsuccessfully to lease North Stars from TCA!).

The T-36

In early 1951, the USAF invited several manufacturers including Canadair to submit proposals for a high-perfor-mance utility trainer/transport, the T-36. Primarily a navi-gation trainer and powered by Wright R-1820s, it was to carry 12-14 passengers in a pressurized cabin at a speed of 740 km/h (460 m.p.h.) at 6,000 m (20,000 ft.). As a cargo plane, the T-36 could accommodate 14 m³ (500 cu. ft.) or 1,800 kg (4,000 lb.). Canadair had nearly finished its pro-posal based on the use of the stipulated engine when word was received that the USAF now wanted the big-ger P&W R-2800.

Canadair's proposal, the CL-60, won the com-petition from a technical standpoint but Beech Air-

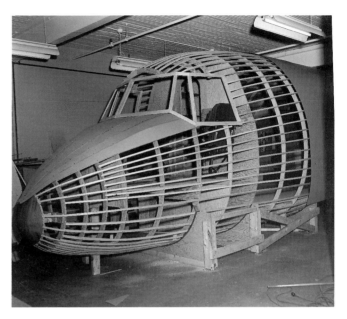

While the T-36 was underway Canadair was developing the CL-21 as a DC-3 replacement. This mock-up is as far as the CL-21 went. (CL D6301)

T-36 wing construction in B102 in May 1953. Canadair also built the fuselage aft of the cockpit. This was the first time it had participated in an all-new project. No sooner had Beech assembled the first T-36 than the project was cancelled. Karl Larsson of Canadair marketing was talking corporate aircraft in those days. He saw potential in the T-36 so Geoff Notman sent Dick Richmond to Wichita to appraise the proto-type. Richmond's conclusion was that too much work would be needed to adapt the design to civilian certification so the T-36 was scrapped. (CL 36-2085)

craft was awarded the contract. Beech, however, did not have the manpower to meet the production schedule. Canadair had surplus capacity, so it undertook about 40 per cent of the main component design. When the Beech-designed tail turned out to be too small for the R-2800, Canadair sent Gord Rosenthal to Beech to help them design a new one.

In 1952, Beech and Canadair were contracted to produce 227 T-36s. This was the first time the United States had placed such a large aircraft order outside its borders. Canadair took over the design, tooling and manufacture of the fuselage aft of the flight deck, building the centre wing, and subcontracting the outer wings, rear fuselage and tail. Harry Whiteman was made project engineer. He was a McGill graduate who had joined Canadian Vickers in 1939 but left to join the RCAF after the outbreak of war. He spent most of this time at Air Force Headquarters in Ottawa, looking after technical requirements for a variety of aircraft types.

Canadair built three pre-production sets of T-36 components, instrumented the wing with strain gauges and thermocouples and assembled the prototype. Gerry Barabé, Dick Richmond and Harry Whiteman were at Beech preparing for the first flight on June 11, 1953, when the program was abruptly cancelled by the newly elected Eisenhower administration as part of its defence spending cuts.

The cancellation caused a major lay-off at Canadair. Tony Natlacen of industrial engineering recalled the morning when his boss, Bob Peachy, was called to Dean Stowell's office. He came out at around 10 a.m. with a quota of people to be laid off by noon. In a scene reminiscent of the PBY cancellation, shop personnel were lined up for hours awaiting clearance. Many staff employees avoided lay-off by becoming instant direct charge workers with their time billed to the T-36 cancellation charges.

Canadair considered adapting the T-36 for the executive transport market. After examining the drawings of the forward fuselage and flight deck (which Barabé had managed to "acquire") and other data obtained from Beech, Canadair decided that the military features of the design made it difficult for civil certification.

CHAPTER TWO

INTO THE JET ERA

SABRE AND T-33

The Sabre was *the* highlight at Canadair in the early 1950s. Here is some of the activity on the line as Sabre No. 19 nears completion in March 1951. (CL D6871)

Canadair had a roller-coaster existence for the 29 years that it was a subsidiary of Electric Boat and General Dynamics, from the beginning of 1947 to the end of 1975. From 1947 to the early 1960s, 80 per cent of production output went to the Canadian military. The early 1950s were marked by a rapid growth in manpower as hundreds of Sabres and T-33s were turned out. Meanwhile engineering spent a million manhours redesigning the Bristol Britannia airliner, first as a long-range maritime patrol/anti-submarine warfare aircraft, and later as a transport. Total employment, which averaged slightly over 3,500 in 1950, peaked at 13,495 in April 1953.

In the early 1960s, changes in Canada's role in the North Atlantic Treaty Organization (NATO) brought new defence policies. Government purchases from Canadair declined to about 45 per cent of the company's total dollar output. Employment fell steeply during the first half of the decade, then climbed steadily as management's efforts to diversify began to bear fruit. The decline in military orders, however, continued and when Canadair was reacquired by Ottawa in 1976, government business represented only about 30 per cent of sales.

It has been suggested that during the 1960s and 1970s, Canadair lacked management direction, its technological activities lacked a competitive focus, and its design and engineering capability was not linked to a market strategy, nor integrated with strategic planning. This is not a fair criticism. Management was aware that large military programs had become a thing of the past. It was exploring every opportunity to maintain its workforce and put its 20 years of expertise to good use. In all, the 29 years of American ownership were particularly noteworthy for the large number of aircraft produced and the variety of programs in-house at any time.

Electric Boat and General Dynamics

Through 1949 Canadair president Oliver West continued to bring in expertise in the form of senior personnel. From the United States came William K. (Ken) Ebel, Everett B. (Ev) Schaefer and Robert Higman. Ebel came from Curtiss-Wright to be vice-president engineering. Schaefer and Higman came from Boeing as chief technical engineer and manager of plant engineering, respectively.

Canadians appointed to senior positions included: Harry McKeown who came from Martin via Boeing to be

As Martin Aircraft's chief test pilot W.K. "Ken" Ebel made the first flight of the famed "China Clipper" in December 1934. He came to Canadair as a vice-president soon after the Electric Boat takeover. In 1994 Dick Richmond recalled at trip in 1952 when he, Ebel and Bob Ross went to the UK to evaluate the Britannia. Ebel asked about how its tab-driven ailerons performed in tight turns then scared everyone aboard by throwing the airplane around the sky to see for himself. He was a hands-on kind of guy whom Richmond described as "a real asset to Canadair". He oversaw such projects as the F-86, CL-28, CL-41 and CL-44. In 1960 he returned to General Dynamics where he helped resolve difficulties with the Convair 880. Ebel retired about 1970 to grow apples in Maryland. (CL S1022)

chief inspector; J. Gordon Barker, comptroller; James F. Tooley, assistant comptroller; Arthur G. (Tim) Sims, sales engineer; and, later, James. G. (Geoff) Notman, executive vice-president and general manager. Peter H. Redpath, formerly executive vice-president of Scandinavian Airlines System (SAS), joined as vice-president, sales.

As Canadair's president and general manager, West had a four-year contract initially paying him $40,000 a year. In March 1948, an unusual contract amendment was made stating that $25,000 Canadian per annum would be paid him, or his estate, for 17 years after his death, or the termination of his contract. In December 1948, West accepted a board offer of $385,000 in lieu of the previous arrangement.

West was shrewd, a stickler for quality, and he could be thorny. A flight across the United States in the nose of a B-29 bomber convinced him that airline passengers should have a similar opportunity to see more from their seats, so he told Tom Harvie (a power plant designer) and

E.B. "Ev" Schaefer of engineering who came to Canadair from Martin. The CASI golf trophy is named for Ev, who died suddenly in 1958. (CL D9726)

A.G. "Tim" Sims grew up in Montreal and got into aviation as a youth. He flew with Ferry Command during the war, then took the Bristol B.170 Freighter on a tour of North and South America in 1946. He next joined Canadair, where he spent many years in sales. (CL D9714)

Dick Richmond (an aerodynamicist) to produce a concept of a four-engined aircraft carrying the maximum number of passengers in the nose and with the pilots in bubbles atop the fuselage. The two produced a conventional four-engined transport concept, and a three-engined version with one engine in the tail driving a pusher prop but West blasted them for wasting time on a three-engined design and not showing him drawings for his own futuristic concept.

West added more work space at Plant 1. On December 22, 1947, he authorized the purchase of 46,800 m² (504,000 sq. ft.) of land across the road from the main Cartierville plant, at 10 cents per square foot, and bought another 13,600 m² (146,000 sq. ft.) north of the first lot at the same price. These areas became the site of Buildings 114 and 115 and two parking lots.

West strove to bring in more work. In early 1949 Canadair won a contract to build F-86 Sabres, a program that promised to tax production facilities to the limit. Even so, West sent Roger Lewis to the United Kingdom to talk to Vickers and de Havilland about Canadair building Vickers Viscounts and de Havilland Comets. Later Richmond and R.F.O. (Bob) Smith visited de Havilland to compare the Comet with the Douglas DC-6 and the Lockheed Constellation.

About this time the British asked Canada to build a medium-range jet bomber, or else to reserve facilities for such production in case of conflict. Ottawa turned this down. In 1950, Britain reintroduced the matter but again was rejected. The bomber, the English Electric Canberra, did not meet Canadian needs (which were standardized with those of the United States). The British then approached the United States and reached an agreement whereby Martin Aircraft would build Canberras.

Perhaps the reason for these failures was contained in a memo of August 16, 1950, from Notman to West. It stated that C. D. Howe was much against building anything British in Canada. Though a proclaimed Canadian nationalist, Howe was American-born. He claimed a relationship to Nova Scotia Liberal statesman Joseph Howe, but his Canadian connections had been remote until he came to teach in Halifax.

When West joined Canadair, the C-47 program was almost complete. Although North Star production was starting, employment was declining. Alec Wright of industrial relations, a close friend of Ralph Stopps, recalled how, on the day West arrived at Cartierville, Stopps took him on a plant tour. West later commented, "You've got a nice little plant here but you could do with some new machinery." "Name one thing we can't do with what we have here," snapped Stopps. That was not the kind of reply West expected; he didn't like people who answered back. According to Wright, West and Stopps never saw eye to eye thereafter, but the plant got its new equipment, and lots of it.

Re-equipment was the second major change in manufacturing at the Cartierville plant. The first had been during the Depression of the mid-1930s when Canadian Vickers began work on the Northrop Delta. Before that, nearly all Vickers products had been of wood or tubular metal framework covered by fabric. The Delta had an all-metal, "stressed skin" wing, meaning that part of the loads on the wing were carried by the metal skin as opposed to fabric-covered wings which carried no bending loads.

By the time West arrived, Canadair had some skill in producing "sheet metal" aircraft, made of parts cut and formed from sheet aluminum and covered with a thin aluminum skin held in place by aluminum rivets. The parts were assembled on relatively simple tooling by skilled workers. Because the structure was mostly sheet metal, fabrication was done using unsophisticated equipment such as conventional lathes, drilling and milling machines, a few grinders, a mechanical press, a couple of hydro-forming presses, a stretch press along with shears, brake presses, hand-wheeling machines and planishing hammers.

Now Canadair was to take a big step into the era of sophisticated, high performance aircraft. In anticipation, West had 18,600 m² (200,000 sq. ft.) of additional floor space added as Building 103 (B103), at the south end of

(Facing page) Aerial views from 1949 (looking northeast) and 1955 (westward). By the mid-1950s Buildings 114 and 115 had gone up across Laurentian Blvd (empty fields in 1949). B114 (northerly) housed payroll; B115 was for materials stores. B119 (most southerly building in main complex) was later connected via B104 (an open lot in the first view) to B103, the first of the postwar additions to the original Canso plant. The new pre-flight hangar (B117) had been added along the main tarmac by 1955. Note the flight test hangar (B106) on the north side of P1—B118 had been added to it by 1955. The course of Imbeault Creek (which crossed Laurentian south of B119) changed from photo to photo. Opposite the north corner of P1 is Forget's greasy spoon. Notice the well-worn footpaths across the fields in the 1949 view. These led to the streetcar and the local neigh-borhood. Compare the size of the parking lots. Most of the growth seen here was connected to the Sabre program. (CL PS3173)

(This page) B106 in 1954 and 1956. In the meantime the North Star nose hangar had been removed and B118 added. In photo two, P1 looking south with B106 and B118 between the Laurentide Aviation hangar and the main plant. Next, the paint shop. (CL P1-2000, '2535)

The parking lot at the north end of P1 in 1954. The variety of employees' cars went from a mini Nash Metropolitan to a tank-like Buick Roadmaster. Except for a lone GM pick-up, nearly everyone drove a car, unlike later trends in pick-ups, vans and jeeps. Over the fence, Laurentide Aviation was putting up a new hangar. (CL PL2388)

the main building (B102). Then he began a massive buying program which introduced over the next four or five years about $2 million of new equipment of every type: skin mills, spar millers, engine and turret lathes, massive drop hammers and presses, some of which were not available anywhere else in Canada.

After he retired, Walter Allatt of plant engineering recalled the ease with which this machinery was obtained. "It was called the 47C4 program and applied to all machine tool equipment. When we wanted a particular type of machine, we by-passed purchasing, got our own quotation from the manufacturer and sent a requisition to the in-plant representative of the department of defence production. He would forward it to Ottawa and back would come the purchase authorization—it was as simple as that. There are possibly some machines still in Plant 1 with 47C4 identification on them [in 1995]."

West Leaves Canadair

The first indication of trouble between West and Electric Boat came when he told a crowd of employees from the C-5 assembly stand, that rumors of his leaving Canadair were not true. An article in the *Montreal Gazette* of No-

vember 24, 1950, stated that West was on extended sick leave, having been in poor health for years. The December 1 issue of the same paper said West admitted breaking with Canadair but claimed his reasons had nothing to do with health.

West had indeed asked the board of directors to relieve him of his duties or grant him leave of absence until his contract expired on January 24, 1951. The board did both and also authorized West to use a company-owned house in Westmount for a further year. The minutes of the board of directors show only gratitude to West. They express "our appreciation for his effective and devoted services to the company and for his outstanding contributions to its success during his incumbency... His leadership of the company during the past four years has resulted in its becoming the primary producer of aircraft in Canada and one of the outstanding aircraft manufacturing concerns in the world."

The Globe and Mail of January 27, 1951, reported that West had slipped quietly from the Canadian aviation scene and that two months previously he had packed a briefcase with personal documents and walked out of the plant. It was rumored that he had come into conflict with

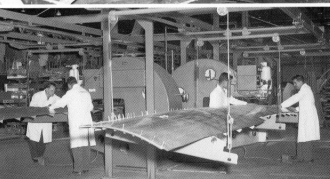

Some of the vital postwar machinery. First, a view across the machine shop with a series of Chambersburg Cecostamp machines in the foreground. Next, a hydro press arrives in still-unfinished B103 in 1950. Canadair's first autoclave—a Foster Yates & Thom unit reaches the Port of Montreal in October 1954. It was a pressure vessel for metal bonding mainly on the CL-28. The four men are riveting panels. Note the overhead rails for moving skin panels. A General Drivmatic machine drills sheet metal and inserts rivets. Canadair made some of its own drilling machines. The Farnham machine rolled sheet metal for leading edges, etc. (CL D15186, D8958, P1-2625, P1-3025, 34926, P1-1934)

the officials at Electric Boat. Insiders later said that he argued with Hopkins over the future of Canadair. West wanted the company to concentrate on building complete aircraft; Hopkins was prepared to build parts for Martin Aircraft.

Electric Boat announced that West had gone on leave and that John J. Hopkins had assumed Canadair's presidency and appointed Geoff Notman as vice-president and general manager. West moved to Nanaimo, British Columbia, where he died in the early 1960s.

James Geoffrey Notman

Geoff Notman was born in Westmount, Quebec. A grandson of renowned Montreal photographer William Notman, and a cousin to Brooke Claxton, Canada's minister of defence in the early postwar years, Notman graduated from McGill University in 1922 with a BSc in mechanical engineering. He joined Dominion Engineering Works Ltd. in 1922 as a junior engineer in the production office, and worked his way up to vice-president of engineering by 1950. During the Second World War he served the government in various capacities while still employed by Dominion Engineering.

After the defeat of Japan, Notman continued as associate director general of industrial conversion, joint organizer of the Canadian Industrial Preparedness Association, and member of the Industrial Defence Board. He was awarded the Order of the British Empire in 1946 for his services. Appointed executive vice-president of Canadair in January 1950, he became president and general manager in March 1952, a position he held until his retirement in 1965.

A big man and an all-round athlete, Notman was well liked by all his employees. He took a genuine interest in their welfare and frequently visited the shop floor. His presidency was noteworthy for the number of employee-related activities that were introduced—annual winter carnivals, large Christmas parties, summer picnics, open houses—all involving employees' families.

Notman was one of Tom Harvie's favorite people. "He was a good president," said Harvie. "Everyone would follow him. He tended to be what was called an Old Boy Circuit type who picked the people he judged could do the job and let them run with it. He did a good job with Electric Boat too. He stood up to them, for Canada and for Canadair." Walter Allatt remembered Notman's fond-

ness for Chrysler products. While he was president all the company cars were Chryslers.

Early Evolution of General Dynamics

In April 1952, John J. Hopkins combined Electric Boat, Canadair and Electro-Dynamics into a single corporation. With Canadair a subsidiary and the first nuclear submarine under construction, Electric Boat was clearly a misnomer, so Hopkins went looking for a new name. Gordon Stringer of Canadair's public relations department recalled that Hopkins kicked names around for hours. "He wanted to be on the New York Stock Exchange near General Motors and General Electric," said Stringer. "That was his niche, right beside the big guys. Eventually, he came up with General Dynamics."

A year later, Hopkins persuaded Floyd Odlum, president of Atlas Corp., to sell General Dynamics a controlling 17 per cent interest in Consolidated Vultee Aircraft Corp. (Convair). It was a case of the mouse swallowing the elephant for, even with Canadair's 12,000 employees, General Dynamics totalled only 19,000 people, while Convair had 49,000.

On April 25, 1955, Hopkins merged General Dynamics with Stromberg-Carlson, a leader in the production of communications and electronic equipment, and on September 30, 1957, Liquid Carbonic Corp., a major producer of industrial gases, joined GD.

The Sabre Program

From 1949 to 1975 Canadair was involved in nine aircraft production programs (not counting variants), two that reached the prototype stage and one that looked promising but never made it. The first was the F-86 Sabre. In terms of the 1,815 Sabres built, it became Canadair's largest program.

The North American F-86 was the foremost Western day fighter in the early postwar years. In 1948, the RCAF selected it as its next fighter, primarily to fulfil part of

Geoff Notman (left) with the famous WWII RAF fighter pilot Sir Douglas Bader, who was with Shell aviation products. (CL D5683)

The aesthetically pleasing North American F-86A Sabre was the RCAF's choice for a new day fighter for the Cold War era. Its design was greatly influenced by German wartime research, especially its 35° swept-back wing. The Sabre prototype, shown here, first flew on October 1, 1947. From 1950-58 Canadair would build 1,815 Sabres, more than any other type in the company's history. (CL D6402)

Canada's commitment to the NATO air defence plan. Four RCAF wings of three F-86 squadrons each were to be formed.

North American Aviation of Los Angeles had begun F-86 development late in 1945. At the same time it was developing a straight-wing fighter for the U.S. Navy, the FJ-1 Fury. In the summer of 1945 the United States obtained German research data disclosing the virtues of wing sweepback, together with a sample swept-back wing from a captured German Messerschmitt Me.262 jet fighter. After examining this material, North American decided to put a swept wing on the F-86. This delayed the project but made the F-86 a better fighter.

A letter of intent of February 23, 1949, proved Canada's commitment to have Canadair build the F-86E Sabre under licence. The announcement that the RCAF was getting the U.S.-designed fighter generated a brief campaign in the Toronto press, as de Havilland also had competed for the contract. It was claimed that, for the announced price to be paid for the 130 Sabres, Canada could buy 800 de Havilland Vampires. The campaign lost credibility when one writer had the gall to claim the Vampire was the world's top performance fighter.

Sabre 1

Sabre production started in August 1949. The first order was for 10 aircraft to verify the accuracy of the tooling on which subsequent aircraft would be built. The 10 would

then be mothballed until needed. However, with war in Korea threatening, a contract for 100 Sabres soon followed. It stipulated a delivery rate of five aircraft a month, with the first ready for acceptance by September 1950.

The Sabre program brought many changes. Factory procedures that had been wedded to those of Douglas during the C-47 and North Star programs had to be changed to match North American's methods. Canadair personnel like Ray Campbell, Bill Montgomery and Stan Russell visited North American's subcontractors to study the manufacture of many components that would eventually be made in Canada. They found that U.S. subcontractors were reluctant to divulge details to the Canadians who were going to be taking work away from them.

Canadair also became involved in its first major tooling program. As North American was still producing F-86s, it could not release any of the tooling on which Sabre parts were made and components assembled. Canadair therefore had to manufacture its own tooling, ranging from small to massive. The initial production rate later hit 20 planes a month, and peaked at 50. This required a moving assembly line, more like those found in the automobile industry than in aircraft manufacture.

Its added facilities enabled Canadair to make more Sabre parts in-house, but the company also launched a campaign to establish Canadian sources of supply to ensure maximum Canadian content and labor in the aircraft. Canadair assisted subcontractors and suppliers in establishing facilities, provided complete design data, and trained subcontractor personnel in specialized processes and techniques. The result of the made-in-Canada policy was dramatic. In the beginning, Sabre components were almost 90 per cent U.S.-made; by 1956 Canadian-government-supplied parts (with the exception of the engine) and components built to Canadair specifications were 95 per cent Canadian-made, and raw material was 83 per cent Canadian.

At first Canadair depended heavily on the United States for certain critical instruments. All USAF procurement was handled through Air Materiel Command at Dayton, Ohio, and when the first Canadair representative showed up there, he was told abruptly: "You can't just come in here, slap down your business card and expect to get action." Thus Canadair was launched into the important business of contract administration. Ivan Manley, who had gained contract administration experience while at Douglas, set up a Canadair office at Dayton and installed Henry Cruise to run it.

The Sabre program spawned several new companies and propelled some existing ones into the big time. Among these were Enheat of Nova Scotia; J.H. Connor of Hull, Quebec; Héroux Machinery of Longueuil, and Jarry Machine Shop of Montreal. Jarry's history is an example of entrepreneurship. An offshoot of Jarry Automobiles, a Montreal car dealership, it began by producing Sabre hydraulic system components, changed its name to Jarry Hydraulics, became part of Menasco, and by 1995 was recognized as one of the foremost manufacturers of aircraft landing gears.

The first US-built F-86A uncrated at Canadair in early November 1949. Sabres were soon rolling off the line at Cartierville. As each came out the door it was towed down the line for an engine run. Then Ray Courteau or Moe White would sign it off for test flying and delivery. (CL D6410)

(Facing page) P2, where Canadair built Sabres. The first view looks west down Bois Franc in 1946 when DC-3 conversion was in full swing. P2 had been Noorduyn's wartime complex where some 800 Norsemen and 2,800 Harvards were built for the military. In 1945 those contracts were lost and Canadair took over the facility and reorganized it for the Sabre. Numerous changes appear in the second (1955) photo. At the left are a new tarmac, engine test cell, jet engine silencers and three small utility sheds for the Sabre. The biggest building at P2 (where Harvards were once made) was B202, the main Sabre facility. T-33s were built in the next building west. The long black-roofed building (originally Quinlan Cut Stone, then repair and overhaul in Noorduyn days) was B203. The two hangars to the east along Bois Franc were used successively for Sabre, T-33, CF-104 and CF-18 servicing. Notice how they and the long shed in front of them grew between DC-3 and Sabre days. South of B202 is a small boxy structure put up by the DOT, and the Montreal Flying Club's hut. (CL D2626, PS3176)

The Northrop C-125 Raider was a rugged post-war transport considered by Canadair as a licence project, but the idea was ultimately bypassed. (CL D5431)

The key Canadair people responsible for the Sabre program included Ken Ebel, vice-president, engineering and program manager; Bob Neale, vice-president, manufacturing; Ev Schaefer, chief technical engineer; Jim Schaffer, chief of design; Ted Larrett, chief of stress; Dean Stowell, manager, industrial engineering; and Dan Gilmore, manager, manufacturing engineering. The design team included Ray Hebert, Joe Knap and Saul Bernstein. Ray Campbell was in charge of production along with Cy McNeil, Jimmy Appleton, Bill Tousigneault, Bernard N. Harte and Harvey Slough.

Bob Raven was the first Sabre project engineer. A graduate of the University of Detroit, he had been working in Vancouver, first for Boeing and then CPA, when he joined Canadian Vickers in 1944. He was one of the engineers who went to Douglas as an employee of Canadian Vickers, and returned an employee of Canadair.

The first F-86 and the sole Sabre Mark 1 produced by Canadair (RCAF No. 19101) was an F-86A made from U.S.-components assembled at Cartierville. It was completed on July 28, 1950. As the main Cartierville runway was being lengthened at the time, 19101 was towed to Dorval Airport where Al Lilly took it on its first flight on August 8.

Structural engineer Bob Raven was from Windsor, Ontario. He started his aviation career with Boeing in Vancouver. Later he held various posts at Canadair including project engineer on the North Star and F-86. (CL 25781)

Lilly had previously visited North American in Los Angeles for briefings on the F-86. While in the area, he also visited the Northrop factory in Hawthorne and flew the Northrop C-125 Raider, a three-engine, high-wing transport with fixed landing gear. Canadair obtained the rights to build the Raider but eventually decided not to go ahead with it. Lilly next visited Wright Patterson Air Force Base in Dayton for his Sabre checkout.

Major Charles E. (Chuck) Yeager of the USAF is thought to have been the first pilot to fly supersonically. This he did on October 14, 1947, in a Bell X-1 rocket-propelled aircraft launched from an NB-29 mother ship. On August 10, 1950, it was Canada's turn to enter the age of "breaking the sound barrier." On Lilly's second test flight in the F-86A he dove vertically from 15,240 m (50,000 ft.) to become the first to exceed the speed of sound in Canada. His euphoria was tempered when an electrical failure caused his engine to flame out, forcing him to make a "dead-stick" landing on a crosswind runway at Dorval and blow a tire.

Sabre 2

The RCAF wanted the "E" version of the F-86 but North American had not completed its design when Canadair started production. To avoid having to stop production and restart when the final F-86E design details became available, the first 20 or so Sabres produced at Cartierville were all F-86As. As soon as they came off the line, however, they entered a modification and retrofit program to convert them to F-86Es. The E-model differed from the A in having many of the improvements of the all-weather F-86D, the major change being the introduction of the "all-flying" tail.

The Sabre had power-assisted flight controls. In contrast to earlier aircraft in which the pilot's "stick" was connected directly to the ailerons and elevator, Sabre stick movements operated hydraulic actuators which in turn moved the control surfaces. Whereas on the F-86A back-and-forth stick movement controlled only the elevator, on the F-86E when the pilot moved the stick forward both tailplane and elevator moved as a unit. When he pulled the stick back, the tailplane and elevator moved first as a unit and then the elevator alone. The ultimate effect was an improvement in overall manoeuvrability.

Sabre production was consolidated in the former Noorduyn plant, now designated Canadair Plant 2. There quantity production was brought to a fine art. Everything took place on one floor, with all associated operations feeding into the major sub-assembly and final assembly lines. Alongside the final line, which could accommodate 12 aircraft, were three major sub-assembly operations. Fuselage assembly took the form of two oval, roundabout lines: one covered the build-up of the forward fuselage; the other covered the rear fuselage and tail assembly. These were brought together at the end of the forward

fuselage roundabout, and the completed unit was moved over to the beginning of the final line. Meanwhile the wing was being assembled on a small four-unit line, positioned so that the wing joined the fuselage at the beginning of the final line.

Assistant chief test pilot Bill Longhurst flew a production Sabre 2 for the first time on January 31, 1951. A native of Saskatchewan, Longhurst had learned to fly in Canada, and then joined the RAF in England at the out-

The Sabre Mark 1 ready to fly. Then defence minister Brooke Claxton, A/M Wilf Curtis and Geoff Notman greet Al Lilly after the plane's initial flight on August 8, 1950. Looking on is Omond Solandt, who was chief of the Defence Research Board. (CL D6512, '6537)

When Al Lilly moved to sales in the early 1950s, Bill Longhurst became chief pilot. He was an inveterate aviator but was often at odds with the pilots under him (he got along with the others at Canadair). Longhurst was always around the plant, and even during the 1965 strike found things to do—he would come in and ask Gerry Barabé to find him some odd job on the shop floor. Barabé recalled Longhurst as a gutsy pilot. Even after he had to eject from the CL-84 Longhurst appeared unfazed. "Just get me a scotch," he told the boys in pre-flight when he was brought in after the crash. (CL 29620)

break of war. He flew two operational tours with Coastal Command before returning to Montreal to join Ferry Command. In 1943, he became a part of aviation history when he piloted a C-47 towing a Waco CG-5A glider from Montreal to Prestwick, Scotland, via Goose Bay, Greenland and Iceland. Longhurst joined Canadair in 1948 and replaced Lilly as chief test pilot in 1953. During his 23-year career with the company he would conduct many first flights and much experimental test flying on the Sabre, T-33, Argus, Yukon, CL-44D4, CF-104, CF-5, CL-215 and CL-84.

Like the F-86A, the Sabre 2 was powered by a 23-kN (5,200-lb.) thrust General Electric J47-GE-13 engine. A total of 350 Sabre 2s was produced in 1952 and 1953 for the RCAF. In the first half of 1952, 60 early Sabre 2s were supplied to the USAF in Korea. They were modified with U.S. equipment and allocated USAF numbers 52-2833 to -2892. American pilots who flew the Canadair Sabres were impressed by their excellent performance and there was considerable competition to fly them.

This superiority was partially due to the level of quality control at Canadair, but also to the smoother functioning of the Canadair Sabres' flight control system. Barry Coleman, who was in charge of the functional test procedures section at that time, credited Tom Harvie with devising the modification that eliminated the abrupt movements of the North American system. Harvie developed a method of hydraulically honing the spool valve that metred the flow of hydraulic fluid to the flight control actuators. Thus he gave the pilot infinitely precise control of the aircraft. A graduate of McGill, Harvie had joined Canadair in 1946 after RCAF wartime service in the aircraft development branch of the Department of National Defence (DND) where his responsibilities had included the Vickers/Canadair PBY production program.

The RCAF sent 22 pilots to Korea to fly with USAF F-86 squadrons. They destroyed nine enemy aircraft, probably destroyed two more and damaged 10. One of these pilots was Canadair's Bruce Fleming, who had been

A classic view of the first Sabre 2. Its colors are those of 410 Squadron, then based at St-Hubert. In 1954 the RCAF gave 19102 to Greece where it was eventually lost in a crash. (CL D6882)

an RCAF pilot during the Second World War. In Korea he flew 82 missions between March and June 1952, 11 more than any other Canadian pilot. He was credited with one MiG-15 fighter probably destroyed and two damaged, and was awarded the U.S. Distinguished Flying Cross.

In late 1950, 410 Squadron's Sabres were ferried to the United Kingdom on Canada's lone aircraft carrier, HMCS *Magnificent*. In May 1952, the RCAF began ferrying Sabre 2s across the Atlantic in a series of operations named "Leapfrog." The first to go was 439 Squadron. Between May 30 and June 14 its 21 aircraft covered the 5,730 km (3,560 mi.) from Ottawa to North Luffenham, England, via Bagotville, Goose Bay, Greenland, Iceland and Scotland. Three further Leapfrogs moved two more squadrons to England and three three-squadron wings to continental Europe (one to France and two to Germany) all by September 4, 1953. The Canadair Sabre soon proved to be the fighter of choice in Europe. It became the mainstay of Canada's contribution to the NATO tactical fighter force for the next 14 years.

Sabre 3

From the beginning the RCAF had intended to use an engine other than the GE J47 in the F-86. The Canadian-designed Orenda engine was favored, which required alteration to 30 per cent of the airframe structure in the engine bay. These tasks took much longer to complete than had been anticipated.

In mid-1952, Canadair installed a prototype of the 27-kN (6,000-lb.) thrust Orenda 3 engine in the 200th

Bruce Fleming won the USAF Distinguished Flying Cross for his Sabre tour in Korea. Ken Ebel admires Fleming's decoration. (CL F4929)

On September 11, 1952 Canadair hosted the famous 421 "Red Indian" Squadron from St-Hubert. In a few days 421 gave the Sabre its ultimate test of reliability by ferrying en masse to RCAF Station Grostenquin, France. The Sabre passed with flying colors. In this photo from the left are: Fred Evans, Maurice Lajeunesse (Canadair tech rep), Jack Doyle, Dusty Keinholz, Al Turnbull, George Northrop, Bob Hallowell, Don Eckert (behind Hallowell), Bob Middlemiss (commanding officer), Tim Sims (manager, sales and service), Des Peters, Neil Pringle, Frank Wagner, Ralph Heard, Doug Hogan, Jerry Tobin, Buzz Buzik, Ken Thorneycroft (behind Buzik), Scotty McKay, Lloyd Skaalen, Al Young, George Fulford, Bill Carr-Hilton, Gerry de Nancrede, Hal Harris and Gordon Eldridge. Many of these young pilots went on to careers in aviation *e.g.* Thorneycroft and Skaalen became air force generals, Middlemiss commanded the first RCAF CF-104 Squadron, and de Nancrede flew for Canadair. Others, like George Fulford, became airline captains. (CL G1054)

Sabre, the first and only Sabre 3. Flown initially by Glen Lynes on June 14, 1952, No.19200 made 12 flights with a J47 before the Orenda 3 was installed. Bill Longhurst made the first flight in the Sabre 3 on September 25, 1952.

The same plane nearly claimed Longhurst's life on an early test flight. At 12,000 m (40,000 ft.) he had put it into a high speed dive. Suddenly a wrench left by one of the ground crew jammed the stabilizer actuator. Longhurst radioed that the elevator was stuck but that he would stay with the aircraft as long as possible. Through five miles of altitude he fought to pull up. With the aircraft down to minimum recovery altitude, he succeeded. A post-flight inspection revealed that the elevator had become free only when Longhurst pulled so hard on the stick that he bent the wrench, enabling it to slip out from under the actuator. The wrench was displayed on the preflight notice board along with an invitation for its owner to claim it. Nobody ever did.

Jacqueline Cochran

Jacqueline Cochran of California was an internationally recognized pilot with many aviation awards from over three decades of flying. In 1952, at age 47, she decided to challenge the women's speed records held by Jacqueline Auriol of France. First she tried to borrow an F-86 from the USAF, but the chief of the U.S. Air Staff, General Hoyt Vandenberg, refused. At a dinner party in New York in November 1952, Jay Hopkins introduced Cochran to Air Vice Marshal W.A. Curtis, chief of the RCAF.

She appealed to Curtis to let her use an RCAF Sabre for the record attempt, emphasizing that she was no mere aerial acrobat, but a practised and dedicated pilot. Curtis took her request to the defence minister, Brooke Claxton, who authorized Canadair to let Cochran use the Sabre 3.

A plan to make the record attempt between Montreal and Ottawa was abandoned because the route was not instrumented, nor could the vital insurance coverage be obtained. Instead Cochran came to Montreal to be briefed on the Sabre and checked out on the T-33. Hedley Everard, Canadair's assistant chief test pilot, was supposed to run through the Sabre pilot operating instructions with Cochran, but she was preoccupied with an endless succession of receptions and cocktail parties. When she finally showed up for her briefing, she pushed the

Jacqueline Cochran talks shop with Bill Longhurst from the wing of the Sabre 3. (CANAV Col.)

Some of the personnel involved at Edwards. In front are mechanics Bill Gyuricsko, Norm Frechette and Leo Lahaye, and Bert Wall (inspector). Behind are Jack Jones (Orenda), Ian Renwick (instrumentation), Barry Gilmore (electrical), Lewis Chow (chief experimental engineer), Jacqueline Cochran, Art Childs (crew chief) and George MacFarlane (radio). (Chow Col.)

book aside and said to Everard: "If I put everything to the firewall, how long do I have before the thing blows up?" Hedley replied: "Until you smell something burning." Said Cochran: "That's all I need to know, honey," and left.

While in Montreal, Cochran was still concerned that the USAF would try to stop her record attempt. Dick Richmond recalled being in Notman's office and hearing

The Sabre 3 during an engine run at Cartierville. The screen at the nose, a safety device, was once left off and a Canadair employee lost his life when sucked into the Sabre as it ran up at full blast. (CL H48)

Test pilot Glenn Lynes had been a wartime fighter pilot. In 1994 Moe White of flight test noted: "Lynes was like Longhurst, Fleming and the rest of our pilots—they flew to live and lived to fly." Lynes got into trouble at Canadair when he flew a Sabre low across the field, greatly impressing a tour of foreign dignitaries. (CL D9758)

her say over the telephone to General Vandenberg, "If you try to stop me on this, Van, I'll go to Ike." ("Ike" was President Dwight D. Eisenhower.)

Longhurst gave Cochran some training in the T-33 at Cartierville in November 1952. In early May 1953, he ferried the Sabre 3 to Edwards AFB in California, for airspeed position error calibration. It was accompanied by a 16-man Canadair support crew led by Lewis Chow. His team included crew chief Art Childs; George MacFarlane, radio; Barry Gilmore, electrical; Ian Renwick, instrumentation; Bert Waal, inspector; and mechanics Normand Frechette, Bill Gyuricsko and Leo Lahaye.

Chuck Yeager flew 19200 on May 6 and Cochran made her first flight on May 12, with Yeager flying chase. She flew three more times before starting her record attempts. On May 18, she set a 100-km speed record of 1,050.15 km/h (652.552 mph), eclipsing the earlier record of

A view of the Sabre line "going full tilt". Jack Forbes, Ray Campbell, Frank Clarke, Bob Cockerill, Barry Coleman, Albert Kemp, Stan Russell, Harvey Slough, Art Thomas and Charlie Ulsh were some of the Canadair men who initially spent time with North American at its Sabre plant in California. Once home Forbes set up the line in P2 and became foreman. Ray Campbell was plant superintendent with Stan Russell and Mike Doyle his assistants. (CL 15728)

In and around Plant 2. First a view of the east end of B202 with the main control tower attached, then, at left, a Sabre 5 ready for a run-up in one of the noise suppressers. (CL P2-1430, '1253)

(Below) When Canadair decided to install the Orenda in the Sabre 6, North American Aviation and the RCAF were dubious. Its extra power needed 111 lb. (50 kg) of air per second, versus 86-88 lb. (39-40 kg) for the Sabre 2 and 105 lb. (48 kg) for the Sabre 5. Canadair engineers Figueroa and Rosenthal studied the problem in the wind tunnel with a model that had a redesigned engine nose cone (but no change to the duct). This "straightened out" the air pouring through the intake and guided it into the engine. The RCAF accepted the modification but only after Dick Richmond and Orenda's Harry Keast signed that it would work. (CL D6940)

(Below) A scene on the under-wing tank line, and the wing for Sabre No. 72 comes out of the jig. (CL D6953, '32)

1,023.01 km/h (635.686 mph) set by Colonel Fred Ascani in an F-86E in August 1951. On May 23, carrying drop tanks for extra fuel, she flew a 500-km (300-mi.) circular course at 949.93 km/h (590.273 mph), and on June 3 she set a 15-km (9 mi.) closed circuit record of 1,078 km/h (670 mph). Between the record attempts, she took the Sabre up three times to 15,000 m (48,000 ft.), and each time put it in a vertical dive and exceeded 1,270 km/h (790 mph) to become the first woman in the world to break the sound barrier.

It was rumored that Cochran bent the Sabre wing during her record runs but this could not be verified. If it had bent, the effect must have been minimal, for Longurst flew the aircraft back to Montreal without complaint. The Orenda was removed and a J47 installed. A new "6-3" wing (six inches more chord at the root, three inches more at the tip) was substituted and the aircraft was flown again, this time as a Sabre 4, by Scotty McLean on April 13, 1954. After completing its RCAF service, it was donated to the Western Canada Aviation Museum at Winnipeg, Manitoba.

Sabre 4

In mid-1952, Sabre 2 production gave way to the Sabre 4. Apart from some minor structural and system differences, including a change of gunsights from the A-1C on the Mark 2 to the A-4 on the Mark 4, the two variants were identical. The introduction of the Sabre 4 also marked a change in Sabre project engineers. Bob Raven moved to the T-33 program and George Burlton took his place. He reported to Ed Higgins, chief project engineer. Higgins, like Dick Richmond, was a graduate of the University of Michigan, and had been an aeronautical engineer in the RCAF during the war. Now he reported to Ken Ebel.

Company pilot Hedley Everard flew the first Mark 4, No.19453, on August 28, 1952. Of 438 Mark 4s built, 10 were initially taken by the RCAF but these and all subsequent examples were eventually turned over to the RAF.

When the Korean War began in June 1950, the RAF recognized that, following the decline in British industry after 1945, a new swept-wing fighter would not be developed at home in time to meet intended service entry by

1951-52. Unable to wait three to four years for an indigenous fighter to rival the MiG-15, the RAF sought the F-86, and it turned to Canadair as the only possible supplier. Canada and the United States agreed, as a measure of mutual aid, to supply the RAF with 400 Sabres, Canada donating the airframes, the United States the engines. Sabre 4 production was delayed on occasion because GE could not supply more than 30 engines a month, 20 for North American and 10 for Canadair. At one stage the delivery ratio was reversed.

The RAF flew its Sabre 4s from Montreal to the United Kingdom between December 1952 and November 1953 in a series of operations called "Bechers Brook." The title was a bit of wry British humor for Bechers Brook is a notorious fence-and-water obstacle on the Aintree Grand National race course near Liverpool, England.

The RAF Sabre 4 served in Britain and Germany until replaced in mid-1956 by newer British fighters, primarily the Hawker Hunter. Though its tenure was brief, the Sabre played a vital role bolstering Britain's air defence during a critical period, and the aircraft was held in esteem by RAF pilots. As the RAF's Sabres became redundant, they were overhauled and passed on to Italy and Yugoslavia.

Sabre 5

At about the start of the Sabre 5 Canadair adopted the "CL" model numbering system to replace the earlier "C" used with the North Star and its derivatives. The PBY was designated CL-1 and subsequent programs were numbered consecutively regardless of whether they reached the hardware stage. Thus the Sabres 1 through 4 became

RAF Sabre 4s at the preflight shed (east end of P2) in 1953. Aircraft XB962 on the right was the 725th Canadair Sabre. It was reregistered XB938 and ended its days in the Yugoslav Air Force. (CL P2-1421)

CL-13s and the Sabre 5 the CL-13A. The C-47 program was somehow overlooked and was subsequently designated CL-0.

The RCAF had intended installing the more powerful Orenda engine in the Sabre 4, but production slow-downs at Orenda forced a wait until Sabre 5 production had begun. C.D. Howe was livid. Maurice Holloway was the GE engine technical representative at Canadair during Sabre 2 and 4 production. Arriving for work one Monday morning he was astonished to find that every J47 engine had mysteriously disappeared and no one would tell him where they were. The reason for their removal became obvious—later that day Holloway heard Howe explaining to a number of visiting parliamentarians that the Sabre program was being delayed by a lack of GE engines, and that positive action was required to speed up the Orenda.

While in service most Sabre 4s were modified to the "hard wing" configuration of the Sabre 5. This entailed removing the moveable slats which formed the wing leading edge, and replacing them with a fixed leading edge. A small vertical fence was added midway along the leading edge upper surface. This "mod" was also referred to as the "6-3" wing because the wing chord was increased by six inches at the root and three inches at each tip. The modifications were the result of experience gained in Korea. The increase in chord improved manoeuvrability at high speed while the fence counteracted the poorer slow-speed

characteristics caused by the removal of the slats. In addition to the 6-3 wing, the Sabre 5 had a Vee windshield, an A-4 gunsight, a new oxygen system and the 29-kN (6,500-lb.) thrust Canadian-designed Orenda 10 engine. Bill Longhurst flew the first Sabre 5 (No.23001) on July 30, 1953. Canadair would produce 370 Sabre 5s with the majority going to Europe to replace the RCAF Air Division's Mark 2s and 4s.

Early in Sabre 5 production, a problem surfaced with the fuel system, and for a time grounded Sabres littered Cartierville. What confused the experts was that the CF-100 had a similar engine and fuel system and it was working perfectly. Pat Campbell credits Tom Harvie with solving the problem. Harvie traced the trouble to the line from a small pitot head located in the engine air intake which metered fuel in accordance with dynamic pressure. It turned out that while the Sabre had a long line, the CF-100 had only a short one. Once the Sabre's line was shortened, the system worked perfectly.

When Sabre 5s began arriving at No. 2 Wing in Europe in March 1954, the Sabre 2s and 4s there were ferried to the United Kingdom for overhaul, and then 107 aircraft were given to each of Greece and Turkey under the mutual aid program.

The thousandth Canadair-built Sabre was presented to Defence Minister Brooke Claxton at a ceremony on April 20, 1954, slightly less than four years after the roll-out of the F-86A.

Classic views of Sabre 5s on test flights from Canadair. Three Canadair test pilots had hair-raising experiences with the Sabre 5 while they had their heads down in the cockpit recording engine data on their kneepads. Bill Kidd caught a flash of movement out of the corner of his eye and looked up to see a giant Convair B-36 bomber bearing down on him. A little later, Don Simmons and Ed Coe were both flying at maximum altitude in an apparently empty sky when they felt their aircraft lurch suddenly as they passed within a few feet! (CL)

Sabre 6

The final Canadair Sabre was the Mark 6, powered by a 33.10-kN (7,440-lb.) thrust Orenda 14. Bill Longhurst flew the first example (No.23371) on October 19, 1954, and deliveries to the RCAF in Europe started shortly thereafter. The early Sabre 6s retained the unslatted hard wing of the Sabre 5 but this was soon changed, and all subsequent "6s" had slatted wing leading edges like the Sabre 4.

Pilots called the Mark 6 the cream of the crop. It out-

government wanted no direct involvement in Suez and cancelled the deal. Israel bought French Mystère 4s instead.

In the summer of 1957, Canadair sent two borrowed RCAF Sabre 6s, with the Canadian civil registrations CF-JJB and -JJC, to Switzerland to compete against the Hawker Hunter for a large Swiss Air Force order. Hedley Everard was accompanied by field service representative Reg Thatcher and technicians Od Cleven, Keith Lathey,

The Canadair pilots who made the Sabre flight test program a success: Bud Scouten, Ed Coe, Hedley Everard, Bill Longhurst, Al Lilly, Ian MacTavish, Bill Kidd and Scotty McLean. (CL F3106)

performed everything else over European skies. With it, Canadian pilots were the indisputable "Top Guns" in friendly competition against other NATO air forces flying fighters like the Hunter, Mystère, Super Sabre and Swift.

Sabre 6 production totalled 655 of which 390 went to the RCAF. As these entered service, the Mark 5s became surplus. Starting in September 1957, 75 were transferred to the West German Luftwaffe. In July 1955, the South African Air Force ordered 34 Sabre 6s; in April 1956, the Colombian Air Force bought six; and in December 1956, the Luftwaffe ordered 225. Israel ordered 24 in 1955. When the Suez War broke out in 1956 the aircraft were sitting on the dock at Montreal, but the Canadian

Sandy Sandbach and Herb White. The demonstrations included gun- and rocket-firing, bomb- and napalm-dropping as well as fast taxiing in and out of hangars hidden in the mountains. These secret locations were out-of-bounds to all non-Swiss nationals. To get around this the Swiss appointed Everard and Bill Bedford, the Hunter pilot, honorary colonels in the Swiss Air Force for the duration of the trials.

Though the Sabre won all other phases of the competition, the Swiss chose the Hunter on account of its 30-mm cannon, by far more lethal than the Sabre's six .50 cal. machine guns. Everard also felt that Hawker had an advantage by being able to take the Swiss adjudicators flying in a two-seat Hunter, while they could only admire the

Ian MacTavish in the cockpit of Sabre 1000 which the preflight crew have polished to a beautiful shine. This aircraft became RCAF 23210 and was lost in May 1956 when the engine flamed out over New Brunswick. (CL F01785)

Sabre from the ground. Canadair lost other sales, mainly in South America, when the United States began selling their Sabres for 15 per cent of cost.

Experimental Sabres

Canadair modified two Sabres for experimental purposes. At the request of the National Research Council, the first (Sabre 6 No. 23544 designated CL-13C) was fitted with an afterburner. An afterburner provides increased short-duration thrust but increases fuel consumption. Tests showed a thrust increase of 21.5 per cent at all altitudes, but the concept never saw production.

A second experiment involved Sabre 5 No. 23275 (CL-13E) which was modified following the disclosure of Richard T. Whitcomb's "area rule". It suggested a possible increase in the speed by adding volume to certain portions of the fuselage. Aluminum blisters were added to the Sabre's fuselage by Al Stone and Vic Fangor, but the marginal performance improvement did not justify such a major modification.

What Happened to All Those Beautiful Sabres?

In the mid-1960s, David McEwen of Moncton, New Brunswick, bought a large number of Sabre 5s and 6s from Crown Assets Disposal Corp. He sold one each to Lockheed and Boeing as chase planes; most of the others went to W.R. Laidlaw of Flight Systems at Mojave, California. As a condition of the sale to McEwen, the government ordered saw cuts to be made in the centre section rear spar to render the aircraft unflyable. Flight Systems, however, devised a repair scheme, had it approved by the U.S. Federal Aviation Administration (FAA), modified a number of the aircraft as pilotless target drones, and in 1995 was still using a few Canadair Sabres for target towing and the development of new avionics, electronics and ordnance.

One Sabre 5, sold to a private operator in the United States, crashed on takeoff from Sacramento, California, on September 24, 1972, killing 22 people in an ice cream parlor. The subsequent court case determined that the pi-

RCAF pilots from No.1 Overseas Ferry Unit (St-Hubert) at Canadair to ferry new Sabre 5s overseas: Bruce Merklinger, Mike Bradley, Bob Middlemiss, Howie Webb of Canadair, Bob Hallowell, Ben Simard and George Fitzgerald. (CL F6031)

New Sabre 6s for the Luftwaffe await flight testing at Canadair in June 1957. (CL)

lot had flown only six hours in the Sabre and had over-rotated the aircraft when trying to take off from too short a runway.

In 1963, Italy sent some of the Sabre 4s it had received from the RAF to support UN peacekeeping efforts in the Congo. While there they were flown by members of a Philippine contingent who took several home with them.

In January 1966, Germany sold 90 Sabre 6s to Iran which quickly transferred them to Pakistan. Neither Canada nor Germany approved of this transfer. When they queried Iran for an explanation, it claimed the Sabres had gone to Pakistan for maintenance and would be returning to Iran.

The Sabre 6 was the leading Pakistan Air Force day fighter during the brief but furious 1971 war with India. It is the official Pakistani view that the tenacity of its air force and the way it established air superiority in the face of India's superior numbers, including its state-of-the-art MiG-21s, led to India's sudden acceptance of a cease fire. Without control of the skies, India apparently felt victory could not be assured.

Several Sabre 4s that had been transferred from the RAF to Yugoslavia were resold as surplus in the late 1970s. They later operated with the Honduran Air Force. South Africa's Sabres were in service until 1979 when 10 were sold for £110,000 Sterling. Some of these were still flying privately in the U.S. in 1995.

When Canadair tried to locate a Sabre to exhibit at the company's 40th anniversary celebrations in 1984, a Texan dealer offered a choice of six low-time Sabre 6s in fly-away

The Colombian Air Force took six Sabre 6s. This photo from June 4, 1956 shows the planes in front of B117 about to depart on the ferry to Bogotá. The last Colombian Sabre retired in 1970. (CL F3682)

The 1,815th and final F-86 about to be pushed off the line at Canadair in October 1958. It was destined for the Luftwaffe and had a later career in Pakistan. In the second photo, Sicotte Transports loads Luftwaffe Sabre 6 No. 1592 in September 1957 for the Montreal docks, where it went aboard ship for Hamburg. Final destination was Dornier's Oberpfaffenhofen assembly facility near Munich. No. 1592 later became one of the infamous Pakistani Sabres. Then Lt. Bruno Bieger at the door of the No. 17 streetcar. He was the Luftwaffe's man at Canadair during Sabre 6 production. (CL 86-4193, F4859, CL)

condition, including guns, for $500,000 each, more than double the original cost.

The original F-86A is on display at Canadian Forces Base Edmonton. The Sabre 3 is at the Western Canada Aviation Museum in Winnipeg, and many others are displayed in museums and on pylons at sites around the country.

After-Sales Service, Sabre Style

The Sabre program included hundreds of aircraft at many locations on three continents. This provided a challenge to Canadair's emerging sales and service organization under Lou Adamson. The major responsibility for keeping the customers happy lay with Canadair's tech reps. As the customers' main source of information about technical and all other matters, they were truly Canadair's ambassadors. Their job often meant spending years in a foreign country with all the associated problems of language, customs and schooling; being prepared at any hour to rush off to investigate an incident or solve a problem; and having the patience to suffer the petty bureaucracy of the home office which seemed unable to relate to the world outside.

Tech rep Jack Forbes joined the company in 1945, working for chief inspector Jan de Vries. His first major job was repairing the Argonaut at Hong Kong. He then became a tech rep on Sabre 2s, first at St-Hubert, then went on to Moncton to dismantle some RCAF Sabre 2s

South African Air Force pilots (above) at Canadair in 1956. Then a Sabre being cocooned for sea delivery to Cape Town, where local workers peeled off the rubber cocooning material and recycled it into raincoats and boots. The last of these Sabres left service in 1979; most were then sold in the US. (CL F3403, 86-3253)

Sales that didn't materialize. First, one of the Sabre 6s sold to Israel in 1955. The Suez War broke out before the planes could be delivered, and Ottawa decreed that the deal was politically too sensitive to approve. Two Sabre 6s made a sales visit to Switzerland in 1956. Civil registrations were carried due to Swiss neutrality. Hedley Everard headed the demonstration team; handling negotiations were Peter Redpath and Jack Davis. Here CF-JJC is seen with a brace of rockets underwing. (CL H178, C5809)

Two experiments: No. 23544 (upper photo) was the only Canadair Sabre with a short afterburner (extra fuel injected in front of the turbine rather than behind the turbine in a normal afterburner). It was flown by F/L Norm Ronaasen, seen here in an experimental partial pressure suit while he was an RCAF test pilot. Ronaasen later flew for Canadair and lost his life in the first Challenger accident. Canadair also experimented with the area rule or "Coke bottle" concept. In 1955 it modified a Sabre in B106 with glued-on bulges of balsa wood covered in sheet metal and glass fiber. Test flying showed no performance benefits. The area rule Sabre was eventually involved in the US Army target drone program at White Sands, where it crashed in February 1980. (DND PCN314, CL 86-3151)

Princess Elizabeth and the Duke of Edinburgh tour the Sabre line during a Royal Visit in October 30, 1951. (CL D5888)

Al Lilly briefs F/L Omer Levesque on the Sabre's cockpit details. Levesque was the first RCAF Sabre pilot and the first Canadian to shoot down a MiG-15 jet fighter in Korea. (CL D5808)

From 1959 to 1963 the RCAF's Golden Hawks air demonstration team thrilled crowds throughout North America with splendidly painted Canadair Sabres. Here the team visits Canadair. The pilots in front are Ed Rozdeba, Fern Villeneuve, Dave Tinson, Bill Stewart, J.T. Price, Jim McCombe and Ralph Annis. Standing, from the left, are Scotty McLean, 2 unknown, Bill Kidd, W/C Jack Allan, team commander, Don Freeborn and Rocky Van Vliett, the team's PR officer. (CL 22671)

Canada's champion figure skaters, Otto and Maria Jelinek, during a tour of the Sabre line in March 1957. (CL M2683)

Canadair's George Keefer, a renowned WWII fighter ace, shows W.F. Murphy (right) through the Sabre line in November 1955. Murphy was a senior man from the Department of Defence Production in Ottawa. (CL G1327)

and pack them for Europe. When the RCAF decided to fly its Sabres to Europe, he went back to Moncton to reassemble the ones he had packed! Then he was off for three years on RAF Sabre 4s at Wildenrath, Germany. After that came Turkey and Sabre 2s and 4s for 30 months; South Africa on Sabre 6s for two years; and Germany on 5s and 6s for seven years. That was just the beginning for Forbes. Between Sabre postings, he went to Antarctica with the CL-70 Rat and to several countries in Europe with the CL-91 Dynatrac. After the Sabre, he went to Venezuela with the CF-5, Malaysia with the CL-41, and Argentina and Thailand with the CL-215. Forbes retired (one would suspect with a sigh of relief) in 1982.

Many more tech reps spent their years with, but sel-

This pristine Canadair Sabre visited P3 at Dorval in June 1994 to participate in the company's 50th anniversary celebrations. In the background is Canadair's administration centre. (CL) (Inset) An ex-South African target-towing Sabre photographed by Canadair's Bill Upton at Holloman AFB, New Mexico, in 1989. Its "dart" gunnery target can be seen under the wing.

Canadair sales and service reps at a February 1954 seminar. In the back row are Reg Thatcher, Charlie Kane, Jack Forbes, Lyne Nesbitt, Tim Stapleton, Ed Norsworthy, Gerry Dutrie, Maurice Lajeunesse and Gordon Eldridge. In front are Jack Heine, Peter Redpath and Tim Sims. Typical of this experienced group was Ed Norsworthy, who earned an engineering degree before the war. Through WWII he was in a branch of the British Air Ministry, then was an air engineer in the navy. He joined Canadair in 1946, first in the DC-3 program; by 1958 he was manager of Canadair's service department. (CL F01649)

dom at, Canadair including: Matt Andrews, Dick Armour, Jim Cutler, Jim Curtis, Jim Fitzpatrick, Ed Keeping, Tom Kelly, Maurice Lajeunesse, Bob Lording, Charlie Massé, Bill Staruch, Jim Steel and Reg Thatcher. As members of the service department, they reported to Charlie Kane and, through him, to service manager Jack Heine, and later to Ed Norsworthy.

The Sabre program brought the first wide use of mobile repair parties (MRPs). These were largely the brain-child of Jack Heine who had used them at Douglas and had already organized one major MRP at Canadair—the Argonaut repair at Hong Kong. An MRP consisted of a team of up to 10 technicians, selected from a core in the service department. They were supplemented by others from manufacturing or preflight. An MRP went out—often at short notice and occasionally to the other side of the world—to fix Canadair aircraft damaged or otherwise unserviceable. They were controlled by the service depart-

A spare parts provisioning conference in September 1954 that brought Canadair and the air force together to discuss Sabre matters. Lou Adamson (seated centre) was presiding. He had first joined Canadian Vickers in 1942 working in such jobs as storeskeeper, sales and service manager, head of the DC-3 conversion program, production manager, assistant plant manager and general sales manager before becoming director of product support in 1960. (CL G1055)

Tech rep woes—crashed or broken Sabres meant extra work. In the first case F/O W.H. Thompson of the RCAF managed to land 23428 when an emergency arose on June 13, 1955. He ended up in a potato patch near Bois Franc Rd. After engine failure on takeoff F/O D.A. Deans walked away after pranging 19253 on the farm of Paul Jasmin near Cartierville on December 6, 1954. In the snowy scene, the recovery crew is about to cart 19230 in for repairs after a nose gear collapsed on January 31, 1955. Moe White (wearing cap) then John Munro are on the right. Peering into the cockpit is Cy McNeil, an old Canadian Vickers man who was superintendent of pre-flight. Finally one of many Sabres that came back to Canadair for refurbishment. (CL 86-3117, '2635, '2717, '1386)

The Sabre Mark 1 ended as a museum piece in Edmonton. (Larry Milberry)

ment and organized by Émile Laviolette, Bill Palmer and Larry Roy.

The last RCAF Sabre went into storage on February 24, 1969. With it went Canadair's direct involvement with the program that had played a major role in developing the company's technological competence, international credibility and financial stability.

Tech rep Kurt Joseph (left) spent years posted abroad with Sabres. Here he displays the honorary pilot wings he received from the Yugoslavian Air Force. (Right) Veteran tech rep Bob Lording. At the rollout of the Sabre 1815 he described the type as "the Spitfire of this era". (CL 5445, R. Lording Col.)

T-33

Never the subject of loud acclaim, the T-33 is nonetheless one of the most successful aircraft of all time. When the RCAF planned to switch to jets and needed a jet trainer, the choice was the Lockheed T-33. It had evolved from the P-80 Shooting Star, the USAF's first operational jet fighter and one of its main combat aircraft in the Korean War. In mid-1947, Lockheed took a P-80, lengthened it by 98 cm (3 ft. 2.5 in.), added a second cockpit and created the TF-80C trainer. Its maiden flight was on March 22, 1948. In May 1949, the USAF renamed it the T-33A.

On September 13, 1951, Ottawa announced that Canadair would build a version of the T-33 for the RCAF. It would be powered by the 23-kN (5,100-lb.) thrust Rolls-Royce Nene 10, not by the Allison J33 used in U.S. T-33s. A contract for 576 aircraft was signed on April 1, 1952. Canadair would design the engine installation, manufacture all but an initial quantity of 200 wings, build the forward and centre fuselage sections, and do final assembly. Beech Aircraft of Wichita, Kansas, would supply the initial wings, and Canadian subcontractors would supply rear fuselages, tail units and intake ducts.

Tom Harvie became T-33 project engineer, reporting to chief project engineer Ed Higgins. Later in the program,

Bob Raven became project engineer. When Raven moved to the newly formed special weapons division, George Burlton took over the T-33, leaving his former Sabre project engineer's job to Bob Deans. Later still, Deans became T-33 project engineer when Burlton went on to the Tutor.

The T-33 program should have been relatively easy since differences between U.S. and Canadian aircraft were minimal. However, installing the larger, more powerful Nene proved time-consuming and expensive. New forgings had to be made for the engine support structure, and three different tailpipe designs were tried before satisfactory performance was obtained. Problems also arose with one of the subcontractors. Canadair had given Ford of Canada a contract to produce the wings, but a labor dispute held up production to such an extent that Canadair was forced to bring the work back to Cartierville. Nonetheless, Ford did manufacture the nose and main landing gears.

As an adaptation of the P-80, the T-33 represented Second World War technology. A sheet metal airplane, it required no special machinery, but the method of assembling the airframe was new to Canadair. The fuselage was built in two halves, split vertically from nose to tail. Incorporating the cockpit and the engine bay, these moved down the assembly line parallel to each other, but wide apart. This enabled all the equipment, wiring, piping and other systems to be installed conveniently at waist level before the halves were joined farther down the line.

T-33 production was in the capable hands of people like Norm Holbrook, Jim Moffatt, Bill Montgomery, Ed Platt, Art Thomas and Tommy Whitton. Charlie Ulsh was factory manager, and Bob Neale was vice-president, manufacturing. Jack Waller ran the material and process group. He had just succeeded in reconciling the differences between Douglas and North American specifications when saddled with a totally different set of Lockheed specs; all three sets then had to be incorporated into a common Canadair set of specs.

With initial program delays solved, T-33 production increased at a remarkable rate, reaching one aircraft a day by the end of the first year. Canadair later received a contract for an additional 80 aircraft, bringing the total to 656.

Barry Coleman recalled a problem with an incorrectly

(Right) While it awaited its first Canadair T-33s, the RCAF borrowed 21 of them from the USAF in 1951. They had Allison J33 engines, underslung tip tanks and no ejection seats. (CL 12008)

(Below) A-NX (USAF No. 51-4198) was the original Nene-powered T-33. Its first engine run was on September 13, 1952 and it flew on October 28. The first Canadair-built T-33 went to the RCAF January 3, 1953. (CL)

The T-33 line hums along at Plant 2. The aircraft in the foreground was delivered in April 1954. (CL F01768)

designed T-33 wingtip fuel tank fixture which caused one tank to be misaligned with its opposite number. Until a new fixture was designed and built, the problem was handled by slackening all the fasteners on the underside of the misaligned wing, twisting the wing into shape and retightening the underwing fasteners. This worked, provided an over-energetic pilot did not throw the aircraft around.

Bob Lording, while a T-33 tech rep at RCAF Station MacDonald, Manitoba, reported that 98 of the 103 T-33s on his station had cracks in their wing flaps. The answer he received from Cartierville–"It's an isolated case"– con-

vinced Lording that certain people should get out of their offices and into the field more often.

In RCAF service, the T-33 rapidly became one of the most versatile jets in Canadian skies. A quantum improvement over previous trainers like the Harvard, it handled all the basic jet training chores. During the 1950s, all RCAF and NATO pilots training at RCAF schools flew a minimum of 80 T-bird hours before getting their wings. After graduation, pilots selected for jets took a further three-week instrument rating qualification course on the T-33, and those chosen to be flying instructors also trained on it.

(Above) A typical Nene engine for the T-33, then (right) a kit full of tools for servicing the Nene. (CL 33-1294)

T-33 celebrities… Moe White (pre-flight), pilots Bruce Fleming and Les Benson, Kenny Reardon, and Ray Courteau (pre-flight) in November 1957. Reardon played for the Montreal Canadiens. White had played for them over the 1945-46 season when "the Habs" won the Stanley Cup. He pulled the strings to get Reardon a T-bird familiarization ride. (CL 5222)

In addition to training, the T-33 was widely used as a communications aircraft. It was popular with desk-bound pilots flying a mandatory number of hours to keep their ratings current, and, many would agree, the T-bird was just perfect for getting around to far-flung weekend parties!

Easy and pleasant to fly, the T-bird had one vice, the "tumble," or as the USAF called it, the "out-of-control manoeuvre." Both names were appropriate. If a pilot flying at high altitude got really sloppy on the controls and let the airspeed drop too low the aircraft would begin to tumble. Once that happened, all the pilot could do was centre the controls, try to stop his head bashing a hole in the canopy, and wait until the aircraft recovered when it entered denser air below 7,620 m (25,000 ft.).

Every so often, the RCAF T-33 fleet went through an upgrading. Although its numbers dwindled, there always seemed to be plenty for the T-bird to do, for the RCAF had distributed it liberally among both the regular and the reserve squadrons.

Canadian Forces students on the last basic T-33 course graduated at Cold Lake, Alberta, in 1974. After that, many Canadian T-birds were scrapped. Some were given, as part of mutual aid, to France, Greece, Portugal and Turkey, and 21 were sold by private interests to Bolivia where they were put to dual use as trainers and counter-insurgency aircraft.

The 50 or so T-33s still in RCAF service in 1995, the youngest of which was 37 years old, were performing a variety of missions including communications, target towing and enemy aircraft simulation during electronic warfare training. Practically all had exceeded 10,000 flight hours; they were only supposed to have a life of 4,000 hours!

A large number of Canadair T-33s are on public display. The first production T-33, No. 21001, is at the CAE plant at Edmonton International Airport. No. 21574 is in the National Aviation Museum at Ottawa. It sports the bright red colors of the Red Knight aerobatic display aircraft that was a regular performer at airshows across the country between 1958 and 1969. T-33 No. 21630, flown by the original Red Knight, Roy Windover, sits outside the Air Force Association Wing at Saskatoon, Saskatchewan. No. 21075 is at the Western Canada Aviation Museum, while others are on pylons around the country.

(Left) Capt W.M. "Turbo" Tarling during a visit to Canadair from CFB Cold Lake. With 7,651 hours, Tarling was the undisputed high-time T-33 pilot. (Right) Hedley Everard and director of aircraft manufacturing Charlie Ulsh, who was about to experience his first ride in the T-33. (CL 41238, F3910)

The T-bird was still in Canadian service in the mid-1990s. It always made an interesting subject for the camera. This example from 414 Squadron was photographed near North Bay in 1991. (Larry Milberry)

(Left) By 1995 most of the 656 Canadair-built T-33s had gone to the scrap yard. No.232 survived the wrecker and "flies" at the end of a pylon over a Winnipeg park. (Larry Milberry)

(Facing page) Contrasting views of Canadair: a fairyland scene one Christmas in the 1950s, then a look inside at the heart of manufacturing—the machine shop. (CL 2146, 2081)

CHAPTER THREE

CANADAIR'S GIANTS

ARGUS, YUKON AND "44"

It was late 1949 when Ken Ebel, Ev Schaefer (chief technical engineer), Jim Schaffer (chief of design) and Dick Richmond (chief aerodynamicist) first discussed getting the RCAF to buy a long-range maritime patrol aircraft to replace its aging Lancasters. They assumed the RCAF would need an aircraft capable of patrolling for eight hours 1,600 km (1,000 mi.) from base, at about 60 m (200 ft.) altitude and a speed of 266 km/h (165 mph). The proposal submitted to the DND was for a stretched version of the North Star with either Wright R-3350, Bristol Hercules 763 or Bristol Centaurus 661 engines.

When the RCAF finally issued its specifications in 1952, it called for an aircraft with greater payload, interior room and comfort than the Canadair submission. Lockheed answered with a version of the Super Constellation while Bristol proposed a version of its Britannia 100 turboprop airliner.

The RCAF contracted with Canadair to carry out a detailed study of the Britannia with various engines to enable the air force to assess its performance against other types. The RCAF discarded the Lockheed proposal since the Constellation would be unable to manoeuvre safely at low speeds and low altitudes. Then Canadair produced a study of a minimum-cost alternative, the CL-33, primarily for comparison with the Britannia. It resembled a large unpressurized Lancaster powered by R-3350s and

weighing about 9,000 kg (20,000 lb.) less than the Britannia. The chief of the air staff, Air Marshal W.A. Curtis, preferred the Britannia which could be converted to replace not only the Lancaster in a maritime patrol/anti-submarine warfare (ASW) role, but also the North Star in a passenger/cargo transport role.

In mid-1953, Ebel, Richmond, Longhurst and Robert J. Ross, an aerodynamicist newly arrived from England, visited Bristol as part of a joint RCAF/Canadair team, to evaluate the Britannia as a suitable platform from which to develop a maritime surveillance and ASW aircraft. They had a major concern: whether or not the Britannia's tab-operated ailerons would provide the essential manoeuvrability at low speeds. Ailerons control the aircraft's rolling motion and are normally operated by a direct linkage from the pilot's control wheel. On the Britannia, however, when the pilot turned the control wheel, the linkage moved only a small tab on the trailing edge of the aileron and that tab, in turn, moved the aileron. The team decided that this concern could readily be handled by the addition of spoilers to augment roll control.

The Argus

At the end of 1953, the RCAF decided on the Britannia. On February 23, 1954, Ottawa announced that Canadair would build the new plane. On March 16 the licence

The Britannia airliner on which the Argus was based. This example was seen at Dorval's old international terminal in 1959. Then a model of Canadair's proposed maritime patrol Britannia conversion. (Merlin Reddy, CL M1425)

mond was chief development engineer and Jack Waller was chief materials and process engineer. The design section chiefs were: Issie Finkelstein, electrical; Hugh Gosnell, fuselage and furnishings; Bob Smith, power plant; and Bob Stapells, mechanical. The other section chiefs were: Dave Bogdanoff, dynamics; Ray Hebert, weights; and Ted Larrett, stress. The detail work fell to people like Saul Bernstein, Jeff Harwood, Joe Knap and Bob Ross. On the manufacturing side, reporting to vice-president Bob Neale, were managers Dan Gilmore, manufacturing engineering, Dean Stowell, industrial engineering, and Charlie Ulsh, factory, assisted by Ray Campbell, George Hannah, Albert McIvor and Fred Nuttall.

The Design Task

The designers chose to retain the Britannia's wings, tail and flight control system, but to design a completely new fuselage to accommodate two 5.5-metre (18-ft.) long weapons bays, a new forward crew compartment and a transparent nose. To help them, a team which included Barker Bates, Keith Lancaster and Vic Southin built a full-scale fuselage mock-up and stub wing with all compartments detailed using actual items of equipment where available. The mock-up also had operative mechanisms such as escape hatches, flap retraction, landing gear uplocks and bomb hoists. Lacking a better source of power, Gerry Barabé fitted up an ordinary bicycle to raise and lower the wing flaps. Several other smaller mock-ups and test rigs were constructed.

One of the biggest tasks facing engineering was the conversion of some 9,000 Bristol drawings to Canadian and U.S. standards, materials and processes. A group of engineers under Jack Greeniaus prepared a thorough "Americanization" manual for use when converting drawings for those portions of the aircraft where Bristol design

agreement with Bristol was signed; on May 27 the government awarded Canadair a contract to produce an initial 13 maritime patrol/ASW aircraft based on the Britannia. Canadair designated it the CL-28.

Development of the CL-28 was a tremendous challenge to Canadair. The task of converting a fast, pressurized, high-flying turboprop airliner into a low-and-slow-flying, unpressurized piston engine patrol plane loaded with tons of sophisticated electronic equipment and weapons was enough to deter the most experienced design engineers. Fortunately, Ebel had the foresight to include a large number of core designers in the preliminary team which carried out the Britannia study. In preparing it, they had also established the aircraft's configuration so that, for the first time at Canadair, a product's configuration was settled before the contract was signed.

Ebel appointed Tom Harvie as CL-28 project engineer and Harry Whiteman as Harvie's assistant. Harvie reported to Ed Higgins, chief project engineer who reported to Ev Schaefer. Jim Schaffer was chief design engineer, Ben Kaganov was chief structures engineer, R.D. Rich-

was still usable. It was a massive job, yet the first detail drawings were issued seven months after the RCAF decision—a remarkable achievement.

Turboprop engines were not ideal for low altitude operations, so the designers replaced the Britannia's Proteus turboprops with 3,700 bhp Wright R-3350 turbo-compound piston engines to provide the combination of high power and low fuel consumption required.

To withstand the beating it would take in a turbulent wave-top environment, the airframe required considerable strengthening. As a result the CL-28 became the first Canadian design to make extensive use of metal-to-metal bonding instead of riveting or spot welding. Bristol engineers had been weight conscious, and in some cases, parts to be mated were only 0.30 mm (0.012 in.) thick. Canadair introduced a tape-type adhesive which, inserted between the parts and then subjected to heat and pressure, produced a bond which increased the resistance of the structure to fatigue by distributing the loads over a larger area. The CL-28 program also marked the first wide use in Canada of titanium and high strength 7079 aluminum alloy.

An entirely new flight deck was installed in the CL-28. The nose landing gear was redesigned to allow the fitting of a large chin radome. This along with a 5.59 metre (18 ft.) magnetic anomaly detection boom protuding from the end of the fuselage, gave the CL-28 its distinctive silhouette. A portion of the vertical fin was made of a structural plastic material to isolate the upper part of the fin electrically, thereby allowing its use as an antenna. This was another first in Canada. A one-fifth scale model of the fuselage and fin covered with a copper screen and mounted on a raised platform was built for fin antenna development.

The two massive weapons bays could accommodate up to 3,600 kg (8,000 lb.) of offensive weapons including torpedoes, bombs, depth charges or mines, and hard points under the wings could carry a variety of other weapons. A 70-million candlepower high intensity searchlight was mounted in the right wing for night target identification.

The CL-28 was the first Canadian aircraft with a fully paralleled AC electrical system, and its avionics and ASW systems were the latest. These sophisticated systems enabled the CL-28 to be flown, navigated and fought more

Jack Greeniaus led the group that converted 9,000 Bristol drawings for the Argus program. (CL 39388)

Harry Whiteman tours RCAF officers around P1 (Jack Henry is on the left—he was later vice-president, flight operations at Canadair). Whiteman enjoyed the Argus program for its hands-on nature. Early on he supervised the mock-up and personally helped in proving one of the escape hatches. For this he had to roll out the hatch into a pile of hay. All in a day's work! The second photo shows Dean Stowell, who managed the industrial engineering side of Argus production. (CL)

Some of those involved with the Argus wind tunnel program: G. Thivierge, P. Bourget, L. Plamondon, A. Thivierge, R. Audette, Gerry Barabé, Ed Payne, Ken Kimber, Bob Werrett, unknown, Keith Walker, Keith Lancaster. (CL)

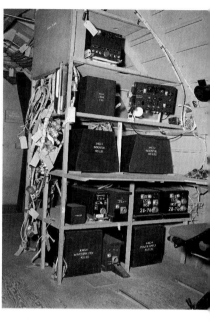

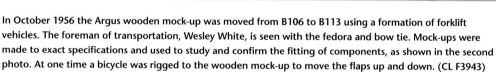

In October 1956 the Argus wooden mock-up was moved from B106 to B113 using a formation of forklift vehicles. The foreman of transportation, Wesley White, is seen with the fedora and bow tie. Mock-ups were made to exact specifications and used to study and confirm the fitting of components, as shown in the second photo. At one time a bicycle was rigged to the wooden mock-up to move the flaps up and down. (CL F3943)

Canadair's stress department in 1957. Most were on the Argus. The occasion was Ted Larrett's farewell party. Those squatting are Joe Heyman, Bob Woodberry, Nick Gentilo, Reg Ringrose, Lorna Barrett, Shelna Brace, unknown, Jim Henry and Dave Turner. Behind are Antone de Smit, Jean Vaillancourt, Saul Bernstein, Jim Grant, Ken Goodall, Eric Aubrey, Ted Larrett, unknown, Ron Wyke, Andy Anderson, Steve Brochocki, Don Joseph, unknown, John Taylor, Ron Regan, Keith Walker (the 3 behind unknown), Peter Deneeve, 2 unknown (over Deneeve's left shoulder), Harvey Delane (no tie), Willi Krause, unknown (wearing cardigan), Len Coombs (behind, with mustache), 2 unknown, John Southwell (barely seen), John Male and Mike Chobotof. (CL)

The CL-28's many systems required much testing: an R-3350 runs up on the massive stand designed by Vic Fangor of experimental; testing one of the main Jarry undercarriage units; a mock-up weapons load; finally the 1/5 mock-up for evaluating electrical installations. One of those who worked on the Argus early on recalled of trials with the bomb bay, "We had a hell of a time getting things to fall out of that thing." (F3421, 28-2207, 28-4044, PL3110)

effectively than any other aircraft in its class. It would be many years before any ASW aircraft would appear to challenge its capabilities.

Barry Coleman of functional test procedures went to Boeing to get some advice on setting up the AC electrical system. After he explained what Canadair was about to do, the Boeing engineers told him, "You'll be the first in history to parallel and synchrophase four 400-cycle systems in an aircraft–we wish you luck." It was indeed a problem. Canadair had to set up a rig consisting of four 150 hp diesel engines driving DC generators which, in turn, drove aircraft AC alternators in order to simulate the CL-28's system.

Manufacture and Test

A CL-28 static airframe, tied down on a huge iron grid, was thoroughly tested. During these tests the frames over the side cargo-loading door collapsed and the rear end of the fuselage drooped about 30 degrees. Saul Bernstein had done the stressing of the design and was devastated. When he got a call from Ebel's office he was sure he was about to be fired. Instead, Ebel said, "I know you feel badly about what happened on the 28 fuselage but, as a result of that failure, we ended up with about $1 million extra profit." (Those were the days of "cost plus" when the government reimbursed Canadair for every dollar spent, plus a fee, and sometimes a bonus.

The Argus static test airframe secured to its grid, then a view showing the results of load simulation. The skin has wrinkled after thousands of hours of rigorous "flying". (CL 43563, 43561)

Sadly for industry, but to the relief of the taxpayer, those days are long gone.)

In late 1954 and early 1955, two new buildings were added to provide more floor space at Plant 1. One was an engineering laboratory (B118); the other housed a new foundry, pattern shop, template shop, jig shop and offices for clerical staff from production control, tool design and planning (B119). At this time there were some senior staff changes. Kelly Smith departed; Dean Stowell became assistant to the president, and Bill Jolliffe took over his job managing industrial engineering. Harry McKeown became director of operations, and Fred Phillips joined the company as chief of aerodynamics and preliminary design.

The first CL-28 (No. 20710) rolled out on December 21, 1956. On February 5, 1957, it was named "Argus" after the all-seeing monster of Greek mythology. After ground

Seen in February 1956, the first Argus fuselage is slowly built up in Bay 1, Plant 1 (the old PBY fuselage line). Then it is shown in August being moved to join the wing centre section (last photo). (CL F3346, 28-3000, F3836)

tests, it made its first flight on March 28, 1957, with the crew of Bill Longhurst and Scotty McLean (pilots), Smokey Harris (flight engineer), George MacFarlane (radio operator) and Peter Wreford-Bush (experimental flight test engineer).

The prototype then entered a prolonged flight test pro-gram which eventually involved seven aircraft. 20710 was used for stability and control testing; 20711 for systems and environmental testing; 20712 for cold weather trials; 20713 for structural integrity and RCAF performance/handling; 20714 for weapons systems evaluation; 20715 for operational evaluation under maritime patrol conditions.

A festive day at Cartierville as the Argus is officially dedicated, then a nice portrait of the prototype coasting along the St. Lawrence with the Royal Yacht *Britannia* in the river below. (CL)

On a blustery December day, the first Argus rolled off the final line into the open air and workers gathered for a souvenir photo. Below is a grand view of VN-710 on its first flight near Montreal, and on the facing page the Argus line is in full swing. (CL F4086, CL, PL3771)

Another view of the Argus line. A new door was installed in October 1957 so that the Argus could move in and out of B117 without its nose being jacked up. (CL 16238)

The Argus in Service

Before completion of the first batch of 13 aircraft, Canadair received a contract for 20 slightly modified versions, designated the Argus Mark 2. The first Mark 2, No. 20723, flew on August 27, 1958, with pilots R.M. (Bill) Kidd and W.J. (Bill) Clark, flight engineer Paul Del Rizzo and radio operator Bill Knibbs. The obvious difference between the two versions was the size and shape of the nose radome—

the Mark 1's was bulbous to hold the American APS-20 radar, the Mark 2's was smaller for the more compact British ASV 21. Eric Haines designed the Mark 2 radome—a remarkable exercise in geometry by today's standards. Argus production continued under a new project engineer, Bob Deans, until the roll-out of the 33rd aircraft (No. 20742) on July 13, 1960.

The Argus flew with 404 and 405 Squadrons at Green-

"I KNOW THIS IS A SUB HUNTER, BUT ARE YOU SURE THIS IS WHAT THEY HAD IN MIND?"

wood, Nova Scotia; 415 Squadron at Summerside, Prince Edward Island, and 407 Squadron at Comox, British Columbia. It became known for its impressive records. For example, in October 1959 Argus 20725 of 405 Squadron, returning from a goodwill visit to Australia and New Zealand, flew non-stop 7,350 km (4,570 mi.) from Hawaii to North Bay, Ontario in 20 hours 10 minutes; and May 31 to June 1, 1974, a 407 Argus was airborne for 31 hours.

On February 10, 1968, the Argus squadrons were integrated with Royal Canadian Navy Trackers and Sea Kings to form Canadian Armed Forces Maritime Command. In

The Argus first flight crew: Bill Longhurst, Smokey Harris, George MacFarlane, Scotty McLean and Peter Wreford-Bush. (CL C1482)

1970 the Argus became the CP-107. The serial numbers, too, were altered by changing the first digit from "2" to "1", thus 20710 became 10710.

Between 1961 and 1965, the Argus fleet was rotated through Canadair in a Calendar Aircraft Inspection and Repair (CAIR) program. All electrical and avionics were updated. Some structural changes were made and each Argus was overhauled in a program which took 20,000 manhours per aircraft. The program was administered by Jim Maskell and Bill Palmer, who reported to Ed Norsworthy. Andy Throner, preflight foreman, headed the work crew. Throner's supervisors, supplemented by

A big day at Greenwood as the Argus makes its official RCAF public debut on May 17, 1958. The first Argus operation was flown by 405 Squadron on August 11, 1958. (CL 5993)

An Argus wind tunnel model with a shape simulating an anti-shipping missile. Near it is the leading edge search light. Photo 2 shows the co-pilot's yoke. The small handle on the right controlled the search light. (CL 28-1368, 4721)

The CAIR line on the go. Closest is No. 710, the original Argus in for refurbishment. (CL 41554)

dozens of designers and technicians from engineering, completed the CAIR program on three aircraft during the Canadair strike in 1965.

The last operational Argus flight took place on November 10, 1980. The last time employees saw an Argus at Cartierville was February 10, 1982, when 10742 flew over enroute to its new home in the National Aviation Museum at Ottawa.

Only two Arguses were lost during the airplane's 24-year military career. 20727 of 404 Squadron crashed near Puerto Rico during a night exercise on March 23, 1965. There were no survivors. 10737 crashed on landing at Summerside on March 31, 1977. It then collided with CF-NAZ, a Lockheed Electra which Canadair had earlier modified for ice reconnaissance work. Three from the Argus crew died.

In May 1981, 24 Arguses were assembled at Summerside for disposal. A Crown Assets sales brochure listed possible uses: cargo transport, forestry management/water bomber, aerial spraying, search and rescue, sovereignty surveillance and fisheries patrol. Some maritime nations were interested in the Argus for military purposes. Perhaps to prevent the planes from falling into the wrong hands, Ottawa decided to scrap the fleet. In 1982, Bristol Metal Industries of Toronto paid $71,936 for the 24 Arguses and melted them down on the spot.

Several Arguses were saved from the melting pot. No.

An Argus in the preflight hangar. The slot in the door was cut out to accommodate the huge tail. (CL PL3685)

(Right) The last Argus (No. 742) rolled out July 13, 1960 (through the door that was modified in 1957 to accommodate the height of its rudder). The final service mission (July 24, 1981) was a ferry flight from Greenwood to Summerside, where most of the fleet was scrapped. The last Argus flew on February 10, 1982 when No. 742 was delivered to the National Aviation Museum in Ottawa. The second photo shows its arrival there. (CL 28-21596, DND REC 82-909)

(Below) George Tait of inspection. He started at Canadian Vickers and his many projects included the Argus. He passed away on the job while preparing to go to Mojave on the Challenger flight test program. (CLD9742)

Geoff Notman, president of Canadair, oversaw the Argus program from start to finish. (CL F3967)

Three Argus and a Sabre fly past at Toronto's Canadian International Air Show about 1960. (Larry Milberry)

(Facing page) A 415 Squadron Argus on patrol from Summerside, PEI. Argus 10712 may be seen at CFB Comox on Vancouver Island. On the fin is the emblem of 407 "Demon" Squadron. (Douglas J. Fisher, Larry Milberry)

10739 is at Summerside; 10717 is at Greenwood; 10718 is at Comox; 10742 is at the National Aviation Museum; 10715 belongs to the Western Canada Aviation Museum. In 1994 No. 10732 was still at the air force depot at Mountain View, Ontario, being used for battle damage repair and anti-terrorist training.

When the Argus was new, there had not been much of a foreign market for it. In 1958, Peter Redpath, Al Lilly and Ken McDonald found sufficient interest in Australia and New Zealand to warrant opening an Australian sales office. Both those nations eventually re-equipped with the Lockheed P-3. There was also some Argentine interest, but nothing became of it.

Ken Coochey of product support later carried out a study of the Argus as a freighter. He concluded that the need for new electrical and electronic systems, the Argus's relatively weak floor, and an impending global shortage of 115/145 octane aviation gasoline made the project unfeasible.

Yukon

In January 1957 Ottawa announced plans for a fleet of long range transports based on the Britannia. Shortly after, Canadair received a contract for eight aircraft (later increased to 12). Designated the CC-106 Yukon by the RCAF and the CL-44-6 by Canadair, the new type would have Bristol Orion turboprop engines. Ken Ebel appointed Frank Francis senior CL-44 project engineer and program manager. A graduate of the University of British Columbia, Francis had joined Canadair in 1955 from TCA where he had been project engineer on the Super Constellation.

Detailed design had already started when, on February 24, 1958, Canadair advised the RCAF that the British ministry of supply had dropped its interest in the Orion. It could not support two new engines, the Orion and the Rolls-Royce Tyne. Canadair now switched to the lower-powered Tyne 11.

The Yukon design used modified Argus wing and tail surfaces, and a redesigned landing gear to handle higher weights. The fuselage was similar to the Britannia 300, or

3.76 m (12 ft. 4 in.) longer than the Britannia 100. It had cargo doors front and rear on the left side, and was pressurized to maintain a cabin altitude of 2,400 m (8,000 ft.) at 9,000 m (30,000 ft.). The Yukon could carry 134 passengers and a crew of nine. In the casualty evacuation role it could take 80 patients and a crew of 11; and in the cargo role it could carry a payload of 27,562 kg (60,763 lb.) for 5,043 km (2,723 nautical mi.).

Since Bob Neale was on extended leave of absence as vice-president of manufacturing, Dean Stowell headed Yukon production. He had moved earlier from manager of industrial engineering to assistant to the president, a position he relinquished to an up-and-comer named Fred Kearns.

Hélène Beauchamp of graphic reproduction recalled the Yukon roll-out as something of a fiasco. Although the Argus and Yukon were theoretically the same height, the door opening was, for some unexplained reason, too low for the Yukon. The problem was easily solved by deflating the main landing gear and lifting the nose slightly.

The first Yukon reached flight status amid a confusion of late engineering changes, unorthodox introduction of changes, negotiation of post-flight modifications and temporary acceptance of deficiencies to be corrected later. It eventually flew on November 15, 1959, with Bill Longhurst, Scotty McLean, Smokey Harris and George MacFarlane as crew. To everyone's relief, the ensuing flight test program was routine—plenty of problems but no disasters.

If there was anything that approached disaster status, it was Rolls-Royce's inability to meet engine delivery schedules. Airframe production outpaced engine availability to the extent that Yukon 'gliders' were still being parked around Cartierville airport as late as 1961.

Yukon Recollections

Barry Coleman recalled that one of the problems with Rolls-Royce was the need to change all the engine fittings to American standards. Proud, aristocratic Rolls-Royce said, in effect, "Nobody changes Rolls-Royce fittings,"

(Top) Tyne and Eland engines are off-loaded at Dorval from a KLM DC-7C in November 1960. (CL 22976)

(Above) The guts of a newly installed Tyne. A note on one of the access doors is "A/c 5", so this would be CL-44 15925 of the RCAF, delivered May 23, 1961. At the rear of the engine is a large unit with its data plate visible. This is the gear box, which delivered 350 hp to six attached accessory units (cabin pressurization, hydraulics etc.). Gearbox design was done by Canadian Pratt & Whitney, Canadair's neighbor in Longueuil. There a group of young engineers headed by Hugh Langshur tackled the job and tested their prototype in October 1958. This was CP&W's first all-Canadian venture and it proved a great success. From here it went on to design the PT6, the world's most successful small turboprop engine. (CL 20488)

(Facing page) The Yukon line at Cartierville in September 1959. (CL 44-18798)

The stately Yukon on roll-out, then on its first flight. Don Freeborn and Stan Lebedis fly chase in a T-bird. When the air force purchased Boeing 707s in 1970, its 12 Yukons were sold. No. 501 went to a Colombian operator and crashed near Medellin on February 22, 1975. (CL 18842, '702)

(Below) Everyone wanted to see the mighty Yukon when it was handed over to the RCAF at Trenton, June 9, 1961. Unlike the later "swing tails", the Yukons had side cargo doors. (CL 26937)

Canadair's photographers floodlit the prototype Yukon to capture this run-up scene, then an air-to-air of the 10th Yukon (No.15929). After its RCAF career, it became a tramp freighter in Zaire and was last seen derelict at Kinshasa. (CL)

One of Canadair's Sabres flies chase on the prototype Yukon. Then, a view of the complex flight engineer's panel, with Flight Sergeant Bud Risely checking his instruments. (CL 44-18770, 27466)

and thereby forced Canadair to make a whole series of weird adaptors.

In a CL-44 article in the *Journal* of the Canadian Aviation Historical Society, Harry Whiteman described several incidents related by Yukon pilots including: having to cope with solidly frozen rudder and aileron controls when a water tank sprang a leak just above the aileron-rudder interconnect; having an engine try to shake itself off its mounts after tangling with a weather balloon; and flying on battery power alone following a double electrical system failure.

Joey Wilkinson recalled the RCAF sending an aircraft to Canadair to have its integral fuel tanks re-sealed. Sounds simple, but it wasn't. The Yukon's outer-wing tanks were integral—fuel was not contained inside a separate fuel cell, but the wing itself was the tank. All joints between the skin and the rest of the wing structure had to be carefully sealed to keep fuel from leaking. Re-sealing meant removing the old sealant and putting in new, and

that meant someone had to work inside the confined, vapor-laden wing. Special equipment—ventilating fans, gas masks, gloves, coveralls, boots and hats—had to be obtained, medical advice sought, special training given, and safety procedures instituted, before the job could start. As work progressed, leadhands monitored the workers to ensure safety. The old sealant was removed with plastic scrapers, then the tanks were cleaned and new sealant applied. The last step was the worst because of pungent fumes. Finally, after the sealant had dried, the tanks had to be cleaned again, tested and, where necessary, repaired. It was a long, unpleasant job, and Wilkinson and the others were glad the RCAF never sent another Yukon in for resealing.

In service, the Yukons performed well. In December 1961 a Yukon set a world record for its class when, on the last leg of a round-the-world flight, it flew 10,860 km (6,750 mi.) from Tokyo to Trenton, Ontario, in 17 hours three minutes, at an average speed of almost 640 km/h

For CL-44 icing trials this USAF KC-135 tanker was modified to spray water from its refuelling boom. The CL-44 would be sprayed as it trailed the tanker causing an ice build-up. Then its anti-icing systems would be activated to evaluate their effectiveness. (CL 26161)

CF-MKP-X, the 9th CL-44 during fuel dumping trials. It became TF-LLH of Loftleidir, where it served a number of years before moving to subsequent operators. It was scrapped in Dublin in June 1986. (CL 26235)

(400 mph). In June 1962, a Yukon captained by Squadron Leader Robert Simmons (later CL-84 marketing director at Canadair) flew 9,080 km (5,640 mi.) non-stop over all 10 provinces and two territories in 15 hours. The following month a Yukon stayed airborne 23 hours 51 minutes.

The RCAF's Yukons retired in April 1971 after 11 years of service. They were replaced by five Boeing 707s. In November 1971, Crown Assets sold 11 Yukons and spares jointly to Beaver Enterprises Ltd. of Montreal, and Compania Interamericana Export-Import, S.A., Miami, Florida, for Cdn $1.1 million. In explaining this apparent give-away, Crown Assets noted that the Yukons did not qualify for certificates of airworthiness under Canadian, U.S. or British regulations; that both the Department of Transport and Canadair estimated the cost of modification would exceed $250,000 per aircraft; and that some jet transports could be purchased for less than $200,000.

Certification centred on the Yukon's Britannia-type windshield. Windshield certification requirements for civil aircraft were amended just after the Britannia received certification, and its design no longer met visibility requirements. Finally, on March 22, 1974, Canadian type approval was granted for the Yukon (cargo only) on the strength of its safe military record. Two Canadian operators toyed with operating Yukons in Canada, but their plans died. Several foreign owners, however, ran Yukon cargo planes for a number of years.

The "Forty-Four"

At about the same time as the Yukon contract, Canadair announced its intention to re-enter the civil transport market with a derivative of the Britannia. Its proposal was the CL-44, a version of the Yukon. It created little interest among passenger airlines which had their sights set on jets. On the other hand, cargo airlines found the cost projections developed by Karl Larsson, Eric McConachie and their sales engineers, attractive compared with the high cost of operating Constellations. In early discussions the two major cargo carriers—Seaboard and Western Airlines, and the Flying Tiger Line—asked Canadair for a better way of loading/unloading aircraft than the traditional side doors. They wanted a system for handling 29,500 kg (65,000 lb.) of freight in 45 minutes, allowing aircraft turn-around in an hour. If the U.S. Navy could fold the wings on some of its aircraft, they asked, why couldn't Canadair swing the tail on the CL-44? It had been done before, by H.P. Folland for a "goods carrying aircraft" manufactured by Gloster in England in 1922, but that aircraft had a payload of only 730 kg (1,600 lb.).

Eric Haines did the preliminary design of the swing tail after examining and discarding the possibility of rear

clamshell doors. A full scale mockup of the swing tail showed the design worked, and management gave the go-ahead. Haines's design was remarkable in its simplicity and flexibility. It allowed the rear fuselage to be swung aside, through more than 90 degrees, to allow straight-in loading of pieces of cargo up to 26 m (87 ft.) in length. The tail could be fully opened in 90 seconds and remain open in winds up to 100 km/h (60 mph). Eight locks around the periphery held it closed, and an inflatable seal kept out the elements. An ingenious system of gearboxes designed by Dave Wright allowed the door to be opened and closed without disconnecting and reconnecting the controls to the rudder and elevators. Others involved in the design included Maurice Bate, Emile Beaujolais, Tom Brown, Dave Campbell, Peter Cross, Ken Deegan, Maurice Gally, Hugh Gosnell, Angelo Hébert, Lloyd Hess, Tony Karanek, Joe Knap, Phil Laroux, Danny Lebeuf, Tony Leath, Fred Newell, Ross Richardson, Joe Smith and Ron Smith. The swing tail CL-44 was now designated the CL-44D4.

A major problem arose when the FAA refused to certify the Britannia windshield for its vision standards. Help came from General Dynamics which provided details of the windshield design for the Convair 880/990. It was sufficiently compatible with the CL-44 flight deck structure that Alec Thompson's design group readily adapted it.

Another certification requirement called for fatigue testing the fuselage. This stemmed from two de Havilland Comet disasters, crashes traced to fatigue failure of the fuselage. International certifying agencies ordered that all future pressurized airliners undergo fatigue testing before certification. The D4 was the first Canadian aircraft to undergo such testing. This required aircraft cabin pressure to be cycled up and down thousands of times, eventually reaching about one-and-one-half times the highest pres-

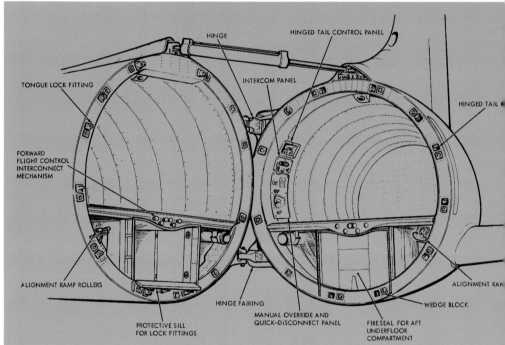

A bare bones look at the static test rig for the swing section of the CL-44 rigged with a host of strain gauges. A diagram from the CL-44D technical manual identifies the main elements in this complex system. (CL 20837)

sure the cabin would ever experience during its lifetime. To lessen the possibility of damage and injury should the fuselage fracture during the tests, and also to speed the cycling rate, Canadair did the tests under water.

An L-shaped tank, with the main part 43 m (141 ft.) by 7 m (23 ft.) by 5.0 m (16 ft.) deep, was built in Plant 4. The test fuselage was placed in the tank, and the tank and fuselage were filled with water. As the tests proceeded, a team of test engineers watched constantly for leaks. The short arm of the "L" provided room for the tail to be opened during the fatigue tests of the swing tail mechanism. The tests ended in March 1961 after completion of the equivalent of 80,000 flight hours and the granting of a service life of 40,000 hours.

Seaboard and Flying Tigers

In May 1959, Seaboard and Western (later Seaboard World) and Flying Tiger Line ordered five and 10 D4s respectively, on the basis of Canadair's design and cost predictions. They took options on a further five aircraft each. Seaboard eventually bought seven and Flying Tiger, 12.

Before the sale to Seaboard was finalized, Fred Kearns,

period, Seaboard was in such dire straits that it was using employees' income tax deductions to pay for fuel.

The initial D4 sales were financed by selling instruments known as "Equipment Trust Certificates," devices originally developed for the purchase of railway rolling stock which used the acquired hardware as surety for the investment. This was probably the first time the device was applied to the sale of commercial aircraft.

The first D4, CF-MKP-X, flew on November 16, 1960, with the crew of Longhurst, McLean, Harris and MacFarlane. Peter Redpath and later Bob Conley headed the CL-44D sales drive. Salesmen Les Kottmeier, Cliff MacKinnon, Eric McConachie, Ken McDonald and Earl O'Mara were out beating the bushes for customers. They faced competition, particularly in dealings with Flying

The famous water tank used for CL-44 pressurization tests. Various potential CL-44D loaders were evaluated by Canadair. In the right photo, an Allen Cargolift is mated to a CL-44 mock-up. (CL 27275, 26111)

Canadair's vice-president and comptroller, sent his assistant, Peter Aird, to examine Seaboard's finances. Aird found the company in such poor shape that he advised against the sale. Despite this, the sale went through. Canadair even advanced Seaboard several million dollars to keep it going. Within three months Seaboard asked General Dynamics for a further advance. At GD's insistence, Kearns sent Aird to sit on Seaboard's board of directors to guard Canadair's interests. Aird was on the board for three months until kicked off by the U.S. Civil Aeronautics Board whose rules forbade manufacturers to be represented on the boards of operators. During one

Tiger. Convair was marketing its Convair 600 jet freighter (predecessor to the Convair 990 airliner). Many carriers still had Douglas DC-7s and Lockheed L-1049s at high residual value on their books; they could not afford to scrap them to buy D4s. Politics prevented the sale of five aircraft to Pakistan and two to Saudi Arabia when Canada refused to issue an export permit for Pakistan (for fear of offending India), and the Saudis lost interest when Pakistan withdrew.

Japan Cargo Airlines ordered three CL-44s, only to cancel when the purchase was opposed by Japan Air Lines. BOAC appeared certain to buy until a sudden

Squeezing a CF-104 into a
Swingtail, then a PR photo of
new General Motors cars rolling
off a Slick "44" at Cartierville in
September 1962. (CL 27448,
32981)

Frank Pace, Jr. (chairman of
General Dynamics), Geoff
Notman and Earl D. Johnson
(president of GD) at the rollout
of the Swingtail in 1960. (CL
22050)

(Right) Although this CL-44
briefly wore German markings,
Lufthansa did not buy the type.
(CL 30263)

The heyday of the CL-44. Three Flying Tiger "44s" and an RCAF Yukon are in this summer 1961 photo. Then, a striking air-to-air of a Seaboard CL-44. (CL 57577, 26729)

change of management." (BOAC and Lufthansa later leased D4s from Seaboard.) Canada's Wardair would have bought CL-44s had Ottawa offered better terms. Instead it was encouraging TCA (which wanted the Douglas DC-8F) to buy them.

The MATS Deal

Canadair experienced its own mini-Avro Arrow debacle in 1960 when Prime Minister John Diefenbaker's conservative government scuttled a planned purchase of D4s by the USAF Military Air Transport Service (MATS). The United States wanted Canada to bolster its northern fighter defences and proposed a deal whereby MATS would take up to 232 D4s in exchange for 100 F-101 Voodoo fighters plus possible participation in the maintenance of the Pinetree early warning radar line. The quantity of D4s had dwindled to 37 D4s when Ontario conservatives close to the prime minister objected on the grounds that it would be politically unacceptable for the government to award a major aircraft con-

Frank Francis worked on a variety of Canadair designs and was senior project engineer on the CL-44. (CL 49791)

tract to Quebec so soon after having cancelled the Ontario-built Avro Arrow.

Curt Fincham (assistant to president Geoff Notman), George Keefer (director of contract administration) and Air Vice Marshal W.A. Curtis (chairman of Avro) went to Toronto to brief members of the Ontario Conservative caucus as to the true amount of work the program would bring to the various provinces. Faced with the fact that Ontario was to get a large share, the politicians appealed to Diefenbaker to change his mind, but it was too late. The USAF had already decided to buy Boeing C-135s.

A USAF purchase could have had far-reaching effects at Canadair. Retired salesman Ken McDonald said Canadair almost had a sale to Pan American, and other carriers would have followed had the USAF deal gone through. As it was, Canadair was forced to cancel plans to build a CL-44 assembly plant on company-owned land at Dorval airport.

Dave Hanchet was D4 project engineer at the time of the delivery of the first Flying Tiger D4 to Newark, New Jersey: "The planned welcoming celebration went awry when the pilot parked the aircraft at the passenger terminal instead of at the freight terminal where the welcoming committee was waiting. Unable to restart the engines without ground power, or raise anybody by radio, they finally lowered the engineer to the ground on a rope. He eventually located a starter and the aircraft made its way back to the freight terminal. By then, the edge had gone from the celebration."

Slick Airways

Slick Airways, the third D4 operator, took delivery of the first of four D4s in January 1962, bringing sales to 23 aircraft. Three months later, a Slick D4 damaged its horizontal stabilizer when it hit a beacon on landing at Wake Island in the Pacific. An MRP led by Ken Dawson, and consisting of Yves Chanfournaus, Vince Fagan, Walter Jacyk and Robert Paton, left Montreal two days later and arrived at Wake on April 19. Meanwhile a new 16.5-metre (54-ft.) stabilizer left Montreal on April 20 on board a Seaboard D4 for San Francisco where it was transferred to Slick. The stabilizer arrived at Wake on April 22, was in-

Early operators of the CL-44D keenly promoted their new capability.

stalled on the 23rd, inspected on the 24th, and the airplane flew back to San Francisco on the 25th.

Service representative H.D. (Cherry) Cherrington related another incident involving Slick's second aircraft in June 1968. It made a heavy landing at Saigon, Vietnam causing major damage to the rear spar and main landing gear attachment. Conditions at Saigon were too dangerous to permit a permanent repair. A temporary fix was made and the aircraft was ferried, wheels down, to Hong Kong where a team of Cherrington, Jack Anstead, Louis Bedard, George Cayford and Ed McCallum, working with the Hong Kong Aircraft Engineering Co. Ltd., had the aircraft repaired by July 30.

Tech rep Ken Hale was stationed in San Francisco when he heard that a Slick D4 had taken off from Guam Island in the Pacific en route to Hawaii with its nose landing gear hanging loose. He hopped a flight to Hawaii, arriving there just in time to radio a Slick mechanic, who happened to be aboard the D4, exactly where to cut through the cabin floor and how to close the gear downlock. The aircraft landed safely. Hale and the mechanic removed the unserviceable actuator, installed a new one, made temporary repairs to the floor and sent the aircraft on its way, all in six hours.

N127SW loads the 54-foot (16.5-m) CL-44 stabilizer for Slick at Dorval in April 1962. Another job for the CL-44 about this time was airlifting a 90,000-pound (40,860-kg) IBM 7030 computer from New York to London for the UK Atomic Energy Authority. At the time, the "7030" was the world's most powerful computer. Two CL-44s made the delivery and the operation saved $50,000 in packing costs had the computer gone by sea. (CL 31349)

The pilots who took delivery of the last Slick CL-44D (N605SA) in October 1962. Note the straightforward panel and controls. N605SA was the aircraft thought to have been shot down over Soviet territory in 1981. (CL 33123)

The Conroy "Guppy" in flight off the California coast. (CL 29798)

An ex-Slick aircraft, s/n 34, was reported to have crashed near Yerevan, USSR, on July 18, 1981. The aircraft, operated by Transporte Aereo Rioplatense of Argentina, was reportedly carrying arms from Israel to Iran during the Iran/Iraq war, when it strayed across the border into the USSR. It either collided with, or was shot down by, an intercepting Soviet fighter.

An ex-Flying Tiger D4 was bought by Jack Conroy Aviation of California and converted into a special "Guppy" version for carrying Rolls-Royce RB-211 engines to Lockheed for the L-1011. The upper fuselage was removed and replaced by an enlarged section which raised cabin height by about 1.5 m (5 ft.) Designated the CL-44-0, the Guppy first flew on November 26, 1969. In late 1984, it carried 21 rare reticulated giraffes from East

Africa to Florida for breeding after the ceiling of the Boeing 747 that had been reserved for them turned out to be too low. On June 10 and 11, 1994, as the sole CL-44 still in service, the Guppy visited Canadair for a 50th Anniversary open house.

CL-44J

The CL-44J was a D4 stretched 4.62 m (15 ft. 2 in.), making it the largest aircraft ever produced in Canada. Four D4s were converted to CL-44Js for Loftleidir Icelandic Airlines. They were used on its passenger route between New York, Iceland and Luxembourg. The United States had awarded Loftleidir much-coveted New York landing rights in return for the use of a military base in Iceland, and the airline had chosen to exploit that advantage. It was not a member of the International Air Transport Association (IATA), so was not bound by IATA's fare struc-

President Geoff Notman with Governor General and Mrs. Georges Vanier, who were touring Canadair and looking at the swingtail in April 1962. Pilots Ian MacTavish and Don Freeborn complete the group. In the second photo, Notman presents 25-year pins in June 1961 to some of Canadair's veterans. From the left are W.O. "Bill" Montgomery (superintendent CL-44), Greg Kilcullen (production control), Ralph Stopps (research and development), Freddy Nuttall (production CL-44) and J.W. "Jim" Saunders (planning and tool design). (CL 31057, 26832)

TF-LLG being stretched at Canadair in early 1966. It had first gone to Loftleidir in October 1964 as a CL-44D. It was sold to Cargolux in August 1970 and crashed at Dacca that December. Next, the first-takeoff photo of CF-SEE-X the prototype "J". It soon became TF-LLI of Loftleidir then went on to fly with other carriers from Colombia to Senegal to Uraguay and the U.S.A. Its days ended in a crash at Barranquilla, Colombia on July 6, 1988. (CL)

ture. Loftleidir offered low fares to Europe to anyone willing to accept a tight seat spacing, no meal service and a slightly longer flight.

Conversion of the "Js" involved inserting two fuselage plugs, one 3.07 m (10 ft. 1 in.) forward, the other 1.55 m (5 ft. 1 in.) aft of the wing. Eddie Arnold and Ross Richardson designed the front plug, Maurice Bate and Ken Reid, the rear, under the direction of Eric Haines. Joe Knap was the designated airworthiness representative.

Loftleidir's first D4 went into service on June 1, 1964. The first CL-44J, CF-SEE-X, flew on November 8, 1965, piloted by Longhurst and crew, and was delivered to

CF-SEE-X and TF-LLF at Cartier-ville. Then a Loftleidir group taking an in-service class at Cana-dair, and the handover of the first CL-44J by Canadair's Merle C. Curtis (ex-Convair, right) to Loftleidir's Halldor "Tiny" Gudmundsson. (CL)

Loftleidir on March 13, 1966. The swing tail features had been largely eliminated during conversion. The hydraulics were removed, the latching points permanently locked and the flight control systems restored to a continuous run across what had been the fuselage break line. These changes, together with the passenger interior, increased empty weight by just over 11,300 kg (25,000 lb.) but still allowed up to 188 passengers (compared with 160 in the D4). Until the stretched DC-8 entered service, Loftleidir had the largest western commercial aircraft. Thousands of American students could thank Loftleidir for giving them an opportunity to visit Europe "on the cheap."

Four D4s and the sole 44-0 still existed in early 1994. Only the Guppy was still flying. They had passed through many hands since Seaboard, Flying Tigers and Slick replaced them with jets. Although those three airlines disappeared, their survival during those times of keen competition was due largely to the profits brought in by the CL-44. Kevin Crichton was a flight manager for the global airfreight company Airfoil. He had worked earlier for rival company Heavy Lift which operated Short Belfast freighters and the CL-44-O. Crichton often crewed on the "O" and recalled in 1994 that it had been Heavy Lift's most profitable aircraft during that era.

N602SA went to Slick in January 1962 thence to a long list of freight carriers, the last being Tradewinds. It was damaged beyond repair while landing at Nairobi's Wilson Airport in July 1978. (CL)

The prototype Swingtail on rollout day. (CL C2148)

N228SW of Seaboard World Airlines wore BOAC markings from Sepember 1963 to October 1965. When BOAC introduced dedicated 707 freighters it returned the Swingtail to Seaboard. In November 1965 it was leased to Flying Tiger for military resupply contracts to Vietnam. It crashed at Da Nang in 1966. (CL C2390)

The replacement tailplane is transferred from Seaboard's N127SW to Slick's N603SA at San Francisco for the trip on to Wake Island.

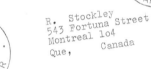

In June 1994 the CL-44-O Guppy EI-BND visited Plant 3 at Dorval as part of Canadair's 50th anniversary celebrations. It came in from Smyrna, Tennessee, where it was based with Buffalo Airways. The Guppy was originally N447T of Flying Tiger. Canadair family members lined up to tour the mighty Guppy. One little keener tries out the first officer's seat. (CL 71223-19, 71472-13)

(Above) Iceland featured the CL-44 and Boeing 727 on these 1969 stamps celebrating 50 years of aviation in the island nation. (Pat Campbell Col.)

A Flying Tiger Line CL-44D on a pre-delivery flight. (CL)

Plant security has always been important at Canadair. In this photo a guard mans his post at the main P1 gate. (CL F3275)

LIFE AROUND THE COMPANY

Always a good time of day—lunch is served in the Canadair cafeteria in March 1956. (CL F3511

The Canadair fire department lines up its trucks in this May 1954 scene; then (right) practices on a clapped out Cornell training plane. (CL M1925, '24)

(Left) Security and fire personnel take part in a Red Cross life-saving course in March 1956. (CL F3445)

Staff from the photographic department discuss the day's work in this November 1954 scene; Art Ford is at the top. Then, Vic Davidson of the *Canadair News* at work with a Speed Graphic and flash. (CL F2424, '434)

(Below) The boys in technical publications grind away on a hundred-and-one daily tasks; then the Canadair library—always an important company resource. The print shop, shown in May 1954, was equally important, especially when it came to producing technical manuals. (CL P2-1776, M1743, P1-1065)

With thousands of employees, suppliers and clients Canadair had no end of paper work. In this 1955 scene a clerk plods away at her SorterGraf, a high tech system for its day. (CL PL2661)

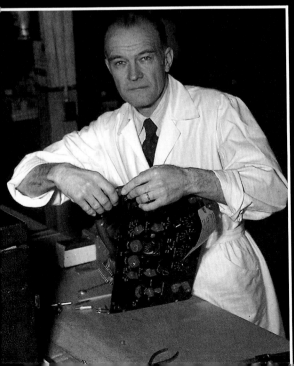

(Above) Canadair's army of draftsmen slog it out over their finely-detailed drawings in a scene from October 1951. Subject matter included projects like the Sabre and CL-21. (CL D15733)

Out in the plant an hourly worker solders wiring (upper left), technician Alex Cones (left) works on a radio unit, a lift operator (above) restacks a tool in a February 1958 scene, and the overhead crane operator transports an engine oil tank for the Argus. (CL 15767, D9783, F4935, 5488)

Plant 4 looking east about 1950. The long, black-roofed Curtiss-Reid factory (B402) parallels Bois Franc Rd. Later it became the CL-41 skunk works where the first three airframes were made. The building at an angle to B402 was used later to test the curtain wall. The one east of B402 was for storage, but later housed an architectural model of the Lafontaine Tunnel (built under the St. Lawrence River). The hangar with the curved roof later housed the CL-44 water tank. There were machine shops in the annex on its north side. Leveiller's curbside restaurant was on the southwest lot at Laurentian and Bois Franc. Across the street was the Sunset BBQ/Pierre Motel. Old wartime staff houses and a Shell station were opposite the Curtiss-Reid hangars on Laurentian Blvd. Inset is the old Sunset, last used by the Canadair credit union and demolished in 1964. (CL P1190)

Training is always on-going at Canadair. The old Curtiss-Reid building at P4 was for years a focal point of classroom work. These "Canadair College" employees were doing an in-service in soldering. For 1961 some 2,000 students completed about 7,000 courses. (CL 28496)

Winter at Cartierville was always a challenge. Here a stranded employee gets a hand, and snow on the roof of Plant 1 is checked. Such an accumulation called for quick action to prevent structural or water damage. (CL 34644)

CHAPTER FOUR

THE "COSMO"

CL-66 COSMOPOLITAN

Mention of the Cosmopolitan first appeared in a *Canadian Press* report of December 6, 1957. It reported that English Electric had disclosed to a visiting Canadian trade commission that it was trying to interest the RCAF in twin-engined Convairs with Eland turboprops to replace 100 or so Dakotas. The Eland was built by D. Napier & Son Ltd., an English Electric company. Canadair would build the Convairs. The report came as a shock, for Ottawa had recently ordered 10 Vickers Viscounts for the RCAF. In March 1958, despite strong protests from the RCAF and TCA (which had itself recently ordered Viscounts) the government cancelled the RCAF Viscount order and announced one for 10 turbo-Convairs from Canadair. The new type was designated CL-66 and later christened "Cosmopolitan" by the RCAF.

Canadair built three CL-66 variants—the CL-66A or Canadair 540, a 48/64 passenger airliner; the CL-66B, a cargo and passenger version with a 6,850-kg (14,300-lb.) payload for the RCAF; and the CL-66C, the designation given to three aircraft received from Convair when it phased out Convair 440 production and which Canadair intended to re-engine with Elands. In general, the civilian CL-66 was called the "Canadair 540."

Ken Ebel appointed Harry Whiteman as senior CL-66 project engineer, reporting to Tom Harvie. Jim Pope became project engineer and Dave Hanchet, assistant project engineer. Dean Stowell was in charge of manufacturing;

Ray Campbell was factory manager. Bill Diamond, Bob Ramsay and Stan Russell were among those involved in production.

The 3,500 shp Eland NE1.Mark 504A engine was chosen because Napier had already installed it in a Convair 340 and was in the process of getting U.S. certification. Canadair obtained the engine and nacelle installation drawings from PacAero in Burbank, California, and the production jigs and tools from Convair. The first shipment of Convair 440 tooling arrived at Canadair in March 1958, and the first Eland came two months later.

The Convair airframe used for the Cosmopolitan was an example built for the USAF as the C-131F. It had a cargo door on the left side and the fuselage had been strengthened by increasing the number of under-floor beams. These changes reduced the number of floor fittings for seats, increased the structural weight and thereby reduced payload. The changes had not been certified by the FAA because the aircraft was not for commercial use. It was Canadair's and Napier's job, therefore, to get the 540 civil version (without the cargo door, but with the standard 440 fuselage and the Eland engine) certified by the FAA before U.S. airlines could be expected to show interest.

The first CL-66C was flown on February 2, 1959, by Bill Longhurst and Scotty McLean. The FAA certification program which followed was done at PacAero at the same time as Lockheed was getting certification for its first turbo-

156

The original Convair 440 converted to Elands was N440EL seen on a 1959 visit to Cartierville. Allegheny Airlines evaluated it that year, then it went to Venezuela to fly for AVENSA. It was converted to Allison engines in 1965. Some of those who worked on the CL-66 recall a Napier engineer who routinely commuted from England to Convair in San Diego. He would spend a day or two there, push on to Canadair, then fly home and perhaps be back the following week! (CL 66-16545)

prop airliner, the Electra. The day the FAA awarded certification for the CL-66, Bud Scouten and the rest of the Canadair crew were celebrating in a bar. Over the television came the announcement that the FAA had certificated its first turboprop airliner, the Canadair 540. Scouten turned to his neighbor and proudly told him that he was the 540 pilot and that they'd just beaten out the Electra. It turned out that Scouten's neighbor was the Electra pilot!

In the months that followed, 540s CF-LMA and CF-LMN went on extensive sales demonstrations. CF-LMA, with pilots Bud Scouten, Scotty McLean and Doug Morrison, plus Smokey Harris, salesmen Ken McDonald and Eric White, tech rep Ken Hale, and mechanics Louis Gauthier, Stan Newlove and Stan Williams visited every

South American country, while CF-LMN, piloted by Longhurst and Scouten, with salesmen Reg Avey, Ken McDonald, Cliff MacKinnon and B.G. Smith completed a United States tour and later appeared at the Paris Air Show.

The *Financial Post* of July 28, 1958, reported that final details were being settled on a deal to sell $100 million worth of Canadair airliners in South America. A condition was that Canadair must build and operate a plant in Brazil; this would ensure an order for a hundred 540s and other Canadair products such as the CL-44. The *Post* said that the first seven 540s would be finished in Montreal; the next 18 would be manufactured in Montreal but assembled at a Brazilian plant operated by Canadair International. Meanwhile, two CL-66Cs were in service with the Quebec regional airline, Quebecair, while the RCAF was using the third for crew training.

The first production CL-66B, designated CC-109 Cosmopolitan by the RCAF, flew on January 7, 1960, with Scotty McLean and Ian MacTavish, Vern Groves (flight engineer), and George MacFarlane. Deliveries began in May, and all 10 were delivered by March 1961.

Normally a certifying authority allots a new engine a

An Eland is installed on a CL-66. All CL-66s were converted from Elands to Allison 501s. Canadian Pratt & Whitney was Napier's Eland sales and service representative in North America. (CL 66-1141)

A typical CL-66 cockpit layout. (CL 66-16160)

The first Canadair CL-66 nears completion in the same production bay with the Argus. (CL 7195)

relatively low time-between-overhauls (TBO) rating, and increases it as the engine proves itself. With the Eland's unreliability, however, the Department of Transport *reduced* its TBO in light of its unreliability. The Eland's poor showing and the 540's projected high price of $1,250,000 Cdn finally killed the project. At the time, the Canadian dollar was strong; potential U.S. customers discovered that, by the time taxes and duties were added, their price would be $1.4 million US. With Convair 440s and Fokker F-27s selling for $760,000 US, the writing was on the wall for the 540.

In 1966 eight "Cosmos" were re-engined with Allison 501-D36 turboprops. The remaining two were not re-engined—by the time the RCAF ordered the change, PacAero had phased out its re-engining program—so the aircraft were scrapped. One of the eight Allison-engined "Cosmos" was later destroyed by fire; the other seven were retired in June 1994 and offered for sale by Crown Assets. By the mid 1990s many Allison-powered Convairs were still in service, long after the Eland had slipped into oblivion. Included among the survivors was CF-LMA. After stints with Canadair, Quebecair and the RCAF it wandered from one operator to the next in the U.S. and Latin America before returning to Canada in 1985 as C-GKFR.

CL-66 No. 11159 fresh from the final line makes a test flight over the Quebec countryside in 1961. The RCAF had 10 CL-66s which it designated the CC-109 Cosmospolitan. Re-engined with Allisons, this example remained with the Canadian air force till the summer of 1994. (CL C1152)

(Above) A Quebecair CL-66 at Dorval. Beyond it is a Viscount, one of the most successful postwar airliners. Had the RCAF Viscount order been pursued Canadair would have escaped the CL-66 debacle. This CL-66 went to the RCAF as 11161. It later served as a Convair 580 (Allisons) with General Motors and North Central Airlines. (Below) Re-engined with Allisons, Cosmopolitan 109157 of 412 Squadron visits CFB Toronto (Downsview airport) on August 31, 1972. (CL C1128, Larry Milberry)

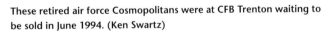

CL-66 production in Plant 2 in July 1959 where the Desjardin brothers were the foremen in charge. This was one of the projects Canadair wished it had never started. As one of the old timers expressed it in 1994, "The 66 was a lemon from day one." (CL 17481)

RCAF "Cosmo" No. 11155 at Dorval in the freighter configuration. It's framed by a Yukon but what is the Yukon doing with its nose in the air? Someone had forgotten to put the tail pole in place. As the Yukon was loaded the tail suddenly dropped. (CL 35691)

These retired air force Cosmopolitans were at CFB Trenton waiting to be sold in June 1994. (Ken Swartz)

Some of Canadair's family during the first Christmas party, December 1944. Then, Santa (Glen Campbell) doing his rounds. In 1961, the Christmas party was attended by 14,000 employees/family. (CL 3416C, 'E)

Throughout its history, Canadair management has provided solid support for employee extra-curricular activities, whether that involved providing facilities for a recreational club, financing speakers for self-improvement groups or administering a community-related activity. Management support alone, however, cannot guarantee a successful employee activity—the employees themselves must provide the major effort. Fortunately, Canadair has always had in its ranks people willing to contribute the necessary time and effort to organize a wide range of activities.

HAVING FUN AND KEEPING FIT

Recreational Activities

For several years after the founding of Canadair, employee recreational activities were carried out on an ad-hoc basis with each club operating as a separate entity. Then, on September 28,1948, the Canadair Employees Recreational Association (CERA) was formed by a group of employees to coordinate the various activities. The founders included Bill Shuttleworth, temporary chairman; Bill

Canadair families and friends crammed the Forum in April 1961 for the CERA Winter Festival. Here a performer circles the ice high above a Triumph TR-3. (CL 25934)

Baker, Adrien Bardonnex, Doug Bruce, Jean-Paul Douville, Thérèse Edisbury, Fred Fairbrother, Guy Lapointe, Joe Menard and Frank Valois.

Management contributed $15,000 initial funding and arranged to deduct five cents a week from each employee's wages. Over half the labor force joined within the first two weeks and in no time

20 clubs, ranging from darts to flying, were in operation. At the first election in March 1949, Conrad Petelle was elected president, Stan McGarr, vice-president, and Frank Valois, secretary/treasurer. Other officers included Ben Locke, Dick Faucher, Jean-Paul Roy, Kay Robinson and John Agnew. Garth Thompson was appointed recreational director, and Gerry LaGrave, his assistant. Management was represented by Bill Shuttleworth as chairman.

As the number of CERA clubs grew, the demand for funds increased, and the association decided to increase the weekly contribution to 10 cents. However, whereas the five-cent contribution had been an automatic pay deduction,

Three of CERA's "originals": Ben Locke (top left), Dick Faucher (left) and Bill Shuttleworth. (CL S1071, S1211, 26227)

161

Hockey was just one of the many activities during the Winter Festival, but in this case the team comprised employees from Commonwealth countries who had never been on skates! (CL F3430)

Skiing was one of many CERA activities. This group from 1957 was on a Saturday outing in the Laurentians. (Below) When it came to winter sports, some preferred curling. (CL 5535, 30508)

The Canadair and Avro teams of the mid-1950s. Far left is defence minister Brooke Claxton. Behind him is Canadair coach George Tait. Geoff Notman is far right. Moe White of preflight is standing centre with the Sabre model. Then, Canadair plays Avro in one of the always-exciting games between two fierce rivals. (CL D5926, M1610)

employees were now asked to sign a card authorizing the 10-cent deduction. Many rejected this and CERA membership dropped by half overnight.

In an effort to raise additional funds and provide an added service, CERA opened a store in Plant 1. Managed by Conrad Deschênes, with assistance from accountant Maurice "Cab" Calloway, it resembled a miniature department store, offering a wide selection of goods ranging from toothpaste to major appliances. It even extended credit. Deschênes' motto was: "If I don't have it, I'll get it." He later opened a branch store in Plant 2 but it closed in the early 1960s. The Plant 1 store closed shortly after Les Galeries St-Laurent opened opposite the plant in the mid-1970s.

The combined revenue from employee contributions and store profits swelled CERA's coffers so rapidly that, in 1953, with over $100,000 in the bank, its executive considered building a recreation centre beside Plant 1. This was opposed by the union executive which wanted all CERA funds spent on activities

Part of entertainment troupe "in flight" at one of the stops along the way during the January 1962 Mid Canada Line tour to Knob Lake, Great Whale and Winisk. This annual Canadair-sponsored affair brought some fun to remote settlements where the RCAF operated radar stations. All the performers were company employees. In the second photo, the audience, made up largely of Inuit, is clearly turned on. Jack Graham of CERA managed this tour. (CL 30026, 29981)

and not on investments which would benefit only a few.

Stan McGarr was elected CERA president in 1954 and held that post until 1962. Later presidents included Eddie Moore and Rollie St. Amour. Gerry LaGrave was recreational director from March 1954 until his retirement in 1971. LaGrave played a key role in the organization of many employee activities. An all-round athlete, he was a former Canadian cycling champion, army boxing and rifle champion, Ottawa Rough Riders footballer, and a hockey referee-in-chief. In 1994, at age 91 the oldest living member of the original Canadian Air Force, he was treated to a one-hour flight in a supersonic CF-18. Herbie Brehn took over as recreational director when LaGrave retired. Tom Harvie followed Shuttleworth as chairman. He, in turn, was followed by Ray Campbell, Walter Meacher and Dick Faucher. Barbara Coleman was CERA secretary for many years.

Other CERA Activities

Besides its numerous clubs, CERA organized regular activities involving all employees. During the 1950s and early 1960s, the CERA Festival Committee, led by George Tait and John Agnew, organized annual Winter Festivals at the Montreal Forum. These featured skating exhibitions by such World and Canadian champions as Maria and Otto Jelinek, Barbara Wagner and Robert Paul, Barbara Ann Scott, Carol Jane Pachl and Don Jackson, as well as a hockey game between the Canadair Aces and teams from

Avro or the RCAF. The highlight of the show, however, was the British Commonwealth hockey game which starred employees, mainly British engineers cajoled by Eddie Cross, who, in most cases, had never before been on skates. These games were, to say the least, hilarious.

The original Canadair Aces included former National Hockey League players, including "Moe" White (Montreal Canadiens 1945/46); Bud Kerland and

Basketball and soccer were always popular team sports with CV and Canadair. (CL)

The height of summer fun has always been the big CERA picnic, this one in 1957. Other staff took an employee charter flight to the UK. This crowd is boarding one of Flying Tiger's new Super Constellations. (CL 4613, 4674)

The CERA auto club had a year-round schedule. Here Roy Nishizaki and Robin Edwardes display the Mont Gabriel Perpetual Trophy, won in the 1961 Canadian Capers Rally. Their car, the grille well-pitted by bugs and stones, is a Peugeot 403. (CL 27219)

Some of Canadair's avid sailors build a "Y Flyer". On the left are Keith Lancaster, Al Stone and Maurice Gallet. (CL M2522)

Canadair employees and friends at the August 1956 Stromberg-Carlson golf tournament. Jim Schaffer (design office), and Bill MacKenzie (hydraulics design) are on the left with two Stromberg-Carlson men from Rochester, NY. (CL F3794)

Flying was big with CERA. The gliding club was operating at this time (1953) at the old wartime training base at St. Eugene, Ontario. The flying club outing dates to July 1957, when the club was at Cartierville. (CL M1285, F4702)

CERA president Stan McGarr awards the team cup to the 1961 company bowling champs as Gerry LaGrave looks on. (CL 26698)

"Mo" Mosco (both of the Detroit Red Wings organization), Eddie Emberg and the Courteau brothers, Ray and Paul. They played in the Montreal Mercantile League against teams from Molsons, Hydro-Quebec, CNR and Northern Electric, but it was the games against Malton's Avro team that packed both Montreal's Forum and Toronto's Maple Leaf Gardens. The Aces' career ended ignominiously, however, when, following an incident between some of the Ace's players and spectators at a game against Avro in Toronto on January 30,1953, the coach was barred from the game and several players drew lengthy suspensions.

A special CERA event on May 29, 1954 featured an evening of dancing to the renowned Duke Ellington Band. Over 6,000 employees, spouses, friends and a host of interlopers, danced from 8:00 pm to 2:30 am for only $1.50 each. During the Ellington band's rest periods, dancing continued to the music of Russ Dufort and his band. Dufort spent 30 years in

For those not keen on the more strenuous CERA activities there were always the stamp and ham radio clubs. (CL 52545, F4995)

Montreal's greatest sports hero was Maurice "Rocket" Richard, the Canadiens' top-scoring forward of the 1940s and 1950s. Here The Rocket signs autographs at one of Canadair's family days. The ever-present Gerry LaGrave is on the right. (CL M3075)

Duke Ellington poses with Canadair men Ben Locke, Dick Faucher and Maurice Scarpaleggia. Local band leader Russ Dufort is at the far right. (via Ben Locke)

The Duke at the keyboard as his boys belt it out. In 1995 Ben Locke's yellowing notes showed that CERA had picked Ellington from a list that included such other greats as Ray Anthony, Les Brown, Billy Butterfield, Xavier Cugat, Harry James, Guy Lombardo and Teddy Wilson. CERA's budget for the night included $2,750 for the band, $500 —Dufort, $2,300—food, $720—waiters, $200—tickets, $500—door prizes. The bottom line on expenses was $8,216; the expected gate was $9,000. (via Ben Locke)

accounting at Canadair. In addition to running his own band, he played drums with the John Holmes Orchestra which featured a pianist who would later become world famous—Oscar Peterson. Peterson's first recordings with RCA Victor featured Dufort on drums.

CERA also had a variety show, led by John Agnew, Jack Graham and Fred Steppings, with performers Linda and Vladek Cierniak, Louise and Madeline Derouin, the Huard sisters, Claude Plante, Les Proulx, Muriel Steppings and Roman Szydlowski. They travelled throughout the province, to the Far North and to the Maritimes, giving concerts at isolated RCAF stations, hospitals, and other institutions. They also appeared at many Canadair annual kiddie's Christmas parties.

CERA also combined with the company to organize and host annual family days, picnics and Christmas parties. Always popular, the family days generally attracted large numbers of visitors to the plant. The first official family day, held on May 16, 1954, attracted 62,000 visitors—32,000 more than expected.

The organization of these events entailed hours of work by representatives from practically every department. No one deserved more credit than Gaëtan Brais, the security guard who played Santa Claus at every Christmas party since 1977. He went on a special diet for several days before the party to avoid having to leave his seat during the eight hours he spent listening to the kiddies' wishes.

CERA activities decreased during the early and mid-1970s as the company population slipped to below 1,600 and, in the late 1970s, the company assumed responsibility for recreational activities by creating a Department of Physical Fitness, Motivation, Recreation and Safety under director Jean-Guy Boisvert. Canadair continued to administer the activities until 1989 when the Motivational Department was renamed the Employees Recreational Activities Department, and administrative responsibilities for the 15 clubs in operation were turned over to the clubs themselves.

Employees Charity Fund
Another activity with a long history is the Canadair Employees Charity Fund. Since Canadair formed, employees have donated hundreds of thousands of dollars annually to an ever-growing list of humanitarian organizations in the Montreal area. Prominent among the fund's organizers were J.C.Cochrane, the first chairman; Jim Tooley; Robert Lavoie; Garth Thompson; Guy Lapointe, who was chairman for seven years; and Dick Faucher, who, in six years as chairman saw the total amount of employees' contributions double. More recently, Pierre Louergli has helped contributions grow to over $200,000 in one year. Other key fundraisers over the years were: Jean Léo Côté, Gaétan Daneau, Lucien Gignac, Dave Gormley, Tony Guyon, Wilf Héroux, Gerry LaGrave, René Loiselle, Yves Perron and Liette Proulx. Tony Guyon was company representative to Centraide for four consecutive years. A cancer survivor, in November 1988 she was awarded the Canadian Cancer Society trophy of the year for her efforts to raise money to fight cancer.

Jock Cochrane, first chairman of the Employees' Charity Fund. (CL F3049)

CHAPTER FIVE

THE TUTOR

CL-41 TRAINER

Two views of the prototype CL-41 in different paint schemes. Ian MacTavish, who had also been on the design team as an advisor, made the first CL-41 flight on January 13, 1960. When it was first proposed by Canadair, the RCAF was not interested in a new trainer.

Canadair persevered, preparing models of various layouts. The RCAF finally gave tentative approval and picked the side-by-side version (mainly since the USAF had recently chosen the side-by-side Cessna T-37 for its jet trainer). (CL)

So far, Canadair's activities had focused on adapting and producing other companies' products. However, in 1956 the company began its most ambitious project—the design and construction, from concept to finished product, of its first aircraft, and Canada's first indigenous jet trainer.

Several years earlier, Canadair design engineers Karl Irbitis and Bob Lindley had done some preliminary studies anticipating the RCAF eventually would need a jet trainer. In the early 1950s, Ken Ebel assigned Al Lilly and Dick Richmond to get the RCAF interested. After discussions with the RCAF, Richmond drew up a preliminary specification and he, Gord Rosenthal and Bob Ross prepared some concepts with tandem and side-by-side seating. At first, these were for the Armstrong Siddeley Viper engine, but later for the Rolls-Royce RB-108. The project was then put on the back burner because of other priorities.

In 1956, Canadair decided to reactivate the jet trainer project and to produce a prototype. One challenge was to design an aircraft with the desired spin characteristics. Because it is vital that a pilot learn why an aircraft spins and how to recover from an unplanned spin, a training airplane must be able to get into a spin easily, always spin predictably, and be able to recover easily. On their own time, two aerodynamicists and amateur model makers, Keith Matheson and Jim McManus, built accurate scale models for spin tunnel testing. The tests showed that fore and aft movement of the vertical fin was critical to good spin entry and recovery. If the fin was too far forward, the model wouldn't enter the spin: too far back and it would not recover. When they got the correct position, they moved the tailplane up the fin until they got the best spin mode. Then they cut off the fin above the tailplane and this gave the aircraft its distinctive "T" tail.

On September 7, 1956, Ottawa accepted a Canadair proposal to build and test two prototypes for the RCAF, the cost to be borne 40 per cent by Canadair and 60 per cent by Ottawa. Canadair would pay the government two per cent of the net price of all sales until that amount equalled the share it had paid. If Ottawa bought the aircraft for the RCAF, the government would reimburse Canadair its contribution.

The preliminary design, prepared largely by Karl Irbitis, Bob Ross and Bob Werrett, was for a side-by-side cockpit and a Fairchild J83 engine, a new lightweight powerplant being developed in the United States for a drone program. The *Canadair News* of February 1958 reported that two J83s were in the plant, but nobody involved in the program can remember seeing them. The trainer never flew with the J83 which was cancelled along with its drone. Instead Canadair installed the Canadian Pratt & Whitney JT12 with a rated thrust of 10.68 kN (2,400 lb.).

Skunk Works

Designated the CL-41, the new program brought two innovations. One was the introduction of the "skunk works" method of protoype construction. This was introduced in 1943 by Clarence L. (Kelly) Johnson of Lock-

CL-41 beginnings. Aerodynamicists Jim McManus (left) and Keith Matheson discuss their hand-made spin test models with project engineer Fred Phillips. The models were used in a vertical wind tunnel to evaluate empennage arrangements. (CL 5536)

Overall CL-41 program manager E.H. Higgins explains the cockpit mock-up to Prince Bernhard of the Netherlands (closest). Watching are project test pilot Ian MacTavish, project manufacturing manager Ralph Stopps, and project engineering manager Fred Phillips. A graduate of the University of Michigan, Higgins was in the RCAF during the war. He joined Fairchild in 1944 and helped design the Husky bushplane. (CL 48761)

Side-by-side wooden mock-ups at Canadair—the CL-41 and the CL-44 in B113. This was in October 1957, some months before the company decided to go ahead with the CL-41. The first two CL-41s are seen below being assembled by hand in Canadair's skunk works. (CL)

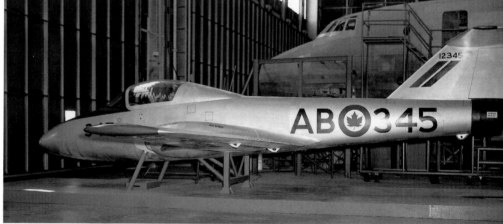

Hank Volker (sales and service) and Karl Irbitis (preliminary design), who were involved in the CL-41. Irbitis had been in aircraft design in Latvia in the 1930s. (CL 5123)

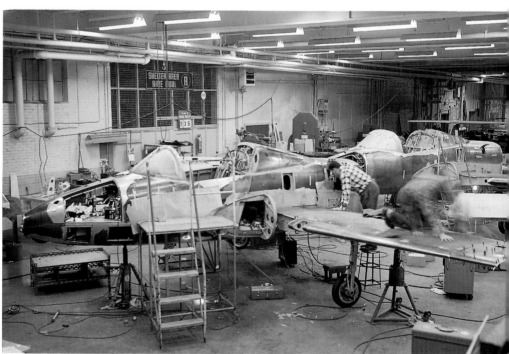

The CL-41 "fatigue test article" moves from the skunk works over to P1 in July 1958. Gerry Barabé is directing from the flatbed. Next, the fully instrumented fatigue article with simulated loads being applied. The CL-41 was Canadair's first project to go from design to flight test. Fred Phillips ran the skunk works at this time. (CL 41-1288)

(Above) The prototype CL-41 with its JT12 engine installed. The second photo shows the ingenious rotatable jig used in production. (CL 41-19111, 34934)

Departments 110-112 in B104. Here parts from the hydro press–heat treat–ice box processes were checked and hand-straightened before they hardened totally. The nearest desk was quality control. (CL 36610)

Forward and centre fuselages on the line, then details of the CL-41 cockpit and a J85 engine awaiting installation. (CL 40806, 46761, 38930)

The neatly proportioned CL-41 prototype whistles across one of Montreal's suburbs in January 1960. This aircraft now sits on a pedestal at the Southport Aerospace Centre at Portage la Prairie, Manitoba. (CL 19231, 31606)

heed when he was given 180 days to design, build and fly the prototype XP-80. Johnson's solution was to form a team of selected personnel from engineering, manufacturing, tooling and procurement and co-locate them separate from the main plant. In this way, he short-cut the system and produced an XP-80 prototype in 143 days. The name "Skunk Works" originated from the mythical booze factory featured in the popular *Lil' Abner* comic strip. The skunk became the symbol of Lockheed Advanced Development Projects which later produced the prototypes of such advanced aircraft as the SR-71 Mach 3 "spy" plane and the F-117 stealth fighter.

The CL-41 skunk works was in Plant 4 under chief design engineer and program manager Ed Higgins. Ralph Stopps was manufacturing manager and the others involved in the early days included Gerry Barabé, Vic Crosby, Eric Elkerton, Joe Knap, Willi Krause, Ron Lake, Odd Michaelsen and Jorge Sobolewski. Barabé was skunk works shop supervisor, Herbie Gregoire, the inspector, and Ian MacTavish, cockpit designer and pilot. Fred Phillips joined the program as project engineer in late 1957. Together they built the aircraft foot by foot.

A second innovation was an Irbitis idea—making the engine intake ducts from fibreglass honeycomb to avoid the cracking that had occurred in the riveted ducts of the Sabre. The honeycomb also provided stiffness for the support of the fuel tanks which were contained entirely in the fuselage.

CL-41 fuselages were assembled on a rotatable barrel-type jig which facilitated assembly, inspection, cleaning and, much later, the required 2,800-hour inspection. Two additional airframes were assembled and subjected to the usual static and fatigue testing. Ian MacTavish flew the prototype CL-41 on January 13, 1960. The plane had previously been painted in four different schemes. Bob Lording recalled that the changes were the result of negative comments made by influential wives!

Though the CL-41 performed well from the outset, the program had some glitches. The first occurred during an early engine run when a bunch of keys was sucked out of Willi Krause's pocket into the engine, setting testing back a few weeks. The second happened when an engine oil relief valve failed just before a scheduled demonstration to the West German air force. Pratt & Whitney engineer

(Left) A CL-41 fuselage set up for ejection seat trials beside P4. A dummy was ejected and caught in the netting behind. The ramp in the distance was built for CL-70 Rat climbing trials. (Right) In another program, through-the-canopy ejections were conducted. Seat and dummy landed on the air bags behind. (CL 41-17117, 37033)

Mike Saunders, finding the P&W plant gate closed for the weekend, climbed over the fence, ripping his pants in the process, and located a valve which, though not the correct one, was sufficiently close to permit a successful demonstration.

The third incident also occurred before a demonstration to the RCAF. The cockpit canopy blew off while MacTavish and flight test observer Colin Harcourt were airborne. MacTavish brought his "convertible" back to Cartierville successfully. With no replacement canopy available and the demo scheduled for next morning, it seemed the program was in for another setback. Flight safety officer Ian McDonald took Harcourt up in a chartered light plane to search, and they caught the reflection of one of the last rays of sunlight from an object lying in the snow behind St-Vincent-de-Paul penitentiary. It was the canopy! Apart from two slightly bent de-misting tubes, it was undamaged and the demonstration went off without a hitch. On another occasion, following a series of high speed runs, MacTavish lost all but two feet of the elevators but landed without incident.

In February 1960, after the prototype had flown 30 hours, it was evaluated by an RCAF survey team. The Hunting Jet Provost from the United Kingdom, the Fouga Magister from France and the Cessna T-37A from the U.S. had already been evaluated. Although these were operational and in production, the RCAF found them unsuitable for the intended role of "all through" training—it required an aircraft whose performance was

sufficiently wide-ranging that a new pilot could progress from first flight through to "wings" standard and beyond in one aircraft type.

The RCAF liked the CL-41 and in September 1961 ordered 190 CL-41A "Tutors." In May 1962, with engineering underway, the government announced that the Orenda-built General Electric J85-CAN-40 engine would power the Tutor, despite Canadair's preference for the JT12. As usual, the decision was political. Installing the heavier J85 increased aircraft weight, so a portion of the tailpipe was removed. That spoiled the hard-won spin characteristics and called for strakes

Ian MacTavish's errant canopy. A CL-70 was used to recover it from a field close to St-Vincent-de-Paul penitentiary. Tech rep Bob Lording is on the left. (CL 19893)

on each side of the nose. Meanwhile Pratt & Whitney transferred development of the JT12 to the United States where it later powered such types as the Lockheed Jetstar, North American Sabreliner and Sikorsky Skycrane.

More time than usual was spent "productionizing"

Engineer Fred Phillips (left) with pilot Ian MacTavish ready for a rare experience—a flight in the airplane he designed. A native Pennsylvanian, Phillips was a graduate of the Guggenheim School of Aeronautics (New York University). Before joining Canadair in 1955 he learned to fly, did graduate studies at MIT, worked for Martin Aircraft and taught at Johns Hopkins University and in Brazil. In 1980 he retired in New Hampshire. MacTavish was the project pilot on the CL-41. In the war he had been a flying instructor, then flew Mosquito night fighters with 410 Squadron. He studied photography when he got home, then flew for KLM before joining Canadair in 1952. Someone from early CL-41 days recalled, "You'd always think of Ian when it was anything to do with the cockpit, since this was going to be a pilot's airplane." (CL, via F.C. Phillips)

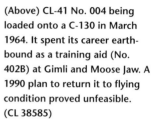

(Above) CL-41 No. 004 being loaded onto a C-130 in March 1964. It spent its career earth-bound as a training aid (No. 402B) at Gimli and Moose Jaw. A 1990 plan to return it to flying condition proved unfeasible. (CL 38585)

(Left) Four early CL-41s near completion. CF-104 components are on the floor to the left. (CL 37914)

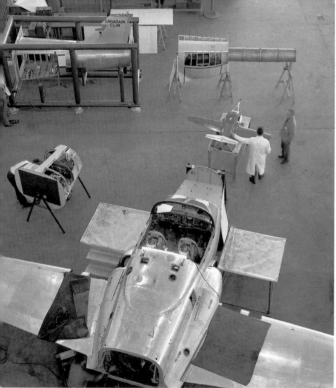

CL-41 No. 2 is modified to CL-41R specs in P4 in March 1962. Mock-ups and a model are being used as aids. Next, the CL-41R is loaded aboard CL-44 CF-PBG in May 1963 for shipment to the Paris Air Show. Then, showing off its slow speed limits, the CL-41R hangs in with a CERA Flying Club Piper PA-12. (CL 30700, 35427, 35290)

A Malaysian Tebuan on a local test flight from Cartierville. (CL)

CL-41 design–taking it from a prototype to the assembly line. Engineering took advantage of a slack period to incorporate RCAF-requested changes and introduce value engineering to achieve some weight and cost savings.

On October 29, 1963, the first production CL-41 was christened by Mrs. C.R. Dunlap, wife of the chief of the air staff. The gremlins were present once more. Breaking a bottle of champagne over the aircraft's nose was still a tradition at that time, and plant engineering had devised a system that would ensure the bottle broke without damaging the nose, and in particular, the nose light. Mrs.

Dunlap duly named the aircraft, wished it well and triggered the bottle release. The release functioned but the bottle did not break. President Geoff Notman and plant engineer Dick Faucher both grabbed the bottle and smashed it against the protective plate. It broke, and so did the nose light.

The first Tutor was delivered on December 16, 1963. The RCAF experimented with its plan for "all through" jet training, and the first all-jet trainees graduated at Christmas 1965. After two courses, however, the plan was judged impractical–up to 60 per cent of students were failing it. In June 1967 primary training reverted to piston-engined aircraft, with students advancing to "wings" on the Tutor. In 1973 the Tutor replaced the T-33 as the Canadian Forces' advanced jet trainer.

The second CL-41 prototype was eventually completed as the CL-41R, an electronic systems trainer for

The RCAF's Red Knight demonstration pilots flew the T-33 (inset) then the CL-41 between 1958 and 1969. (CL)

Canadair board member Chuck Rathgeb and fellow pilot Jim Monteith flew a Tutor in the July 1971 London-Victoria Air Race. They ferried to Abingdon, near Oxford, routing Toronto-Montreal-Schefferville-Fort Chimo-Frobisher-Sondrestrøm-Keflavik-Glasgow. This was the first time a Tutor had flown the Atlantic (other than as cargo). In 1994 Rathgeb recalled what a dicey trip it had been. They reached Frobisher just before the airport was engulfed in fog. Heading to Keflavik, fuel became critical—their tanks ran dry while taxiing in! Going westbound to Victoria, they stopped at Kenora, where Rathgeb planned a quick turn-around, getting his race papers certified while the engine ran. As an official stood by the cockpit, a rag in his back pocket was sucked into the Tutor's J85, causing major damage. So ended its participation, but the air force loaned Rathgeb a replacement Tutor to finish flying the route. Here Rathgeb and Monteith are departing Toronto on June 16, 1971. The oversized fuel tanks were from a Sabre. (Larry Milberry)

(Below) A dramatic view of the CL-41G. (CL)

The CL-41G (upper left) with stores on six sets of hardpoints, then "G" wind tunnel work at the NRC in Ottawa. (CL 42133, 51709)

The CL-41G launches Zuni air-to-ground rockets during trials at NAS Patuxent River, Maryland in 1965. (CL 42860)

future CF-104 pilots. It was fitted with an F-104 nose and "saddlebags" on each side of the fuselage to accommodate electronic systems matching those of the CF-104 strike-reconnaissance aircraft. Ian MacTavish flew the CL-41R for the first time on July 13, 1962, and the aircraft and systems performed well. However, it proved impossible to form a consortium of F-104 operators to justify setting up production so the concept was scrapped.

Tebuan

Canadair borrowed RCAF Tutor 26015 for conversion to a prototype tactical version, the CL-41G. It featured a strengthened landing gear, and underwing and belly hard points for ordnance and fuel tanks. Ian MacTavish took the prototype on its first flight on June 9, 1964. In March 1966, after a protracted effort led by military sales director Hedley Everard, the Royal Malaysian Air Force ordered 20 CL-41G-5s. This was a combination pilot trainer and close-support version of the 41G powered by a more powerful GE-built J85-J4. The Malaysians called it the Tebuan, the Malay equivalent of "Wasp."

By this time, all the CL-41 tooling had spent two years

rusting in the "boneyard." Mel Curtis, vice-president of operations, gave Andy Throner his first program and, with it, the job of recovering the tooling, restoring it, and building the first few G-5s before turning responsibility for production over to Joey Wilkinson.

MacTavish flew the first production Tebuan on April 3, 1967. The first was delivered on May 17, and all 20 had been delivered by the end of November. Jack Forbes spent three-and-a-half years as a field service representative with the Royal Malaysian Air Force. He found that the Malaysians liked the aircraft and operated and maintained them efficiently until they eventually ran out of spares.

Canadair marketing, first under Peter Redpath and later Bob Conley, made vigorous efforts to sell the CL-41 to other countries including Australia and New Zealand; as a carrier-capable version to the U.S. Navy; and, in combination with the CF-5, to several European countries. All were unsuccessful, one reason being the preference of some air forces for tandem seating, another being strong competition from the Italian Macchi MB-326.

The last CL-41A was delivered on September 28, 1966. About 130 Tutors were still with the Canadian Forces in

Although Canadair worked diligently to sell the CL-41 to the U.S. Navy, no order resulted. The North American T-2 Buckeye became the Navy's basic jet trainer. Here graphic designer Ray Legault shows a CL-41 model in US Navy colors. (C4982)

(Above) The Tebuan cockpit included gunsights mounted atop the dash. (CL 53357)

(Left) Tebuans No. 23 and No. 26 are loaded into a CL-44 for the trip to Malaysia. (CL 838-4)

1995. They had logged over one million flight hours and were expected to stay in service past the turn of the century. The Tutor became familiar to millions across North America as the aircraft used by Canada's famed 431 Squadron "Snowbirds" who have thrilled millions of on-lookers at airshows throughout North America since 1970.

(Right) Canadair also promoted the CL-41 as a business jet and as a low-cost trainer for the airlines. (CL)

(Left) Ken McDonald (director of international sales) and Fred Phillips show the Tutor to Air Vice Marshal Morrison of the New Zealand air force. (CL 34923)

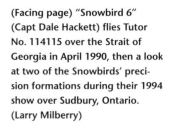

(Facing page) "Snowbird 6" (Capt Dale Hackett) flies Tutor No. 114115 over the Strait of Georgia in April 1990, then a look at two of the Snowbirds' precision formations during their 1994 show over Sudbury, Ontario. (Larry Milberry)

(Left) To make room for the 1992 Saskatchewan Airshow held at CFB Moose Jaw, many of the Tutors flown by No. 2 Canadian Forces Flying Training School were pushed out of the way. By 1995 Moose Jaw was still home to more than 100 Tutors. (Larry Milberry)

Harry Halton looks on as Bob Humphries of core engineering presents Fred Phillips with a gift on his retirement. (CL 15467)

The first CL-41, CF-LTW-X, became a gate guardian at Portage la Prairie, Manitoba, home of the Canadian Aviation Training Centre. The second CL-41 was donated to the Edouard Montpetit technical school at St-Hubert, Quebec, to be used as a maintenance trainer. (Larry Milberry)

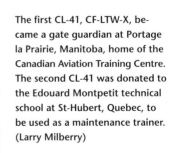

CHAPTER SIX

SUPER-SONIC YEARS

CF-104 AND CF-5

The 1960s saw average annual employment at Canadair drop from 10,500 in 1960 to 5,100 in 1965, climb back to 9,500 in 1968, and fall to about 5,000 in 1970. A number of familiar faces departed the scene including most of the Americans who had done so much to get the company moving in the right direction. Ted Emmert and Roger Lewis had been the first to leave in 1950, Emmert to become president of Ford Canada, and Lewis to become vice-president of Curtiss Wright Corp. Bob Neale took extended leave of absence in 1957 and did not return, but joined GD in 1962. Ev Schaefer died in 1958; Ken Ebel left in September 1960 for Convair and Dean Stowell, who had replaced Neale as vice-president, manufacturing, returned to Boeing in 1961. Charlie Ulsh replaced Stowell, but he left in 1965. Peter Redpath retired in 1964 and his replacement, Bob Conley from GD, also left before the end of the decade.

Two important changes took place at the very top. John J. Hopkins died in March 1957; his position as president and CEO of GD and chairman of Canadair was taken over by Frank Pace Jr. Pace resigned in April 1962. He was replaced by Roger Lewis who, since leaving Curtiss Wright had been U.S. assistant secretary of the Air Force, and executive vice-president of Pan American World Airways.

Canadair president Geoff Notman retired in 1965, and executive vice-president Frederick R. Kearns became president and CEO of Canadair.

Frederick R. Kearns

Fred Kearns was born in 1924 in Quyon, Quebec. He joined the RCAF and at age 20 was flying Spitfires in Europe. He completed 140 operational sorties in nine months. From 1946 to 1949, he attended McGill University's School of Commerce on weekdays and flew with No. 401 "City of Westmount" Auxiliary Squadron on weekends.

Kearns joined Canadair in 1949 as a timekeeper. He transferred into cost accounting, became assistant comptroller in 1954; assistant to the president in June 1957; vice-president and comptroller in September 1957; executive vice-president, finance and sales in 1960; a member of the board in 1961; and president and chief executive officer in 1965, at age 41.

Of medium height and red-haired, Kearns was a

Fred Kearns joined Canadair's accounting department soon after the war. He became the head of the company in 1965. (CL S1034)

Nos. 750, 731 and 763 in a tight formation that shows the stubby wings of the CF-104. This profile gave rise to one of the the CF-104's nicknames, "the missile with a man in it". (CL 39500)

man of strong likes and dislikes. Peter Aird and John MacKenzie were close to him, as senior finance officers throughout much of Kearns' presidency. Aird described him as a tremendous visionary, the person who, though not always right, provided most of the drive at Canadair. According to Aird the CL-215 was one example of a good product that would not have existed but for Kearns's strong stand against GD president Roger Lewis.

Mackenzie recalled that Kearns was shrewd but autocratic: "He was a person who didn't worry about the niceties of organization. He had people he relied on, no matter their title. Probably half the people shown on the organization chart as reporting to him seldom got to see him."

Those who knew Kearns intimately had no doubt that he always had Canadair's best interests in mind. Ever the optimist, he worked tirelessly to bring in work when the

big military contracts dried up, and fought to hold the company together when others were prepared to close it down. The testimonial given him by the Canadair board of directors in 1979 in recognition of his 30 years service was a fitting tribute to his achievements. Yet, less than four years later, his career at Canadair came to an unhappy end.

CF-104 Starfighter

In 1959, NATO proposed to Canada that the RCAF assume a nuclear strike role in Europe. Neither major political party was anxious to become embroiled in the nuclear game; nevertheless, Prime Minister John Diefenbaker's Conservative government accepted the role for the RCAF's Air Division. Now the RCAF needed a new aircraft to replace the Sabre.

With many types to choose from, the list was narrowed

An October 1960 view in P2 shows how the CF-104 fuselage was constructed in matching halves. This was the first of 200 CF-104s for the RCAF. The lower photo shows GE J79-GE-11A engines for CF-104s in the engine bay in P2. (CL 22795, 27241)

(Right) Don Dixon who was in charge of CF-104 production when that program began. (CL 54304)

to the Grumman Super Tiger and the Lockheed F-104 Starfighter. From the RCAF test pilots' point of view, the Super Tiger had the inside track, but on July 2, 1959, the government announced that it had chosen the F-104G to be manufactured by Canadair under licence. The aircraft was initially designated CF-111, but this was quickly changed to CF-104.

The CF-104 represented a major change in the concept of aerodynamics. It had a thin wing with a span of only 6.63 m (21 ft. 9 in.), an average thickness of 7.6 cm (3 in.), and a leading edge with about the same ratio of thickness-to-span as a razor blade. Its long, slim, slightly area-ruled fuselage made it appear more like a missile than an airplane, and it had a bad reputation as well. In the United States, the F-104 had already been dubbed "a second lieutenant's airplane" following a series of accidents which, it was said, made pilots of higher rank reluctant to fly it.

The advent of the CF-104 introduced RCAF pilots to several new features such as supersonic level flight, afterburners, drag chutes, leading and trailing edge flaps, artificial stall warning, boundary layer control and an approach speed of 314 km/h (195 mph). Power was provided by a General Electric J79 turbojet, delivering 44 kN (10,000 lb.) of static thrust and 70.3 kN (15,800 lb.) in full afterburner, giving a top speed over twice the speed of sound.

As the recent cancellation of the Sparrow missile program had left Canadair's missiles and systems division with a considerable surplus of engineering talent, the CF-104 program was first established in Plant 4 under Dick Richmond with Bob Raven as project engineer. As a partial concession to Canadair for the loss of the Sparrow program, the government decided that much of the electronic equipment would be Canadian made—and there

was a lot of it. The wiring was massive. Testing circuits individually would have taken forever, so Canadair and a company with the unusual name of the Drive-in Theatre Movie Company (DITMICO), developed an electronic computer-controlled circuit tester which enabled

Geoff Notman views the cockpit of No. 701 during the CF-104 rollout ceremony at P2. Then, with Bill Kidd at the controls, No. 703 trails its drag chute at Cartierville on August 14, 1961. (CL 25310, 27632)

30,000 wire terminals to be tested for continuity, resistance or breakdown at the flick of a switch. To do the same job manually would have taken 30 days. Another innovation was the aircraft's dielectric nose radome which was produced by a filament winding process developed by Canadair's chief of materials and process, Jack Waller.

Soon after Dick Richmond left Canadair, the CF-104 was moved to Plant 1 under Ed Higgins, chief engineer, aircraft programs. Harry Whiteman was senior project engineer and Harry Louis, project engineer. When Ken Ebel left, Higgins became vice-president and Tom Harvie, chief engineer. Shortly thereafter, Dean Stowell left and Charlie

Ulsh took over manufacturing; Don Dixon became director, aircraft production; Jock West, director, production; and Bob McCall, director, manufacturing engineering. Harry McKeown director, quality control.

Roll-out

When the first CF-104 rolled out in May 1961, it was taken to Lockheed at Palmdale, California, where it flew for the first time on May 26. The first flight at Cartierville was a two-aircraft display on August 14, with Lockheed test pilot Glen (Snake) Reaves putting on a remarkable show of low-speed manoeuvrability by "walking" the first

CF-104 final assembly in late 1963, then a photo of horizontal stabilizers in their jigs. Harry Whiteman and Harry Louis were two of the early Canadair men to visit Lockheed (1961-62) for briefings about F-104 engineering, planning, tooling, etc. (CL 36604, 23866)

F-104G wings for the Luftwaffe are readied for shipping from Canadair in April 1962. (CL 31247)

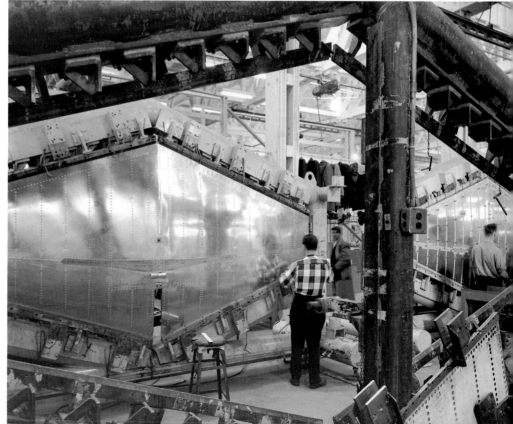

No. 721 ready for a "Rho Delta" trip. It met an untimely end near RCAF Station Baden-Soellingen, West Germany. It was landing there on January 7, 1970 when it crashed killing the pilot, Capt K.M. Wright. Then a night view showing how snuggly a Starfighter fit inside the C-130. (CL 32550, 25353)

During Canada's nuclear weapons era the RCAF's NATO CF-104s were fitted with a nuclear flash shield to protect the pilot from being blinded in an atomic explosion. Here the shield is shown neatly stowed, then deployed across the cockpit. (CL 37862, '861)

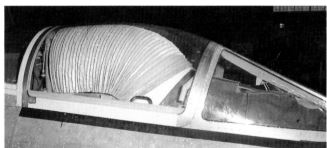

Bruce Fleming's CF-104 after the crash of November 25, 1961, then a happy-looking Fleming with his poodle after he was rescued and brought back to Cartierville. (CL 29209, '194)

Flight Lieutenant Lumsdaine coming down by parachute near Henri Bourassa on September 4, 1962. His CF-104 (No. 803) is seen on the old Bois Franc Road near the home of Dr. Bergeron, a local veterinarian. As a precaution, Canadair's fire department foamed down the wreck, parts of which were used later to restore a CF-104 on display at CFB Cold Lake. (CL 32754, '755, '666)

production aircraft, nose high, across the airfield, while Canadair's Bill Kidd burned a hole in the cloud as he rocketed the second aircraft vertically through the low overcast.

Wary of the CF-104's reputation, the RCAF directed that only pilots with at least one tour on other fighter types be allowed to join the early trainees. The first Canadian pilot to fly the CF-104 said it was easy and pleasant to fly. Others reported that it was easier to fly than the T-33, yet all admitted that it did not provide the same margin for error as the T-bird. The emergency section of the pilot's handbook contained a list of 17 situations considered critical and 21 less critical; the final solution to many of them was one word—eject!

Over three years, Canadair produced 200 CF-104s for the RCAF and 140 F-104Gs, under a mutual aid program, for Denmark, Norway, Spain, Turkey, Greece and Taiwan. Under a separate subcontract agreement, Canadair also supplied Lockheed with over 600 F-104 wing sets, aft fuselages and empennages.

Starting in October 1962, 139 CF-104s were delivered by C-130 Hercules to the RCAF Air Division in Europe in an operation known as "Rho Delta." Tom Kelly was the Canadair tech rep in Germany at the time and he accompanied the first aircraft to Germany. The welcoming party included several local burgomeisters prepared to protest the arrival of the noisy 104s. Their hostility dissolved rapidly, however, during the course of what Kelly describes as an "immensely successful happy hour."

When Canada opted out of the nuclear strike role in the early 1970s, the RCAF reconfigured the CF-104 for a conventional weapons role by installing a 20-mm Gatling gun and adding provisions for air-to-air missiles, rockets and iron bombs. The CF-104's 24 years of service were costly—102 were lost. The explanation is that the CF-104 generally operated at low altitudes where it had to contend with birds, terrain and foul weather. The CF-104 was the mainstay of the Canadian NATO air effort from 1962 until phase-out in 1986.

Canadair test pilot Bruce Fleming was forced to eject from a CF-104 on a test flight in November 1961 when an improperly closed main landing gear door deactivated the stall warning system and he got into a deep stall. As he was coming down by parachute, he saw an airplane fly by just below him and thought, "It didn't take them long to catch up with me." He then realized it was his own airplane in a flat spin. Investigators found that the aircraft had been flying at only 140 km/h (86 mph) when it hit the ground.

Pilots Bud Scouten and Les Benson in a CL-44 spotted

The CF-104 was Canadair's high-profile program for the early 1960s. In this photo CF-104s Nos. 750, 754 and 780 of 417 Squadron are at British Columbia's 1976 Abbotsford International Airshow. No. 750 ended its days as a battle-damage-repair training aid, No. 754 ploughed into a hill during a training mission in February 1979, and No. 780 was one of 44 serviceable and six non-serviceable CF-104s transferred to Turkey in 1986. Down the line are four Canadair-built CF-5s, a C-130 Hercules and an Avro Vulcan bomber. (Larry Milberry)

the flash from Fleming's heliograph mirror in dense bush. He was picked up by helicopter and phoned the plant as soon as he landed. Nora Pennance was manning the phone in public relations when Fleming ejected. She was told not to accept any calls until they had heard from Fleming. When the phone rang, Nora picked it up and said, "I'm sorry I can't accept any calls." The caller persisted and Nora repeated that she had to keep the line free for an emergency. With a blistering stream of invective, her caller informed her that he was the emergency—it was Fleming.

One of the few accidents at Cartierville in nearly five generations of flight operations happened shortly afterwards, when RCAF Flight Lieutenant L.S. (Jack) Lumsdaine clipped a tree on the final approach to runway 10 and ejected at a height of about 20 m (65 ft.). The aircraft

On September 11, 1963, Jack Lumsdaine, commanding officer of the CEPE detachment at Canadair, accepted the final RCAF CF-104 from pre-flight inspector Ray Courteau. On the left is Ray Ledoux, engine run-up mechanic. (CL 36386)

landed on the airfield and broke its back. Lumsdaine landed, unhurt, on the north side of Henri Bourassa Boulevard, his ejection and parachute descent having been recorded on film by an amateur photographer who had stopped to watch the landing.

Sadly, Lumsdaine became the first Canadair pilot to lose his life on the job. During a test flight from Cartierville in March 1966 he ejected unsuccessfully from a CL-41 near St-Lucie in the Laurentians. Lumsdaine was a popular member of the RCAF test pilot group at Canadair. He had served with distinction in the RAF during World War II, and had been a member of Britain's pentathlon team at the 1952 Olympics.

When the Canadian Forces phased out the CF-104 in 1986, 44 airworthy and six non-airworthy examples were transferred to Turkey. Of these, 20 had already been given their periodic inspection which extended service life by 200 hours; the remainder were to be used as spares.

The CF-104 that is on display at the National Aviation Museum in Ottawa is the first prototype, No. 12700. It was manufactured by Canadair but assembled by Lockheed. This aircraft holds the Canadian altitude record of 30,514 m (100,110 ft.). In 1994 the first Canadian-built 104, No. 12701, was sold for scrap at Mountainview, Ontario.

CF-104s await delivery at Cartierville. Nos. 850 and 851 (far right) later served with the Norwegian and Danish air forces respectively. No. 715 (top right) crashed on December 11, 1974— Capt Youngson had to eject when his controls jammed. (CL H77)

Once lowered, this belly panel (below) revealed some of the inner details of the CF-104. In assembling this intricate aircraft Canadair depended on hundreds of skilled workers, but also on a host of valued suppliers. Then, a nice detail of the CF-104's cockpit. (CL 29897, 51218)

(Below) Pilots Frank Gilland and Bruce Fleming at the handover of the 340th and final Canadair-built MAP F-104 on September 20, 1966. Gilland, a long-time RCAF acceptance pilot, was the first Canadian to log 500 hours on the F-104. (CL 50001)

There were bound to be accidents in a big operation such as Canadair. One snowy night in March 1964 a CF-104 was being towed across Cartierville. A company VW operating between P1 and P2 collided with the plane in the dark. As the tip tank impaled his car the driver ducked. He was only slightly injured, but the VW was not so lucky. (CL 38850)

Aircraft No. 746 waits for the snow to melt after a spring storm in 1962. This aircraft was lost with its pilot in December 1966 while on a night exercise from Cold Lake. (CL 30670)

(Left and below) Canadair test pilots enjoy a bit of fun away from the eyes of "head office". No. 845 later went to Turkey, No. 887 to Denmark. (CL H215, 35263)

Starfighter "No. 872" looking good at CFB Cold Lake, Alberta. It's made from parts left over from No. 816, which burned in Germany, and No. 803, which crashed at Cartierville in 1962. (Larry Milberry)

CF-5 Freedom Fighter

Geoff Notman's personal files contain a report of a meeting at the 1964 Farnborough Air Show with the U.K. minister for air, who "spent the best part of an hour pleading with me to get the Canadian government to build 150 McDonnell-Douglas F-4 Phantoms, worth $500 million, for the Royal Navy, rather than buy them from the U.S. The *quid pro quo* would be that Canada would accept the F-4 as a replacement for the CF-104 and that the airplanes would be equipped with Rolls-Royce Spey engines." Notman noted that he was in favor of the British proposal but that "in their wisdom, the Canadian cabinet decided against the F-4 and [minister of defence, Paul] Hellyer announced he will be buying $200 million in Freedom Fighters of some sort or another that will ultimately produce something less than $100 million work for Canadair."

Ken McDonald was manager, military sales at the time. He recalls discussions with British Aerospace and Rolls-Royce regarding a joint licence production program of F-4s for the RCAF, RAF, Royal Navy and U.S. Marine Corps. According to McDonald, the F-4 was the RCAF's choice for a tactical fighter to fulfil both its NATO commitment and the domestic defence requirement. The RAF and the Royal Navy wanted the F-4, and the U.S. Marine Corps was interested if the project went ahead. According to McDonald, "Everyone stood to gain. Canada from the export of Canadair-built airframes to offset the cost of the RCAF's order; the British from the sale of engines and electronics for the RCAF order, and the Americans from the sale of the manufacturing licence and technical support. There were months of negotiations in the U.S.A., the U.K. and Canada among the three gov-ernments, the military and the companies. When everything was finally in place, Ottawa decided that the program was too expensive and the project fell through. Instead of Canada mounting a production line of over 300 technologically advanced aircraft, the 210 aircraft for the RAF and the RN [Royal Navy] were built in the U.S.A., and the RCAF was left with the CF-5."

In 1965, at the direction of Hellyer, the RCAF had considered several aircraft types including the Northrop N-156, Vought A-7 Corsair and Fiat G-91. The RCAF preferred the A-7, and after doing considerable work on possible program offsets, Canadair sent Eddie Altimas, Mike Doyle, Ivan Manley, Bob McCall, Herb Miller and Tony Natlacen to Vought to complete the offset agreement. They arrived to find that only those with a U.S. Navy security clearance were allowed in the plant. McCall had clearance so he worked alone while the others stayed in their hotel. After four days, the clearances came through, but they had hardly sat down with Vought when they were told that the Northrop F-5 had been chosen and they could go home.

The RCAF had evaluated the F-5 when it was the N-156; they found it nice to fly but lacking in range, so placed it low on their list. But the F-5 had one big plus—it was cheap—a fact that influenced the politicians, especially Defence Minister Hellyer. He had been sold on the F-5 by Robert McNamara, the U.S. defense secretary, who was pushing its sale, or in some cases giving it away, to friendly nations around the world. Hellyer seemed determined to make the F-5 the RCAF's new fighter, regardless of the Air Force's needs and heedless of its protests. His office issued a memo indicating that he did not want to hear any further negative comments about the F-5.

The CF-5 line in P2 at the peak of production in 1968. CF-5D two-seaters are in the foreground. Then, a detail of wing final assembly. (CL)

Shortly thereafter, the government contracted with Canadair to build the aircraft under licence with Orenda supplying the General Electric J85 engines.

In October 1965, Canadair sent a team of 12 engineers led by senior project engineer Jack Greeniaus, and including Eric Haines and Stan Paskins, to Northrop to do some design work and incorporate changes the Air Force wanted, including provision for the larger engine and a heated, birdproof windshield.

Frank Francis was Canadair's F-5 program manager in the initial stages of the program, and Andy Throner was in charge of production. Francis remembered problems since some of the engineering and manufacturing planning supplied by Northrop was incomplete: "They had used a short-cut system of recording changes as a way of saving money. We didn't get copies of the changes so went through the same growing pains as if we were making a new airplane. As a result the costs were very high."

Tony Natlacen said he had never seen an aircraft that resembled its drawings so little. Jack Waller found Northrop hard to deal with, possibly because the company had limited experience with licensed production and provided little support. He got into hot water when he misinterpreted the contract agreement and made changes to Northrop's process specifications without first obtaining Northrop's approval. Harry Whiteman and Harry Louis went to Northrop to pick up whatever information they could, but found that most of what they needed was contained in the little black books the foremen carried in their back pockets.

What looked like a simple, lightweight fighter was quite a complex aircraft to build. The fuselage and the bifurcated intake ducts leading to the engines, though of conventional construction, contained many complex curved surfaces which required forming. Like the CF-104, the wing skins were tapered and machined all over and the "boat tail"–the end of the fuselage, the jet pipes and the vertical and horizontal stabilizers–contained light gauge titanium parts that necessitated purchase of a hot forming and sizing press: a first application for Canadair.

Andy Throner remembered the CF-5 for its ever-present wing twist problem: "The wing had a twist designed into it. If it wasn't riveted up in precisely the correct order, it

The first NF-5s are handed over to the Dutch. For the 115 CF-5s and 105 NF-5s on order in 1967, 189 centre fuselage sections were made in Holland by Fokker and shipped to Canadair for assembly. (CL C5526)

would also have a manufacturing twist, and then it would have to be taken apart, and that was a big, big job!"

The first F-5 produced was a single seat CF-5A, one of 89 for the Canadian Forces (CF)–the name had been changed from Royal Canadian Air Force under the Canadian Forces Reorganization Act of February 1, 1968. The CF-5A was rolled out on February 6, 1968, and shipped to Edwards Air Force Base, California, where it was flown for the first time on May 10 by Henry Chouteau of Northrop. An initial quantity of 26 CF-5Ds (a two-seat trainer version) was built for the CF. Longhurst and Chouteau took the first on its maiden flight on August 28, 1968.

When the CF-5 was first ordered, it was meant to equip four tactical fighter squadrons, but while production was in full swing, a combination of tightening purse strings and changes in defence requirements resulted in 44 aircraft being delivered straight into storage.

The situation changed in 1970 when a new role was created for Canada–the protection of NATO's northern flank (i.e., Norway). In October 1970, six CF-5s flew to Europe for exercises to determine the aircraft's usefulness in the NATO environment. It proved reliable and adaptable. An in-flight refuelling system was introduced in 1972, and on June 6, 1973, eight CF-5s flew non-stop from Canada to Norway in Exercise Long Leap 1. Such exercises became routine proving that, having overcome its range deficiency, the CF-5 was a respectable little fighter.

With a top speed of nearly one-and-one-half times the speed of sound, the CF-5 carried two 20-mm cannons and either five 230-kg (500-lb.) bombs or 76 70-mm rockets, or a combination of the two. The reconnaissance version had three 70-mm cameras in a Canadair-designed nose.

In 1971, Whiteman, Louis and Matt Zaleski of contract estimating, went to Venezuela to discuss a potential sale of 20 CF-5s to the Venezuelan Air Force. Since the licensing agreement prohibited Canadair from selling the CF-5 to any country other than the Netherlands, the Canadian Forces sold 16 of its CF-5As and two CF-5Ds to Venezuela. Then the CF bought 18 new CF-5Ds from Canadair to expand its advanced training program and ease the load on the aging T-33s. At the same time, Canadair supplied two CF-5Ds to Venezuela, bringing total CF-5 production to 135.

Northrop considered the sale to Venezuela a contravention of the licensing agreement and sued the Canadian government. Canadair, too, made a multi-million dollar claim against the government, as licence-holders, for reimbursement of the additional costs of clearing up the mess created by the early Northrop deficiencies. Fortunately, Louis had recorded Northrop's shortcomings, in writing to Northrop, and this helped lay the groundwork for the claim. The government settled the Canadair claim when it purchased the company in 1975, and presumably also reached a satisfactory settlement with Northrop.

In December 1993, the Canadian Forces reported that 35 CF-5Ds and 27 CF-5As were still in service. Many had been through a modernization program at Bristol Aero-

space in Winnipeg and Canada planned to keep the type in service till about the year 2000.

The NF-5

In 1966, the Dutch government ordered 105 F-5s (75 single-seat versions, designated NF-5As, and 30 two-seat NF-5Bs) from Canadair under a contract negotiated by Frank Francis, Ben Locke, Ambrose Mosco, Julius Serafin and Ernie Walford. Fokker of the Netherlands supplied the centre fuselages, built on tooling supplied by Canadair. Canadair supplied the rest and assembled the aircraft. Ken O'Neil was appointed NF-5 program manager and Hugh Cavanagh, project engineer. Cavanagh later became CF/NF-5 program manager.

The differences between the CF and NF versions were slight: the NF version had a wing leading edge flap which improved low-speed manoeuvrability, and could carry 1,250-litre (275-imp. gal.) underwing fuel tanks.

The first NF-5A was rolled out on March 5, 1969, and flew on March 24 with Bill Longhurst at the controls. On May 9, it flew to Edwards AFB, California, for testing. The Royal Netherlands Air Force accepted delivery of the first NF-5 at Cartierville on October 8, and on November 7, it flew with three others to Twenthe in the Netherlands. The first NF-5B was flown by Seth Grossmith on July 7, 1969.

Canadair registered another first when the Netherlands awarded it a contract to furnish the data required for doing its own third- and fourth-line maintenance. This covered the servicing, repair and overhaul of equipment which, if unserviceable, was generally sent back to the vendor for fixing. The job meant that for the first time in its history, Canadair had to obtain maintenance, repair and overhaul publications and parts lists for all items of equipment, and recommend what spare parts the air force should procure. To make matters worse, the Dutch insisted on a fixed price for the contract. Jim Maskell, and later Fred Agnew, were the product support managers who handled the program. It did well and brought in a good profit.

By 1991 Canadair had completed 10,000+ hours of CF-5 durability and damage tolerance tests using this specially rigged and instrumented airframe. This resulted from a 1987 Air Command request for Canadair to determine the airframe life of the CF-5 (originally 4,000 hours, later extended to 6,000 by Northrop). In its study, Canadair induced various failures in the CF-5 wing and tail, devised long-term repairs for these and passed on this technology to Bristol Aerospace in Winnipeg, the primary CF-5 repair and overhaul contractor. Modification kits for 58 CF-5s were manufactured by Canadair for Bristol. (CL C57619)

(Above) Three CF-5s of 433 "Porcupine" Squadron lift off in tight formation from CFB North Bay on May 22, 1980. Ottawa's 1994 defence white paper recommended that the CF-5 finally be retired from Air Command after more than 25 years of service. (David Thompson)

(Right) A pair of 419 Squadron CF-5s during an aerial refueling exercise in April 1989. Pilots advancing to the CF-18 learned the basics of fighter tactics flying the CF-5 with 419 Squadron at CFB Cold Lake. The CF-5 was retired from the Canadian Forces in 1995. (Larry Milberry)

(Below) This Dutch NF-5 took part in Exercise Maple Flag at CFB Cold Lake in July 1988. (Larry Milberry)

CHAPTER SEVEN

VERTICAL FLIGHT

THE CL-84

Although the CL-84 never went into quantity production, it deserves recognition as the most important research and development project undertaken by Canadair while the company was a subsidiary of General Dynamics.

In the early 1950s, Canadair management began to show interest in vertical takeoff and landing (VTOL) aircraft. In late 1954, Ken Ebel hired Fred Phillips as chief of aerodynamics and preliminary design. A graduate of New York University and the Massachussetts Institute of Technology, Phillips had spent the four years prior to joining Canadair as senior design engineer on helicopters and convertiplanes at McDonnell Aircraft Corp.

Soon after he joined Canadair, Phillips asked Karl Irbitis to prepare a review of all known principles which could be used in V/STOL (vertical and short takeoff and landing) aircraft design. Irbitis was a design engineer who had

come to Canadair from Latvia in 1951. He had done some research and preliminary VTOL design. On May 4, 1956, at the annual general meeting of the Canadian Aeronautics and Space Institute in Montreal, Phillips presented a paper which combined the results of Irbitis's review and Phillips's own experience in VTOL aircraft.

Shortly after, John Orr of the Defence Research Board (DRB) proposed that Canadair carry out further VTOL

Wings rotated for slow-speed flight and hovering, two CL-84-1s manoeuvre at Cartierville. The tilt-rotor CL-84 was the most advanced of the so-called convertiplanes. Aircraft that could transition from vertical to high-speed level flight first appeared in the 1950s. Designs included the Convair XFY-1 Pogo and Lockheed XFV-1 Salmon experimental fighters. Other were the Bell X-14 with thrust vectoring jet exhaust nozzles, the Doak VZ-4DA with pivoting ducted airscrews, and the Hiller X-18 tilt rotor. Until the Bell/Boeing V-22 Osprey (first flown 1989), the CL-84 was the most advanced of the convertiplanes. (CL C7173)

In 1954 Canadair completed a V/STOL design study designated CL-43; other studies followed. Shown here are wind tunnel models for the CL-73 (top) and CL-74 army reconnaissance V/STOL aircraft proposed in August 1958. Allison T63-A-3 turboprop engines were envisioned for these designs. (CL 84-19394, RD9013)

(Left) In 1958 the CL-62 was envisioned as a two-, four- or eight-engine turboprop tilt-wing transport weighing up to 53,000 lb. (24,000 kg). Canadair described it as using the "tilt-wing/deflected-slipstream principle, to obtain vertical as well as short-field take-off and landing capability". This mobile test rig gathered data for the CL-62. From such studies the CL-84 concept emerged in 1960. (Right) A test rig for studying CL-84 propeller performance in different flight modes. (CL RD8958, 48969)

and V/STOL research. As a result, Canadair, the National Research Council (NRC) and the DRB agreed to sponsor joint studies to determine the configuration of aircraft best suited to the support of ground forces. Canadair would build models of three versions (tilt wing, tilt engine and fan-in-wing). The NRC would test the models in its wind tunnel, and the DRB would provide money for the analysis. The first studies established tilt-wing/slipstream-deflection V/STOL transport configurations as the most promising for further work.

Between 1957 and 1963, Canadair conducted analytical, design and experimental work in tilt-wing technology with financial assistance from the Department of Defence Production (DDP). This included a considerable amount of powered-model testing in wind tunnels and on an open-air mobile rig. A static-thrust propeller test rig was developed; various propeller designs were tested at about half-scale; and a computer-controlled flight simulator was developed.

The decision to fund a tilt-wing V/STOL prototype was announced in February 1963. Designated the CL-84, the prototype was conceived as a small research vehicle, but was built as a larger machine capable of development into a useful military aircraft.

The final configuration of the prototype was established, and in August 1963 the DDP and Canadair agreed to share the $10 million cost of building and developing the aircraft to the stage where military demonstrations could be made. Canadair contributed a quarter of the amount and the DDP, the balance.

The CL-84 was a fairly conventional looking, high-wing, twin-engined design, but it could fly in a way that was definitely *not* conventional. It could take off, fly and land like an ordinary airplane but also take off, climb, descend and land vertically, like a helicopter—and like a helicopter it could hover. What made this possible was its tilt wing. With a flick of a switch, the pilot could tilt the wing and the engines to any position from horizontal to past the vertical. With the wing horizontal, the CL-84

Building the CL-84 mock-up, March 1964. After it had served its purpose, it was kept around by some of the engineers for nostalgia. Plant manager Mel Curtis asked chief plant engineer Dick Faucher several times to get rid of it, as it was occupying valuable space. The engineers always procrastinated so Curtis said to Faucher one day, "Get rid of that thing by 4 o'clock today, or I'm getting myself a new chief plant engineer." The mock-up went to the dump. (CL 38866)

The first CL-84 takes shape in P2. In the second view the wing is mated to the fuselage on November 1, 1964. (CL 6595-7, 42127)

(Above) The CL-84 is shown on rollout day. It was a brilliant aerodynamic concept built without a particular role. It taught Canadair much about the V/STOL concept, but no production orders came in. (CL 42715)

(Left) The prototype CL-84 runs up while shackled to its immovable test bed. It ran on the test bed for months before making its first free flight (below). (CL 43351, H129)

operated like an ordinary airplane. With the wing tilted half-way up, it could make short takeoffs and landings and tight turns. With the wing vertical, it flew just like a helicopter.

The design, manufacture and installation of the V/STOL features of the CL-84 were all new to Canadair. The features included engine, oil and fuel systems which would function equally well whether horizontal or vertical; a mechanism which tilted the wing and engines; complex shafting linking the engines so that, if one engine failed, that engine would disengage and the aircraft would be powered by the remaining engine, and finally a mixing

Configured for high-speed, level flight, the prototype CL-84 whistles over Quebec farmland on a bright winter's day. (CL C3098)

box which produced the same reaction to the pilot's control movements regardless of whether the aircraft was flying vertically or horizontally.

This box, designed by Karl Irbitis, was an ingenious arrangement of cams and levers which enabled pilots to fly the CL-84 without having to learn a whole new technique: the mixing box did the thinking for them. For example, to bank the CL-84, the pilot moved the control column to one side or the other as in a normal airplane. In conventional flight, this operated the ailerons, but in vertical flight it varied the blade angle of the propellers. In either case the result was the same: the airplane banked. Similarly, a turn, normally made by moving the rudder, was produced in vertical flight by deflecting the ailerons. A climb or dive, normally the result of moving the elevator, was achieved by varying the thrust of the tail rotor when hovering or flying vertically.

The CL-84 prototype was built in the experimental shop in a skunk works operation similar to the one that turned out the first CL-41s. It used many of the same personnel. Fred Phillips was the program manager. Gerry Barabé headed up the manufacturing team and Longhurst took over as project pilot with Doug Morrison as back-up.

When the CL-84 rolled out on December 9, 1964, its most noticeable features were its short, square wing with full-span leading edge flap and trailing edge flap/ailerons; its two engines located at mid-span to enable their huge propellers to "wash" the entire span; a variable-incidence tailplane but no elevator, and two horizontally mounted, contra-rotating tail rotors.

Inside the cockpit, the pilot had a conventional stick and rudder but only one throttle lever. Termed a "power lever," it controlled not only the power of both engines but also (in V/STOL flight) propeller blade angle. A switch on the top of the lever controlled wing tilt.

After lengthy ground testing, Bill Longhurst made the first flight on May 7, 1965. It consisted of four short ex-

CL-84 flight control system. (CL)

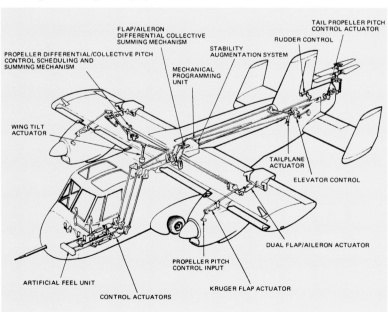

199

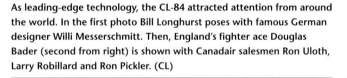

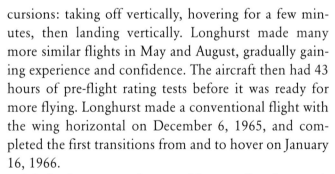

As leading-edge technology, the CL-84 attracted attention from around the world. In the first photo Bill Longhurst poses with famous German designer Willi Messerschmitt. Then, England's fighter ace Douglas Bader (second from right) is shown with Canadair salesmen Ron Uloth, Larry Robillard and Ron Pickler. (CL)

Bob Simmons is winched aboard CF-VTO-X during trials at Cartierville in January 1966. Note the CL-84's large belly door. Simmons had been an RCAF Sabre pilot before joining Canadair in sales. Always an adventurous fellow, he volunteered for these search and rescue trials. (CL 45956, 51085)

cursions: taking off vertically, hovering for a few minutes, then landing vertically. Longhurst made many more similar flights in May and August, gradually gaining experience and confidence. The aircraft then had 43 hours of pre-flight rating tests before it was ready for more flying. Longhurst made a conventional flight with the wing horizontal on December 6, 1965, and completed the first transitions from and to hover on January 16, 1966.

Much of 1966 was taken up with expanding the experience envelope. In September, the director of CL-84 marketing, Bob Simmons, earned the uncontested title of the first person to be uplifted from the ground by a tilt-wing VTOL aircraft. During search and rescue trials the following month Longhurst lifted Simmons out of a rubber dinghy on the Rivière des Prairies, after first dipping him gently in the water. Also in September, five visiting pilots flew the CL-84, one each from the Canadian Army, Canada's National Aeronautical Establishment and the RAF, and two from NASA. Their assessments ranged from complimentary to enthusiastic.

The failure of a small part during testing in January 1967 proved the effectiveness of the engine cross-shafting. While the plane was making a turn in transition from hover at under 55 km/h (35 mph) and a height of only 12 m (40 ft.), the part failed causing an abrupt loss of power on one engine, but the pilot was able to land, under full control, on the remaining engine.

During the spring and summer of 1967, seven U.S. military pilots flew the CL-84 for a total of 21 hours and declared it mechanically simple, generally easy to maintain and easy to fly.

Two views of the prototype CL-84 following a heavy landing at Cartierville. In the front view Bob Lording is by the propeller. Pilot Doug Morrison, Fred Kearns and Eric McConachie are to the right in the second view, with George Robinson by the nose. VTO was destroyed in 1967 after becoming uncontrollable at about 3,000 feet (900 m). (CL 48887, '887)

Unfortunately, the failure of a standard off-the-shelf bearing caused the prototype to crash on September 12, 1967, after it had flown 145.5 hours in 305 flights. Bill Longhurst and flight test observer Colin Harcourt ejected safely. The bearing that failed was hidden within part of the propeller control system where it could not be inspected.

CL-84-1

Some time before the accident Canadair had become hopeful of selling a few CL-84s. It began preparing for further production, and in February 1968 the DND and the Department of Industry, Trade and Commerce ordered three updated CL-84-1s for military evaluation.

The CL-84-1 was engineered and built in a shop more like a production assembly facility than a skunk works. Fred Phillips continued as program manager; Harry Louis was in charge of production; Gerry Barabé was production general superintendent, with B.N.(Slim) Harte and Bas Daniels as assistant superintendents; Jack Crowshaw and Al Fitton were in charge of assembly;

Bill Longhurst (left) with one of the visiting pilots who flew the CL-84-1. (CL C7575-35)

Henri Lafrance was in planning; M. Duplanty was in tool design; R. Laferrière was in sheet metal fabrication; and Herbie Gregoire was in inspection. The manager of design, Mike Telford, was seconded to the project on several occasions. Some of the prototype engineers were still available but most were busy on other programs. The factory too was busy which meant that more work had to be farmed out to subcontractors. As a result, it was two full years from go-ahead before the first aircraft was ready to fly.

The CL-84-1 incorporated over 150 engineering changes, mostly resulting from criticisms and suggestions of the 16 pilots who had flown the prototype. It was 1.6 m (5 ft. 3 in.) longer than the prototype; its engines produced 100 shp more and its maximum weights had in-creased to 5,720 kg (12,600 lb.) in the VTOL mode and 6,580 kg (14,500 lb.) in the STOL mode. The cabin con-tained bench seating for 12 passengers. Three under-fuse-lage hardpoints could each carry a 450-kg (1,000-lb.) store. The two outer hardpoints had provisions for two 460-litre (100-imp. gal.) jettisonable fuel tanks.

Bill Longhurst flew the first CL-84-1 on February 19, 1970. It then entered an evaluation program to determine its suitability for roles in support of ground forces, which included stores-dropping and gun-firing trials.

In January 1971, Longhurst retired from Canadair and his place as chief pilot was taken over by F.D. (Doug) Adkins. A native of Medicine Hat, Alberta, he had joined the RCAF in 1951 and flew as a fighter pilot in Europe and Canada until 1956 when he transferred to the RCAF

CL-84-1 No. 402 hovers before landing on the helicopter carrier USS *Guadalcanal*. It was on joint Canadian, US Navy, US Marine Corps and RAF trials off Norfolk, Virginia in March 1974. Then an overall view of the ship with the CL-84-1 over the deck. (CL C7482-7, 7503)

Auxiliary and entered the University of Toronto. Graduating in 1961 with a bachelor of applied sciences in engineering physics, he joined the engineering division at Canadair. From 1962 to 1966 Adkins was a production test pilot flying the F-86, CF-104, F-104G, CL-41, CL-28 and CF/NF-5. In 1966, he became involved with the CL-215 program, initially in the aerodynamics section and subsequently as project pilot on the flight test development and certification. In 1971 he became project test pilot on the CL-84-1. Adkins first flew the CL-84-1 on April 4, 1971. He became familiar with the aircraft in a very short time and was a tower of strength in both development and demonstration flying.

In February 1972, at the invitation of the U.S. Navy, Adkins took a CL-84-1 on a demonstration/evaluation tour to Washington, D.C., and Norfolk, Virginia. He gave demonstrations at Andrews AFB and Dulles International Airport, and three separate displays of precision flying to large groups of military and civilian personnel at the Pentagon, while operating in gusty winds from a 30-metre (100-ft.) square helicopter pad.

He then flew the "84" to a U.S. Navy assault carrier, the USS *Guam*, steaming 30 km (20 mi.) off the Virginia coast. There he demonstrated a series of vertical and short takeoffs and landings. Though he had no previous deck-landing experience, he managed to make the whole operation look completely routine.

When Adkins left the *Guam*, in winds gusting to 65 km/h (40 mph), he made a high speed, low level pass

No. 401 over the fan deck of the USS *Guam* during trials off Norfolk in the spring of 1972. A Marine Corps CH-46 Sea Knight hovers beyond. (CL C6929)

A group of CL-84 men at Canadair *c.* 1973: Lawrence Rowley (project engineer), Tom Sullivan (marketing engineer), Maurice Holloway (tech rep/field maintenance supervisor), Odd Michaelsen (chief aerodynamicist), Doug Adkins (chief test pilot), LCdr Ken Rauch (US Navy), Fred Phillips (program manager) and Doug Morrison (Canadair pilot). (CL 21647-24)

This Royal 22nd Regiment platoon lined up on a sunny day in October 1965 to illustrate the CL-84's potential as a troop transport. (CL 46184)

Maryland, for a 12-month tripartite test program involving pilots from the U.S. Navy, RAF and Canadian Forces. The aircraft was equipped with a head-up and head-down electronic display system developed by Smiths Instruments of England. Phase 1 of the program dealt mainly with the evaluation of the electronic display system as it would relate to the British Harrier V/STOL aircraft. It was conducted by two RAF pilots and a team from Britain's Royal Aeronautical Establishment and Smiths Instruments. It was during this phase, on April 5, 1973, that an RAF pilot, Flight Lieutenant Ron Ledwidge, completed what was probably the first descending transition from conventional flight to hover ever made on instruments in a V/STOL aircraft other than a helicopter.

Ledwidge took control of the aircraft from the safety

alongside the ship. As he passed the bridge, to everyone's surprise and delight Adkins did a slow roll.

The shipboard operation demonstrated the CL-84 could provide anti-submarine warfare capability and radar surveillance when operating from ships with limited deck space like the proposed U.S. Navy sea control ship or the Royal Navy through-deck cruiser.

On December 7, 1972, Adkins ferried the second CL-84-1, to the Naval Air Test Center, Patuxent River,

Canadair also touted the CL-84 as an attack aircraft. Here it is raking a target with fire from its belly-mounted machine gun pod. The artist's conception shows a gunship development. (CL C6616, 42600)

pilot, Canadian Lieutenant Commander Barry Gartner, at a height of 450 m (1,500 ft.) on the downwind leg of the circuit at 275 km/h (175 mph). Flying on instruments, he intercepted the glidepath and made a descending, decelerating approach to hover and make a vertical landing. That "five minutes of sweat," as Ledwidge puts it, helped earn him a bar to his Air Force Cross and the prestigious Douglas Weightman Flight Safety Award, the first time it had been awarded to a serving member of the RAF.

Phase 2, which started on May 30, 1973, was conducted by the U.S. Navy and focused on the development of display systems for naval aircraft.

No. 8401 crashed on August 8, 1973, while being used to train U.S. Navy and Marine pilots at Patuxent River. It was in a maximum power climb when the left propeller gearbox failed and the propeller and supporting structure of the gearcase fell away. The two U.S. Navy and Marine Corps pilots ejected safely with only scrapes and bruises.

With this loss, No. 8402 was assigned to Phase 2 for two weeks of sea trials aboard the USS *Guadalcanal* helicopter carrier. This included several days of the worst weather ever encountered by the ship. The violent rolling caused considerable damage to furnishings and loose equipment, but thanks to good preventative measures by Maurice Holloway and his maintenance crew, the CL-84 came through unscathed.

Phase 3, flown by RCN Lieutenant Commander Gartner and civilian W.S. Hindson, was to develop a display system for future versions of the CL-84. It began on April 8, 1974, and included a night evaluation on May 2, 1974.

While the evaluation programs were going on, Canadair's CL-84 salesmen, Bob Simmons and Tom Sullivan, and several contract administrators led by Harold Buhr, had not been idle. Between 1961 and mid-1973, Canadair made eight formal marketing proposals, mainly to the United States, but also to Germany, Holland, Italy, Scandinavia and the United Kingdom. Four of these were in competitions. In two (the Tri-Service V/STOL Transport competition of 1961, and the Advanced Aerial Fire Support System in 1965) the CL-84 lost out to other competitors, but in each case the program was cancelled without any aircraft actually going into service. For another of the four competitions (Combat Aircrew Recovery Aircraft —CARA), General Dynamics/Convair provided proposal assistance and there were definite indications that GD/Convair/Canadair were going to get a development

contract, but the bombing of North Vietnam ended and the immediate need for a CARA aircraft disappeared.

The last, and possibly the best proposal in a competition, was prompted by U.S. Navy interest in aircraft compatible with the sea control ship concept. The proposal resulted in Canadair receiving two contracts: one for further studies of a CL-84 derivative, the CL-84-8, and another for flight testing the CL-84 to evaluate its compatibility with the sea control ship. (The demonstration on the *Guam* was part of this contract.) An advanced design team under Jeff Harwood worked on the study of the CL-84-8, but just when it seemed certain that a development contract would be awarded, the Navy dropped the sea control ship concept.

In September 1974, the CL-84 program died for want of a customer. Technically the program was a success, based on the comments of the 40 pilots who flew the three aircraft for 476 hours in 709 flights. (The third CL-84-1 was never completed.) Fred Phillips attributed the lack of sales to two main reasons: "For one thing, it's difficult to sell in a foreign market if the product is not in use in one's own country. Also the need for V/STOL capability was not sufficiently important in the military mind at

Flight Lieutenant Ron Ledwidge of the RAF who did some pioneer flying on the CL-84-1. (via R. Ledwidge)

The CL-84-1 maintenance crew at NAS Patuxent River in mid-1974: George Lewinski (crew chief), Mike Baraguy (quality control), Ian Rowan (tech), Jacques Canuel (tech), Fernand Poirier (tech), T. Crosby (instrumentation), Maurice Holloway (supervisor) and J. Nagle (instrumentation). (USN via F.C. Phillips)

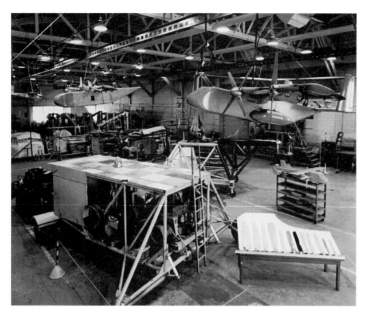

Test models in the early days of V/STOL development at Canadair. Hanging (far left) is the CL-73, then two models of the CL-62 concept. At floor level on the shelf is a CL-84 model. (CL C4687)

On the table is the "US Army Advanced Aerial Fire Support System" CL-84 proposal made by Canadair. Jack Greeniaus (project engineer) and Fred Phillips (program manager) pose with the mass of paperwork. (CL 43159)

the time to warrant expensive development and deployment of new aircraft types such as the 84." As with the CL-44, Canadair was cursed with having the right aircraft at the wrong time.

The CL-84, a product at the leading edge of technological innovation, was unceremoniously mothballed. No. 8402 is displayed at the National Aviation Museum in Ottawa; 8403 belongs to the Western Canada Aviation Museum.

The CL-246 Tilt-Wing Transport

In response to a 1970 request by American Airlines, Canadair proposed a STOL passenger airliner for city-centre to city-centre operation along the Washington-New York-Boston corridor. Canadair's design, the CL-246, was prepared by a team which included Saul Bernstein, Albert Brown, Ernie Currington, Jeff Harwood, Karl Irbitis, Wally Remington, Ross Richardson, John Skomorowsky and Dave Wright.

A 48-seat aircraft, powered by four T53 turboprop engines, the CL-246 used technology developed during the

An artist's conception of the CL-246 STOL-liner... another idea that was stillborn. (CL C6410)

The program was canceled before CL-84-1 No. 3 could fly. Canadair later donated it to the Western Canada Aviation Museum in Winnipeg. It left Cartierville in October 1985. (CL C33645)

CL-84 program to obtain STOL performance by tilting the wing 15 degrees. American Airlines chose the CL-246 over its rivals, the de Havilland Buffalo and Breuget 941, but before the prototype could be built the program was abandoned, in part because of environmental concerns and high projected operating costs.

The CL-84 had a pair of 1500-shp Lycoming T53 turbines. The T53 was primarily a helicopter engine, made famous in the Bell UH-1 Huey. (CL 49999)

After a flight out to sea, No. 402 gets the salt washed from its back at NAS Norfolk. (CL C7552-11)

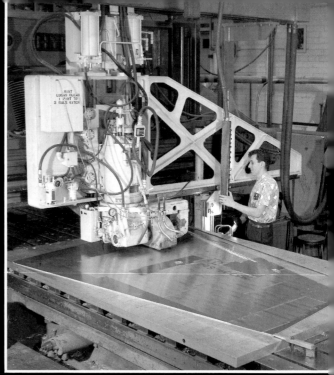

With new machinery and processes, manufacturing became more sophisticated in the 1960s. Here CL-44 panels are cleaned in a bath of nitric acid before being bonded. In the second photo, work is underway on CF-104 wings with a Giddings & Lewis skin mill in P1, June 1961. (CL 27053, M21502)

SNAPSHOTS AND SKETCHES

(Right) Canadair had a contract for Sikorsky CH-53 helicopter components in the 1960s. In this scene in B118 a craftsman molds a plaster master needed in that program. He is using a template to check contours for a perfect shape. (CL 37622)

(Left) A massive Watson-Stillman 5,000-ton hydro press seen in September 1961. A certain amount of spring-back in parts made by such machines necessitated a manual stage called "check-and-straighten". (CL 28307)

(Below) Some of Canadair's firemen with their new FWD foam truck in front of B117 in June 1961: driver Robert King, with André Ducharme at the foam cannon, then Gerald Smith, William Young, Sid Naylor, A. D'Aoust and Dan McKay. (CL 27001)

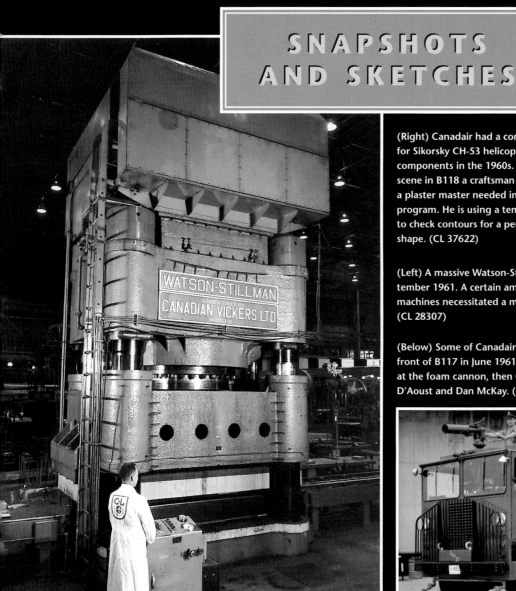

WATSON-STILLMAN
CANADIAN VICKERS LTD

To take over the work done by its famous DC-3 CF-DXU, Canadair added this executive Grumman Mallard and a Convair 240 (CF-UOJ) in the 1960s. The Mallard was ideal for VIP trips to Canadair's fishing camp at Lac Piraubé, north of Lac St-Jean. Later the Mallard was converted from R-1340 radials to PT6 turbines. (CL C4557)

(Below) This view from the late 1960s looks down Runway 28 and may be compared with the photos on pages 20, 68 and 84 to see the changes over the years. By now Runway 06/24 had been grassed over. The big shopping mall had been built on the east side of Laurentian Blvd. and housing developments had gobbled up the golf course north of the railway yards. (CL C7592)

(Left) Lou Adamson presents 15-year pins to Art Battis, Johnny Altimas and George Henderson of spare parts sales. (CL F3026)

Some of the visitors at a Canadair family day in the early 1960s. (CL M1892)

Also well-known in the infirmary was Dr. Bob Brodrick, Canadair's medical officer for more than 30 years. Later in his career he was medical director of the Montreal Expos. (CL C33756)

Canadair's infirmary always had work to do and nobody there was better known and loved than nurse Rolande Martel. She joined Canadian Vickers in 1943 and stayed on for 39 years. One retiree recalled in 1994 how Martel knew all the employees by their first names. She is seen with patient Jim Crowshaw (industrial relations). Canadair illustrator Bob Dallabona sketched "Roly" Martel in the cartoon for the *Canadair News*. (CL F2635)

Canadair's Sheila Ward was Dean Stowell's secretary in 1957 when she was proclaimed "Queen of the Secretaries", in a continent-wide competition organized by the Executive Furniture Guild of America. Here she is congratulated by Montreal's mayor, Jean Drapeau. (CL 4790)

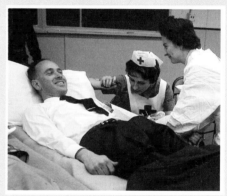

Canadair employees have always been ready to help a good cause. Red Cross blood donor clinics have been held since the Second World War. This one was in January 1961. (CL 24118)

Dave Clark, supervisor of technical illustrations, produced these impromptu pencil sketches of activities on the shop floor in the mid-1950s. Clark later moved to the financial planning department, then went into the banking world.

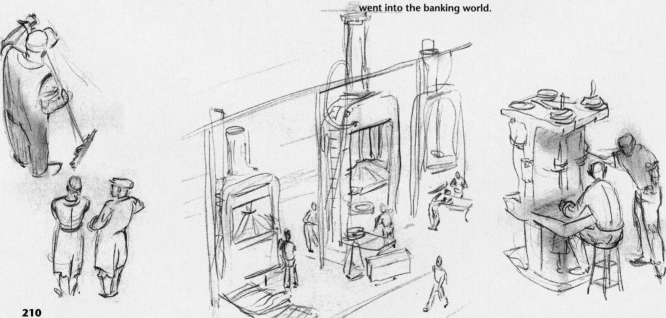

Canadair had dozens of employees named Roy on the payroll over the decades. Each year the "clan" assembled for a luncheon celebration in the cafeteria. (CL 5496)

The strike of 1965 ended that June. The principals in the settlement gathered for this historic photo. At the head of the table are Lodge 712 business agent Charles Phillips and Fred Kearns. Also at the table are Maurice Litalien (lodge president), Adrien Villeneuve, Merle C. Curtis (V-P, operations) and W.D. Shuttleworth (director, industrial relations). Standing are union and management men Marc Lapointe, Aimé Gohier, Jack Smith, Wilfrid Héroux, Ovila Leblanc, Normand Cherry, André Martin, Marcel Fournier, Maurice Norton, Bernard Langlois, Hervé Rivard and Stewart Willis.

Captioned in the *Canadair News* as "the smiling family," the Vigers at this stage had 53 years of company service. Shown here are Johnny, Henry Jr., Lorraine, Henry Sr., George and Freddie. (CL)

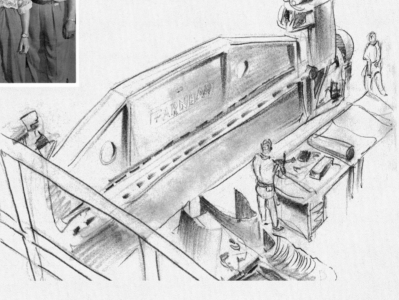

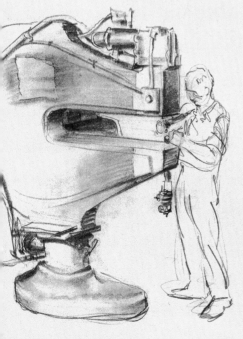

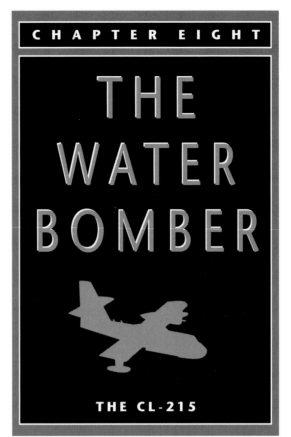

CHAPTER EIGHT

THE WATER BOMBER

THE CL-215

The CL-215 aircraft program became the longest-running production program in Canadair history. When the company celebrated its 50th birthday, 27 years had passed since the first flight of the CL-215.

Popularly known as the "Waterbomber" or the "Super-scooper," the CL-215 joined the CL-44D as the only two Canadair products without official names, though the French dictionary *Le Petit Larousse illustré*, defined "Le Canadair" as a forest-fire-fighting plane equipped with water tanks. The only aircraft in the world designed specifically to fight forest fires, the CL-215 became the third product, following the CL-41 and CL-84, designed and developed from scratch by Canadair.

How the Program Got Started

In the early 1960s, Canadair market research indicated a need for a specialized transport to open up the Canadian North for civil and military purposes. Preliminary studies favored a twin-engined floatplane with a gross weight of 5,670 kg (12,500 lb.) powered by either 540 hp Curtiss Wright or 550 hp Alvis Leonides piston engines.

Around 1961, Canadair marketing manager Tom Watt mentioned the studies to Richard "Moose" Murdoch, a pilot with the Quebec's government air service, which had recently begun fighting forest fires with converted Cansos. Murdoch suggested Canadair abandon the transport idea and concentrate on building an aircraft designed to fight fires.

Watt brought the air service director general, Paul Gagnon, to Canadair. Gagnon told Eric McConachie, manager of sales engineering, that he was concerned the Cansos would not survive many seasons of firefighting, and he was looking for a replacement. As a starting point, Gagnon and McConachie agreed that Canadair should base its initial studies on an aircraft capable of carrying a water load of 5,400 litres (1,200 imp. gal.) or 50 per cent more than a Canso load.

McConachie and sales engineers Bob Agar, Gil Dunkin, Les Kottmeier and Ken McDonald produced a concept of a simple, inexpensive twin-engined floatplane which they passed on to executive vice-president Fred Kearns for comment. Geoff Notman spotted the proposal on Kearn's desk. It caught his imagination, and he told Kearns to "get on top of this."

A preliminary design study by Jeff Harwood, Eugene Kazilow, Keith Matheson and Ed Payne proposed a 16,000-kg (36,000-lb.) gross weight floatplane using four Wankel-type rotary combustion engines, but this was discarded when it became evident the engine needed further development.

The next preliminary design was the CL-204, a 17,000-kg (38,000 lb.) floatplane powered by two 2,100 hp Pratt & Whitney R-2800 piston engines. It was a development of the CL-43 military transport proposed by Karl Irbitis in 1954. Meanwhile, engineering and marketing personnel were talking to forest fire experts. On December 9, 1963, Harwood of engineering and Cliff MacKinnon of marketing were invited to a workshop meeting on aircraft in forest fire control organized by the NRC. One subject was "The Desired Aircraft" during which the participants agreed on desirable characteristics for the ideal fire fighting aircraft: they could have been cribbed from the specs of the CL-204.

Further engineering design studies, however, established that a floatplane would not be able to operate safely in rough water. The design was changed, first to a flying boat with a strut-braced, pylon-mounted parasol wing, then to an amphibian with the full fuselage, shoulder wing configuration of today's CL-215. The configuration finally chosen was a twin-engined amphibian with R-2800s; able to attack forest fires for over four hours with successive drops of 5,400 litres (1,200 imp. gal.) of water scooped as the aircraft skimmed along the surface at about 130 km/h (80 mph).

The CL-215's intended roles provided problems of compromise for its designers. Its structure had to be strong enough to withstand the pounding of scooping and the buffeting over the fire, yet it could not be heavy because then it would not be able to carry a large enough load. It had to fly safely at low speed yet be fast enough to reach a fire quickly. And it had to be manoeuvrable enough to fly at low altitudes in hilly terrain.

Long before the CL-215, Canadair was researching water bombers. It consulted Quebec's *Service aérien* to learn about the best system of the day—that designed for the Canso by Knox Hawkshaw of Field Aviation. Here Canso CF-PQM makes a demonstration drop at Cartierville. (CL 37377)

(Below) A schematic showing water bombers of the 1960s. These ranged in capacity from the 90-gallon Beaver to the 6,000-gallon Mars, the world's largest. (CL 48678)

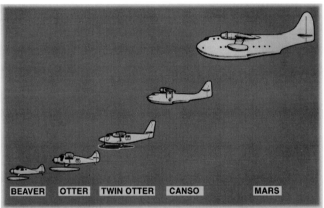

BEAVER   OTTER   TWIN OTTER   CANSO   MARS

The 1962 CL-204 (left) was a pioneer study—the first purpose-designed water bomber. Canadair described it as "of rugged construction with manufacturing processes and tooling kept as simple as possible... Detail tooling shall be kept to a minimum by the extensive use of interchangeable parts... Skin panels shall be flat and of single curvature with snap or mushroom head riveting." The CL-204 was to have a 5,400-litre (1,200-gallon) plywood water tank behind the cockpit. This idea evolved into the CL-215 (right), of which the early conception included a T-tail, slab wing and stabilizer, and raised cockpit. (CL C2302, 42910)

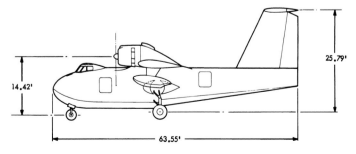

The forward fuselage mock-up of the CL-215 with Pat Campbell trying out the cockpit he built. (CL 44929)

Pilots from the Quebec government air service visit Canadair to see the CL-215 mock-up. Standing in front, from the left, Ron Pickler, unknown, Jean-Guy Rioux, unknown, J.-Paul Demers, W. Casselman, Jules Ringuette, Ralph Lord, Yves Mahaut, Camilien Verret, Frank Desmarais, Martin Renaud, Louis Morin, Cliff MacKinnon. Above, Yvon Vaillancourt, Léo Lejeune, Jacques Robert, Ghislain Boivin. (CL)

Notman had already retired when the time came to get General Dynamics's approval for production; his successor, Fred Kearns, had to use all his powers of persuasion to convince GD president Roger Lewis that the project was worthwhile. Lewis was not enthralled at the prospect of Canadair building an old-fashioned flying boat, and felt that the water bombing market was already well served by conversions of ex-military landplanes.

Reminiscent of Canso production scenes 25 years earlier, the hull of the first CL-215 (CF-FEU-X) takes shape in P2 in late 1966. With all the sharp angles (right), this looks more like a house than an aircraft! (CL 51902, 53581)

(Facing page) Nose on the left, hull on the right CF-FEU-X comes together (early 1967). Don Regan (final assembly) is standing in the middle. Norman Holbrook, in charge of CL-215 final assembly, is second from the right. Next, the scene in July 1967 with FEU's wing in place. The third view, taken a month later, shows three aircraft in the making. (CL 52821, 53793, 54126)

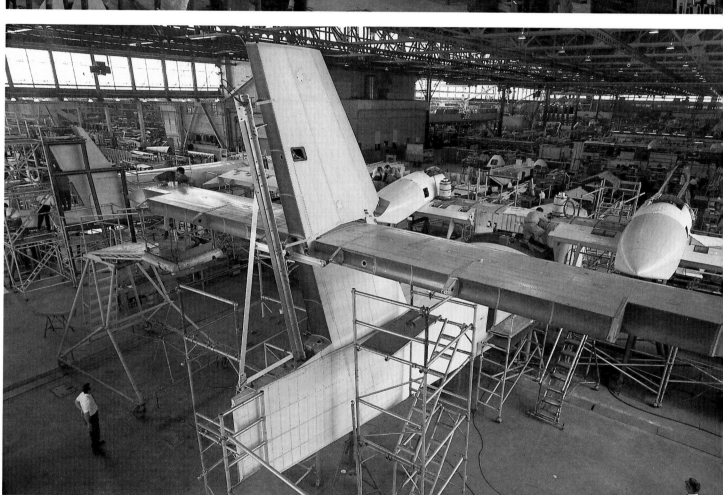

The static test CL-215 (top) in mid-1968. Results from this program earned the CL-215 a utility type approval in addition to its restricted (fire-fighting) certificate. Other behind-the-scenes work involved wind tunnel studies at the NRC in Ottawa. (CL 57663, 45945)

Celebrating the Quebec order for water bombers, Paul Gagnon of the *Service aérien* accepts an original CL-215 painting from Fred Kearns. (CL 1155)

Program Go-ahead

Lewis finally gave the nod in February 1966, on the basis of the sale of 30 aircraft—20 to the province of Quebec and 10 to France. Kearns appointed Bob Stapells as program manager. Norm Holbrook was appointed manager of production with George Moffatt in charge of fabrication; Tommy Bingham was in the machine shop; Bill Montgomery was in bonding; and Bud Kerland was in preflight.

The CL-215 was designed to be simple and inexpensive to manufacture. It didn't turn out that way, despite the efforts of successive vice-presidents, all of whom were convinced it could be built more cheaply. The fuselage was slab-sided and angular, with only a few simple curves around the nose. The wing was thick and square on the theory that costs could be saved by making all the wing ribs the same size; but this was not true because the strength, and hence the weight, of each rib varies in accordance with the load it has to bear. As a result the CL-215 became, in these days of smooth, flowing lines, something of an anachronism. As Dave Hanchet, one of the many people who worked on the program in its early days, quipped: "It set the aviation industry back 50 years."

A CL-215 fights a forest fire by repeatedly drenching it with 5,400-litre (1,200-imp. gal.) drops of water. The water load is carried in two fuselage tanks located below the wing. The lower two-thirds of the tanks are below the cabin floor and form part of the permanent structure of

The CL-215 line is organized on paper. (CL 40771-21)

Two early views of CF-FEU-X during water trials on Lac Simon in the Laurentians. (C4540, 4385)

the hull. The upper one-third are fibreglass and are removable.

The tanks can be filled on the ground through fittings in the side of the fuselage, but are almost always filled by scooping. When scooping, the water is picked up through two small probes which extend below the aircraft's hull. It takes about 10 seconds and a run of approximately 600 m (2,000 ft.) for the CL-215 to pick up a load. Over the fire, the pilot can drop the contents of the two tanks together or separately. In an average three-hour firefighting operation, a single CL-215 can drop nearly 77,000 l (17,000 imp. gal.).

The first CL-215, appropriately registered C-FEU-X, made its maiden flight on October 23, 1967, with the crew of Bill Longhurst, Doug Adkins and Smokey Harris. By this time Doug Follett had replaced Stapells as program manager, and he was followed in quick succession by Harry Halton, Gordon Arnison, Eric Aubrey and Harry Louis.

The first flight revealed a problem that had not surfaced during over 1,000 hours of wind-tunnel testing: the aircraft had insufficient rudder control. The rudder was reshaped and testing commenced. A directional stability problem showed up during later tests and required further modifications to the tail area. Certification was delayed because a special certificate was needed to allow passengers to be carried. Canadian type approval was received in March 1969, and deliveries started with the ferrying of two aircraft to France in June and two more later in the year. A change of government in Quebec resulted in the province reducing its order to 15 aircraft. Four were delivered in 1970 along with the remaining six for France. Two of the five unsold aircraft were first leased and then sold to Spain, and one was sold to Greece, leaving two unsold.

France

As soon as the French *Protection civile* received its first two aircraft, it began a series of open water tests in the Mediterranean Sea off Marseilles. These produced some spectacular flying by Adkins who demonstrated water scooping in seas which eventually reached a height of 2 m (6 ft.). Unlike other CL-215 operators, the *Protection civile* used only one pilot, the right seat being occupied by a flight engineer with sufficient flying ability to land the aircraft safely.

Charlie Massé was the Canadair field service representative in France for the first seven years. He recalled that, shortly after operations started in August 1969, one aircraft scraped a float on a rock outcrop when attacking a fire in the mountains. That aircraft landed safely, but on July 4, 1970, another struck a tree on a mountain in Corsica and crashed, killing all three aboard. The next year, s/n 1025 began to porpoise during scooping, also off Corsica, and landed heavily, fracturing the hull skin. Although severely damaged, the aircraft remained afloat long enough for the crew to be rescued. The French government bought the two remaining aircraft from the first

(Above) Dramatic views of water bombers at work in southern France. (CL)

30-aircraft production run, but with no further sales in sight the line was dismantled.

United States

From early in the program, Canadair marketing had considered the United States, particularly California, a good prospect for the airplane, and lost no time in demonstrating it there. In 1970, a CL-215 flown by Adkins and Yves Mahaut received rave reviews for its performance on a massive fire in the Malibu area of Los Angeles County. (Mahaut was an experienced Quebec government pilot who had joined Canadair.) At a subsequent enquiry into the cause of the fire, the enquiry board thanked Canadair

Spanish government water bombers No. 404-09 and 432-14. The latter is bombing in typical Mediterranean brushland. Fires destroy countless hectares each year in countries like Spain, Italy and Greece. Especially costly are fires that consume olive groves and vineyards. Every year the CL-215 saves great stretches of these valuable resources. (CL)

Tanker No. 35 of the Quebec government. Its angular lines are known far and wide—across Canada, in the Amazon, the Mediterranean and the Far East. Conceived in the early 1960s, the world's most famous water bomber spent more than 30 years on the production line in one version or another. (CL C7368)

for its help and promised that the company's suggestion that Los Angeles County acquire two CL-215s would receive careful consideration. Nonetheless, the enquiry's published findings contained no mention of either Canadair or the CL-215 but recommended that a U.S. aircraft manufacturer produce a firefighting aircraft.

Selling the CL-215 presented its own problems. Canadair's salesmen, among them Bill Kidd, Cliff MacKinnon, Lou Mehl, Ron Pickler, Don Simmons and Jim Sowers, were accustomed to selling an aircraft on its merits, but now they found themselves trying to sell the concept of using airplanes to fight forest fires to people unfamiliar with aviation. It became a long learning process during which many approaches were attempted and many lessons learned. More than two years passed before the

production line was restarted for a 20-aircraft run based on an order for eight dual-role firefighting/search and rescue Series II aircraft for Spain.

Water bombers for Wine

The Spanish sale was unique. Peter Aird, vice-president, finance, while in Madrid to finalize the sale of the two leased aircraft, was entertained to dinner by the Spanish minister of agriculture. Though he seldom drank wine, Aird complimented the minister on his choice of wine, to which the minister replied: "I have warehouses full of the stuff."

"Would you be prepared to consider buying the CL-215 in exchange for wine," enquired Aird. "Certainly," was the reply. On his return to Montreal, Aird contacted Paul Durocher, adviser to Quebec Premier Robert Bourassa, and a deal was quickly arranged. Spain bought eight aircraft and paid for them over eight years

Peter Aird, whose career involved not only the CL-215 but many other projects. He put together the planes-for-wine deal with Spain. (CL 48347)

In April 1977 No. 404-09 (s/n 1037) ran into a stone pier in the harbour at Fuenterrabia, Spain. Salvagers towed it ashore and trucked it to the nearby airport where the Spanish air force decided that the aircraft was too badly damaged to repair. (CL)

from the proceeds of the sale to Quebec of an equivalent value of wine over the same period. Spain kept on profiting from the deal because Quebecers acquired a taste for Spanish wine and the provincial liquor commission continued buying large amounts of it.

Quebec

Meanwhile Quebec had ample opportunity to prove the effectiveness of the CL-215. On May 31, 1972, two fires

broke out simultaneously at opposite ends of Val d'Or, population 20,000, located 520 km (325 mi.) northwest of Montreal. One fire threatened a road/rail junction, the site of a propane storage plant, three large gasoline tanks, a brewery and a lumber yard. The other was approaching a school and a row of new homes when two CL-215 water bombers and two Cansos arrived to supplement the two CL-215 aircraft based in the area. In under two hours and 65 drops both fires were out, but not before one had reached within a metre or two of the propane tanks.

Later that season, a single CL-215 controlled a fire burning in a pulp mill at Desbiens, Quebec, by using the weight and impact of successive drops of water to break through the roof and wet down the interior. Those two operations saved far more than the total cost of the province's water bomber operations for that year.

On another occasion, two CL-215 aircraft rescued 43 inhabitants of a tiny Indian settlement in the James Bay area of Quebec from a forest fire that threatened them. When efforts to evacuate the people by landplane had to be aborted because of heavy smoke, the water bombers picked them up at a nearby lake.

Production of a batch of 20 Series II aircraft began in 1973. The major differences between them and the Series I aircraft were: the engine, with the civil R-2800-CA3 replacing the military R-2800-83AM-2 version; the auxiliary power unit, which was moved from the rear cabin to the right nacelle; and the two main entry doors which were hinged to open rather than sliding back along the outside of the fuselage.

The beginning of Series II production signalled further management changes in production and marketing. Production became the responsibility of a new vice-president of operations, Andy Throner, who took over the job from Conrad Kunze. George Moffatt was director of manufacturing, and Joe Daly manufacturing manager. Frank Francis took over as vice-president of marketing, the sixth person to hold the job in seven years. Another group of salesmen arrived to try their luck including John Bisson, Bob Burns, Wayne Cannon, John Nicas and Will Page. The first 10 Series II aircraft were delivered in 1974—eight to Spain, one to France and one to Greece.

The Japan Trip

In 1974, Japan leased a CL-215 for evaluation, which presented the problem of how to get a short-ranged aircraft across the Pacific Ocean. When the United States reneged on its permission to use Shemya Island at the end of the Aleutian chain, it was back to the drawing board for the sales engineering staff, and on September 17, 1974, a leased Quebec aircraft—crewed by pilots Adkins and Mahaut, with Stan Newlove, maintenance technician, and George Morgan, flight engineer—left on the long haul across the Atlantic, Europe and Asia to Bangkok, then on to the Philippines and Tokyo.

Mahaut had been recalled from Greece where he had been training Greek Air Force pilots to fight fires. It was a rough assignment. The Greek pilots were all fighter types who had never handled multi-engine aircraft nor flown from water. Mahaut had to accompany each one on every flight, and because it was the peak fire season, he flew almost continuously for 25 days, sleeping overnight on a cot in the hangar.

Crossing Iran en route to Japan, one engine failed and the aircraft force-landed at Zahedan. So Mahaut got a welcome, if uncomfortable, week's rest, sleeping under the aircraft's wing, awaiting the arrival of parts.

The team's problems did not end in Zahedan. When they arrived in Japan on October 7, 1974, after a 21,000-km (13,000-mi.) trip, they discovered the national fire agency had set up a drop test site at Mito, some 80 km (50 mi.) north of Tokyo. Although the site was only about 100 m (330 ft.) from the ocean, the environmental agencies refused to allow the CL-215 to scoop there. Instead it had to fly nearly all the way back to Tokyo to ground load after every test drop.

The aircraft gave demonstrations at Fukuoka in the south, Sapporo in the north and Wakiyama, in the centre of the country, all to the satisfaction of the fire agency. Everything appeared to be a "go" for a sale until the Japanese navy representative voiced his service's objection to a purchase on the grounds that heavy drops of water from a low-flying aircraft could be dangerous. Japan eventually converted one Shin Meiwa US-1 amphibian for firefighting using a system very similar to the CL-215's, but it never saw service.

On its way back to Canada, the CL-215 gave demonstrations in the Philippines, Hong Kong and Turkey. An overnight stop (but no demonstration) had been planned for Bangkok; however, the Canadair agent in Bangkok had invited a large group of Thai Navy officers to view the aircraft. That initiative resulted in the sale of two aircraft

to Thailand while the pre-planned demonstrations in the other countries had produced nothing.

Before and after shots of the CL-215's target at Sapporo. (Ron Pickler)

Salt Water

CL-215s were not always appreciated by the residents of the areas they were protecting. Jim Fitzpatrick was CL-215 field service representative in Spain from 1969 to 1976. For his years of valuable service, Spain awarded him the prestigious Spanish Air Force Medal. Fitzpatrick recalled that people in the north believed that the salt water the aircraft dropped was ruining their land. Agronomists from the Department of Agriculture were frequently called upon to persuade farmers the nutrients in the salt water were actually good for the soil.

Several years after Fitzpatrick returned home, he was asked to accompany a group of Spanish officers on a tour

On December 2, 1974, Yves Mahaut, Doug Adkins and George Morgan returned from their sales trip to Japan. On the way home they did demonstrations in the Philippines, Hong Kong, Thailand and Turkey. Here they are greeted at Cartierville by Fred Kearns. (CL 22298)

Quebec's CF-TXI (s/n 1016) up on the step and ready for flight off calm waters in the St. Lawrence River. (CL C20267-8)

of Plant 1. A minor commotion arose when the general leading the party demanded to know why a Canadair guide was wearing a Spanish decoration. A colonel hastened to explain that the guide was *the* Señor Patrick and that he had been awarded the medal, rarely given to foreigners, for meritorious service to Spain.

The subject of salt water drops harming the forest cropped up so often that CL-215 salesmen wondered whether some foresters would rather see the forests burn than allow salt water to be dropped on them. When a forestry officer expressed his concern as to the effects of the drops, Canadair's negotiator produced reports attesting to the beneficial effects of salt water, only to have the forester say: "I'm not concerned about the salt, it's the pollution in our coastal waters that I don't want dropped on my forests."

Other Roles

Though CL-215 sales and production activities continued at a very slow pace for several years, it was not for want of innovation. Engineering and marketing produced prototypes or concepts of spray systems to apply pesticides and oil dispersants. In 1970, the U.S. military allotted funds to buy 20 CL-215 aircraft to spray defoliant in Vietnam, but Canadair had no aircraft to sell at the time and it is doubtful the Canadian government would have granted an export licence.

Quebec used the CL-215 to spray spruce budworm infestations for two seasons before having to stop because budworm outbreaks and spring forest fires inevitably occurred in different places at the same time. France later bought two spray systems for oil pollution dispersion, and Yugoslavia bought four.

Designs were produced for solid spreader systems for aerial fertilizing or fire ant bait, but none were ever built. And there were studies of many other applications like maritime patrol, search and rescue, passenger transportation to remote locations, and flying medical and dental clinics for countries ranging from Chile to Indonesia. Nonetheless the buyers stayed away in droves. Only one CL-215

Spray plane CF-TXE (s/n 1012) at Rimouski ready to fight the spruce budworm plague in Quebec forests along the south shore. Note its underwing spray bar. In the background are Avenger fire bombers. The advent of the CL-215 hastened the decline of these once-popular forestry workhorses, the last of which operated in New Brunswick in 1994. (CL C7286-15)

was delivered (to France) in 1975. This brought the total delivered during the General Dynamics era to 41 aircraft.

CL-215 activity in 1976 concentrated on the production of 15 Series III aircraft and the delivery of four Series IIs: one to France and three to Greece.

The Greek aircraft were operated by the Royal Hellenic Air Force which, like all military services, occasionally used inexperienced personnel as fill-ins. Such was the case at the Elefsis Air Base in January 1977. After washing down CL-215 s/n 1015 with gasoline, two ground crew slipped into the cabin for a quiet smoke, with the inevitable explosive result. Canadair sent "Cherry" Cherrington to assess the damage. He found that, although severely damaged, the aircraft was repairable. The damaged portion of the fuselage extending from the back of the wing to the fin would need to be removed and a new piece inserted.

Unfortunately, none of the repair crew spoke English and Cherry could not speak Greek. The air force officer detailed as translator never showed up, so Cherry used sign language and pencilled markings to show which rivets to drill out, which parts to remove and where to cut. The aircraft which resulted had a Series I front and a Series III rear, yet the pilots reported it flew better after the explosion than before. An appreciative air force general presented Cherry with a plaque which served as a constant reminder of the nightmares he suffered that some morning he would arrive on the job to find that, during the night, the tail section had slipped off its supports! During 1977, production continued on a batch of 15 Series III aircraft. Three Series IIs were delivered: two to Greece and one to Manitoba (its first). In 1978, two CL-215s went to Greece and two to Thailand.

Thailand

The two aircraft the Thai Navy received in 1978 were Series III maritime patrol and search and rescue versions, with radar, additional radio equipment, navigator and flight engineer stations, two observer positions, a small galley and a toilet.

Yves Mahaut and Doug Morrison ferried both aircraft to Thailand. On the first training flight with a Thai pilot, Mahaut spotted a fire burning near the airport and extinguished it with one drop. The Thais were impressed.

Jack Forbes, who spent several years in Thailand as a field service representative, experienced one of those incidents that occasionally haunt field service reps (FSRs). It

began with being routed out of bed at midnight by gun-toting soldiers who insisted he come immediately "for lost airplane." It transpired that the most senior Navy pilot had run out of fuel during a naval exercise and had landed, "dead stick," in the sea despite strong winds and high seas. Now the Navy wanted Forbes to get the aircraft back to base.

Forbes was taken to the flagship where the admiral told him that if he could not salvage the aircraft quickly it would be sunk, as it was drifting towards Cambodian waters. The Navy put Forbes, plus fuel drums, pumps and hoses into an inflatable Zodiac then headed through heavy seas to the aircraft.

Realizing it would be impossible to refuel the aircraft where it was, Forbes had it towed 30 kms (18 mi.) to the lee of an island. There it was refuelled at the cost of one broken arm suffered by a sailor when the fuel drums broke free. The aircraft then flew to base with Forbes as passenger. He had no intention of returning to the destroyer in the Zodiac.

The Navy wasn't sure what to do with their pilot—punish him for running out of fuel or give him a medal for landing safely under appalling conditions. The decision must have been favorable for, when this was written, he was Admiral of the Fleet.

Phos-Chek System

During a 1975 CL-215 tour of U.S. Forest Service and state firefighting bases in the western United States, regional firefighters presented such a strong argument in

The Thais sign for two CL-215 aircraft as Bob Wohl (vice-president administration) and Norm Forget (contract administrator) look on. (CL C10629)

C-GUKM at Kinston, North Carolina, in 1977. The Phos-Chek bins stand ready to be installed. Then, a group photo of the Canadair people involved in the project: Paul Sagala (photography), Ian McDonald (co-pilot), Ron Pickler (marketing), Yves Mahaut (pilot), Billy Moore (North Carolina forest service pilot), Garth Dingman (photography), Stan Newlove, Harvey Fournier and Roger Demers (all from maintenance), and Saul Bernstein (design). (CL 24302-22)

favor of long-term chemical retardants that Canadair decided to design a retardant-mixing system for the CL-215. In co-operation with Monsanto Chemical, manufacturer of Phos-Chek retardant, a team led by Saul Bernstein devised a method of mixing the heavy retardant powder with incoming water during scooping.

The system used an eductor, or venturi-type mixer, which functioned like a paint spray gun. The retardant chemical was carried in 10 aluminum canisters dubbed "Phos-bins." Each group of five bins was connected to a mixer. During scooping, the inrushing water flowed through the eductor manifold, sucking up and mixing the chemical as it went and depositing the mix in the water tanks. The system held sufficient chemical for five separate drops.

Tests conducted in North Carolina in February 1977 proved the system, but a lack of funds prevented further development. Subsequently Bernstein, Ross Richardson and Harry Oakes were awarded certificates and cash awards under the company's inventions and patents program for their contributions to the design of the system.

Pilot Yves Mahaut recalled an incident that occurred during the tests. While controlling one drop, the North Carolina forestry pilot got his signals crossed and directed Mahaut to drop on a spot occupied by Canadair photographer, Paul Sagala. With true photographer's dedication, Sagala never moved. As a result he got classic footage of a direct hit, and a thorough drenching with sticky red mud.

China

In September 1978, president Fred Kearns visited China with a delegation of Montreal businessmen. He proposed Chinese participation in the development of a turboprop water bomber. The Chinese showed interest, so Kearns sent John Nicas and John Reid of marketing, Henry Kruszynsky of contract estimating and Pat Campbell of outside production to Harbin, Shenyang and Xian to work out the details. Following this visit, the Chinese told Kearns they were interested in the CL-215 but did not have the money for a development program. Instead, Kearns offered them contracts to produce CL-215 components with no offsetting obligation. The Chinese were happy to accept. From 1981, when the first agreement was signed, to the time of writing, China produced all CL-215 and (later) CL-415 doors, hatches, float pylons and ailerons. Their prices were good and their quality excellent. Campbell recalled that Kearns said at the time: "This is a long-term contract, but it will bear no fruit in my lifetime." Kearns's gesture paid off handsomely, for China subsequently bought five Challenger jets, three in Kearns' lifetime.

A reverse Challenger/CL-215 swap occurred in April 1983 when Ontario's premier, Bill Davis, was forced by public and political pressure to exchange the province's Challenger for two CL-215 aircraft.

Venezuela

Deliveries picked up in 1979 with seven CL-215s going to Spain, two to Greece and two to Venezuela. Production began on a batch of 15 Series IV aircraft. Marketing was now being handled by Bob Auer, John Bisson, James Clarkson, Curt Fincham and Dave Wood, all reporting to vice-president John Nicas. Production was directed by Sid Gleadhall, reporting to vice-president, manufacturing, Vince Ambrico.

The first of the only two transport versions of the CL-215 left Cartierville on February 27, 1979, on delivery to the Ferrominera Orinoco mining company of Venezuela. They were configured for up to 26 passengers, and ferried crews to and from a mammoth dredge working a channel used by large ore-carriers negotiating a 240-km (150-mi.) stretch of the Orinoco River. These amphibians could be converted rapidly whenever needed to fight fires in the pine plantations north of the Orinoco.

Canadair's demonstrator, s/n 1049, was also in Venezuela in 1979. On one occasion pilots Yves Mahaut and Larry Roluf responded to a call to fight a fire in a paint store in the centre of Caracas. Mahaut described the operation in these words: "To get to the fire meant flying around and among the skyscrapers. As we came in for the first drop, I could see the streets surrounding the fire were crowded with spectators so I dropped a little high and drenched them. When we came in for the second drop the area was clear. It's a good job it was, because when the drop hit the fire, the building collapsed."

Back to the United States

On September 16, 1979, Canadair's demonstrator and a leased Quebec aircraft were in California at the invitation of Los Angeles legislator Bob Ronka, when fires broke out in Laurel Canyon, a community of expensive homes in rolling hills northwest of the city. The LA fire department quickly dispatched both aircraft to the fire. The CL-215 knocked down fire after fire, saving homes, opening paths to allow fire equipment to get into the area, and cooling hot spots so firemen could get in and extinguish them. Local residents and the media were full of praise for the CL-215 and clamored for the city to buy some.

Ronka succeeded in getting a proposition added to the ballot at the time of the presidential election. It called for a $50 per household, per year, addition to

the municipal tax for a period of two years to cover the cost of two aircraft. The approval of two-thirds of the voters was needed for acceptance. But with the fires out and the sense of urgency gone, only 58 per cent voted in favor, so the proposition was defeated.

More Action, More Travel

Only one CL-215 was delivered in 1980, the first Series IV, which went to Manitoba. In the summer of 1980 two Quebec CL-215 aircraft fought a fire in a shopping centre at Chicoutimi, Quebec, on a bright Sunday morning. A sharp drop in the town's water pressure forced the fire brigade to ask the air service for help. After some delay clarifying insurance liability, the water bombers were dispatched. In 1.5 hours, they made 47 drops, breaking through the roof and extinguishing the fire which was advancing in the space above the ceilings.

In January 1981, Mahaut, Roluf, co-pilot Mike Ross, mechanics Maurice Langlois and Jose Ribiero, and FSR Jack Forbes spent four months on a marketing tour in Argentina. Later that year the Quebec government sent two aircraft to help fight fires in Argentina, but they made a hurried exit when the Falkland Islands War began. No sale resulted from either effort, but two aircraft were delivered to Yugoslavia during the year.

The first two of five water bombers delivered during 1982 went to Italy. The first set a different kind of record when, on July 6, it went into action within two hours of arriving in Italy. Over the following three weeks it flew more than 76 hours and helped control 30 fires. Canadair CL-215 instructor pilot Bill Casselman spent 26 months in Italy training pilots. He was supported, from time to time, by pilots Bob Galac, Bill Hind, Michael Holliday, Yves Mahaut and Michel Ross; contract administrator Norm Forget; mechanics Alain Sylvestre, Jose Ribiero and Frank Pistilli; and FSR Claude Côté.

Federal/Provincial Fleet

On July 21, 1983, the federal government announced it had negotiated with several provinces to purchase jointly 29 water bombers: 12 by the provinces and 17 by Canada. Alberta, Newfoundland, Quebec and Saskatchewan each agreed to buy two,

I think we went a little too low on that last drop.

(Facing page) With scenic Quebec as a backdrop, CL-215 No. 25 of Quebec's fleet scoops water from the St. Lawrence during a demonstration. In the second photo, action on the front line in Hollywood Hills, California, in 1979. Mahaut plasters a raging brushfire. (CL C9233, C17152)

A number of radio-controlled scale models of the CL-215 have also taken to the skies. (CL)

(Right) Canadair's "flying fire truck" has proven its value controlling special fires. In the top photo, CF-TUU attacks the supermarket fire in Chicoutimi in 1980; then, another dramatic scene as Ontario's Tanker No. 262 drops a load on the famous Hagersville tire fire in 1990. (CL)

A nice close-up as a CL-215 water bomber taxis for takeoff. (CL C33274)

Manitoba one and Ontario three. Ottawa would match the provinces' purchases on a one-to-one basis except for Ontario. Since Ontario had recently bought two, Ottawa would contribute four to Ontario's three. The federal government also bought two each for the Northwest Territories and the Yukon. Basic price per aircraft was $6.1 million. Marketing director Larry Robillard deserved much of the credit for this sale.

The program got off to an unhappy start. On September 29, 1983, a CL-215 crashed following the ceremony marking the go-ahead. Yves Mahaut and Michael Holliday, flying s/n 1078, had given an impressive demonstration of the manoeuvrability of the CL-215 and

Canadair president Gil Bennett, Ontario Minister of Natural Resources Vince Kerrio, and federal Minister of State for Transport Suzanne Blais-Grenier at the delivery of the first federal-provincial CL-215, October 10, 1985. (CL C33674-1)

were starting a single-engine low-level pass when they experienced a propeller overspeed on the live engine. Unable to correct this or restart the feathered engine in time, they crashed near the boundary of Dorval airport. The co-pilot regained consciousness to find himself hanging almost upside down. Crawling from the cockpit, he noticed fire in the aft fuselage. Ignoring the possibility of an explosion, he re-entered the cockpit to release Mahaut who was hanging unconscious in his harness. In doing so, Holliday fell backwards, injuring himself.

Meanwhile, a local truck driver, Jocelyn Hamelin, realizing an accident was imminent, climbed a fence and ran to where he thought the aircraft would crash. He arrived only moments after the impact. Overcoming his fear of fire, he ran forward and helped Holliday pull Mahaut clear. Both pilots recovered quickly from their injuries. Holliday and Hamelin were subsequently awarded Canada's Medal of Bravery. The diminutive Hamelin was unable to explain what force propelled him over that 2.5-m (8-ft.) fence.

A 10-year Record

A water-bombing record that still stands was set on July 14, 1983, when Yugoslav Army pilot Maj. Radovan Katanic and co-pilot Capt. Kujundjic made 225 drops in a single day on fires on the island of Hvar. Dropping 1,200 tonnes of water in 11 hours 25 minutes, they helped control the fires and save the village of Cara.

By the end of 1986, CL-215 deliveries totalled 92: 19 to Spain; 15 each to France, Quebec and Greece; six to Ontario; five to Yugoslavia; four each to Italy and Manitoba; two each to Thailand, Venezuela, Alberta and Northwest Territories and one to the Yukon. Market surveys and technical studies of a proposed turboprop version of the CL-215 were complete, and a go-ahead decision from Bombardier was awaited.

The Northwest Territories and Manitoba took part in the federal-provincial deal for water bombers. Here the NWT's C-GCSX taxies at Yellowknife, and Manitoba's C-GUMW is seen at Winnipeg. (Larry Milberry)

The Manitoba aircraft at Chico Airport, California, fall 1982, following hydraulic failure and a wheels-up landing. Ted Leeder was the pilot. (John Reid)

One of the Ontario Ministry of Natural Resources's CL-215s. (CL)

Two views of a water bomber at work on a roaring fire in Spain. (CL)

CL-215 production at the height of activity in the mid-1970s. Aircraft 1044, seen in the middle, went to Manitoba as C-GMAF. (CL C7580)

(Left) Thai and Venezuelan water bombers. These aircraft were purchased not as fire fighters but mainly for search and rescue (Thai) and air transport (Venezuela). (CL)

Baker Denis Lacourse puts the finishing touches to a commemorative cake that sports the flags of 16 CL-215 operators. (CL C33634)

CHAPTER NINE

MISSILES AND DRONES

CL-89 AND OTHER PROJECTS

Velvet Glove

Canadair's involvement with missiles and surveillance systems began with the Velvet Glove program.

In 1951, the Canadian Armament Research and Development Establishment (CARDE), a Defence Research Board (DRB) laboratory at Valcartier, Quebec, was developing the Velvet Glove missile. The goal was to design and develop an air-to-air guided missile for the CF-100 all-weather fighter, and establish a nucleus of expertise for future industrial expansion in this field.

The Velvet Glove was powered by a solid rocket motor and equipped with a semi-active radar homing device. The radar transmitter was carried in the aircraft and the receiver in the missile, so the pilot had to keep the transmitter aimed at the target while the missile was in flight. The missile was about 3 m (10 ft.) long and weighed about 200 kg (500 lb.).

CARDE's technical team was led by Dr. Gerald Bull who was featured on the cover of *Life* magazine and hailed as "a boy genius." Bull later achieved international notoriety as the suspected designer of Iraq's Doomsday Gun in the late 1980s. CARDE had neither the staff nor the knowledge of the practical aspects of manufacturing to build a missile, so the DRB asked Canadair to help by

productionizing drawings, building parts and designing and producing the missile control system.

In the belief that guided missiles would play an increasingly important role in Canadian defence, Canadair established a Special Weapons Engineering Department with Mel Espy as section chief and Peter Bellinger, Len Box, Jack Burnside, Larry Clifford, Merv Devine, Ralph Hayward, Herb Miller, George Parker and Jack Rawlins. In early 1954, Espy reported to chief development engineer Dick Richmond. The company committed a capital expenditure of some $4.5 million for missile equipment and facilities, and began to recruit scientific and engineering personnel.

These new employees, together with those hired for the

A Velvet Glove fitted to the launch pylon of a Sabre. (CL T1250)

Activity in the P4 missile lab. A Velvet Glove tail section is on the stand to the right. (CL P4-1217)

Britannia/Argus conversion program, were among the first of several hundred Canadair would bring to Canada over the next few years. Most came from the United Kingdom, others from other European countries. Some used their Canadair jobs as a way of gaining entry to the United States. Unable to get clearance to enter the States directly, they stayed in Canada only long enough to obtain U.S. entry permits. At one point, the turnover of technical personnel at Canadair reached two per cent per month. Nevertheless, many of the immigrants remained at Canadair for long periods, some until they retired.

Canadair became more heavily involved in the Velvet Glove program and, when problems arose in the management of the program, DRB asked the company to assume control of the project. Richmond gave the job to Bob Raven.

Sections of the Velvet Glove–particularly the hydraulic control system–were designed, assembled and ground-tested in a special weapons manufacturing facility in Plant 4, the former Canadian Car & Foundry facility (near the corner of Henri Bourassa and Marcel Laurin boulevards) which Canadair had acquired in the spring of 1952.

The whole Velvet Glove program was carried out under a heavy security blanket. The first view any outsider had of the missile was when Bill Longhurst flew a Sabre with the Velvet Glove mounted under its wing. The installation was carried out behind a wall in B106. When all was ready, the wall was removed and the aircraft taxied out

Dick Richmond, who headed Canadair's missile activities. (CL S1158)

with the missile wrapped up to hide its shape. Longhurst taxied quickly to the runway, the missile's covering was removed and the Sabre took off, only to return almost immediately, minus the missile. Insufficient slack had been left in the cable to the jettison release, so when the Sabre's wings flexed after takeoff, the missile was jettisoned (and never found).

A total of 131 Velvet Gloves had been completed when the program was terminated in 1956 due to lack of support from the RCAF. Meanwhile, the program had been overtaken by U.S. missiles including the Sparrow II and Sparrow III. The Velvet Glove was nonetheless beneficial to Canadair. It helped establish a missile test facility, obtain sophisticated test equipment and recruit an expert team, which was kept intact while the Canadian government negotiated an agreement with the U.S. regarding the Sparrow II.

Sparrow II

In March 1958, the Canadian government contracted with Canadair, in association with Douglas Aircraft and Bendix Aviation, to supply 900 Sparrow II Mark 1 air-to-air missiles. Canadair was co-ordinating contractor with overall responsibility for the manufacture, assembly and flight test of the missile.

Intended to provide the long range clout for the Avro Arrow, the Sparrow II, with its solid rocket launcher, was 3.76 m (12 ft. 4 in.) long, 20 cm (8 in.) in diameter and weighed 184 kg (406 lb.). It had a fully active radar guidance system which combined both transmitter and receiver in the missile and made it unnecessary for a pilot to keep his aircraft aimed at the target.

In preparation for what promised to be a rewarding program, Canadair built new offices, a computer facility and an environmental test facility, complete with a centrifuge, at Plant 4. It also set up a semi-autonomous Missiles and Systems Division under Dick Richmond, with Bob Raven as manager of engineering, Bob Higman director of manufacturing, Jim Egbert manager, manufacturing engineering and Peter Grier in contract administration. The inclusion of the word "Systems" in the title was in recognition of the fact that future programs would invariably involve the development of a system rather than a single piece of equipment.

The centrifuge was used to check components exposed to heavy gravity loads by spinning them at high speed on the end of a 4.5-m (15-ft.) arm in a specially reinforced pit. On a very early test run, a piece of depleted uranium about the size of a shoebox was being taken up to speed when the container distorted, allowing the load to slip out, whereupon it ricocheted off the pit wall, and passed through the wall of the building and the wall of

A Sparrow II connected for telemetry tests in P4. (CL P4-1453)

the adjoining manufacturing building before coming to rest, fortunately without hurting anyone.

Dick Richmond sent about 20 engineers to the Douglas, Santa Monica, and Bendix plants in California for on-the-job training. He also sent along Len Box to supervise the job and ensure that the thousands of drawings and technical data were shipped to Canada on time. Another 20 engineers went to the General Dynamics missile plant at Pomona, California, for missile training.

In 1957, shortly after Canadian participation in the Sparrow II program began, the U.S. Navy withdrew support for the Sparrow II when it cancelled its new Douglas F5D-1 Skylancer that was to carry it. The Navy, however, let the RCAF and Canadair continue using its test range at Point Mugu, California.

In the latter part of 1958, there were indications that the Arrow program was under critical review by Diefenbaker's conservative government. As any adverse decision was bound to affect the Sparrow program, Geoff Notman sent vice-president manufacturing Dean Stowell and Richmond to Boeing to look for work on the Bomarc ground-to-air missile which Canada was considering acquiring. While they were at Boeing, the Canadian government cancelled the Sparrow program. Raven said: "It's a good job Richmond was on the West Coast when the program was cancelled or there'd have been blood on the government's conference room floor." To that point, Canadair had manufactured only two Sparrow vehicles and modified five others, manufactured by Douglas. The

Sparrow cancellation had two effects: it left Canadair with 250 spare engineers and technicians, and it left some government funds unspent.

While still on the West Coast, Stowell and Richmond were able to persuade Boeing to rent a number of spare Canadair engineers and technicians to work, at so much an hour, on the Bomarc missile. Eventually 180 of them were placed for a period of 12 months, and they and their families travelled to Seattle, just before Christmas 1958, in two special trains. The arrangement turned out to be beneficial to all parties and many of the people who went west never returned to Montreal.

As for the unused funds, Ottawa allowed Canadair to use some of them to pursue a number of studies aimed at identifying new product lines of interest to the Canadian military. This was in appreciation of how Canadair had saved so many jobs by "renting" employees to Boeing. One of the studies was a battlefield surveillance program for the Canadian Army—a program that eventually led to development of the CL-89.

Bomarc Wings and Valves

In addition to finding work for spare personnel, Stowell and Richmond obtained some manufacturing work on the Bomarc. Between 1959 and 1962, Canadair produced 550 sets of Bomarc wings and a quantity of valves for the ground system. This was the first of several important subcontracts Boeing would award Canadair over the next 30 years.

The first Bomarc wing ready for shipping to Boeing on March 6, 1959. Looking on are Bob Higman, Raymond O'Hurley (Minister of Defence Production), Curt Fincham, Dean Stowell, Dick Richmond and Ken Ebel. The Bomarc was Canadair's first contract with Boeing. (CL 16885)

"Well, back to the drawing board, John."

This cartoon by the renowned Duncan Macpherson showed how John Diefenbaker and George Pearkes killed the Avro Arrow then replaced it with a supposed dud—the Bomarc. This simplified reality, but made for entertaining material on the editorial page. (via D. Follett)

After its tour in NORAD, this Bomarc "B" escaped being shot down as a target drone (the fate of most Bomarcs). It was restored for display at CFB Edmonton. In the background is the prototype Canadair Sabre. (Larry Milberry)

The Bomarc equipped two Canadian squadrons, No. 446 at North Bay, Ontario and No. 447 at La Macaza, Quebec. They were disbanded in September 1972. Their Bomarcs were returned to the United States to be used as target drones.

Drone Surveillance System

As aircraft production continued dwindling, management searched for new areas of diversification. Two which produced significant long-term benefits from both a financial and stability enhancement point of view were surveillance systems and component subcontracts. Both were supported and encouraged by General Dynamics.

Surveillance system activities began with the cancellation of the Sparrow II in early 1959, and the resulting need to find a program to occupy spare engineers. A systems engineering team produced a concept for a robot dispatch carrier, a rocket-launched missile-like vehicle (CL-85), about the size of the Sparrow II, to carry messages and maps across a nuclear battlefield. Convair was working on a similar concept called the Lobber.

One concept had a spike on its nose—a feature that evoked considerable amusement when the brainstormers contemplated what might happen if the spike struck a

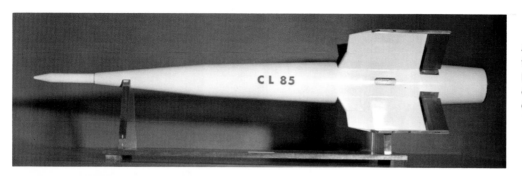

A model of the CL-85 as proposed to the Canadian army in 1959. From the CL-85 discussion process evolved the concept for the CL-89. (CL 85-17766)

Doug Follett (program manager CL-89), Air Chief Marshal Frank R. Millar (RCAF chief of the air staff), Joe MacBrien (CL-89 marketing manager) and Major Eric Illot (Canadian army CL-89 project office) in a photo from about 1965. Follett is holding a CL-89 distance-measuring turbine. (CL 48874)

rock on landing. In fact, Gordon Lloyd recalls the team tried dropping a test vehicle onto a 45-gallon drum of frozen muskeg. The spike bent.

The team members took their idea to DND headquarters in Ottawa and showed it to two Canadian Army majors, Hal Roche and Denny Badenoch, members of a NATO working group concerned with battlefield surveillance. The majors turned it down but said the army would be interested in a vehicle which could photograph a 30-km (20 mi.) strip of the front line and return within 30 minutes. Their position according to Raven was, "Diefenbaker has given us 'Honest John' [an artillery missile], now we have to find the target."

Joe MacBrien had recently joined the special weapons department as marketing manager after lengthy service with the Royal Canadian Navy. From numerous military staff college courses, he knew it was a waste of time trying to sell anything to the military unless the military had an operational requirement. So he, Roche and Badenoch wrote an operational requirement for an unmanned airborne surveillance system.

John Kerr, an engineer from the advanced design de-

partment, took the requirement and conceived a drone configuration, designated CL-89, based on studies he had done on target drones for Sparrow missile testing. One of these, the CL-36, was about the right size, but was based on a ramjet engine and Kerr needed a sustainer engine. By a stroke of good fortune, he saw an advertisement in a magazine for a small gas turbine engine manufactured by Williams Research in Detroit, Michigan. Raven and Kerr visited Williams and found that the company had only been in business for a year and its small staff had no idea what a drone was. The engine had potential but Sam Williams wanted over $10,000 to develop a 125-pound thrust version. Raven told him he was authorized to spend a maximum of $10,000 so they settled for $9,990. Thus Williams got its first-ever contract. Williams International eventually became one of the largest private suppliers to the U.S. government.

In May 1959, Dick Richmond became a vice-president but he left Canadair the following year for Pratt & Whitney Canada. The Missiles and Systems Division was dissolved and the direction of the surveillance system program reverted to engineering under vice-president Ed Higgins. CL-89 development became the responsibility of Doug Follett as program manager. Harry Halton and Len Box were assistant program managers. Jim Egbert was director, manufacturing; Peter Grier was director, sales and administration; Tommy Whitton was superintendent, manufacturing; Roy Hall was in purchasing and materiel control; and Ken Rowley was in contract administration. Gordon Lloyd ran the test labs, Hugh Cavanagh was in charge of test planning and Fred Agnew conducted some of the tests. Bob Raven continued as director of engineering for two years; then he too moved to Pratt & Whitney.

The Sponsors

In June 1963, the governments of Canada and Britain agreed to jointly sponsor the design, development, test

A CL-89 ready for launch from its stand at the US Army test site near Yuma. Fred Forsyth is on the right. Then, two views of drone recovery. The air bag shock absorbers automatically deflate on touchdown. (CL48407, C5583, '317)

and evaluation of the CL-89 medium range drone system. They were joined later by West Germany. The United States was invited to participate but declined. The U.S. Army, however, offered the use of its test facilities at Yuma, Arizona, free of charge.

Designed for army division deployment, the CL-89 system's key component was a small drone 2.4 m (8 ft.) long and 33 cm (13 in.) in diameter that initially carried an optical sensor—a camera capable of photographing from horizon to horizon. Later in the program the camera could be replaced by an infrared linescan sensor, able to photograph at night and through haze.

Fired by a rocket booster from a truck-mounted launcher, the drone flew a preprogrammed course, taking photographs or infrared images at preset intervals. Its mission completed, it homed to a radio beacon and was lowered to the ground by parachute. Large landing bags inflated automatically during descent to prevent it from being damaged on impact. Each drone was designed to survive 10 flights with only unit-level repair. It was a difficult target for the enemy. It flew at high subsonic speed,

its noise and heat emissions were low, and its flight was preprogrammed and could not be jammed. Not only was it hard to see, it was very hard to shoot down.

Gerry Barabé and his experimental shops team built 18 prototype drones. The first made its maiden flight at Yuma in March 1964, but did not get very far. An electrical wiring fault commanded the drone to elevate and launch simultaneously and it shot off almost horizontally and flew into the ground. This signalled the beginning of a long, often frustrating period of experimentation on this new technology. Although initial plans had assumed the use of off-the-shelf system components, it soon became apparent that Canadair was pushing the state of the art in almost every element.

The three customers established a joint program office

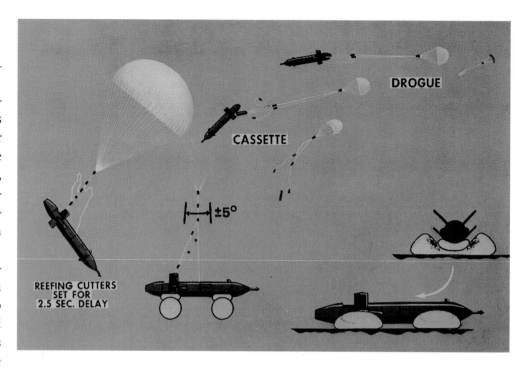

Schematic illustrating the CL-89 parachute/air bag recovery system. (CL 56827)

in Ottawa, staffed by contractor and technical officers who inundated Canadair with hundreds of phone calls and dozens of letters, not to mention loads of visits and demands for meetings all over the place in each of the three countries.

Len Box especially remembered one Canadian major who would dream up the most peculiar technical questions which took hours of work to answer. On one occasion, recalled Box, he wrote concerning the availability of brine for a brine-activated drone battery. "How do you envisage the logistics of brine supply, particularly in cold weather," he asked. "Can they be activated by fresh water or, in an emergency, by urine?" The reply, prepared by avionics section chief Mike Stevenson, said in part, "Urine should be excellent because of the dissolved salts. In fact, this might be the answer to the logistics problem since it is generally on tap, temperature-controlled at 98°F, at minimal cost, and provides the user with a unique opportunity to comment in a practical manner."

The British became the real backers of the program.

It is a practice in the British Army to ensure that systems and equipment are "soldier proof." Major C.S.H. (Cliff) Frater set up a maintenance advisory group which reviewed every item from the aspect of how it affects the soldier and provided invaluable help to the Canadair engineers.

After several successive test flight failures, Ed Higgins asked General Dynamics for help. GD sent an engineering team led by George Schwab of the Convair astronautics di-

A dramatic scene as a CL-89 takes flight. The CL-89, which entered service in 1972, proved valuable during the Gulf War, where it served with the British Army. Superb reconnaissance photos were obtained for the army's 32nd Heavy Artillery Regiment. About 500 CL-89s served with Britain, France, Germany and Italy into the mid-1990s. (CL C9421)

vision, San Diego, and Irv Buckler from the Pomona missiles division. Schwab introduced the science of reliability engineering into Canadair. Buckler was a systems engineer. With their help, Canadair's engineers got the program back on the rails. Even so, Fred Kearns felt compelled to defend the program strenuously before GD's board and chief executives, some of whom would have preferred to see the missiles and systems engineering department disappear altogether and Canadair to buy technology from GD with Canadian government funding.

In 1966, Follett left to become CL-215 program manager and Box took his place as CL-89 program manager. Dave Race became CL-89 project engineer for a time, and then left to join CAE where he eventually became president. Several others joined the program including Tony Ferrey, Dave Hanchet, Derek Higton and Herb Mahaffey. Production was formalized under Ray Campbell. Brooks De Gere was responsible for procurement and Ken Rowley and Bill Stephen for contract administration.

The first complete CL-89 system was delivered to West Germany in 1969, the same year that John Kerr received a Canadair award for engineering achievement for his contributions to the CL-89 design concept.

During the early 1970s, marketing made strenuous efforts to sell the CL-89 throughout NATO. Following a 1971 demonstration in Sardinia, Italy bought and assembled components for two systems. France later became the fourth CL-89 customer by buying two complete and one reserve system.

The CL-89 entered service with the West German army in 1972. The first unmanned surveillance system to enter service with NATO, it established Canadair as a world leader in such technology. NATO designated the CL-89 the AN/USD-501.

Black Brant Research Rocket
Between 1962 and 1964, CARDE contracted with Canadair for work on the Black Brant IIa high altitude research rocket vehicle. This included carrying out analyses of configuration, performance and aerodynamic heating as well as the design and manufacture of nose cone and stabilizer assemblies. The Black Brant's role was to carry 90 kg (200 lb.) of measuring equipment to a height of 190 km (120 mi.) to scan the earth's horizon and determine the shape of the infrared horizon gradient in several spectral bands. Canadair activities were under the direction of Dr. Hans Luckert.

A Black Brant departs the rocket range at Churchill, Manitoba. A scientific research vehicle, the Black Brant was developed for upper atmosphere research by Bristol of Winnipeg in conjunction with the Canadian Armament and Research Development Establishment at Valcartier, Quebec. In 1960 Canadair delivered its first 15 sets of Black Brant components—nose cones, forward bodies and fins. Also in this era, Canadair manufactured 506 tailcones for the Raytheon Hawk surface to air anti-aircraft missile. (Inset) Dr. Hans Luckert, who worked on several of Canadair's research projects, including the Black Brant. He had worked on jet aircraft with the Arado company in Germany during the war. He came to Canada in 1952 and was hired by Canadair as a theoretical aerodynamicist. (CL 35281, 35048)

CHAPTER TEN

SUB- CONTRACTS AND SPECIAL PRODUCTS

CL-91 AND OTHER PROJECTS

Automatic Mail Sorter

In January 1959, William Hamilton, Canada's new postmaster general, told his friend Geoff Notman that the Post Office had a prototype automatic mail sorter on which it had already spent $3 million, but it was going nowhere. He asked if Canadair could take the prototype and bring it to production standards. Ken Ebel, Dick Richmond and systems engineer Stuart Geddes looked at the sorter and decided it was worth the effort. Project engineer Doug Follett and design chief Ken Cole determined what needed doing and what it would cost. Their estimate was accepted, and a Canadair team, with the help of the inventor whom Canadair hired, undertook the job of productionizing the sorter and designing and manufacturing new coding desks for the operators to use when applying destination codes.

The sorter was 21 m (70 ft.) long. Driven by what Follet described as "the world's biggest bicycle sprocket chain," it could sort letters into 31 destination boxes at a rate of

A test run with the CL-77 letter sorting machine in 1958. It had been developed by other companies, but the Canadian Post Office asked Canadair to perfect it. The sorter entered service in 1961. (CL 25994)

Jim Rollo, André Guyon and Ken Cole were three members of the CL-77 mail sorter team. (CL 25997)

seven letters a second. The team also designed and produced six coding desks. Ian Geddes wrote in the *Canadair News* that, during a test in which undelivered *Reader's Digest* letters were used to simulate the mail, the operators heard a continuous pinging noise. It was the sound of pennies being ejected from the letters and hitting the wall. Geddes claimed to have pocketed $5.97.

The completed system was installed in the downtown Ottawa post office. The Post Office's director of research and development later told Follett that while the development program provided the information the Post Office needed, the high cost of continuing development had persuaded them to modernize using American equipment.

Subcontracts (1950-1975)

In addition to the numerous aircraft design and production programs of the 1950s and 1960s, Canadair undertook several subcontract programs involving primarily the production of major components for other manufacturers. These were frequently won in the face of strong competition from other companies.

Between 1955 and 1958, Canadair produced 99 rear fuselages and 150 radomes for the Grumman CS2F-1 and -2 Tracker anti-submarine aircraft under a subcontract from de Havilland Aircraft of Canada Ltd. Bob Ramsay was in charge of assembly.

During 1956 and 1957, Canadair was engaged in modifying a Boeing B-47 bomber to use as a flying test bed for the Orenda PS-13 Iroquois engine which was to power the Avro Arrow. A team from experimental engineering, under Mike Telford, and including Gord Little, Dermont Gillespie, Joe Merrick and Reg Ringrose designed and

The USAF B-47 (No. 51-2051) arrives at Cartierville on February 16, 1956. W/C C.R. Thompson (left) was commanding officer of 1102 TSD (RCAF technical services detachment) at Canadair. Bud Sager (contracts) is beside him; Orenda test pilot Mike Cooper-Slipper is on the right. Besides fitting the Iroquois and its instrumentation, Canadair strengthened the B-47 by double-skinning the rear fuselage, reinforcing bulkheads, and adding bulkheads and longerons. The B-47 left for Malton on April 15, 1957. (CL F3323)

built the pylon and the nacelle, initially around an Orenda 14 engine, later around a mockup of the Iroquois. They modified the B-47 co-pilot's station to incorporate the controls for the Iroquois; converted the navigator's station into a flight test engineer's station, and installed 900 kg (2,000 lb.) of photo recorders, oscillographs, telemetry equipment and other test gear on a platform in the bomb bay. In addition, they put 3,600 kg (8,000 lb.) of ballast in the nose of the B-47 to counter the weight of the mockup on the right side of the rear fuselage.

In subsequent test flights, the B-47 pilot was able on occasion to shut down his six jet regular engines and fly on the single Iroquois. Later, a turbine failure caused considerable damage to the nacelle and part of the fuselage.

Unit one from the Canadair run of Grumman Tracker rear fuselages, July 14, 1955. (CL F2964)

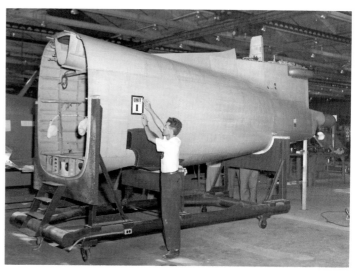

The Iroquois engine died when the Arrow was cancelled in 1959.

Under a contract placed in May 1957 with Republic Aviation Corp. of Farmingdale on Long Island, New York, Canadair produced tooling and wing leading edge skins for the single seat version of the F-105 Thunderchief. In 1962, more tooling was made for the two-seat trainer version.

Between 1960 and 1963, Canadair supplied 201 sets of F-104 wings, aft fuselages and empennages to Lockheed.

The initial Lockheed order was for 106 ship sets; however, Ivan Manley and Bob McCall, who negotiated the deal with Lockheed, managed to acquire all the tooling for the three components from the previous supplier, Vought. As a result, when other F-104 users needed spare components, Lockheed had to get them from Canadair. The program was handled at Canadair by the "four just men"– Ray Campbell, fin; Bob McCall, wing; George Moffatt, aft fuselage, and Réal Lemieux, horizontal stabilizer. They were assisted by Maurice Audet, Don Kennard and Peter

The CL-52 during its year of modifications in P1. The B-47 was chosen as the Iroquois test bed since it met Orenda's criteria: it was fast and high-flying, able to take the heavy engine and its big instrumentation payload, had a reliable record and was available. Canadair's main problem was designing a retractable door to cover the intake to prevent turbine blade windmilling in flight. Beyond the CL-52 the first Argus can be seen taking shape. (CL D11361)

Kukovica. Of the 201 shipsets, 30 went to Holland, 25 to Belgium and 40 to Japan.

In 1961 and 1962, Canadair produced 250 lightweight underfloor cargo containers for the Convair 990 airliner.

Engineering spent over 60,000 manhours through 1962-1964 on the design of portions of the CH-53A helicopter for Sikorsky Aircraft of Bridgeport, Connecticut. Some 20 engineering personnel spent several months at Sikorsky designing the aft fuselage, rotor blade stowage and hinged tail section. Said Ross Richardson: "Sikorsky needed our expertise in heavy airframe design but we learned a lot from them about gearboxes and shafting, which came in very useful when we were working on the CL-84." Meanwhile, in Montreal, another group was busy designing the tooling and manufacturing the tool masters for the tail rotor pylon.

In 1962, the Fort Worth, Texas division of Convair awarded Canadair a contract to design and build the vertical stabilizer and rudder for the F-111 fighter bomber. A Canadair team consisting of George Adams, Freddie Fender, Jim Henry, Ian Lamont and Alec Thompson spent seven months at Fort Worth working on preliminary design of the vertical stabilizer and rudder. Then a design team headed by Joe Knap, and including Eddie Arnold and Bill Sturrock, carried out the production design. Frank Francis was program manager; Steve Barinka was director, assembly; George Moffatt was in charge of fabrication; Tommy Bingham was in machine shop; and George Blandford was in chemical milling.

The vertical stabilizer, or fin, consisted of two outer skins and internal spars. Each skin was made from an aluminum plate 6.4 cm (2.5 in.) thick, tapered by up to 14 stages of chemical milling, then machined to close tolerances in a waffle pattern of approximately 1,000 pockets. The machine that cut out the pockets was devised by Canadair. It used a pantograph principle whereby the routers were guided by a stylus travelling in a pattern mounted above the router table. Later in the program, the skins were routed on newly acquired Cincinnati milling machines. When assembled, the fin required careful sealing as it was also a fuel tank.

Dave Hanchet, who was assistant program manager, described the inside of a completed fin skin as a work of art. "I secretly hoped someone would spoil one so it could be put in a museum," he said.

The rudder consisted of aluminum skins bonded to an

F-111 stabilizers being deburred in January 1967. This component was designed by Canadair and manufactured from a single billet of aluminum. Alec Thompson led the design team (he also designed Canadair's radar dishes used for satellite receiving). Canadair delivered 559 sets of F-111 vertical stabilizers/rudders along with wing pivots and wing carry-through fittings between 1963-77. Later, 46 vertical tail assemblies were produced for Grumman for the EF-111 electronic warfare edition of the F-111 (initial delivery September 11, 1980). (CL 51892)

aluminum honeycomb core and required the development of a method of holding the honeycomb while machining it to shape with "bacon slicer" high-speed cutters.

In 1963, Fort Worth gave Canadair a second F-111 contract, this time to manufacture wing carry-through fittings and wing pivots. The F-111's wings sweep back for high speed flight. The centre section of the wing, which passes through the fuselage, is called the carry-through fitting. It consists of a box structure which holds the wing pivot bearings. The top and bottom of the box came to Canadair as two billets, or forgings, of high-strength D6CA alloy, weighing 3,100 kg (6,800 lb.) each. They required a great deal of machining to produce the desired half-box shape complete with integral stringers. Each completed part weighed only 306 kg (675 lb.) which meant that Canadair had machined away 90 per cent of the original billet. The job of disposing of the tons of scrap fell to Jim Lynch and his special crew of cleaners, and Clive Southall who arranged for scrap transportation and sale.

The wing pivots were machined from D6AC steel on Wilson profilers, 14 of which (two four-spindle and 12 six-spindle) were bought especially for the program. These could machine up to six parts simultaneously from a single pattern.

Grumman had the subcontract to build F-111 fuselage frames. Jim Henry remembered an "interesting interface" between GD's "Texas farmers" and Grumman's "Brooklyn cityslickers," a situation which resulted in Henry and Alec Thompson being cast in the unhappy role of peacemakers.

By the completion of the contract in 1967, Canadair had delivered 559 aircraft sets of fins, rudders and carry-through fittings, as well as a large number of wing pivots, and received a commendation from GD for exceptional performance. The F-111 was a lucrative contract not only for the appreciable profit Canadair eventually made but also for the machines, technology and skills it acquired.

Nuclear Submarine Ball Valves

Between 1962 and 1972, Canadair produced ball valves, hydraulic actuators and ball valve components for the U.S. nuclear submarine program under contract to the Electric Boat division of GD and other manufacturers. Ben Locke recalled: "T.V. Chandler had been assigned to get us some diversification business and he got an opening with Electric Boat. He, Jim Kirkwood and I went to Groton, Connecticut, for our first bidders' conference. Our first order, for about a year's worth of work, was about $4 million and we lost about $1 million on it. It was a nightmare. There were thousands of changes on thousands of valves. At one point, about 30 of us were invited to the board room where Mr. Notman tore a strip of hide off us saying, while he might take a $100,000 loss

Defence Minister Paul Hellyer during a visit to P4 in February 1966, with Mike Doyle of manufacturing on his right. Gordon Stringer of PR is on the far left. They are inspecting a large ball valve for the US Navy nuclear submarine program. CL 47368)

in his stride he couldn't accept a million-dollar loss on such a small contract. He ordered us to claim and collect it, which we did, though it took us a couple of years. At the end of this fiery meeting, Jim Seeley and I were the last to leave and "Uncle" Geoff put his enormous arms around us and told us not to brood as we must be considered pretty important to get personal heck from the president."

Bob Peachy ran the program with key help from Art Agnew, Tommy Bingham, Roger Ramlick, Stan Rose and Cliff Stewart, and they made it profitable, despite the dual problems of meeting Electric Boat's requirements and obtaining suitable castings.

Electric Boat was satisfied with Canadair's performance. When it won a follow-on submarine contract in 1976, it resurrected the ball valve program at Cartierville. Canadair, however, was no longer part of GD. For security reasons, Electric Boat had to set up a separate organization under the title "General Dynamics Manufacturing" in a leased portion of Plant 4. Ball valve production continued there for four more years, using personnel borrowed from Canadair, initially under Conrad Kunze and later under Lynn Farr, before it was moved back to the United States.

Northrop F-5

Over 1,400 boat tails and horizontal stabilizers for the Northrop CF-5, F-5A, F-5B and T-38 were produced between 1965 and the early 1980s under a series of contracts from Northrop and the DND. Don Kennard and Art Drysdale were involved in the manufacture of the boat tails which were the tail end of the fuselage, including the support structure for the vertical and horizontal stabilizers, plus the jet pipes. This was Canadair's first real experience with forming titanium. When Canadair took over the program it received a large number of parts made by Northrop. These could not be made to fit together and Canadair had to make replacements.

The construction of the horizontal stabilizer was unusual. It consisted of a core of aluminum honeycomb sandwiched between a pair of skins, with only a small leading and trailing edge member and a root rib, all bonded in an autoclave. The stabilizer pivoted on a machined forging, dubbed the "shotgun fitting." Canadair also provided the tooling on which Fokker of the Netherlands produced 190 F-5 mid-fuselages under a contract

negotiated by Frank Francis, Ben Locke, Ambrose Mosco and Julius Serafin.

Lockheed C-5A Galaxy

In June 1966, Canadair was awarded a contract by Lockheed-Georgia of Marietta, Georgia, to supply 58 shipsets of ailerons, wing slats, slat tracks, wing leading edges, undercarriage doors and fairings, and aft cargo doors for the C-5A, the largest transport in the USAF. A second contract brought the total to 81 shipsets. Don Dixon was appointed C-5A program manager reporting to Mel Curtis, vice-president, operations. Later in the program, Dixon was replaced by Jock West and two deputy program managers, Bill de Hart and Ed Platt. Andy Throner was director of assembly and Joe Daly, the manager.

Canadair had never handled components as large as those from the C-5A. The landing gear fairings were 18.4 m (60.5 ft.) long, an aft cargo door was 12 m (40 ft.) long and 4.3 m (14 ft.) wide. The fairings and doors were honeycomb-bonded structures which necessitated the purchase of two large autoclaves and the development of methods of manufacturing and handling the huge assemblies. The bonding shop grew almost overnight from a half-dozen people to over 100, and all these required training.

The wing leading edge, slats and ailerons required a great deal of machining, which led to Curtis authorizing the purchase of six large Cincinnati five-axis milling machines, built to Canadair design. These were installed, three per bed, on two 43-m (140-ft.) beds; thus two machines on a bed could be cutting parts while the third was being set up for the next operation.

Canadair also bought electron-beam welding equip-

ment to weld the slat tracks in a vacuum chamber, and gave special training to production personnel in the use of expensive titanium fasteners.

From the start the C-5A contract was plagued by problems, because Lockheed had underestimated the size of the job. A major weight problem during development necessitated a raft of changes to add to those introduced by the USAF, all of which had an effect on Canadair. Canadair's other difficulties stemmed from a poorly defined contract and Lockheed insisting that bids be based on early drawings so incompletely defined they led to inadequate conclusions as to the part/piece count. Lockheed was frequently late with drawing changes, often sending blank drawings in an effort to maintain their schedule. The change traffic was enormous. Tony Natlacen recalled discovering that 100,000 repairs and rejects (R & Rs) had not been posted–that took 40 extra people one year to correct.

In the end, Canadair was forced to claim for millions of dollars compensation for unplanned costs. It took a team consisting of Bill Bishop, Bill Jolliffe, Ben Locke and Ken Rowley 20 months to negotiate a settlement, but they won Canadair an additional $40 million. GD appointed a member of its New York corporate office staff as an advisor to the team. That advisor, Bob Wohl, was destined to play a key role in subsequent Canadair affairs.

The 81 C-5A shipsets were delivered between 1966 and 1972. Canadair later manufactured an additional quantity of slats and ailerons under a spares contract from the USAF. This time there were no problems, thanks to the production team which included Albert Berubé, Dick Faucher, Betty Hamill, Fred Hollylee and Michelle MacLellan.

Maurice Audet of manufacturing had conceived the idea of the five-axis machines and of mounting them on long beds. Walter Allatt had written the specification and negotiated the purchase from Cincinnati Milacron. When the machines arrived, Jolliffe instructed that Allatt be appointed manager of the machine shop, saying, "He bought them, let him install and maintain them." In 1982, Cincinnati Milacron presented Canadair with a plaque commemorating the delivery of its 100th five-axis machine.

Other Subcontract Work
During 1970, Canadair did some tooling and a small amount of manufacturing for the F-14 Tomcat carrier-

based fighter for Grumman of Bethpage, New York. Peter Candfield was project manager.

Between 1971 and 1975, Canadair machined or manufactured 10 sets of wing panels, vertical stabilizers, slat tracks, flap tracks and carriages, and engine pylons for France's short-lived Dassault Mercure 120-passenger airliner. At the same time, seven sets of wing panels were supplied to Dassault for the Falcon 10 business jet.

Don Dixon, then vice-president, manufacturing, signed the contract with Dassault without first consulting GD. As a result, Norm Forget of contract administration and Ben Locke of contract estimating, spent several weeks at GD's headquarters in St. Louis and several more at Dassault in Paris, getting every word, comma and penny approved by GD and Dassault. Jock West was the early program manager with René Royer taking over later. Armand Lavigne and Jim Murphy handled manufacturing.

The Mercure job is remembered for the incredibly close tolerances demanded by Dassault; the requirement to use a particular type of shot-peening equipment called vapor blast which blasted the surface of machined parts with glass beads to resist fatigue cracking; wing planks formed by an oil gear press; and raw material slabs suspected of containing substandard properties which could only be detected by meticulous and time-consuming ultrasonic testing.

Rafe Sherwin, manager, materials and process, and Marcel Henderson, chief inspector, were heavily involved in the raw material problem, one of the reasons Canadair was forced again to claim for unplanned expenses. Don Dixon and Bob Wohl, however, negotiated a satisfactory settlement. The Mercure was considered an engineering success but a marketing failure, and only 10 were built. It represented Dassault's last venture in the commercial airliner business.

In 1972, Canadair received a contract from Nordair to modify two ex-Northwest Airlines Lockheed Electras for ice patrol for Environment Canada. This entailed designing and installing a new interior, nose radome, observation blisters, additional fuselage fuel tanks, infrared linescan equipment, theodolite laser and cameras. Mike Davy led the engineering team, while Bud Kerland led the shop team, Fern Kingsley manufacturing engineering, and John Gilmore liaison engineering.

Neither aircraft was in very good condition; in fact one

was a combination of two cannibalized planes. The electrical wiring was badly deteriorated and required replacing. When completed, however, the aircraft performed well. Operated first by Nordair and later by Canadian Airlines International, they were based at Gander, Newfoundland, and Summerside, Prince Edward Island, in winter and Iqaluit and Resolute Bay, Northwest Territories, in summer. The crew of 10 carried out 3,700-km (2,300-mi.) patrols of the Canadian east coast and the Gulf of St. Lawrence in winter, and Arctic waters in summer. Besides recording water temperature and detecting and measuring icebergs, their equipment could estimate the age and thickness of ice floes to determine if an ice-breaker could get through them. The Electra's presence in the Arctic also helped confirm Canadian sovereignty in the area.

Under a Boeing contract of November 1973, Canadair manufactured 44 fuselage barrel sections for the 747SP airliner. The SP (Special Performance) was an ultra-long-range version of the standard 747. Its fuselage was 14 m (47 ft.) shorter than the standard 747. This required the installation of a 4.6-m (15-ft.) long tapered barrel section immediately forward of the rear door.

The contract was obtained by Conrad Kunze, vice-president, operations. Bob McCall was program manager, Armand Lavigne

was in charge of production and Réal Milaire of quality control.

Early in the program, Canadair developed kid-glove methods of handling and protecting skin material, which had to have a mirror finish. It turned out that most of Boeing's customers wanted this part painted anyway, so the precautions had been unnecessary. Again, Canadair

One of the Electras (CF-NAZ) modified at Canadair for ice patrol. NAZ was wrecked at Summerside, Prince Edward Island in March 1977. Its fuselage was later used in rebuilding ice patrol Electra C-GNDZ. (CL C26020)

(Above) The prototype 747SP is chased on its first flight (July 4, 1975) by Boeing's Canadair F-86. (Boeing)

(Right) Canadair completes Boeing 747SP components. The first SP ("special performance") was rolled out in May 1975. Canadair's involvement lasted from 1973-1985 and included 45 fuselage barrel sections. The SP is the shortest of the 747s but has the longest range—6,900 nm (12,770 km). (CL 22107-3)

had to resort to another claim to regain unplanned costs. In 1985, Canadair supplied one more barrel section to Boeing, bringing the total to 45 units.

Nuclear Projects

In 1953, when it became apparent that Canada would actively develop atomic power for industrial use, Canadair established contact with Atomic Energy of Canada Ltd. (AECL) of Chalk River, Ontario. Between 1955 and 1958, Canadair was involved in three nuclear programs under the direction of Dr. Arthur C. Johnson who had come from AECL.

In August 1955, AECL awarded Canadair a contract to design and build a small, low-cost atomic reactor for research into problems of constructing economical electricity-producing atomic power plants. This "swimming pool" or pool test reactor determined how much reactor fuels absorb neutrons, the agent used to split uranium atoms and produce energy. The first of its kind in Canada, it went into operation at Chalk River on November 29, 1957.

In May 1956, AECL contracted for the design and manufacture of the coils and support structure for a Beta-Ray Spectrometer to measure energy emitted from radioactive sources. The 6,400-kg (14,000-lb.) spectrometer consisted mainly of three pairs of coils, the largest 4.3 m (14 ft.) in diameter. Each coil was an assembly of four sections wound from aluminum strip and mylar tape to fine tolerances. The components were shipped to AECL in November 1957.

In December 1956, the University of Toronto gave Canadair an order for a sub-critical atomic reactor for training purposes. This was a simplified form of reactor which produced a low-level chain reaction that never reached the self-sustaining stage. It was delivered in June 1958.

Canadair Nuclear ceased operations shortly after completion of the reactor because Canadair's activities were overlapping those of a sister GD division, General Atomic of LaJolla, California. Several former Canadair Nuclear personnel, including Johnson, transferred to General Atomic.

Architectural Products (Canarch)

The Architectural Products Division was formed in April 1959 in experimental under chief structures engineer Ben Kaganov, who reported to Tom Harvie, vice-president, programs. Its purpose was to provide design, engineering

and manufacturing service for the construction industry. Its main product was its curtain wall.

Canadair had been pressured to get involved with the curtain wall by an architectural engineer named Joe Wanko of Giffels & Associates. He was convinced Canadair could design systems suitable for Canadian winters and had presented a good case to management.

In curtain wall construction the outer surface of a building consists of panels, approximately 1.2 m high by 1.4 m wide (4 ft. x 4.5 ft.), made of aluminum, steel and glass. Hung on the basic steel and concrete structure like a curtain, the panels transfer wind and weather loads to the structure.

Tom Harvie was responsible for the division, but the mainspring of the curtain wall program was Dick Noe, whom Ken Ebel had brought in from Ford. Ian Wright was in charge of manufacturing; Chris Perunovich was field superintendent and Pat Campbell was test engineer.

Canadair built and installed a curtain wall panel measuring 4.3 x 6.1 m (14 x 20 ft.) in the wall of Building 401 at Plant 4, and used the blast from a J85 or a Merlin, combined with a water spray, to test the panel's ability to withstand hurricane-force winds and extreme heat.

Curtain walls were used in a number of Montreal buildings including CIL House (later called Maison Royal Trust) at the corner of René Levesque Boulevard and University; Westmount Square; "Le Cartier" apartment building; the Montreal headquarters of the Quebec Provincial Police; and the grandstand at Blue Bonnets race track. Some 4,000 panels were used in the construction of the 34-storey CIL House. Other contracts included a facade for the Aeroquay at Toronto's Malton Airport; a load-bearing structural steel wall for the Laval (Quebec) City Hall, and a number of

Work progresses in early 1967 on Westmount Square, a Canarch project at Greene and St. Catherine streets. Established in 1959, Canarch's main product was the curtain wall—a facing of metal and glass designed for Canadian climate conditions. (CL 51298)

Curtain wall trials in July 1961 at Toronto's new aeroquay. Canadair set up a Merlin engine, whose propeller created a hurricane-force wind. (CL 27477)

components for Montreal's Place Victoria Stock Exchange Tower.

In 1965, the division was reorganized on a more commercial and competitive basis under the name Canarch. Gordon Arnison was the new head, reporting to George Keefer, vice-president, plans.

In 1965, an engineering team led by Longin Arenth designed two types of air traffic control tower cabs–the glassed-in portion of an airport control tower. Thirty-two C-1 (CL-231) cabs and six larger C-2 (CL-233) cabs were supplied to the U.S. FAA in the mid-1960s. Pentagonal-shaped and weighing in the region of 18,000 kg (40,000 lb.), they were generally erected on concrete towers from 15 to 27 m (50 to 90 ft.) in height.

Dick Faucher was the program manager for the control tower projects; Tony Ross was test engineer and Nat Eycken the marketing representative. Faucher recalled that Canadair had 100 days to design, build and test the first cab, to prove it could be assembled in a specified number of hours and withstand high winds. "We didn't make the 100 days," said Faucher, "but we came close. Once we had the first cab installed on a 4-ft. [1.2-m] high section of typical concrete shaft, we backed up an F-86, cranked it up to 100 per cent power and blew all the windows out. The structure held up OK, so after some adjustments to the window opening squareness, we re-glazed and the test was successfully completed."

The cabs were installed at such airports as Chicago's O'Hare; Oklahoma City; San Diego; Jacksonville; West Palm Beach, Florida; and at some U.S. air bases overseas. Canarch field representatives supervised.

Canarch designed and built several small transportable tower cabs. With a

floor area of 6.1 m² (66 sq. ft.) and weighing 2,500 kg (5,600 lb.), they could be carried by a small helicopter and assembled by two people. They were supplied to Canada's Department of Transport for temporary airport air traffic control and to the U.S. Navy for missile-firing-range control.

Bill Gibson took over Canarch briefly in 1967. Then the aircraft manufacturing business picked up, and most Canarch personnel were recalled to their former departments, while the rest went to Canadair Flextrac at Calgary.

Dick Faucher recalled that Montreal's mayor, Jean Drapeau, wanted the city to have a tower to rival the Eiffel Tower in Paris. Around 1965, Arnison, Rod Conyers, Faucher and Andy Nowakowsky met the mayor at the Windsor Hotel in Montreal and were shown a model of a 300-m (1,000-ft.) concrete tower he wanted to build on Île Notre Dame or St. Helen's Island for the city's Expo 67 World's Fair. One entire wall was to be curtain wall. Canarch gave the mayor an assessment of the project, which never developed.

Vehicle Programs – The Rat

In a further attempt at diversification, a Vehicles Division was formed in 1956. Tom Harvie was appointed vice-president, with Ralph Hayward in charge of engineering, Peter Greer administration, Roy Hall procurement and Ken Rowley contract adminstration. Jim Egbert was in charge of production, Tommy Whitton was shop superintendent, Cec McCracken was shop foreman, Mike

A prototype one of the Canadair control towers, then one of the mobile towers on a GMC five-ton truck. (CL 43891, C4288)

Wilhelm and Arthur Nichols handled quality control, and Lou Adamson and Paul Oleskevis sales.

The Vehicle Division's first project was the Rat (Remote Articulated Track), a light vehicle for transporting personnel and equipment over difficult terrain. Amphibious and air-droppable, the two-unit vehicle had a gross weight of 1,100 kg (2,500 lb.) and a payload of 300 kg (600 lb.). It could travel at 30 km/h (20 mph) on packed snow and at 5 km/h (3 mph) in water. A 35-hp Volkswagen engine drove both units through a unique articulating transfer joint designed by Andy Nowakowski. The Rat was produced by experimental under George Robinson. Paddy Burke was project engineer.

A total of 36 Rats was built, six prototype CL-61s and the rest CL-70s. Of these, 24 went to the Canadian Army, two each to the Swedish Army and the New Jersey Mosquito Control Authority, and one each to the Canadian Department of Mines and Resources and the Department of Northern Affairs.

Because its low ground pressure enabled it to operate on relatively thin ice, the U.S. Navy used a Rat in its 1957 Geophysical Year activities in the Antarctic. Field service representative Jack Forbes accompanied the Rat and made a photographic record of it carrying supplies on an 80-km (50-mi.) run between the coast at Wilkes Station and the inland base of operations.

Jack Forbes with one of the CL-70s. Forbes grew up in Montreal's suburb of Verdun. He got his first job at Fairchild in 1938 and stayed there through the war on Bolingbroke and Helldiver bombers. He joined Canadair after the war and spent most of his career (30 years) abroad as a field service rep in places like Germany (F-86), South Africa (F-86), Malaysia (CL-41), Venezuela (VF-5), Antarctica (CL-70), Argentina (CL-215) and Thailand (CL-215). (CL F5076)

Field service rep Ken Hale accompanied a Rat on a marketing tour of Scandinavia. In Oslo, Norway, he demonstrated it at an international ski jumping site. Before television cameras and other observers, Hale drove the Rat up and down the steep landing section of the jump. Then, encouraged by the reaction of the onlookers, he decided to reverse up the slope. At the top of the ramp, the gearshift lever broke and the machine slipped into neutral. Without brakes (they were fitted later) the Rat took off down the slope, scattering the audience in all directions, and disappeared into the forest at about 80 km/h (50 mph). Neither Hale nor the vehicle was damaged.

Dynatrac

Around 1958 the Canadian government decided that if Canadian manufacturers could get involved in U.S. programs while still in the development phase, they would be in a better position to compete with U.S. manufacturers for production programs. The Canadian/American Development Sharing Agreement was established for this purpose. It was under this program that Canadair began work in September 1961 on a Canadian government-funded program to design and develop a new multi-terrain, high mobility tracked vehicle for the U.S. Army. This became the CL-91.

Named the Dynatrac by Canadair and designated the XM-571 by the army, the vehicle consisted of two units connected by an articulation joint which permitted relative displacement of the units up to 30 degrees from the centreline in any plane. (The articulation joint was invented by Ian Thomas and protected by a Canadair-held patent). A single 65-bhp General Motors Corvair air-cooled engine drove both units. It could alternatively operate as a single unit or in a three-unit combination.

The CL-91 could travel at up to 50 km/h (30 mph) over snow, mud and muskeg; and, thanks to its relatively lightweight construction and 20-cm (8-in.) freeboard, it could swim at 3 km/h (2 mph) with a full 900-kg (2,000-lb.) payload. In deep snow, with a full payload, it could tow 12 ski troops or a 1,100-kg (2,400-lb.) toboggan, and negotiate a 60 per cent grade and a 40 per cent side slope.

Initially 10 Dynatracs were built, seven for the U.S. Army and three for Canadair test purposes. The vehicle was tested in August 1962 against 22 other off-road vehicles on the U.S. Army proving grounds at Aberdeen,

The variety of non-aviation products in which Canadair had an interest in the late 1960s. Included are the Snoscoot snow machine, the Fisher all-terrain vehicle (ATV), two CL-91 Dynatracs (with a 105mm gun) and two Nodwell ATVs. (CL C4284)

Maryland, and later in Vietnam, Thailand and Alaska. In every case it came through with flying colors.

Lou Mehl was Canadair's representative at the GD office in Washington. An ex-U.S. Army colonel, he was Canadair's contact man with the U.S. Army. He recalled a marketing trip to Australia with Ralph Hayward, Peter Grier, Ken Rowley and a Canadian government representative. According to Mehl, the Australian army wanted 500 CL-91s but had funds for only 384. Canadair wanted to accept the order for 384 and negotiate for the balance later, but the government representative refused to accept anything less than 500, so the sale was lost.

Continuing demands by the U.S. Army for additional accessories and upscaled performance, delayed development so much that production was stopped after 63 vehicles. The U.S. Army accepted 47, and sent 35 to Vietnam. When Mehl visited Vietnam, he found them hauling garbage. It appears intra-army unit disagreements prevented them from being used for their intended purpose—carrying ammunition to forward artillery positions. Two Dynatracs were sold to the Canadian Army and two to the British Army.

A CL-91 during swimming trials in the old CL-44 water tank at P4, then slogging through mud pulling a trailer and a field gun. This versatile little vehicle was one of Canadair's "also rans"—it never reached production, in spite of interest from several nations. (CL C4175)

The CL-91 was readily air transportable. Here one is being loaded onto an RCAF C-130B. Then, a Dynatrac on trials with the US Army is slung by a CH-47 Chinook helicopter and dropped by parachute from a C-130. (CL 43191, C2543, 40407)

Canadair Flextrac

Despite the failure of the XM-571 program, Canadair decided to design the Dynatrac II. To get its production away from the high overheads and aerospace-quality mentality of the Cartierville plant, it bought a Calgary-based off-road vehicle manufacturer, Flex-Track Equipment Ltd., and some assets of the Tracked Vehicle Division of Robin Nodwell Manufacturing Ltd., also of Calgary. In May 1968, Canadair Flextrac Ltd. was formed with approximately 100 former Flex-Track employees, including their top management personnel, and Canadair people from Cartierville, including Bill Gibson as vice-president.

While the Dynatrac II was still in the design phase, the Alberta oil boom began and the demand for the Flextrac Nodwell (FN) range of off-road vehicles skyrocketed. The Calgary work force increased from 120 to 350, and FN vehicle production jumped from three or four vehicles a month to 25 to 30.

Canadair Flextrac eventually built three prototype Dynatrac IIs. Powered by a Ford 3900-cm³ (240-cu.-in.) engine, it had a standard transmission, and sheet metal body and track shoes instead of the expensive aluminum and balsa body and heavy forged aluminum track shoes of the XM-571. In 1975, the Canadian government funded productionizing of the Dynatrac II, but, although the package was completed, it was never implemented.

In 1970 Bob Peachy replaced Gibson when Canadair Flextrac acquired Universal Go-Trac, a Rolls-Royce subsidiary. In 1972, Len Box took over as vice-president and started engineering on a program to redesign the FN vehicles. However, in 1976 Canadair decided to quit the vehicle business and sold Canadair Flextrac.

Flextracs trundle across Arctic terrain during oil exploration in the 1970s. (Inset) A Flextrac unit rigged for seismic drilling. (CL 5858)

Fisher Vehicle

During 1963 and 1964, the company had a brief relationship with the Fisher Vehicle, a two-seat, all-terrain vehicle powered by a nine-hp one-cylinder, two-cycle Rotax engine. Designed by A. Gordon Fisher, a Montrealer and former employee of the Ford Motor Co., the Fisher carried a 300-kg (600-lb.) payload at up to 19 km/h (12 mph), could negotiate a 50 per cent grade, and could swim. Propelled by two sets of seven balloon-tired wheels, it had a peculiar motion resembling that of a creeping animal. Joe Morley was responsible for marketing the vehicle. Phil Hutchinson and Al Lajoie built two, one of which was sold to the U.S. Army. Mehl recalled that the U.S. Marines thought a larger version would have great potential, but Canadair decided to drop the project.

Buses and Transit Systems

During 1965 and 1966, Canadair produced 50 public transport buses for the City of Montreal under licence from the Flxible Co. of Loudonville, Ohio. Canadair modified the Flxible design to meet the rigors of the Canadian climate by adding more stainless steel and glassfibre-reinforced plastic. The first bus rolled out in November 1965 and all 50 had been delivered by the end

Canadair's board of directors meets in Calgary in Flextrac days: John Duquet, Henry Marx, Frank McGill, Roger Lewis, unknown, Robert Winters, unknown, Charles Rathgeb, Fred Kearns, C. Roy Slemon, Rodgie McLagan, unknown, Geoff Notman. (CL)

A Fisher splashes through marshland, an environment where it was quite at home. (CL C2936)

Let's put it another way –
How many of you guys have worked on aircraft before???

of January 1966 at a price of $34,860 each. Bob Higman was in charge of the program. Norm Holbrook and Joey Wilkinson were responsible for production. Only one Canadair-built bus was known to be in existence in late 1994, at Autobus Verrault, Granby, Quebec.

Canadair's involvement with ground transportation systems began with a 1971 study of guided ground transit systems for the federal government made by Bill McClaren, Wally Remington, Dave Turner and others. In June 1975, Ontario's Urban Transportation Development Corp. (UTDC) needed a Canadian company as prime development contractor for its new Intermediate Capacity Transit System (ICTS). UTDC vice-president and a former Canadair vice-president, Doug Follett, recommended Canadair as the only company able to do the job. On June 20, 1976, Kirk Foley, president of UTDC, announced that Canadair would design and build the system and three test vehicles.

Tom Harvie (pointing) conducts a tour of the line on November 18, 1965, the day the first CL-218 bus was officially rolled out. Geoff Notman is on the right. The licence-built bus was 40 ft. (12.2 m) long, weighed 20,684 lb. (9,402 kg) and carried 53 passengers. (CL 46590)

The ICTS is a high-density people-mover system, a step up from streetcars, and capable of carrying 20,000 people per direction per hour. Trains of one, two or three 70-passenger vehicles, run in guideways located at ground level, underground or elevated. Capable of speeds up to 80 km/h (50 mph), they can be controlled manually or automatically.

Bob Cooke was appointed ICTS program manager, Ray Smith was in charge of the engineering and Herb Mahaffey was the project manager. The units were designed by two teams. One led by Joe Knap designed the body; the other under Jorge Sobolewski designed the running gear. Marcel Menard was responsible for purchasing; Gerry Barabé and Johnny Charest handled production.

Designing the ICTS presented several opportunities for innovation. UTDC wanted a quiet system, so the designers reduced noise by substituting aluminum alloy for traditional heavy steel trucks (bogies) and magnetically levitating the vehicles to lift weight off the wheels. They eliminated wheel squeal when making tight turns by designing steerable trucks, and they installed linear induction motors (LIMs) for noiseless propulsion.

A LIM is best described as a squirrel cage induction motor, similar to that in a vacuum cleaner, in two pieces. The armature is split and spread out as a strip along the centre of the guideway; the field is carried on a flat metal shoe under the vehicle. Power for the vehicle is picked up from a rail along the side of the guideway. The levitation system used the characteristics of two magnets' mutual attraction to maintain a constant 11-mm (0.43-in.) gap between the LIM shoe and the centre strip.

The design of the unit bodies, the guideway in which the vehicles ran, and the automatic control system also presented unique challenges, but were rewarded by Canadair invention awards. Joe Knap received awards for four separate items on the vehicle units, and Lawrence Gray for one item; Jorge Sobolewski received three on the trucks, and Harold List one. Dave Turner earned his PhD largely for his thesis on the design of the guideway.

Canadair supervised the construction of a 2.4-km (1.5-mi.) test track at Millhaven, Ontario. When it opened on October 27, 1978, 80 Canadair engineers under vice-president and general manager Len Box moved from Montreal to operate it. With the development and test phase completed, many Canadair employees joined Venturetran, a company formed at Millhaven by UTDC and TIW to produce systems for Vancouver, Scarborough, Ontario, and Detroit. The Ontario government later sold UTDC to Lavalin which in turn sold it to Bombardier.

The Vancouver system was an immediate success. Opened in 1986, it ran initially from the city centre 25 km (15 mi.) to New Westminster. By 1994 it had been extended

A detail of one of the UTDC test cars, then an aerial view of the test track at Kingston, Ontario. Malaysia ordered an updated version of the ICTS in November 1994. (CL)

a further 4.3 km (2.7 mi.) to Surrey. A further extension to either Coquitlam or Richmond was in the cards in late 1994. The 7-km (4.3-mi.) Scarborough system was not very successful because the local authority insisted on building streetcar guideways four times as massive as Vancouver's and using part-manual/part-automatic control, unlike Vancouver's which is completely automatic. Detroit's 3-km (2-mi.) system circles the downtown core.

Doug Follett was at a loss to explain why the ICTS, which was fast, clean, quiet and much cheaper to build than a subway, did not find a market in countries like Japan, China and Malaysia with their high population densities and greater reliance on mass transportation.

Looking for Work

Throughout the 1960s, Canadair continued to diversify into fields other than aerospace. This trend grew from 1970 to 1975, when Canadair took on whatever business it could find, just to keep the plant open and as many people employed as possible.

Through Geoff Notman's affiliation with McGill University, Bill Kowal assisted in the design of the barrel of the gun McGill used in Barbados to fire weather-sounding missiles to the edge of outer space (the gun was designed by Gerry Bull), and also provided the drills the university used to drill into Arctic ice to study climate conditions existing 100 years previously.

Prior to Montreal's Expo 67 World's Fair, Canadair was involved in a number of minor projects including: the manufacture of front and rear panels for Montreal's Metro cars under contract to Canadian Vickers; Drapeau's Tower; the design and manufacture of the stylized wing that stood in front of the Air Canada building in Montreal; and the study of air flows and fume removal in the Louis Hippolyte Lafontaine Tunnel at the east end of the Island of Montreal.

In February 1969, Notman reported that, over the past year, Canadair had contacted 122 companies and made 230 visits, looking for work. The company had received 65 enquiries of which seven were successful. These included some test equipment, value $110,000, for Hughes; Bomarc ramjet engine components for Marquardt, value $15,000; hydraulic valves for Food Machinery Corp. for $58,000: small potatoes for a company used to dealing in multi-millions. Not included in Notman's list were 506 sets of tail cones Canadair made for Raytheon Hawk missiles.

Subsequently, the company took on such diverse tasks as machining castings for Rolls-Royce Tyne engines and combine harvester parts for White Cockshutt; manufacturing tracks for dragline mining vehicles for Bucyrus Erie; making 12-m (40-ft.) diameter frames for spherical containers for Lyte Shipping's liquid gas carrier ships; stretch-forming for Otis Elevators; designing, building and installing a large ring on a Hydro-Quebec helicopter to sense leakage on major transmission lines; designing and building a bomb disposal device during the FLQ crisis; and building a DC-8 tail stand for Air Canada.

Some additional revenue resulted from the 1971 lease of 30 engineering and manufacturing personnel to Boeing for 12 months to work on the Boeing 727, and the rental of Plant 2 to General Motors for the assembly of city transport buses. GM was a good tenant—it left the plant in better condition than when it arrived. Some other activities deserve mention, if only to illustrate the lengths to which the company went to obtain work, acquire expertise and continue the building process.

Antennas

In 1965, Canadair was awarded contracts by Northern Electric to design, construct and erect two antennas. The first was a 9-m (30-ft.)-diameter precision tracking antenna (CL-210) for the Department of Research and Telecommunication establishment at Shirleys Bay, Ontario. The second was a 14-m (45-ft.) diameter antenna for an earth station for domestic satellite communications (CL-225) at Lac Bouchette, Quebec, 110 km (70 mi.) north of Ottawa.

The design team led by Alec Thompson included Ian Lamont, Robin Salmon, Bill Sturrock and Al Vinokuroff. They did an outstanding job of designing to maintain extreme accuracy of the contour of the large receiving dish over a wide range of temperature and wind load conditions. Both antennas performed so well that Canadair was subsequently asked to bid on a number of other antennas but declined because of the high cost of fabrication in an aerospace facility.

Air Cushion Vehicles

Ed Higgins introduced the air cushion vehicle (ACV) concept to Canadair one morning in 1964, when he brought a report of British ACV activities to the engineering "prayer meeting" (when everyone present prays they won't be given another job). He directed Derek Jones,

One of the huge Canadair antennas. (CL 45953)

chief thermal engineer, to research the subject. Jones managed to raise $20,000 from GD, DRB and Canadair, and then built two ACVs.

The CL-212-1A10 had three engines, two 100-hp Mercury outboards for lift and one 50-hp McCulloch drone engine for propulsion. The CL-212-1B11's two 4740-cm³ (289-cu.-in.) Ford Mustang engines provided both lift and propulsion.

Jones tried hard to sell the ACVs to GD and the U.S. Navy, but without success. Then GD decreed that all future ACV activity would be concentrated at Electric Boat, which was then working on a surface-effect vehicle ship.

Hydro Cable Car

In 1965, Canadair designed and built a cable car to travel along Hydro-Quebec's 735,000-volt power line from Montreal to Manicougan, 400 km (250 mi.) northeast of Quebec. The power line consists four 2.5-cm (1.0-in.) cables; the car carried personnel to install cruciform spacers every few metres along the line. Where the line crosses the Saguenay River, the cables sag approximately 150 m (500 ft.), so the car had to carry two people and a load of spacers up and down a 45-degree slope. Designed and built by the experimental department in just six weeks, the car was powered by four 2-cm (0.75-in.) drill motors.

Project manager Ron Regan recalled that, after several successful test runs on a test rig, he and Hydro's chief engineer were walking away when they heard laughter. They

The CL-212 hovercraft in different arrangements. The CL-212-1A10 is seen on the Back River a few kilometres from Cartierville. Al Stone holds the rings used in lifting the hovercraft from the water. Stone is in the driver's seat of the CL-212-1B11 in the scene above, outside B118 in February 1966. This version had twin Ford Mustang 4.7-litre engines. In the third view Geoff Notman observes the machine from his Chrysler Imperial. One of those involved in the project recalled, "The CL-212 made a lot of noise, and that's about all." (CL 42535, 42842, 47286)

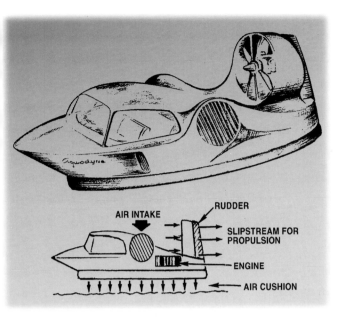

Canadair's Aquadyne was a proposed family recreation vehicle but did not materialize. (CL)

turned to see the car moving up the slope with not two but 12 Hydro workers hanging to it.

Waste Water Treatment Plant

In August 1971, company research and development funds were used to finance initial design activity on a small water treatment plant, in co-operation with École Polytechnique of the Université de Montréal. A team led by Bob Deans and Jim Chatfield designed and built a demonstration pilot plant for treating approximately 230,000 litres (50,000 imp. gal.) of waste water daily, installed it at the Sainte-Rose, Quebec sewage treatment plant, and turned it over to the École Polytechnique for research. Though subsequent tests

The CL-217 hydro cable car during trials. (CL 44772)

confirmed the feasibility of the concept and a U.S. patent was awarded, funding could not be obtained—the project did not relate "to critical research priorities" and it was cancelled.

The Baby Belt

In 1962, a Special Weapons Engineering team of Ken Cole, Ian Gray and Gordie Lloyd designed and built a birth-assist device for St. Mary's Hospital in Montreal. This consisted of an air-tight compression chamber which, when placed across the expectant mother's abdomen, reduced labor pains by means of a vacuum that drew the abdominal muscles out during labor contractions. Vacuum was provided by a shortened version of a standard Electrolux vacuum cleaner, donated by the manufacturer.

The mother controlled the amount of vacuum to coincide with the onset and easing of labor pains. The *Canadian Medical Journal* reported that 85 per cent of the patients using

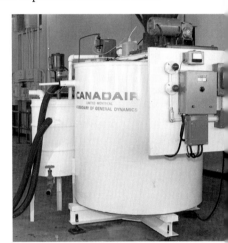

The CL-250 waste water treatment system. (CL 18096)

the so-called "baby belt" found they had less pain—in most cases amounting to 75 per cent relief, while some had no pain at all.

Gordie Lloyd was awarded an application patent for the backboard portion which relieved back strain when the abdomen was lifted. His wife used the belt during the birth of their daughter and pronounced it most effective. Lloyd said the device was used experimentally at St. Mary's and believed it was then sold to a Boston company which marketed it under the trade name Birth Eeze.

At about the same time, the Experimental Department built a hydraulically powered, rotatable chair for the Ortho Reno Larango Department of Notre Dame Hospital in Montreal. The chair, which had seven degrees of movement, was used to detect evidence of Ménière's disease by enabling doctors to study the movement of the patient's eyeballs while the chair was being rotated.

Programs that Never Were

Then there were programs which never got off the ground. In 1949, Canadair obtained a licence to build the Northrop Raider transport aircraft, but the project was dropped before any metal was cut. In 1952, Canadair seriously contemplated building a new aircraft (CL-21) to replace the DC-3. It was to be a 32-passenger, low-wing aircraft, with two 1,525-bhp Wright R-1820-82 Cyclone engines, a cruise speed of 470 km/h (290 mph) and a range of 2,750 km (1,710 mi.). A complete mock-up was made in experimental by a team led by Lew Chow. Needing 300 firm orders for go-ahead, marketing sent technical data packages to 170 civil operators worldwide. While initial reaction was positive, potential buyers were scared off by the high cost. Hindsight suggests the program may have succeeded if Canadair had sold to the military first.

The CL-236 was to have been Canadair's entry in the 1968 Canadian Advanced Multi-Role Aircraft (CAMRA) competition. CAMRA was the brainchild

and were then forced to withdraw because the Canadian government was afraid to get locked into a costly Arrow-type program. With Canada out, CAMRA became MRCA (multi-role combat aircraft), and the United Kingdom, Germany and Italy went ahead with a program which produced approximately 1,000 Panavia Tornados.

In 1952, sales engineer Karl Larsson proposed a series of airliners with gross weights ranging from 68,000 to 114,000 kg (150,000 to 250,000 lb.) powered by five jet engines mounted in a cluster at the tail end of the fuselage. His designs (which, except for the engine arrangement, looked remarkably like a Boeing 707 but predated the appearance of the 707 and DC-8) never progressed beyond the concept stage.

In late 1961, Karl Irbitis produced a concept for a six-engined all-wing freighter with a gross weight of 450,000 kg (one million lb.), a payload of 200,000 kg (450,000 lb.) and a maximum range of nearly 8,000 km (5,000 mi.). Its wing span was

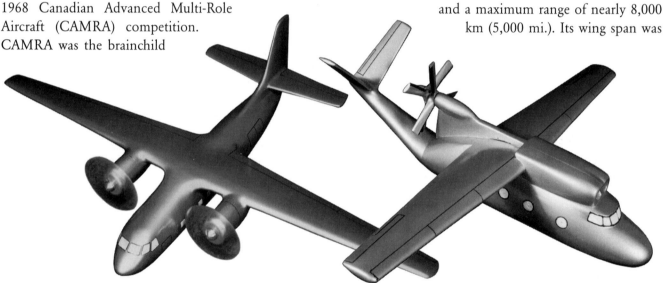

Models of designs that never went ahead. The CL-21 (left) was proposed to replace the DC-3. Proposed in June 1958, the CL-69 series (right) was aimed at corporate, utility and cargo markets. Various layouts went down on paper, ranging from an aircraft 32 feet long/7100 pounds to one 40 feet long/15,000 pounds all-up weight. Engines considered went from 500 shp to 1000 shp turboprops. One version was a triphibian using a bolt-on centreline float. All manufacturers in this era had a host of concepts under discussion. Few materialized, but the process kept the engineers and marketers active. (D6360, CL 16053)

of two RCAF officers, Air Commodore Bill Carr and Group Captain Hal Bridges. They wanted Canada to spearhead a consortium of nations to design and develop a single type of advanced multi-role aircraft for use by all members. The two officers cleared the technology release, designed the production and management plans, obtained the support of the British, Germans and Italians,

99 m (325 ft.) and its wing tips and tip-mounted vertical stabilizers folded upward to expose the cargo bays for loading and unloading. A visionary concept, but alas only a vision.

Other projects never got as far. Canadair once attracted the attention of legendary aviation pioneer Howard Hughes. At Hughes's invitation, Peter Redpath, Ken Ebel and Dick Richmond attended a middle-of-the-night meeting with him in a Las Vegas hotel to discuss a Trans World Airways requirement for a 150-passenger high speed turboprop airliner capable of flying New York to Los Angeles non-stop at 650 km/h (400 mph). Like many of Hughes's ideas, the plane never materialized.

In addition to the C-7, Canadair tried unsuccessfully to interest TCA in a big turboprop (CL-39) similar to the Vickers Vanguard, but long before the Vanguard. Don Long of engineering researched Northrop's XB-35 flying wing in sufficient depth that Canadair prepared a production proposal.

In 1963, Canadair responded to a proposal to build tooling and manufacture wings, empennages and miscellaneous components for the BAC 1-11 aircraft. The project died when Air Canada refused to buy the aircraft. Canadair also flirted with the idea of building the Russian YAK-40 airliner and Swedish Saab cars under license.

Reg Avey of CL-215 marketing invented a method of oil slick removal which consisted of a series of large plastic bags rolled on a drum mounted on a floating rig in a way that the mouth of the bag scooped up the oil as the

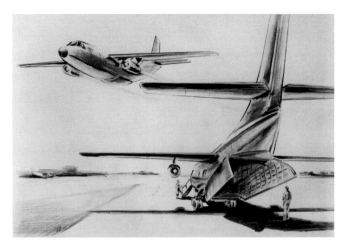

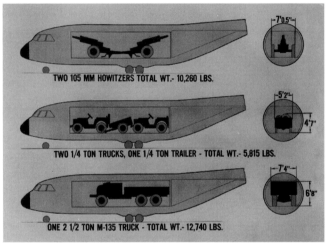

A 1962 concept for a military jet transport was the CL-203. Most military transports in this class (50,000 lb. all-up weight) have been turboprops like the de Havilland Buffalo. (CL 34694, '677)

Two other projects investigated for possible participation but not pursued were the United Aircraft Turbo Train (built by the Montreal Locomotive Works) and the Trident Trigull light amphibian built in Vancouver. (CL 23979, C9718)

rig was towed through the slick. When full, the bag was released and the weighted mouth sank, trapping the oil until it could be recovered. Experimental built a model and Avey demonstrated it to Inland Waters personnel who reported the principle to be sound, but were not prepared to finance further development.

And then there were the variants. Engineering seldom considered only one version of a promising product: they studied no fewer than 57 variants of the CL-44, 54 of the CL-84 and 37 of the CL-41.

CHAPTER ELEVEN

THE CHALLENGER

CL-600 AND CL-601

The early 1970s were tough times in the aerospace industry. Recession and the winding down of the Vietnam War had a severe impact. From an all-time high in 1968 of $150 million, Canadair's sales declined to $40 million in 1973. The average annual employment level of 9,250 in 1968 dipped below 2,000 in 1975. At one point there were fewer than 1,400 direct workers in the company's 320,000 m² (3.4 million sq. ft.) of work space.

When CF-5 production ended (the last of Canadair's big military aircraft programs) the company could barely meet overhead. To reduce expenses, several buildings in Plant 2 were demolished, Plant 4 was closed and snowfalls were piled, not removed. The Plant 4 shutdown was a mistake, for considerable damage was caused by burst pipes and neglect. General Dynamics could not help because its own plants at Fort Worth and San Diego were losing money; in any event, Fred Kearns wanted desperately to escape GD's benign neglect.

As employment plummeted and Plant 1 began to resemble a morgue, Kearns and vice-president of engineering Harry Halton fought to retain a small nucleus of top engineering talent for the day when they surely would be needed to spearhead a new venture. They imagined having to repeat three

programs with which they were familiar: the CL-89, CL-215 and a licensed fighter. Then they decided the type and number of engineers each program would require. They wanted to be able to select any two projects and staff them from an engineering core. They determined they would need at least 235 engineers for two projects, and then listed by name the ones to keep, by hook or by crook. In fact, they never did fall below 250 engineers.

After extensive meetings with industry management, the Liberal government of Pierre Elliot Trudeau decided not to sit back and watch Canada's aircraft industry go under, but to strive to return control of de Havilland and Canadair to Canadian hands. In 1972, Ottawa obtained from Hawker Siddeley, de Havilland Canada's parent company, an option to acquire DHC anytime to the end of June 1974. The option was requested because of Hawker Siddeley's refusal to help fund the DHC Dash 7

Fred Kearns joined Canadair in 1949 then worked his way up in accounting to become vice-president and comptroller in 1957, replacing James F. Tooley. In 1965 he succeeded Notman as president, then saw Canadair into the exciting and controversial Challenger years. Kearns retired in 1983 and passed away in London, Ontario, on November 14, 1987. (CL C7707)

In the early 1970s de Havilland's STOL Dash 7 was Canada's most advanced aviation project. Fred Kearns feared that Ottawa might favor de Havilland to the detriment of Canadair. (Larry Milberry)

program. This forced Ottawa to finance its entire development and prototype production phases. For political reasons, therefore, Ottawa felt compelled to buy DHC.

In September 1973, Air Canada and Comstock International, one of Canada's largest construction companies, jointly proposed a merger of Canadair and DHC. Air Canada and Comstock would control 51 per cent of the merged entity, Hawker Siddeley and GD the rest. Ottawa rejected the idea. Instead, on May 27, 1974, it announced that it had exercised the de Havilland option and intended to obtain another to buy Canadair. On January 15, 1975, Ottawa and GD signed an option agreement giving the government the right to buy all the shares and total GD interest in Canadair for $36 million Cdn, plus $1.5 million representing profits during the option period.

Despite this, GD apparently wanted to retain an interest in the Canadian aviation industry, for on May 15, 1975, GD's executive vice-president, James Beggs, wrote to the minister of industry, trade and commerce proposing a plan for GD's participation in the restructuring program. This suggested Canadians acquire 80.5 per cent control of de Havilland and Canadair, leaving GD with 19.5 per cent. The letter stated that agreement in principle had been reached with two members of a prominent Canadian industrial family to take up to 51 per cent of the equity. GD also claimed to have had discussions with other prominent Canadian businessmen, who were willing to subscribe between $250,000 and $500,000 for a further participation of 29.5 per cent.

A condition of GD's plan was a commitment from the Canadian Forces to buy some 120 General Dynamics F-16 fighters. In return, GD promised to place about $200 million in offset work in Canada. This assumed that Canadair would handle final assembly and flight test of the

F-16s. The GD proposal was possibly a move by GD president David Lewis to pre-empt a similar proposal from his rival and former boss, J.S. McDonnell, who wanted to merge McDonnell Douglas with DHC and Canadair and persuade the DND to buy F-15s. Ottawa turned down GD's proposal. Negotiations for the sale continued through the summer and fall of 1975, with Peter Aird representing Canadair.

For Fred Kearns, convincing the government to buy Canadair was not difficult. It was politically unthinkable that Ottawa would save Ontario's de Havilland and neglect Quebec's Canadair. Kearns' main worry was that some bureaucrats believed that, if both companies were saved, the industry should be rationalized: one company manufacturing aircraft, the other making only parts. Since Ottawa had bought DHC to save the Dash 7 program and Canadair had no production program in-house, it

Artist's conception of an F-16 as proposed by General Dynamics for the Canadian air force. (CL C11503)

followed that de Havilland would be the manufacturer and Canadair would become a "bucket shop." Kearns later said of this period: "It felt like being back in my Spitfire, looking in the rear view mirror and seeing a Messerschmitt on my tail, moving in for the kill."

On January 5, 1976, the government bought Canadair from GD for $38.15 million including $1.5 million Cdn for incremental profits between 1973 and the exercising of the option. Canadair's 54 per cent interest and control of Asbestos Corp., which the company had bought in 1968 and 1969, were not part of the agreement. Immediately before selling Canadair, GD had transferred the shares to General Dynamics Canada and later sold them to the government of Quebec.

Once de Havilland and Canadair were under Canadian control, the subject of rationalization appears to have received only lip service. Ottawa asked David A. Golden, former deputy minister of defence production, to assess its options regarding the two companies. In a memorandum of July 10, 1978, Golden considered the case for general rationalization to be weak, reasoning that the companies were in different businesses. He found the case for greater co-ordination more convincing; however, another 14 years would pass before any real degree of co-ordination would be achieved and that would be under a different owner, Bombardier.

Survival in a Drowning Industry

Regardless of how long Canadair might exist, the period 1975 to 1985 and the birth and development of the Challenger business jet will be viewed as a most significant period in the company. Historians will not have to look far for details, for no other Canadair program has been so well documented. Nor have any, save possibly the Avro Arrow program, been more controversial or attracted so much public interest, particularly in the early phases. Canada's National Film Board made a movie about the Challenger. Three investigative reports criticizing Canadair and the airplane were shown across Canada on prime time CBC television. A book was published, and hundreds of articles appeared in print around the world.

That Canadair survived this decade is a tribute to the determination—despite pressures, conflicts and interference—of a handful of key players. Their efforts were bolstered by the sacrifice of hundreds of people who, by working cruel hours in a climate of desperation to meet crushing schedules, created a product of which Canadians are justifiably proud.

While the government strove to rescue a drowning industry, Fred Kearns and his management staff sought a program with enough engineering and manufacturing potential to thwart any move from Ottawa to turn Canadair into a bucket shop. Regardless of the assumptions in GD's plan, the government had made it clear that there would be no new licensed fighter production program for Canadair.

There was a small amount of pro-

duction work in house, but little to occupy the designers and engineers. A few of them were busy in advanced design on a CL-215 spray system, and comparing a proposed Argus update with the Lockheed and Boeing entries in the long-range patrol aircraft (LRPA) competition. The CL-89 program continued to bring in revenue from the sale of systems and spare parts, but deliveries of the second batch of CL-215 aircraft had slowed from 10 in 1974 to one in 1975. The Mercure subcontract was coming to an end with the completion of the 10th shipset, leaving only the F-111, F-15 and Boeing 747SP subcontracts running, and they employed very few. Canadair stood a good chance of winning a large subcontract to produce major components for the winning LRPA, but that was still months away. The only activity employing high technology personnel was the CL-289 surveillance system—the successor to the CL-89—and that was still at an early stage.

Fred Kearns could not hold his key people indefinitely. He needed a program quickly: a major commercial program, preferably within the company's existing engineering and production capabilities, and one with sufficient potential to get government backing. Then he had to sell it to the bureaucrats and the politicians. Fate did not help. Harry Halton, whom Kearns was depending on to help lead this initiative, had undergone a serious operation and was left paralyzed from the waist down.

Halton had come to Canadair in 1948 as a functional procedures engineer. Involved with every aircraft program from the North Star to the CF-5, he gained recognition for his work on the complex CF-104 electronic systems. From there he moved quickly to program manager on the CL-215, before becoming chief product engineer in 1969, director of engineering in 1970, vice-president, engineering in 1972, and executive vice-president in January 1975. Somewhat of an enigma, he was regarded by some as a good manager while others considered him single-minded and overly optimistic. All agree, however, that it was Kearns's and Halton's optimism that kept Canadair going.

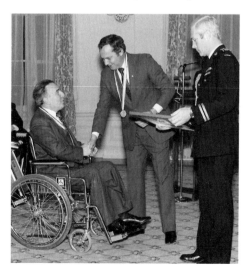

Harry Halton, who spearheaded Canadair's business jet gamble, is congratulated by Governor General Ed Schreyer on being awarded the ORT Centennial Medal in 1980. (CL 19034-9)

LearStar 600

In November 1975, Bernhard (Bundy) Bundesman, president of de Havilland Canada, introduced Fred Kearns to Carl Ally, an advertising man and promoter for inventor William Powell Lear. An electronics genius, Lear held 150 patents and had received many awards for inventions including an automatic pilot and eight-track tape deck. He had developed the Learstar, a corporate version of the Lockheed Lodestar, and the Learjet, the first successful small business jet.

Ally told Kearns that Lear had a design for a new 14-passenger executive jet with an 8,000 km (5,000 mi.) range and a top speed of 970 km/h (600 mph). He called it the LearStar 600. Ally claimed that Federal Express (FedEx), a fast-growing small-package express carrier with a fleet of aging Falcons, was interested in 40 examples in the cargo version, and that he foresaw a market for 1,000 aircraft over the next decade.

When Kearns brought the concept of an executive jet to Halton's hospital room, what caught Halton's attention was its similarity to the idea he had had in mind when he told a 1974 meeting of the Aerospace Industries Association of Canada that he foresaw a need for a new generation small civil aircraft with an advanced technology wing, high-bypass fan engines and a gross weight of 14,000 kg (30,000 lb.). Then and there, Kearns and Halton decided to investigate the LearStar 600.

In January 1976 Halton sent Jack Greeniaus and George Turek of engineering, Peter Candfield of manufacturing engineering, Tony Natlacen of industrial engineering and John Denheyer of contract estimating to look at Lear's Nevada base. They saw little besides a wooden mock-up of an earlier configuration and about three dozen sketches done by a small group working weekends and overtime. Greeniaus's report said that the program had potential and that, " . . . if there is any possibility of Canadian government financial support for such a program, then we should put together an overall proposal, for presentation to the government."

It was clear that Lear had little to offer technically, or in the way of design, although he bandied about such terms as "supercritical wing" and "high bypass turbofan engines," both already known in the industry. A supercritical wing is a thick wing that "thinks" it is thin. Though thick enough for fuel tanks, it generates less drag than a conventional wing. Turbofan engines use less fuel and are quieter

Early in their discussions Bill Lear and Fred Kearns appeared on the cover of *Professional Pilot*, the leading US business aviation magazine.
(CL C11124)

than non-fans, and high bypass turbofans are the quietest and most efficient of all. Put wing and engines together and one has an aircraft that flies faster and farther on less fuel.

Kearns knew there was little substance to Lear's concept; what would be of use, in his opinion, when it came to getting government support for the program was the Lear name. So in late March 1976, he sent vice-president, administration and legal, Bob Wohl, to Reno to negotiate an option agreement with Lear and his lawyer. While Wohl was in Reno, however, Lear changed his mind and left to make a deal with Ling-Temco-Vought (LTV) of Dallas. A few days later, he changed his mind again and agreed to a signing date with Canadair of April 2. On that day, Kearns, Halton and Wohl met with Lear in New York and signed the agreement.

Preliminary design began in Montreal on April 7, 1976, the day Kearns announced that Canadair had acquired worldwide exclusive rights to the LearStar 600 for five months. Greeniaus was appointed project manager, Mike Telford, chief of design, and Turek, head of flight sciences. A few days later, Halton arrived in Reno to get his first look at the Lear facility. He was shocked to find the place "a shambles with about 12 employees, including secretaries and sweepers." All he could see of the LearStar were some disjointed conceptual-type drawings. Halton admitted he was disappointed but not seriously troubled because, as he said: "I thought it really didn't matter what Lear had—we were probably on our own anyway."

Jim Taylor

With advanced design of the new jet underway at Cartierville, Kearns turned his attention to marketing. He, the Canadair board of directors and its government advi-

Jim Taylor with Harry Halton. Between 1963 and 1976 Taylor sold hundreds of business jets for Pan American and Cessna. When he left Cessna, he was hired by Fred Kearns and led the sales team into one of the toughest markets in the midst of economic hard times. Taylor's expertise put Canadair on a rough but eventually happy road to success. (CL C9892-12)

sors had agreed that a minimum 50 firm orders would be required for a production go-ahead. Canadair's small marketing staff had no knowledge of the executive jet market, so Kearns hired, as a consultant, the man reputed to be the top business aircraft salesman, James B. (Jim) Taylor.

Taylor, a former U.S. Navy pilot, had earned his reputation selling Falcon Jets and Cessna Citations. In his six years as vice-president of the business jet division of Pan-American World Airways, he and his staff sold more than $250 million worth of French-built Falcons. He then joined Cessna which, at that time, had only one order for its new Citation business jet, and that was from the manufacturer of its engine, Pratt & Whitney Canada. By the time Taylor left Cessna, his salesmen had sold more than 300 Citations.

Taylor's philosophy was that the marketing department should be involved in the program from the beginning to ensure the product was customer-oriented and not what engineering or manufacturing wanted to build. He told Kearns that, in order to sell 50 "paper aircraft" in five months, he would need to pick his own team and have complete control of marketing, including promotion, after-sales service/support, and demonstration flights. He had found that test pilots usually were not good demonstration pilots: demo pilots were trained to sell.

Given the green light, Taylor brought in the three top members of his Citation sales team—Dave Hurley, Bill Juvonen and Barry Smith—and Peter Ginnochio, a product support specialist. They knew the market inside out, and had a personal relationship with many potential customers. Because the biggest market lay in the United States, Taylor persuaded Kearns to establish a subsidiary, Canadair Inc., with Taylor as president. It was at Westport, Connecticut, near many top U.S. corporations. Taylor later established a demonstration flight team in Connecticut headed by Les McClelland, a former personal pilot to four U.S. presidents. McClelland's team included Maxie Nameth and Doug Glime, former presidential pilots, and one Canadian VIP pilot, Bob Flynn.

Advanced Design and Funding

Activity at Canadair continued at a furious pace. Engineering staff were studying the design, reducing the uncertainties and preparing preliminary data for the salesmen. The task of matching the precise wing shape and engine combination needed to achieve the desired level of performance was formidable. Mike Telford was manager of design during most of the preliminary phase, but he retired in August 1976 and Jeff Harwood took over. Jack Greeniaus was engineering project manager, and the section chiefs were Eric Haines, airframe; Eddie Coates, mechanical; and Lloyd Hess, avionics. Odd Michaelsen and Fotis Mavriplis were working together on the aerodynamics of the advanced technology wing.

Meanwhile, vice-president of finance Peter Aird was identifying potential sources of funding. Since buying Canadair, the government had decided that it was politically inexpedient to put more equity into the company. This left Aird having to arrange outside funding. He and Kearns concluded that about $130 million, plus customer advances and deposits, would be needed to see the program through the design, certification, production and operational phases. A Catch 22 situation prevailed for a few weeks, with the government telling Aird that it would guarantee half the loan if the banks first came up with the other half. The banks were saying that they would provide half but the government must issue its guarantee first!

Aird broke the impasse: the bankers would provide half, the government would guarantee the rest. He was subsequently able to relieve the government of its direct financial responsibility by raising $70 million US via a Eurodollar bond issue based on a government letter of comfort. The issue was immediately oversold.

When Ottawa said it wanted Canadair to take on a partner for the venture, Kearns talked to Saab in Sweden and, with Halton and Wohl, held extended negotiations with Italian manufacturer, Aeritalia. Nothing happened with Saab, but Canadair took on two dozen Aeritalia engineers who spent a year in Montreal supporting early development. Meanwhile, Taylor, working hard to obtain the all-important 50 orders before the option expired, brought 250 corporate pilots, maintenance chiefs and financial officers to Montreal to tour Canadair and hear presentations on the program. "This way they knew we weren't some tiny outfit in the corner of a hangar somewhere," said Taylor.

Those at the first seminar on August 12, 1976, suggested a wider fuselage would give more room for a variety of interior arrangements and for passengers to move around during eight- and nine-hour flights. Halton agreed. Lear had proposed a 2.24-m (88-in.) diameter fuselage. Halton decided that 2.69 m (106 in.) would provide the needed headroom and an attractive width, but Lear was furious. He stormed unannounced into a Canadair board luncheon, holding a model of the aircraft, shouting: "Would any of you guys like to see Fat Albert with a nose job." Few of the board members present even knew who he was.

Crazy Schedule

Lear's staff had also been working, in parallel with Canadair's designers, on their own studies of the LearStar 600. After a classic argument with Lear about the direction of the program and its prospects for the future, Canadair and Lear held a joint review with outside consultants invited to evaluate the two designs. Top engineers from Boeing and McDonnell Douglas agreed pretty much with Canadair's design and performance calculations, though the Boeing engineer commented: "You guys have

Computer technology was opening up as the Challenger jet project moved from concept to reality. It eased the work load on engineers at all levels and accelerated design. Had Fred Kearns not come up with the business jet project when he did, Canadair might not have survived past 1980. (CL)

got a beautiful airplane there, but you sure have a crazy schedule!"

Halton had a simple explanation for that crazy schedule. He knew the LearStar wasn't going to have the market to itself. Upcoming were the Gulfstream G-III, Lockheed Jetstar II, and Dassault Falcon 50. The first on the market would have an edge. Halton figured that the usual time required from go-ahead to first flight for a new design was three years. He estimated an additional 18 months from first flight to certification, though Taylor had told him that the Falcon and Citation had taken 24 months from first flight to certification. Adding another 2 1/2 years to build 50 aircraft meant telling the buyer of the 50th aircraft he would not get his aircraft for seven years. This was unacceptable to Halton, so he cut the three years to two and his 18 months to 12.

Halton admitted that his schedule was crazy, just as he knew that Lear's weight estimates were crazy from the day they signed the option agreement. He was not happy that FedEx wanted changes that would add even more weight. He also knew that without FedEx there would be no program, and with no program, possibly no Canadair, so he "held his engineers' feet to the fire."

Ross Richardson remembered the heat, the long hours and the pressure he and the other design engineers lived with: "We'd estimate the number of hours to do a job, then Harry would halve them. We'd re-do them and find that the new figure was closer to his than our original.

Two of the leading business jets of the 1960s were the Dassault Falcon 20 and Lockheed Jetstar. When they visited Canadair they attracted much attention. These were first generation "biz jets" and it was the goal of Fred Kearns and Harry Halton to lead the industry into a new era. It was Jim Taylor's job to sell one of Canadair's jets to every Falcon and Jetstar operator and to those with other early types like the Citation and Learjet. (CL 45999, 40820)

We'd no sooner get a design laid out than Harry would want to freeze it and get it to Planning. Danny Lebeuf did 14 different wing configurations to suit Harry and every one meant changes to fuselage design. One thing about Harry though, you knew he knew what you were doing because he was always after you to do it better and faster. And, if something turned out wrong, he never said: 'Why did you do that?' he just said: 'What do we do to fix it?'"

Federal Express and the Engine

Fred Kearns always believed that a better market for the aircraft existed in areas such as air freight and air ambulance, rather than business jets. Early in the program he decided to offer a cargo version. Taylor and his staff knew the senior management of FedEx. As its operating certificate allowed it to operate aircraft with a maximum payload of 3,400 kg (7,500 lb.)–right in the Canadair ballpark–Taylor brought some top FedEx people to Montreal. FedEx subsequently ordered 25 of the first batch of aircraft.

The FedEx involvement brought another matter of dissension to a head–the question of the engine. The choice lay between the 30 kN (6,750 lb.) thrust Avco Lycoming ALF-502 and the 38.5 kN (8,650 lb.) thrust General Electric (GE) CF34, but neither was exactly what Canadair wanted. The Lycoming was an adaptation of a helicopter turboshaft engine and lacked the required thrust. A mili-

tary version of the GE engine had already accumulated several million hours of operation in the Fairchild A-10 ground attack aircraft and carrier-based Lockheed S-3A maritime patrol aircraft, but it would need considerable modification for civil use. And it was heavy and expensive.

Lear's concept was based on the Lycoming which Canadair's engineers also preferred for its light weight, ease of maintenance and the fact that a larger version was reported to be near certification. Taylor, however, argued that while Lycoming had never built a fan engine, the GE engine was proven. Also, because an aircraft always gains weight during development and throughout its life, he recommended the more powerful GE engine. FedEx, on the other hand, had had problems with the GE engines in their Falcons. They considered the CF34 unmaintainable because changing any major component required removing the engine. Arguments ensued and relationships became strained before Kearns decided to go with a proposal from Avco to increase thrust on the ALF-502 to 33.4 kNs (7,500 lb.). After he retired, Kearns said he regretted that decision, but the die was cast.

The option with Lear had to be extended two months to allow for completion of the various aircraft comparisons. On October 29, 1976, three days before the revised expiry date, Canadair's board of directors gave the program a go-ahead on the strength of 28 firm orders, plus a conditional order for 25 from FedEx, at a unit price of $4.375 million US. The same day, Ottawa announced that it had authorized Canadair to exercise an option to begin design and development of the LearStar 600.

"Challenger"

The first progress report, dated February 25, 1977, showed 311 people working on the program, 138 short of requirements. Sales were given as 68 aircraft plus 19 under negotiation. First flight date was scheduled for April 1978; first delivery for June 1979.

The organization chart listed Harry Halton as program manager; Jock West as deputy program manager, administration and control; Ron Neal as deputy program manager, technical; Mel Curtis as deputy manager, flight test facility; and Greeniaus as engineering project manager.

Production was the responsibility of Andy Throner, vice-president, manufacturing. He had joined Canadair as a pre-flight mechanic in 1951 then worked his way up the management chain to vice-president, operations in 1973, and vice-president, manufacturing in early 1977. Reporting to Throner were Peter Candfield, director, manufacturing engineering; Tony Natlacen, director, industrial engineering; Bill Harris, director, manufacturing; and Steve Barinka, special assistant, CL-600. Rodney Buy was director, fabrication; Sid Gleadhall, manager, final line; Joe Daly, manager, wing assembly and Gerry Barabé, manager, preflight and mock-up. Walter Allatt was in charge of the machine shop; Stan Rose, sheet metal; Don Kennard, tool design; John Ballard, assembly and installation planning; Terry Chypchar, production control; and John Major, tool fabrication. Other key people involved were Bob Wohl, vice-president, administration and legal; Conrad Kunze in charge of procurement; Bill Woodhouse, director, materiel; Paul Mc-Morran, director, Challenger contracts, and Ben Locke, director, contract estimating.

In March 1977 Canadair renamed its airplane "Challenger", a name recommended by a consulting group which specialized in naming and introducing new products. The renaming was to give better market appeal; besides, the aircraft really had little to do with Lear. "Its performance is a challenge to any other business aircraft existing or contemplated," proclaimed the official announcement. "Its guarantees are a challenge to the aviation industry." One aviation magazine wondered to whom the program presented the greater challenge, the competition or the Canadair engineers tasked with meeting the guarantees. For his part, Lear turned his attention to a new and more radical design, the Lear Fan (which never got into production). He died a little over a year later.

A 1978 view of the shop floor in P2. Raw material, components, a wing jig and other paraphernalia to do with the Challenger program days can be seen. The walled-in area down the floor is the small skunk works where the first Challenger parts were hand made. Beyond is the CL-215 preflight area. (CL C9346)

Harry Whiteman, who directed engineering in the early days of the Challenger. He retired in 1978 but continued to consult for Canadair into the 1980s. (CL 50210)

Assembly of Challenger s/n 1001 began in September 1977 in a small skunk works set up in the centre of the Plant 1 final assembly area, under the direction of Harry Whiteman and Eric Reynolds. The purpose of the skunk works was to produce those parts for the three pre-production aircraft for which hard tooling was not yet available; whose design was likely to change; or which were not designed until the last moment. Engineering, tooling, manufacturing and quality control personnel involved in this phase were co-located in the skunk works, and drawings went straight from design engineering to the skunk works where manager Gerry Barabé and his team handmade the parts directly from the drawings and recorded any required changes right on the drawing. The nose section of the first Challenger was built entirely in the skunk works while the remainder of the fuselage was assembled on the normal production line. Barabé recalled that he had the first Challenger part, a small, formed sheet metal part, encased in plastic and delivered to Halton as a souvenir.

Manufacturing the Challenger presented no major problems for Canadair because the design incorporated much of the technology that Canadair had acquired

on earlier programs, such as fully machined skins, spars and ribs; metal-to-metal bonding and honeycomb bonding.

Structural Testing

Plans called for the manufacture of three pre-production aircraft for the certification program, and two for static and fatigue testing. The test airframes were installed in two massive structures where dozens of hydraulic actuators applied loads—regulations required that 1½ times the maximum expected load be applied to critical structural components. The fatigue tests simulated the loads experienced throughout every phase of ground manoeuvring and flight over the equivalent of thousands of flights. Such tests allowed the engineers to determine whether any part of the structure needed rework. Satisfactory results were needed to prove the integrity of the airframe to the certifying agencies; for in addition to being the first wide-bodied business jet and the first to combine an advanced wing and fan engines, the Challenger aircraft was also the first required to meet new and more stringent regulations under Federal Aviation Regulations (FAR) Part 25. These covered every aspect of design, manufacture and operation. Jack Greeniaus recalled that the requirement to guarantee dispatch reliability was one of the most difficult and mind-boggling parts of the program.

Another part-airframe became the "Iron Bird," a rig for testing the hydraulic

Proof that Fred Kearns was serious about moving Canadair into the future... the prototype Challenger 600 fuselage slowly takes shape in P1 (March 7, 1978). The mid-fuselage and nose section have just been mated. Then an overall view of activity on the shop floor, and a close-up of the first wing in its jig. (CL C9700, 9853, 9852)

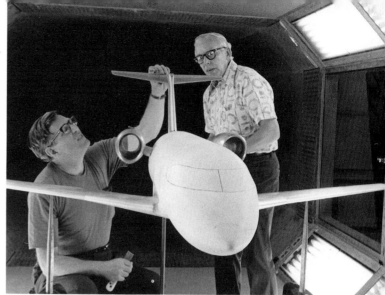

Work on a flying prototype was paralleled by research and development. A fatigue test airframe (above) is pushed into B.117 for trials early in the program. The first CL-600 wind tunnel test was conducted in October 1976. In the photo at top right Ken Kimber (left) of Canadair helps a technician adjust a model in the NRC's low-speed wind tunnel. Then, a study of the intricate set-up required for airframe fatigue testing, and a view of the stabilizer of a fatigue test article being loaded up for stress tests. The same article has been used in bird strike tests—note the bird strike damage to the vertical stabilizer. (CL C10988, 25581-34, 12662, C15565)

(Below) This engineering mock-up of the new jet was essential in proving a thousand-and-one details. The cut-aways showed the placement of various systems, such as hydraulics. The craft of making mock-ups eventually will be lost—all such work is now done on the computer screen. (CL C9486)

and flight control systems. For safety and reliability, the Challenger had three separate hydraulic systems, each with two independent sources of power, and a flight control system divided into left and right halves. If one malfunctioned, the other would be unaffected. It also had four separate sources of electrical power. Other test rigs established the strength of the landing gear trunnions, the windshield and the T-tail joint. A full-scale mock-up helped to determine where best to locate system components, access panels and the like.

TAG

In July 1977, Kearns announced the sale of 21 Challenger aircraft to TAG Finance SA, a Geneva-based multinational organization. He also revealed that TAG would be Canadair's exclusive distributor in 22 countries of the Middle East. Taylor and his team knew TAG well. While with Falcon Jet, Bill Juvonen had sold a Falcon to Aziz Ojjeh, one of two sons of TAG founder, Akram Ojjeh. When Aziz showed up at the Canadair chalet at the Paris Air Show in June 1977, Juvonen invited him to view the Challenger mock-up. Aziz immediately ordered two aircraft. When Akram Ojjeh saw the mockup, he said he

The Challenger marketing mock-up was unveiled April 29, 1977 and is seen here about to "hit the road". On May 10 it sailed for Le Havre aboard the *Atlantic Cognac*, destined for the Paris Air Show. Later it toured North America, turning up at such events as the National Business Aircraft Association convention in Houston, where it was *the* focus of attention. Models in the interior scene are Canadair's Bob Germain (graphic design), Bruce Fleming (pilot), Barry Lingard (contract administration) and France Bouchard (graphic design). (CL 24932)

A view of the Challenger assembly floor early in the program. Aircraft No. 2 is taking shape on the right. (CL 10823)

Canadair's top executives in 1977. (CL 26346)

canadair ORGANIZATION

F.R. KEARNS
PRESIDENT
& C.E.O.

J.B. TAYLOR
PRESIDENT
CANADAIR INC.

B. KERUB
DIRECTOR
PUBLIC
RELATIONS

P.J. AIRD
VICE-PRESIDENT
FINANCE

R.A. WOHL
VICE-PRESIDENT
ADMINISTRATION
& LEGAL

J.E. OUELLET
VICE-PRESIDENT
RESOURCES

H. HALTON
EXECUTIVE
VICE-PRESIDENT

A. THRONER
VICE-PRESIDENT
MANUFACTURING

F.M. FRANCIS
VICE-PRESIDENT
DEVELOPMENT
PROGRAMS

C. KUNZE
VICE-PRESIDENT
PRODUCTION
PROGRAMS

wanted 10 and sent his private aircraft to bring Kearns and Taylor to his chateau to discuss further purchases. Taylor and Juvonen had been there a week when Akram suddenly appeared saying: "I'm going to buy 19. That brings the total to 21 and that's my birth date." Bob Wohl and the TAG lawyer wrapped up the deal in Paris.

A few weeks later, the United States deregulated its air carrier industry. This removed restrictions on the size of the aircraft used by FedEx. Able now to use 727s and DC-10s, FedEx cancelled 20 of its 25 Challenger aircraft. To keep FedEx in the program, Kearns promised to develop a stretched Challenger. In return, on January 30, 1978, FedEx signed a letter of intent to buy 25 of them should the program materialize.

A February 22, 1978, announcement that all engineering drawings had now been released also confirmed that the basic design was complete. Systems were being installed in the forward fuselage of aircraft 1001 and the mid-fuselage was nearly ready for assembly. Nose and mid-fuselage were joined on March 6; wing and fuselage were mated on May 8.

Roll-out and First Flight

On May 25, 1978, only 19 months after go-ahead, the first Challenger was rolled out before 5,000 employees and guests—the work force had mushroomed from 1,600 to 4,500 since the program had begun.

271

While 19 months was not a record, it was a remarkable achievement considering most employees at the roll-out were not even with the company in 1976. Halton and vice-president operations Andy Throner were the first to admit that most of the credit for that achievement belonged to those who had worked long hours, seven days a week, for the first two years of the program.

The Challenger jet appeared from the darkness of the hangar into the sunlight to a burst of applause from the audience. Those seeing the Challenger for the first time had good reason to be impressed. It was state-of-the-art, the first wide-bodied business jet, and the first aircraft designed to the highest standards of safety and reliability. Before guest of honor Jean Chrétien (minister of industry, trade and commerce) took his place on the platform, he put on an Expos baseball cap, climbed onto a tractor and said he would tow the Challenger out himself. Kearns persuaded him to let the experts do it.

Only minutes before the roll-out ceremony, TAG had placed an order for a further 10 aircraft bringing total sales to 127, plus Fed-Ex's 25. Market acceptance had been so favorable that Canadair had raised its price to $7 million US, a 60 per cent increase over the original price.

The prototype's forward fuselage (top) is taken out of the jig March 11, 1978. On May 8, 1978, the wing and fuselage are mated. Then the rear section is added. In the view on the facing page, some days later, Fred Kearns may be seen in the group to the right. (CL 28297-19, 29397-22, C9952, C9977)

With the ceremony over, 1001 went back into the hangar for the completion of much unfinished work. The work tempo continued to increase. Ron Foran of pre-flight remembered the long hours: "What was it? What was the driving force behind a small army of

men who went to work before most people were awake and returned home long after bed time for a few hours rest, and kept doing it over and over again? The achievers must have been motivated by something other than money—I believe it was like a man in love with a beautiful lady."

Life was particularly hard for those in manufacturing, manufacturing engineering and industrial engineering who were struggling to keep up with the heavy change traffic. They had experienced traffic like this before; in fact the number of changes per drawing or per part were less than on the CF-5 or the C-5A programs. The problem here was not the volume of the changes but the rate—the high number of changes per day, or per week, due to the crushing schedule.

Life was also difficult for controller John MacKenzie

Challenger 1001 in B117. It still has a long way to go before completion. (CL C10990)

(Below) The Hon. Jean Chrétien with Fred Kearns at the October 29, 1976, press conference where Ottawa authorized Canadair to take up the option for designing the new business jet. Later to be Canada's prime minister, Chrétien was Minister of Industry, Trade and Commerce and an important supporter of the Challenger. (CL)

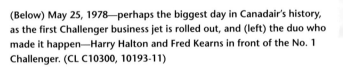

(Below) May 25, 1978—perhaps the biggest day in Canadair's history, as the first Challenger business jet is rolled out, and (left) the duo who made it happen—Harry Halton and Fred Kearns in front of the No. 1 Challenger. (CL C10300, 10193-11)

Building an early Challenger 600 wing. Nearly all airframe components were made in-house, but horizontal stabilizers were subcontracted to Canadian Aircraft Products of Richmond, BC, and rudders came from Fleet Industries of Fort Erie. (CL C9697-7)

and cost estimator Ben Locke who were trying to follow where the flood of changes was carrying the program cost. Every change had an effect on the aircraft's price. Locke remembered being in the board room as often as three times a day, trying to establish price changes: "Taylor had said that getting the airplane priced was like electing a Pope. He suggested we brick up the board room door and windows until white smoke blew out of the chimney with the news."

At the beginning of November, 1001 was ready for taxi tests. Director of flight operations and chief experimental test pilot Doug Adkins first made a number of slow-speed runs over low bumps to check nose-wheel steering. These he followed with a series of simulated takeoff runs, start-ing very slowly and increasing speed a little each time to get the feel of the airplane.

On the clear, unusually warm morning of November 8, 1978, Adkins was ready to go. With Norm Ronaasen as co-pilot, and flight test observers Bill Greening and Jim Martin, the Challenger took off at 9:26 a.m. and flew for 50 minutes. Adkins was all smiles as he left the airplane. "It's the best airplane we've ever built!" he told an equally jubilant Fred Kearns. They flew again after lunch for 45 minutes and would have made a third flight if the light had held. By the end of the first week they had logged nine hours 18 minutes. After 35 hours flying from Cartierville, Adkins and Ronaasen ferried 1001 to Mojave, California, for the flight test and certification programs.

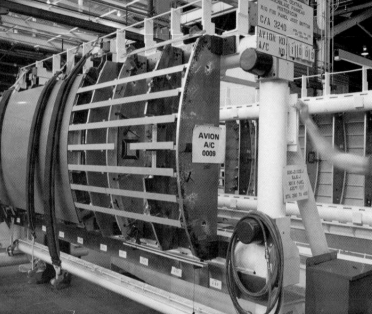

Three stages in building up the centre fuselage of Challenger 1009, going from masonite formers holding aircraft frames and stringers to being skinned. (CL C12221,C12371, C12369)

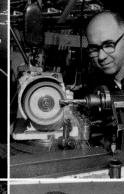

Challenger aircraft workers—the heart of the operation: an operator runs a grinding machine; another runs a Weldon form tool grinder. Next, a tool and die maker works on a jig, a staff engineer at his board, and technicians James Brownie and Bob Harris inspect the first Challenger landing gear members manufactured by Dowty Equipment of Canada. (CL 14336, '333, '331, '339, C9469)

Technicians ready a Lycoming engine for installation on Challenger 1009. The nacelles had recently arrived from subcontractor Rohr Industries of California. (CL 38424)

C-GCGR-X on its first flight on November 8, 1978. (CL)

Mojave

Early on, Canadair contracted with Flight Systems Inc. of Mojave to build a 2,400-m² (26,000-sq.-ft.) facility at Kern County Airport for the Challenger certification phase. On the fringe of the Mojave Desert, 100 miles northeast of Los Angeles, Mojave was chosen for its annual average of over 300 days of perfect flying weather. Flight Systems was run by Robert Laidlaw, a Canadian who had previously been a vice-president at Rockwell. Laidlaw had bought large numbers of ex-RCAF Sabres and T-33s and converted them to target drones for the U.S. Army.

By the end of 1978, a combined team of about 200 Canadair and Flight Systems personnel were at Mojave ready to welcome the first Challenger aircraft. The facility accommodated three aircraft, everything needed to operate and maintain them and all flight, preflight, maintenance, quality control, quality assurance, engine, instrument, purchasing and administration personnel. Adjacent

Test pilots Doug Adkins and Norm Ronaasen, who took the first Challenger on its first flight. (CL C21391, 13739)

buildings contained measuring equipment, equipment calibration labs and a computer complex to process test data generated by the aircraft.

Former USAF test pilot Jim Wood headed the Mojave team. Jack Greeniaus was engineering test manager, and Hugh Cavanagh, chief of experimental engineering. Cy Cockrell was responsible for structures; Robin French, mechanical systems; Dave Miles, propulsion; Derek Marshall, electrical; and Odd Michaelsen and John Taylor, aerodynamics. Gerry Barabé was responsible for the test aircraft; Matt Zaleski and Gordie Campbell for administration.

Flight Test and Certification

Three pre-production airplanes and one production airplane were used for certification: Challenger 1001 for stability, control and performance testing; 1002 and 1003 for power plant, auxiliary power unit and air-driven generator systems testing; and 1004 for the function and reliability portion of the program.

Certification was to have taken 13 months; instead it took 24. Aircraft empty weight was 1,100 kg (2,500 lb.) over estimate; the plan to save weight by using composite materials in place of aluminum was postponed because neither Canadair nor Transport Canada had sufficient data on composite behavior on which to base certification. The increased weight, combined with a higher-than-estimated fuel consumption, brought range well below

estimate. So maximum gross weight had to be increased to allow more fuel, in an effort to meet the guaranteed range.

John Holding, a design engineer who later became executive vice-president, now joined the program from British Aerospace. He found things so chaotic he told his wife not to unpack until he knew what was going on. "Everyone was trying to keep their heads above water," said Holding. "We were on a 24-hour cycle; we'd meet each morning at nine to decide what to do today."

The engines were a particular headache. It was evident that Lycoming had not completed testing and development of the ALF-502. Deliveries were late and reliability poor. It was March 12, 1979, before all the accumulated modifications could be incorporated, and pilots Norm Ronaasen and Al Baker were able to continue the certification program with the uprated engines.

The second pre-production aircraft flew on March 17, 1979; 14 days later, it became the first Challenger delivered to a customer when it was turned over to the Florida Company. This was only a formality because the owner immediately leased it back to Canadair as a test aircraft.

The Challenger flight test centre at Mojave, then a view of the second pre-production 600 before a test mission on a bright but chilly morning in the California desert. The dark shape at the fuselage tip is the spin chute housing. (CL 37764, C12188)

On June 5, Adkins flew it non-stop from Montreal to the Paris Air Show.

Despite the show of optimism at Paris, all was not well with the program. The schedule continued to lag, and by late 1979 the first indications of cash problems were appearing. Program costs were $20 million over forecast. On a new program, the peak financial exposure generally occurs just before deliveries begin. For the Challenger program this was to have happened in 1978 but the schedule was already a year behind. The planned six day interval between roll-out and first flight had been six months. By the end of 1979, only one aircraft had been delivered, instead of an intended 11, a deficiency which, when combined with fewer-than-forecast pre-delivery deposits, resulted in a shortfall of $70 million. As a result of these factors, interest expenses exceeded the forecast level by some $14 million. Aird's credit lines were severely strained, and lenders were now requiring that loan agreements carry a clause guaranteeing payment if the government sold Canadair.

Stall Test Controversy

A problem had developed with the flight test and certification program. It involved Canadair engineers and the Transport Canada (TC) team assigned to certify that the Challenger met all aspects of FAR Part 25. The two groups differed in their interpretation of the requirements regarding stall tests.

Stall tests are vital. They determine the speed at which an aircraft stalls in various conditions of flight and loading. This is critical because it establishes the slower speed boundaries for safe flight: the lower the stall speed, the shorter the aircraft's takeoff and landing run; the shorter the run, the more airfields that can be used. A few knots of stall speed can have a profound effect on the acceptability of the aircraft in the marketplace.

High-speed, swept-wing planes with T-tails often react violently when they stall. Manufacturers therefore equip them with stall barrier systems to ensure they never get into a stall. The Challenger aircraft's stall barrier system has two main components: a stick shaker and a stick pusher. When the aircraft nears the stall, the pilot's control column, or "stick", starts to shake and the shaking increases as the stall point is approached. If the pilot does not take corrective action, just before the aircraft stalls the pusher applies a strong downward pressure to the stick

The cockpit of an early Challenger 600 nears completion. These looks would be greatly changed by the introduction of "glass" (cathode ray tube, or CRT) data displays in the 601. (CL 14647)

that allows airspeed to build up again. The Challenger aircraft has a dual shaker/pusher barrier system so that, in the unusual event one fails, there is a back-up. The system also has a horn which sounds and a light which flashes when the aircraft nears the stall.

The aviation certifying agencies in the United States, Britain and France do not require T-tail jet transports to demonstrate "natural" stalls with the barrier system switched off. Instead, they rely on the proven reliability of modern barrier systems to prevent the aircraft from stalling. TC, however, decided Canadair must demonstrate an acceptable and consistent natural stall without the safety net of the barrier system. To give the Challenger a consistent stall, the engineers put a short strip of metal, called a stall strip, on the leading edge of the left wing. While this ensured that the aircraft would roll left when it stalled, it also increased the stall speed and lengthened the takeoff and landing run.

Loss of 1001

Disaster struck on April 3, 1980. While investigating the stall characteristics of Challenger 1001, with the barrier system switched off, a malfunctioning angle-of-attack indicator misled the pilot, and the aircraft entered a deep stall. A deep stall occurs when the airflow over the tail is blanked out by the wing, causing the elevators to lose their effectiveness, thus making the pilot unable to lower the nose and recover.

Each of the three test Challenger aircraft was equipped with a drag chute as a safeguard against such a situation. The crew deployed the chute and regained control, but the chute failed to jettison and the crew was unable to stop 1001's rapid descent. Co-pilot Dave Gollings and flight test observer Bill Scott escaped by parachute at a low altitude but Norm Ronaasen was killed when the aircraft crashed with the drag chute still attached.

Eric Norman Ronaasen had a diploma in Aeronautical Engineering from the Northrop Aeronautical Institute. He had joined the RCAF in 1950. In 1955, he graduated from the Empire Test Pilots School at Farnborough, England, and was posted to the National Aeronautics Establishment in Ottawa. In 1958, he was one of two RCAF pilots chosen to test the Avro Arrow, but that program was cancelled before he flew the aircraft.

Ronaasen spent the rest of his 25 years in the RCAF test flying, first at the Central Experimental and Proving Establishment (CEPE) at Ottawa, then at CEPE in Cold Lake, Alberta; at Scottish Aviation in Prestwick; and at Baden-Soellingen, Germany. In recognition of his contributions to the development of aviation, he was awarded the Order of Military Merit.

A brilliant pilot and a charming, unassuming gentleman, Ronaasen had done the majority of the Challenger stall tests. His death came as a blow to everyone. In his memory, Canadair sponsored the Ronaasen Award given for the best paper delivered at the Canadian Aeronautics and Space Institute annual flight test symposium. The first award, in 1984, was to Jim Henry of Canadair for his paper on the flutter test program of the Challenger 601.

Challengers 601 and 610

On March 14, 1980, Fred Kearns's promise to FedEx was fulfilled when Canadair's board of directors approved production of a stretched Challenger, initially designated the Challenger E and, later, the CL-610. The board also announced that a variant of the standard Challenger with General Electric engines (Challenger 601), would be made available to customers in the same time frame as the CL-610.

In July 1980, Kearns made some significant changes to the program management team. He brought in Bob Ross, director, surveillance systems engineering and CL-289

program manager, as vice-president, Challenger programs, and made him responsible for technical and design matters, reporting to Halton. Kearns gave Ron Neal responsibility for project engineering and Mojave.

Ross found the program in a sad state. The Challenger 600 was still about 1,100 kg (2,500 lb.) overweight, drag and fuel consumption were up, engine thrust and range were down, and the program was about 12 months behind schedule. A real effort was needed to identify deficiencies and decide how to correct them. Performance improvement and weight reduction programs were started; changes were authorized. Fuselage fuel tanks were ordered to permit an increase in range; and the outfitting allowance–the allowance for additional equipment and

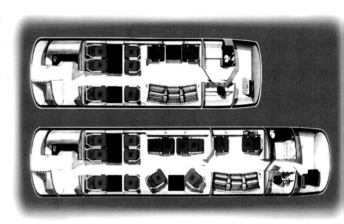

Interior comparison between the CL-600 and the proposed CL-610. (CL 14670)

furnishings installed for the customer at completion centres–was increased. To accommodate higher weights, maximum gross weight was scheduled to be increased to 18,600 kg (41,100 lb.).

Certification

At last certification testing was completed. Only the paperwork remained. This involved preparing nearly 1,500 documents showing compliance with FAR Part 25. Another 1,200 approvals had to be obtained from Canadian authorities. It was a formidable mass of paper–over 8,000 pages which Harry Whiteman, who had retired in 1978, came back to handle with his usual quiet efficiency.

The Challenger 600 received Canadian Type Approval on August 11, 1980, and U.S. Type Certificate on November 7, 1980. These carried a number of restrictions. The aircraft was not permitted to fly into known icing conditions; the thrust reversers could not be used; there were limitations on the autopilot; takeoff weight was restricted to 15,000 kg (33,000 lb.), and the maximum operating speed limited to 592 km/h (368 mph). But at least Challenger jets could be flown and delivered to completion centres. While they were having interiors installed and customer-prescribed equipment added—a procedure which took around 12 months—Canadair could incorporate improvements. By Christmas 1980, the maximum takeoff weight was already up to 16,000 kg (36,000 lb.).

Richmond Returns

In the fall of 1980, Kearns hired Dick Richmond as a consultant. During Canadair's early years he had played a key role in several aircraft programs, the development of missiles and drones and the introduction of the systems approach. Since leaving the company in 1960, he had been vice-president, operations and a director of Pratt & Whitney Canada; president, CEO and a director of McDonnell Douglas of Canada; and president, chief operating officer and a director of Spar Aerospace. Richmond was conservative, gruff, deliberate, and had earned a reputation as an organizer. Of his tenure as president of Spar, Larry Clarke (Spar's founder) said: "Over his five years with the company, he put in place the organization and the people that resulted in the company's most famous success, the Canadarm." Kearns hoped he could do the same for Canadair.

Richmond first looked at the status of the Challenger 601 and stretched CL-610. He found that only Saul Bernstein, Tim Douglass, Bob Ward and a few others were working on them. They had a concept, but not enough design information to substantiate the advertised perfor-

mance of either aircraft. Also major subcontracts had been awarded—to LTV for engine nacelles, and to Rockwell for rear fuselage design—but a lack of adequate definition and monitoring had resulted in both subcontractors making costly, uncoordinated decisions. Richmond asked Kearns for a six-month extension on the program schedules. Kearns gave him three.

In January 1981, Richmond rejoined Canadair as executive vice-president, operations. Two months later, at the urging of the board of directors, Kearns gave him total control of the Challenger program. At the same time,

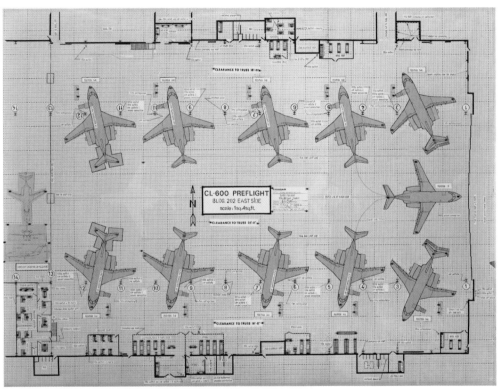

The floor plan for B202 as remodeled for CL-600 preflight requirements. Harvards, Sabres and CF-104s were once manufactured in this space. (CL 36171)

Kearns introduced a program of cash conservation and spending constraints, and appointed Halton to head a small group of members of senior management to oversee it. These were the first of many management changes.

Richmond found the Challenger program still in a state of confusion. Many of the modifications dictated by TC and the FAA as required for certification had not yet been designed. At Throner's suggestion, aircraft on the production line were brought up to a certain status and then moved to Plant 2 where Throner set up two modification lines: one to incorporate the modifications re-

Views of the "600". C-GCGS-X (s/n 1002) was an early flight test model, while N637ML (s/n 1024) was one of the first delivered.

No. 144601 was the first example for the Canadian Forces. It went to 412 Squadron in Ottawa for VIP duties. In the Canadian military the CL-600 was redesignated CC-144. The in-flight photo of 144609 shows it dummied up with antennae for the electronic warfare training role.

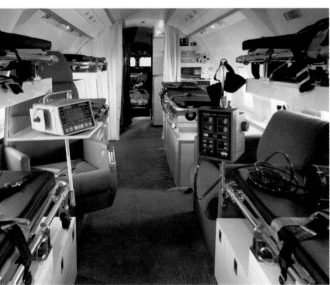

The rear three-quarters view shows C-GCGT-X in flight. Then, the interior of a CL-600 fitted out as a four-litter air ambulance, and C-GBKC-X on its delivery to TAG with the board of directors: Don Watson, unknown, Jean-Pierre Goyer, Charles Rathgeb, Walter Ward, Dave Culver, Leo Lavoie, Fred Kearns, Guy Desmarais, John Pepper. (CL C17977)

quired for certification, the other to install fuselage fuel tanks. Pete Ginnochio, vice-president, customer service, sent teams to completion centres to do the same. Engine deliveries, however, were still so far behind that, after an aircraft was delivered for completion, the engines were removed and returned to Canadair for use on the next delivery.

In April 1981, Dick Richmond got a further three months extension on the decision date for the Challenger 601 and CL-610. At about this time, Neal resigned, Ross became vice-president, Challenger programs, and Eric Aubrey became vice-president, Challenger engineering. Two months later, Vince Ambrico, who had come to Canadair from Fairchild Republic Aviation in 1979, took over as vice-president, manufacturing (Plant 1) including Challenger manufacturing, while Andy Throner became senior vice-president, manufacturing operations (Plants 2 and 3).

Money Problems

By now, funding was a pressing problem. With interest rates and operating costs skyrocketing and revenue just a dribble, Aird had been forced to obtain substantial loans from the banks on the strength of so-called letters of comfort from the government. Though not true legal commitments (they lacked parliamentary approval) the banks accepted them as collateral, confident that the government would not renege if the program failed. The parliamentary opposition suggested that letters of comfort were a political move to hide the facts from parliament, but Aird denied this. "Thousands of copies of every loan offering circular were distributed," he said, "and each contained either a copy of the letter of comfort or an outline of its essential conditions."

Out with the 610 – In with the 601

At a meeting of top management during the summer

meant the loss of some business. There had been 49 firm orders for the CL-610, and another 30 in final negotiation but all was not lost. Offered an incentive of a $1 million reduction in list price, customers for 19 of the 49 units on order switched to 601s.

Peter Aird's financial report to the end of 1981 presented a gloomy picture. He noted the total cost of the Challenger program to date as $1.2 billion, an increase of $530 million over original figures. Thirty-three aircraft had been delivered instead of the forecast 113. Only $377 million had been collected from sales, $370 million less than anticipated. The audit committee and the board of directors considered a write-down of inventory but decided to await the 1982 financial results.

Despite well publicized problems with the program, Jim Taylor's team was successfully selling Challenger aircraft. In 1981, it sold 22 during a worldwide recession which saw record high interest rates. Orders for 600s

The CL-601 prototype (C-GCGT-X) photographed from a Learjet chase plane over the Mojave desert in April 1982. (CL C24063-2)

shut-down of 1981, Richmond reported that the CL-610, instead of being a stretched 600, was a new design and would be too heavy even for a more powerful GE engine. He recommended postponing it, concentrating on fixing the 600, and redefining and speeding up the 601. Kearns realized there was no point in prolonging the agony, and on August 24 announced postponement of the 610. It

stood at 125, of which 40 had been delivered and 12 were in service. Since the start of the program, the aircraft's price had more than doubled to $9.5 million US in 1981 dollars.

Some of the early customers wanted to cancel because of the shortfall in range. For months, Bob Wohl, Bob Lefcort, director of legal services, and Matt Milnes, director, Challenger contracts, worked with customers to keep them on board and their contracts in the backlog. In many cases the range shortfall was countered by an offer to install either extra fuel tanks or winglets, free of charge. The tanks increased range by 445 kms (242 nm) but took six to eight weeks to install. The winglets added 210 kms (114 nm) but only required a week to 10 days to fit, so the majority–55 aircraft–got winglets.

The 601 prototype was the third pre-production 600 (s/n 1003) fitted with a redesigned rear fuselage and nacelles to carry the 38.5 kN (8,650 lb.) thrust GE CF34-1A engines. LTV designed and made the nacelles; Rockwell designed the structural changes to the rear fuselage; and Canadair made the system changes and built the rear fuselage. The new rear end was then flown in a Short Belfast freighter to Mojave where a GE prototype group

fitted it to s/n 1003 (now re-serialed s/n 3991) under the direction of Peter Candfield and Gerry Barabé. Doug Adkins and Jamie Sutherland took the Challenger 601 prototype on its scheduled maiden flight on April 10, 1982.

In June 1982, Ross was made vice-president, Challenger engineering. John Smith, a former Canadair employee who had left in 1964 and had recently returned, became vice-president, Challenger programs and Len Box became vice-president, engineering and technology.

The first production 601 was rolled out on schedule on August 17, 1982, and Adkins and Ian McDonald flew it for the first time a month later. In addition to GE engines, it had increased fuel capacity and winglets which together increased range to 6,365 km (3,365 nm).

Challenger 601 wings are built up in their jigs and on the floor. (CL 38418)

The busy CL-601 final line in 1983. S/n 3014 (later N14PN) is closest. (CL C28809-5)

The first production CL-601 is rolled out at Plant 1 to the joy of hundreds of those who made it possible. (CL C25439-4)

Some of the key men from the CL-601 program: Armand Lavigne (director, final assembly), R.D. Richmond (executive V-P and COO), Fred Kearns (president), Vince Ambrico (V-P manufacturing) and Claude Roy (director, pre-flight). (CL C25443-10)

Production Cutback

By July 1982, Challenger production reached five a month, but few aircraft were being delivered. Many undelivered ones had been ordered by TAG which would not take them because of performance deficiencies. Richmond went to Aird with a proposal that production be stopped until the contractual issues with TAG and the other customers were settled. Aird agreed, and he and Richmond persuaded Kearns to authorize laying off 1,700 production workers for six to eight weeks. In September 1982, 1,300 people were laid off for eight weeks and 400 more, permanently. Halting production also gave time to plan a new schedule based on a two-a-month production rate.

At about this time Ottawa, concerned about the constantly changing schedules and forecasts, set up a committee to study the program. To Aird and MacKenzie's surprise, its forecasts of 1982 deliveries were more optimistic than Canadair's; but the report was critical of Canadair management, in particular its practice of making vital decisions without first consulting its board of directors.

A general perception in government circles was that some Challenger sales were "under the table." Matt Milnes, director of Challenger contracts at the time, remembers three separate groups of lawyers coming to Canadair to scrutinize every Challenger contract for irregularities. They found none, but severely criticized the business decisions made by management.

The worldwide economic recession finally hit the business jet market. Customers began cancelling orders. Inter-

est rates soared so high that, at one point, Canadair was paying 18 per cent on day-to-day credit lines. Then another government committee showed up. It never got a chance to finish its job, because the government withdrew it. On November 25, 1982, Ottawa put Canadair under the control of the Canada Development Investment Corp. (CDIC).

CDIC

CDIC had been incorporated in May 1982 to hold the government's 48.2 per cent of the Canada Development Corp. and in November 1982 CDIC was given responsibility to manage Ottawa's investments in Canadair and four other companies the government wished to sell to the private sector: de Havilland, Eldorado Nuclear, Massey-Ferguson and Teleglobe.

Heading CDIC was Joel Bell, a lawyer and economist who had worked on government missions and committees. Bell was one of the bright boys in the Department of Energy who developed Ottawa's national energy policy with respect to the oil companies and the formation of PetroCan. Kearns and company were convinced that Bell intended to terminate the Challenger program–and maybe Canadair as well.

Just before Christmas 1982, with all indications that the 1982 financial results would show further deterioration, Aird advised Kearns that the financial situation qualified for an inventory write-down. Kearns concurred and so advised CDIC. With Challenger program costs now totalling $1.5 billion and the company's book value at only $255 million, CDIC decided to reduce the $1.5 billion to $127 million as being a reasonable value of in-

The CDIC's Joel Bell in a typical scrum with the media during hard times at Canadair. (CL C28387-7)

ventory. With a stroke of the pen, the company's net worth was reduced from a positive $255 million to a negative $1.1 billion.

Though Canadair as a whole was in trouble, the Challenger was starting to hit its stride. On February 25, 1983, after a relatively problem-free certification program, the 601 received its Canadian type approval, ahead of schedule and meeting all performance guarantees. FAA pilot Jim Plackis came to Montreal on March 11 to do the final test flight for U.S. type certification. After two hours in the air he was so pleased that he called the Canadair radio room from somewhere northwest of North Bay, Ontario, and had them patch him through to the FAA office in New York to report his approval. The New York office immediately arranged for confirmation of the U.S. type certificate to be telexed to Canadair where it was awaiting Plackis when he landed.

The Fifth Estate
Before long, reports of the company's financial problems began to spread. In March 1983, CDIC wrote Kearns that the CBC television network was considering making Canadair the subject of an investigative report for its weekly feature, *Fifth Estate*. The first of three *Fifth Estate* programs was televised April 13, 1983. On CDIC's instructions, Canadair's senior management group viewed the program together in the Plant 1 Harold Room. They witnessed a one-hour mixture of facts, half-truths, distortions and innuendo.

Kearns, the members of the board and senior management were furious. The employees who had worked hard to make the program a success were devastated. They were not surprised at the criticisms levelled at some members of management; what really hurt was the criticism of the airplane. They had put heart and soul into the project. They knew that mistakes had been made but were confident they had turned the corner and now had a good product.

Flight test personnel at Mojave in early 1983. Most were from Flight Systems, but three were Canadair men: Junior Dartois(standing second from the left), Harvey Fournier (front left) and Gerry Barabé (front centre). The CL-601 had just been certified and they were soon to return to Montreal. (via G. Barabé)

The story made front-page headlines, and Challenger customers read them. One important customer cancelled its order for four Challenger jets saying that it could not afford to be associated with a product that was the subject of public criticism. That the negative publicity did not cause even worse damage was due to the fact that, by then, the majority of owners had acquired confidence in the Challenger and knew that, given a little time, they would have a great aircraft. Nonetheless, the program had a negative effect on the market.

Gilbert S. Bennett
On Friday, May 13, Fred Kearns announced his retirement effective June 10. Bell replaced him with Gil Bennett, a corporate lawyer and CDIC vice-president who had been overseeing Canadair. Bell also appointed Dick Richmond chief operating officer. Bennett was a graduate of the University of Toronto and Osgoode Hall Law School. Called to the bar in 1964, he practised in Toronto until 1979, then became president and chief operating officer of Comstock International Ltd., which he refinanced, reorganized and returned to profitability. He had

At a party to celebrate his 30 years with Canadair, Fred Kearns and his wife, Beth, share a glass of wine. The keg was done up to resemble the Spitfire Kearns flew in WWII. (CL C15853)

This crowd of Canadair employees got together to celebrate the certification of the CL-601. Included are: 1 Wally Remington, 2 Bob Mather, 3 Ed Coates, 4 Tony Natlacen, 5 Gordie Rawlinson, 6 Lloyd Hess, 7 John Holding, 8 Martin Eley, 9 Odd Michaelsen, 10 Bob Werrett, 11 Ken Fewkes, 12 Wes Ewanchyna, 13 Andrew Jordan,14 Ralph Gallinger, 15 Gerry Marsters, 16 Dave Turner, 17 Tony Barber, 18 Georgi Comino, 19 Jim Henry, 20 John Carr, 21 Richard Belanger, 22 Bob Ross, 23 Peter Candfield, 24 Tim Douglass and 25 Scotty McLean. (CL C27325-5)

come to Canadair in February 1983 as a CDIC representative.

Bennett proved a good choice for president. His quiet, reasoned demeanor alone brought an atmosphere of calm to the executive offices. He viewed his role as a caretaker and hence was not greatly interested in the operating side of the business. However, he did produce excellent strategic plans and he and Richmond deserve much of the credit for beginning to turn Canadair around.

When Bennett had first arrived at Canadair he found Kearns defiant and senior management demoralized and defensive. Morale was low because most employees expected CDIC to close down Canadair and/or the Challenger program. Interviewed later, Bennett denied such intentions adding that while Bell had an extremely healthy skepticism about the company and its programs, his mandate was to do whatever made good business sense. Bennett's job was to develop a rationale for either shutting down the program or continuing it.

After long sessions with Richmond and MacKenzie, supplemented by discussions with Kearns, Aird, Wohl and Lefcort, Bennett concluded that Canadair's management had a great deal more talent and commitment than previously thought. He advised Bell

Gil Bennett, who took over the reigns at Canadair when Fred Kearns retired in 1983. (CL)

that he felt Canadair could operate profitably for the next two or three years without much difficulty. His main concern was where the company would get the capital to develop new products.

Committee Hearings

Now the government and the public wanted to know the facts about Canadair and the Challenger. Between June 6 and June 30, 1983, Bell, Bennett, Kearns, Richmond, Aird and others appeared on several occasions before two government committees investigating Canadair. On June 30, they appeared before the Standing Committee on Public Accounts to rebut some of the *Fifth Estate* criticisms. At Taylor's suggestion, they brought along an expert witness, Dick Van Gemert, director of flight operations for Xerox Corp, which had three early Challenger jets.

Van Gemert's lengthy answers to the committee's searching questions were supportive of Canadair and the Challenger. Asked his opinion of the *Fifth Estate* assertions, he said, "I believe they were looking for negative support and we could not provide any negative support. We are very positive on the aircraft. I do not believe that issue came across. As I recall it, they photographed our shuttle that runs to Rochester, loading some passengers, and the last comment was, 'and this aircraft only goes 250 miles to Rochester'."

One MP present, Mr. Fennell, commented: "I do not sympathize with this type of reporting, basically. I think it is negative and bad." Bell also criticized the program, but that did not change the opinion of the Canadair representatives and most of their colleagues who remained convinced that CDIC inspired the program to ensure that Canadair management took all the blame. Interviewed later, Bennett strongly discounted any CDIC involvement, saying that many people, in and out of government, thought Kearns, Halton and Aird were hiding something. He felt that an exposé was wanted, and that anyone could have promoted the television program.

The U.S. trade magazine *Business & Commercial Aviation* conducted a survey in mid-July and found that companies flying Challenger business jets were overwhelmingly satisfied. In August, Bennett assured the audience at an operators' conference that the program would continue. The operators' comments were generally very positive about the aircraft which one referred to as "a hell of an airplane."

On October 18, 1983, the CBC aired a second installment of the *Fifth Estate*. This one zeroed in on Taylor's organization, but the tone regarding the Challenger was almost apologetic. Nonetheless, the viewer's impression was that the Canadair situation was still deteriorating.

The axe fell on October 23, 1983. On that day, some members of senior management were fired, others were demoted, several were asked to take early retirement and many were transferred to other jobs. Only Wohl and Ouellet remained from Kearns's 1976 senior team. Halton and Aird left on November 18. Taylor became chairman of Canadair Inc., but he soon left to join Gates Learjet as president and CEO. Hurley and Juvonen left to start their own company. Hundreds of employees were laid off, and morale sank to an all-time low as others awaited the pink slip. The labor force fell from 7,200 in September 1982 to 4,320 at the end of 1983. Now, with Challenger production only 15 a year, Ottawa was set to put Canadair on a new footing.

Bennett Plan

On March 13, 1984, Senator Jack Austin, the minister responsible for CDIC, tabled a report before the House of Commons committee on finance, trade and economic affairs, containing a plan for restructuring Canadair. Bennett had devised the plan under which CDIC would incorporate a subsidiary, New Canadair, to assume the assets and current liabilities of the existing Canadair Ltd. (Old Canadair). Old Canadair would be left with no assets of significance and $1.35 billion in debt, to be repaid by the government as it became due. The plan predicted that, relieved of the interest burden on the past debt, New Canadair should be profitable by 1985.

On March 31, 1984, the government announced approval of the CDIC plan and the formation of a new Canadair Limited. It kept all the assets of its predecessor, the plants, equipment and inventory, plus $350 million in equity. It was debt-free, the debts having been transferred to a paper company, Canadair Financial Corp. Canadair, the Challenger aircraft and 4,000 or so employees, had been given a new lease on life.

The slowdown in production gave the engineers who had worked on the Challenger jet since Day One, a chance to reflect on the reasons for the program's problems. The general opinion was that it was a mix of naivety and over-optimism. Andy Throner summed it up: "We were naive to think we could design and build a state-of-the-art aircraft in such a short time, with a small nucleus of engineers which had neither designed a complete aircraft of such size and complexity nor possessed a basic established philosophy to start with."

The consensus was that only Fred Kearns could have sold the Challenger to the government. Without his and Harry Halton's determination to keep it alive, there would not have been a Canadair. Without Peter Aird to find the funds and Jim Taylor to get those vital initial sales, there would not have been a Challenger. As for the workers, while they hated the program at the time, they wouldn't have missed it for the world.

Fred Kearns died in November 1987. In his eulogy, Peter Aird said: "Every time a CL-215 puts out a fire; every time a reconnaissance drone is launched; every time a Challenger takes off; every time any of these things happens, a little tribute is paid to the initiative and vision of Fred Kearns."

New Canadair

Gil Bennett brought in some new blood. In April 1983, CDIC appointed two former Gulfstream marketing executives, Charles G. (Chuck) Vogeley and Roger L. Hazelton, as president and CEO and executive vice-presi-

With the Challenger at the head, this busy "formation" of Canadair-designed and licence-built projects was put together for the company's 40th anniversary in 1984. (CL C9282)

dent, respectively, of Canadair Inc. CDIC also appointed Bryan Moss vice-president of sales. He had joined Canadair Inc. from Lockheed in 1979 and had been responsible for sales in the southeastern United States.

Bennett hired Carl Perry from Hughes Helicopters as executive vice-president to direct worldwide marketing, business development and strategic planning for all Canadair products. Dick Richmond continued as executive vice-president and chief operating officer.

The last Challenger 600, s/n 1085, was delivered on June 22, 1983. With production concentrating on the more-promising Challenger 601, Canadair once again financially stable, and under almost completely new top management, spirits began to rise. Efforts to reduce operating expenses began to pay off. The operating loss for fiscal 1983 decreased by $61.3 million from the $145.1 million loss recorded in fiscal 1982.

Another major headache was eased in February 1984 when Canadair and TAG signed a new agreement covering sales in the Middle East. Under its terms, TAG would continue as exclusive distributor and representative in 22 Middle East countries. The 100th Challenger jet was delivered on March 15, 1984.

Records

Meanwhile, the reputation of the Challenger was improving by leaps and bounds. At a seminar on June 25, 1984

the director of maintenance for FedEx told the audience: "This is the finest aircraft to come off an assembly line." He asked those present to join him in a well deserved round of applause for Canadair, Avco Lycoming and General Electric. The reaction was spontaneous and enthusiastic.

The Challenger achieved international recognition between July 22 and 24, 1984, when a TAG 601 set a record for its class by flying around the world in less than 50 hours. Captained by TAG's executive vice-president, Aziz Ojjeh, accompanied by TAG pilots Gerard Streiff, Jeff Weber and Duncan Higgins, and Canadair employees, pilot Jerry Westphal and flight engineer François Tessier, the aircraft covered 37,800 km (20,526 nm) in 49 hours 27 minutes at an average speed of 754.94 km/h (469.11 mph).

Some previous Challenger records had gone relatively unnoticed in the heat of the program crisis. On September 1 and 2, 1983, Challenger 601 s/n 3002, flown by Martin Summerard and Ian McDonald, with Roger Booth as flight engineer, Gerry Piat and François Tessier, maintenance technicians, and Howard Goldberg, official FAI observer, had flown 7,023 km (3,814 nm) non-stop from Calgary to London, England, in a record 9 hours 4 minutes. Between July 6 and 9, 1983, the same 601 and pilots had set 18 international time-to-climb records for this class.

The crew of the record-breaking Calgary-London flight: an FAI observer, Martin Summerard (captain), Ian Mc Donald (co-pilot) and Gerry Piat (Canadair flight ops). (CL 49765)

Luftwaffe Sale

Canadair returned to profitability in the second quarter of 1984. Results for the quarter ending June 30 showed a net income of $12.3 million compared with a loss of $24.7 million for the same period in 1983. Adding to this news, Gil Bennett announced that, following intense competition with Gulfstream and Dassault, the West German ministry of defence was ordering seven Challenger 601 aircraft for the Luftwaffe.

The sale was a fitting conclusion to months of work by vice-president, government sales, Bill Carr; vice-president, Challenger programs, John Smith; Canadair's German representative Peter Otto; contracts manager Paul Francoeur; Luftwaffe program manager, Robin French; and a proposal team of personnel from a dozen departments, all under the direction of Bob Wohl. It was one of Canadair's most important sales, for it happened at a time when the international aviation community was still unsure as to the continued existence of the company. The West German government only agreed to the sale after Ottawa provided assurance that it would continue to support the program. During the negotiations Bill Carr made 53 trips between Canada and Germany.

September 1984 brought a federal election and a new Conservative government

Bill Carr, whose strenuous efforts resulted in the pivotal sale of CL-601s to the Luftwaffe. (CL C35884)

to Canada. Joel Bell was replaced as president of CDIC by Paul Marshall. As Gil Bennett was also a government appointee, nobody would have been surprised if he too had been replaced; fortunately for Canadair he was not. Marshall's mandate was to privatize all CDIC's assets including those of Canadair; however, continuity of Canadair's existing programs and operations was to be a number one priority. In September 1984, Canadair Inc. at Westport, Connecticut, was renamed "Canadair Challenger Inc." to focus attention on its role as the marketing group for the Challenger aircraft.

Though Canadair's financial situation was improving—in 1984 it made a profit of $6 million on sales of $376 million—the business jet market continued to be poor. In March 1985, however, the government gave the program a boost by buying eight 600s and four 601s under a contract negotiated by Matt Milnes. Four of the 600s were completed aircraft exchanged by TAG for four green (uncompleted) 601s. Another was the Ontario government's 600, exchanged for two CL-215 water bombers. Still another was the second pre-production aircraft. It was unsuitable for conversion to a business aircraft configuration, so would be used by the Canadian Forces as an airborne electronic test bed. The 601s would replace the aging Jetstars and Falcons in the government's administrative fleet. Derek Gilmour was appointed program manager and Stuart Hill, project manager.

In May 1985, Gil Bennett announced his intention to resign as president and CEO in August and return to CDIC. Ottawa asked him to stay on until a suitable replacement could be found, and he agreed.

The 601-3A and China

At the National Business Aircraft Association convention on September 24, 1985, Canadair launched an improved version of the Challenger, the 601-3A. Powered by uprated GE CF34-3A engines capable of providing rated thrust up to an ambient temperature of 21°C (70°F), the 601-3A featured a state-of-the-art all-digital EFIS cockpit, cockpit voice recorder, additional landing lights and power-assisted passenger door. Expected to have a range of 6,365 km (3,365 nm), it sold for $12.3 million US. First deliveries were scheduled for the spring of 1987.

Another important sale was recorded on October 28, 1985, when corporate vice-president Bob Wohl signed an agreement with Poly Technologies, a government subsidiary of the People's Republic of China, for three 601s. Like the German sale, this was the culmination of considerable effort by a large number of Canadair people, including Chris Anderson, Paul Francœur, George Laforme, John Male and John Nicas. It was also a direct result of the gesture Fred Kearns had made to the Chinese seven years earlier; contrary to his prediction, it happened in his lifetime.

Pierre Des Marais II

On December 26, 1985, Gil Bennett resigned and Pierre Des Marais II became president and CEO of Canadair.

President of one of the largest printing firms in Canada, he was vice-chairman of CDIC, a member of the Canadair board since 1984 and chairman of the board since October 1985. He was formerly mayor of Outremont, Quebec.

Des Marais's role at Canadair was as caretaker pending the sale of the company; as such, he was mainly concerned with day-to-day activities and proved to be an efficient administrator. The financial situation continued to improve. Results for fiscal 1985 showed a profit of $27.6 million on sales of $438 million.

More Uncertainty

On January 24, 1986, Industry Minister Sinclair Stevens reaffirmed the government's intention to sell Canadair. Three months later, he reported receiving proposals from five interested groups: Bombardier Inc. of Montreal; Canadian Aerospace Technologies,

The first Luftwaffe Challenger jet just before its delivery overseas and, at left, some of those involved in the Luftwaffe agreement: Ray Learmond, Dick Richmond, General Obleser (commander of the Luftwaffe) with two of his officers, Bill Carr, Jim Ross and Jack Henry. (CL C21134-6)

An array of new Challenger jets at Cartierville. Closest is 144615 (alias C-GCUR), a Canadian forces 601. Its civil registration allowed it to be flight tested by Canadair. Clockwise are a Luftwaffe 601-1A (12+04, s/n 3049)), C-GCFI (601-1A, s/n 3020) of Transport Canada, a Canadian Forces 600, and a Chinese 601. (CL)

also of Montreal; a consortium led by Fleet Aerospace of Fort Erie, Ontario; the IMP Group of Halifax; and Magna International of Toronto.

In May 1986, Chuck Vogeley retired as president and CEO of Canadair Challenger Inc. and was replaced by former executive vice-president, Roger Hazelton. Bryan Moss was appointed executive vice-president, sales. The first Luftwaffe aircraft entered service on July 9, 1986. That day Hazelton reported total sales of 123–82 Challenger 600s and 41 601s. Bill Carr stated that Canadair had sold 21 aircraft for government and military roles in the previous 15 months, and Dick Richmond noted good progress by a corrective action team in removing a "small number of, but continuing, customer problems." Meanwhile, CDIC's efforts to find a buyer for Canadair eventually bore fruit. On August 18, 1986, Ottawa announced that Canadair had been sold to Bombardier Inc. of Montreal.

Donald C. Lowe

Donald C. Lowe was appointed president of Canadair on September 26, 1986. Des Marais continued as chairman and CEO until completion of the acquisition by Bombardier.

Don Lowe was an Ontarian with a bachelor of applied science degree from the University of Toronto and a master of science degree from the University of Birmingham, England. Employed in the General Motors organization from 1957-1975, he had been assistant general manager of GM's plant at Ste-Thérèse, Quebec, and director of manufacturing at Vauxhall Motors in England. Lowe was president and CEO of Pratt & Whitney Canada from 1975 to 1980, and president of Pratt & Whitney's Commercial Products Division in Hartford, Connecticut from 1980 to 1982. A member of Canadair's board of directors from 1982 to 1984, he had been president and CEO of Kidd Creek Mines Ltd. since 1983.

Tall, grey-haired Lowe had a presence that prompted

(Above) VH-MZL was the first Challenger sold in Australia. (CL C36434-15)

(Left) General Electric engines for the CL-601 are built up at the GE plant in Massachusetts. (CL)

some to consider him the archetypical CEO. Senior staff described him as shrewd, forthright and well respected—a team-builder who had a very positive effect on the early acceptance of Bombardier.

Doug Adkins, Malcolm MacGregor and Bill Greening made the first flight of the Challenger 601-3A on September 28, 1986. This marked the beginning of another phase in recovery of the Challenger. At the end of 1986, sales stood at 148, with 142 delivered (19 in the previous year). This must have been encouraging to the new owner.

(Facing page) A spectacular view of CL-601-1A N602CC (s/n 3065) climbing sharply from the airport at St. George, Utah. (Above) Another superb photograph of the same aircraft, this time over San Francisco. Then (below) staff on the final line proudly receive one of Canadair's quality assurance awards. (CL)

(Above) A Swiss 601-3A of ALG Aeroleasing, Europe's largest corporate jet charter company in the early 1990s. (CL)

(Above) The crowded floor of the Canadair Challenger Inc. hangar at Westport, Connecticut, with 600s and 601s in view. (CL C32231)

(Left) Longtime tech rep Jim Fitzpatrick (left) became general manager of the Challenger Service Centre at Oberpfaffenhofen, Germany. Claude Roy (right) was his director of pre-flight. (CL 55267)

(Right) TAG's first CL-601 visiting Oberpfaffenhofen. (via CL)

(Above) One of the airways inspection 601s used by Transport Canada in calibrating instrument landing systems and other navigation aids at major airports. (CL)

Inside and out... Challenger 601-3A HS-TVA was ordered by Thai Airways International as its corporate jet. (CL)

Canadair-sponsored air cadets leave Dorval in an RCAF North Star on a November 1954 outing to Ottawa. Next, the cadets parade in downtown Montreal in April 1961. Canadair air cadet alumni include many who later worked for the company or went into flying. (CL F2404, 26059)

Since 1954 Canadair has sponsored air cadet squadrons. The goals of the cadet movement include developing in youth the attributes of good citizenship and leadership; promoting physical fitness; raising interest in the RCAF/Canadian Forces; promoting a practical interest in aeronautics; and assisting cadets hoping to pursue a career in aviation.

When recruiting for No. 588 (Canadair) Squadron started in March 1953, membership was limited to sons of Canadair employees. At the time, boys between the ages of 14 and 19 could be admitted. Parliament later authorized participation of girls in the air cadet programme, and the joining age was lowered to age 12. A year later, No. 592 (Canadair Community) Squadron was formed for youths from the local community. No. 592 was then the only squadron in the West Island of Montreal. Because of a lack of public transportation in the mid-fifties, Canadair chartered a bus which ran from Ste. Anne de Bellevue to Dorval along the old Hwy.2-20, picking up cadets from the

Lakeshore communities and transporting them to Canadair and back each week. This continued until the formation of two new squadrons in Pointe Claire and Dorval.

Initially, 588 and 592 accepted both English- and French-speaking cadets, but

AIR
CADETS

bilingual instruction proved too time-consuming. A new French-speaking squadron, No. 621 (Canadair Cartier) Squadron was formed and 588 and 592 became all-English units. With the formation of 621, and with Canadair as their sponsor, the RCAF and the Air Cadet League of Canada authorized the formation of No. 16 (Canadair) Wing in 1956.

For the first five years, the three squadrons trained and drilled in the Plant 2 hangars. One former cadet recalled forming up for weekly inspection between the wings of Sabres and T-33s. Try-

ing to march around was difficult, but to a teenager to be so close to Canada's latest jet fighters and trainers was a dream come true. In 1958, the DND arranged to have a prefabricated building constructed at Plant 2 and leased it to the 16 Wing Civilian Sponsoring Committee for a dollar a year.

The founding of Canadair's cadet squadrons was largely the work of Eric Simms of material control and Eddie Ainger of public relations. Simms had been a senior navigator with RAF Transport Command. In 1948 he was navigation leader for the first Vampire jet fighter formation to cross the Atlantic. Simms had been active with No. 1 (West Montreal) Air Cadet Squadron in Westmount and saw a need for a squadron at Canadair. Ainger was personal secretary to the Hon. Brooke Claxton, Minister of National Defence, before joining Canadair in 1946. As an active director of the Air Cadet League, he was instrumental in persuading Geoff Notman to sponsor the new squadron.

Canadair cadets inspect a Sabre on the line, then typical sports activity on a cadet parade night. (CL 4670, 37650)

The first squadron commanding officers were S/L Eric Simms (588), S/L John Barnes (592) and S/L Harry Johnston (621). Simms commanded 588 until late 1956 when he was promoted to Wing Commander and assumed command of No. 16 (Canadair) Wing. S/L Herbie Brehn took over 588. Some of the many squadron commanding officers who served during the first 40 years were: S/L John Berth-Jones, S/L Frank Green, Major Joe Dubuc, Major Brian Darling, Major Gilles Cuerrier, Captain Jim Mooney, Captain André Courville, Captain Jim Wiechold and Major Hratch Adjemian.

Simms remained wing commander until the wing was disbanded in 1968 with elimination of the air cadet wing

Dr. Hans Luckert lectures Canadair air cadets about the Black Brant in this scene from 1965. (CL)

concept. This resulted from the integration of the RCAF into the new Canadian Forces. From then until his death in 1982, Simms was successively: chairman of the Canadair civilian committee; president of the Quebec provincial committee (QPC) of the Air Cadet League of Canada; and its national director. For a number of summers in the late 1950s and early 1960s, W/C Simms was commandant of the air cadet summer camps, first at RCAF Station St-Jean and then at CFB Bagotville. He also rewrote the national training manual used by all air cadets. Because of his involvement in the air cadet movement at

WO1 Paul Coates of 592 Sqn, attending the annual reunion of the Air Cadet League in 1966, chats with Governor General Georges Vanier. (CL)

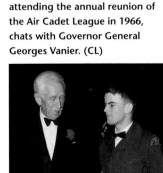

national, provincial and local levels, Simms became known as "Mr. Cadet". Eddie Ainger continued as chairman of the Civilian Committee from 1954 until his death in 1982. Bernie Campbell of payroll then became chairman until he retired in 1992 and was succeeded by Susan Levesque.

The Canadair squadrons have collected numerous honors and awards, including the RCAF Award, the country's highest squadron award and the Air Officer Commanding trophy for the top squadron under the jurisdiction of the Quebec Provincial Committee. The squadrons also excelled in precision drill teams, having won both the Strathcona and Walsh Drill trophies on numerous occasions. A highlight in the history of the Canadair squadrons was the visit by His Royal Highness Prince Philip in 1969 when he presented gold, silver and bronze Duke of Edinburgh awards to cadets who had achieved the required levels.

After leaving the cadet movement, many Canadair cadets served with the RCAF and the Canadian Forces. Notable among the ex-cadets in the forces were Jeff Brace, who attained the rank of brigadier general and was Commander of Air Transport Group at CFB Trenton, Ontario. Mike Capstick became a lieutenant colonel in the Royal Canadian Artillery and at the time of writing was serving at St-Hubert in Land Force Command Headquarters, after a tour of duty in Cyprus with the United Nations.

Several cadets returned to No. 16 (Canadair) Wing as officers. Brian Darling was the first. He eventually commanded both 588 and 592 Squadrons before moving to the Air Reserve with No. 401 (City of Westmount) Squad-

WO Vicki Becker of 588 Sqn receives the Duke of Edinburgh Gold Award from the duke himself on April 16, 1982. (CL)

ron and 1 Wing, where he served for 20 years, attaining the rank of lieutenant colonel. In 1995 he was active with the West Island region of the league, and was involved non-stop with the cadet movement for 40 years. No. 621 Squadron produced a number of cadets who became officers in that squadron before going on to hold executive positions with the Quebec Provincial Committee of the Air Cadet League of Canada. In 1994 Gilles Cuerrier was the provincial chairman, André Courville was past chairman, Pierre Tanguay was executive director. Paul Martin was a vice-president of the Quebec Progressive Conservatives. Gary Bingham, vice-president of marketing and sales was another former Canadair cadet.

Eric E. Simms is remembered as the father of Canadair's air cadet movement. On May 25, 1985 he was honoured with a plaque on the occasion of the 30th annual Canadair cadet annual inspection. Presenting the keepsake is then-LCol Jeff Brace, commander of 437 (T) Squadron at the time, and himself an alumnus of 16 Wing. (CL C32674-3)

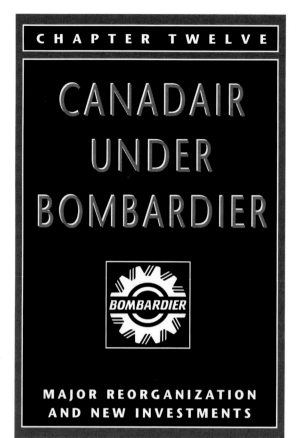

CHAPTER TWELVE

CANADAIR UNDER BOMBARDIER

MAJOR REORGANIZATION AND NEW INVESTMENTS

Bombardier's purchase of Canadair Limited took effect on December 23, 1986. Before deciding to sell Canadair to Bombardier, the Canada Development Investment Corp. (CDIC) and its financial advisors contacted approximately 150 parties throughout the world. Some 25 showed interest; many of these were given plant tours and a chance to talk with Canadair management.

CDIC set April 1, 1986 (later extended to May 20) as the deadline for receipt of letters of intent from serious parties; six were received. On June 6, all six parties made presentations to the CDIC board, following which the board narrowed its choice to Bombardier Inc. of Montreal and Canadian Aerospace Technologies Ltd. (CAT). CAT was a consortium led by Justus Dornier, a member of the famous German aviation family, and Montreal financier Howard Webster.

After further discussions, CDIC received revised proposals on June 17. On June 20, its board recommended the government accept the Bombardier proposal, subject to minor revisions, as being financially superior to the CAT offer. On August 18, 1986, federal minister Barbara McDougall and Laurent Beaudoin, chairman and chief executive officer of Bombardier Inc., signed a letter of intent to sell Canadair to Bombardier Inc. for $120 million plus other financial considerations. The government listed three major reasons for its choice:

• Bombardier manufactured transportation equipment, was based in Canada and registered sales of $515 million in 1985.

• Bombardier had experience in related markets, with exports of transportation equipment and sales to governments.

• Aerospace expert Donald C. Lowe, past president of Pratt & Whitney Canada, was a member of Bombardier's management team.

Bombardier Inc.

Bombardier's founder, Joseph-Armand Bombardier, was born near Valcourt, Quebec, in 1907. As a young man he nurtured the dream of inventing a motorized vehicle that could carry passengers, primarily schoolchildren, and cargo over the snowbound roads of rural Quebec. He received a patent for his first snowmobile, the B7, in 1936. In 1940, he built a factory at Valcourt and, in 1942, founded L'Auto-Neige Bombardier. During the Second World War more than 1,900 tracked vehicles based on Bombardier's designs were built for the military.

With the lifting of wartime restrictions, the demand for snowmobiles mushroomed. Sales rocketed from $211,800 in 1943 to $2,347,000 in 1948. But, in 1949, Quebec decided to clear rural routes of snow and transport the children in school buses. As a result, Bombardier sales plummeted by 50 per cent in 1950.

In the early 1950s, Joseph-Armand Bombardier introduced a line of industrial all-terrain vehicles including the J-5, the first tracked vehicle used in the forest industry. He also perfected a light tracked vehicle which, in 1959, led to the first personal snowmobile. He called it "Ski-Dog," but through a printer's error, it became known worldwide as the "Ski-Doo." The Ski-Doo* snowmobile gave rise to a new sport and a new industry. Bombardier grew rapidly in the following years, maintaining its leadership of the snowmobile industry despite the emergence of a large number of competitors.

J.-A. Bombardier died in 1964 at the age of 57, but he lived long enough to see his company become a great success. His oldest son, Germain, held the post of president for two years before retiring for health reasons. Laurent Beaudoin, J.-A. Bombardier's son-in-law, then assumed the presidency. In 1970, the company bought the Austrian firm of Löhnerwerke GmbH and its affiliate Rotax-Werk AG. It merged them into a subsidiary of Bombardier under the name Bombardier-Rotax GmbH. The Austrian subsidiary manufactures the Rotax* engines which have powered Ski-Doo snowmobiles since 1962 and Sea-Doo* watercraft since 1987.

Bombardier began to diversify in 1973 when a combination of an energy crisis and restrictive legislation ended the snowmobile boom. The company broke into the rail transit field in 1974 with a contract to supply the Montreal Urban Community with subway cars, having acquired the technology for rubber-tired equipment used in the Montreal subway system through a licensing agreement with the French firms CIMT and AT-BL (now GEC Alsthom). To carry out this contract, Bombardier converted its La Pocatière snowmobile plant southeast of Quebec City into a modern rail transit vehicle assembly plant, which it remains to this day.

Bombardier consolidated its position in rail transport by acquiring Montreal's MLW-Worthington, a manufacturer of diesel-electric locomotives and diesel engines. MLW's technology included the LRC* (Light, Rapid, Comfortable) train, North America's first high-speed train. Bombardier then acquired the technology for a full range of transit vehicles through licensing agreements with American, Japanese and European manufacturers and by buying Pullman Technology and Transit America, a division of the Budd Co. In 1980, to better serve the U.S. market, it built a rail transit assembly plant in Barre, Vermont.

In May 1982, only eight years after entering the mass transit arena, the company landed rail transit's most valuable contract to date—an agreement to deliver 825 subway cars worth over $1 billion to New York City. It was the largest export contract ever won by a Canadian manufacturer. In just 12 years in the mass transit business, Bombardier had chalked up over $1.8 billion in orders.

At the time it bought Canadair, Bombardier's main activity lay in the supply of rail transit equipment, and rail and diesel products. The mass transit division produced rail, tramway and subway vehicles in plants at La Pocatière, Quebec and Barre, Vermont. Bombardier had tramway manufacturing facilities in Vienna, Austria, and was a principal shareholder in BN, a Belgian designer and manufacturer of locomotives and transit vehicles. The rail and

The modest garage in Valcourt, Quebec, where Joseph-Armand Bombardier (inset) worked on his early snowmobiles. (Bombardier)

diesel products division designed and manufactured locomotive, marine and stationary power engines in plants at Montreal and Auburn, New York. (Bombardier sold the rail and diesel products division in 1989 but kept the Auburn engine operation.) The logistics equipment division produced military transport trucks, off-road vehicles such as snow grooming machines, and industrial equipment for public utilities, mining and oil operations, at Valcourt, Quebec. (Truck production ended in 1989.) The recreational products division at Valcourt produced the Ski-Doo snowmobile.

In 1978, Bombardier moved its head office from Valcourt to Montreal. The corporate name, which changed successively from L'Auto-Neige-Bombardier to Bombardier Ltée in 1967, and to Bombardier MLW-Worthington Ltée in 1976, became Bombardier Inc. in 1981.

In 1986 Bombardier employed 8,000 people. By late 1994, it had 36,500 employees in eight countries, including 24,000 in the aerospace sector. For the 1994 fiscal year, Bombardier's revenue amounted to $4.8 billion of which aerospace contributed 50 per cent and defence 3 per cent.

Corporate Management

Bombardier management is headed by Laurent Beaudoin, chairman and chief executive officer. Born and educated in Quebec, Laurent Beaudoin earned a bachelor of arts degree from Ste-Anne College in Nova Scotia, and a master of commerce degree from the University of Sherbrooke. A chartered accountant, he joined Bombardier in 1963 as comptroller, was appointed general manager in 1964, president in 1966 and chairman and chief executive officer in 1979.

Beaudoin is highly regarded by his peers in business and industry. In 1992 he was chosen Canadian International Executive of the Year by the International Chamber of Commerce and the Business Advisory Committee. The prestigious U.S. magazine *Aviation Week and Space Technology* named him aeronautics/propulsion laureate for

Laurent Beaudoin, chairman and CEO of Bombardier Inc., was a driving force behind the acquisition of Canadair. (Bombardier)

1993, and the U.K. publication *Flight International* named him Aerospace Personality of the Year in 1994. Referring to the purchase of Canadair and subsequent Bombardier aerospace acquisitions, *Aviation Week and Space Technology* said: "Beaudoin demonstrated not only his mastery of the art of the deal in these acquisitions but also a knack for turning around troubled aerospace companies." Of his role in enlarging the companies' presence in the aerospace markets, *Flight International* said: "All of this development and expansion has been the direct result of Mr. Beaudoin's vision and determination."

Those at Canadair consider Beaudoin a good judge of what makes a product successful. As one employee said, "He has the touch, an intuitive sense of things engineering; he listens to people, encourages them, challenges them and really motivates them."

President and chief operating officer Raymond Royer, a native of Quebec, earned degrees in commerce, civil law and accountancy from the University of Sherbrooke. He joined Bombardier in 1974 to set up and manage the mass transit division, and was appointed president and chief operating officer in 1986.

Royer assumed interim control of Canadair's aerospace activity for six months during 1989 and 1990. He impressed his Canadair associates as being "an absolutely capable, dedicated individual, with a spark complementary to Beaudoin's, which makes them a perfect team."

First Moves

When the privatization of Canadair was completed on December 23, 1986, Don Lowe took over from Pierre Des Marais II as president and CEO. Dick Richmond, although past retirement age, stayed on for a year as executive vice-president and deputy to Lowe but asked to be relieved of the responsibilities of chief operating officer. Vince Ambrico, also past retirement age, stayed on as head of manufacturing for the transition period. At the time of the privatization, Canadair had 5,500 employees.

Bombardier's appointment of Don Lowe as president of Canadair turned out to be a smart move. As a former member of the Canadair board and president of Pratt & Whitney Canada, Lowe was well known to most in Canadair management. He made a significant contribution in getting the Bombardier/Canadair management relationship off on the right foot.

The first member of Bombardier's senior management to join Canadair was Paul Larose, corporate vice-president of finance, who spent two years as Canadair's vice-president, finance, and introduced Bombardier's accounting disciplines and systems. Larose went out of his way to make Canadair management feel part of Bombardier.

Bombardier found that Canadair had a wealth of technology in many areas and a good management team that was doing its best with antiquated facilities, manufacturing methods and equipment. Canadair was seriously undercapitalized, however. Its finances had been handled in the way governments and finance companies generally work, but a way that made no sense in the commercial world.

The new owner's style was like a breath of fresh air. The Bombardier philosophy, which encouraged personal entrepreneurship, offered employees more opportunity in return for a commitment to the company and the job, and an acceptance that they were accountable for their actions. People at Canadair found that if they had ideas for improvement or a new product development that made good business sense, they would receive approval and funding within a reasonable time.

New Programs and Restructuring

Bombardier's first year as Canadair's parent was notable for the introduction of several new programs. One contract, the CF-18 systems engineering support program, had been awarded on October 31, 1986, immediately after Bombardier's arrival on the scene.

Raymond Royer became president and COO of Bombardier in 1986. (CL C43837-3)

Then, in a series of bold moves involving a major investment of development funds, Bombardier gave the go-ahead for two new programs. The first, given on January 16, 1987, only three weeks after completion of the acquisition, authorized the development of a turboprop version of the CL-215 aircraft, designated the CL-215T. This was followed on November 9 by the start of advanced design of a new jet for the regional carrier market, the Canadair Regional Jet airliner. To round out an eventful period, on November 25 representatives from Canada, West Germany and France signed a $411 million contract for CL-289 drone surveillance system production. A year later, Canadair began its largest ever subcontract program following orders from Aerospatiale and British Aerospace for components for the Airbus A330/A340 aircraft.

Donald C. Lowe was the first to head Canadair following the Bombardier acquisition. (CL C36300-16)

On May 20, 1987, Canadair's official name was changed to Canadair Inc. In June 1988, Bombardier introduced its management style by "divisionalizing" Canadair operations according to product lines and markets. The divisions were combined into two groups: the Canadair aerospace group and the Canadair defence group. Don Lowe was appointed acting president of both. Reporting to Lowe in the aerospace group were L. Antony Edwards, president, Challenger division; Vince Ambrico, president, manufacturing division; and Andy Throner, vice-president and general manager, CL-215 division. Reporting to Lowe in the defence group were vice-presidents Yvon Lafortune, surveillance systems; Walter Niemy, military aircraft; and Fernand Boyer, logistics.

Each division was made responsible for its own profitability and was given the means to meet its objectives, including its own engineering and manufacturing functions. Experience would show, however, that engineering and manufacturing functioned more efficiently when centralized, and both would be returned to their original status.

On August 5, 1988. Canadair merged with its parent company and became known as the Canadair Group of Bombardier Inc.

Tony Edwards had joined the company in May 1988. A former vice-president of General Electric, he had spent the previous five years managing an electronics company that competed directly against Japanese companies. In February 1989, he was appointed president of the Canadair aerospace group but resigned in the fall to return to his native England. A warm personality and great motivator, he made a solid contribution during his short stay at Canadair.

New President

Effective February 1, 1990, Laurent Beaudoin appointed Robert E. (Bob) Brown president of Canadair. Don Lowe became deputy chairman of Bombardier Inc.

Bob Brown took over the Canadair presidency from Don Lowe in 1990. (CL)

A graduate of Royal Military College, Kingston, Ontario, Bob Brown spent three years in Germany in the Canadian Armed Forces before joining government service in 1971. He held senior positions in a number of federal government ministries and agencies and was associate deputy minister, Department of Regional Industrial Expansion, at the time of the sale of Canadair though he was not involved in the sale. Brown had joined Bombardier in February 1987 as vice-president corporate development. He was appointed senior vice-president, corporate development and strategic planning in February 1989 and was deeply involved in the negotiations concerning Bombardier's subsequent aerospace acquisitions. Popular and respected, Brown has been described as very competent, strategically minded and a good administrator. Without constantly looking over their shoulders, he encourages people to ex-

tend themselves and assume responsibility.

Change and Reorganization

During the summer of 1989, the first steps were taken in a major remake of Canadair facilities. Subcontract manufacturing was moved from Dorval (Plant 3) to Saint-Laurent (Plant 1), and Challenger final assembly was moved to Dorval, all without missing a scheduled delivery.

In December 1989, Bombardier launched a five-year, quarter billion dollar expansion program, entitled "Building our Future." Directed by Roland Gagnon, vice-president, manufacturing (who had joined Canadair from Bombardier's Rail and Diesel Products Division), it included the addition of a new administration building and a complete rearrangement of manufacturing facilities to bring departments with frequent and regular links closer together and to group similar parts-manufacturing activities into specialized departments. A program management system improved the flow of material through the plant from receiving to final assembly.

To prepare Canadair for future competitiveness in the industry, Gagnon began changing manufacturing from the traditional aerospace system to the Bombardier system. He introduced the Bombardier philosophy of management by commitment, changing the way management dealt with employees by delegating authority and accountability to lower levels in the organization. It also streamlined activities and workloads.

Gil Bennett's retirement luncheon at the end of 1985. Bennett is at the head of the table (at the right). His colleagues (going clockwise from his left) are Dick Richmond, C.D. Perry, R.A. Wohl, J.P. MacKenzie, F.M. Francis, R. Hazelton, A. Throner, A.M. Guérin, A.B. Marquis, K. Jacob, V. Ambrico, T.G. Hill, J.E. Ouellet and Pierre Des Marais II. (CL)

Roland Gagnon oversaw many of the changes at Canadair into the 1990s. (CL)

Production was simplified by amalgamating the former industrial engineering, manufacturing engineering and material control departments into departments called "methods" and "work and material planning." Now, engineering had the responsibility for recommending what to build; methods for deciding how to build it; work and material planning for deciding when to build it; and fabrication for building it. The need to carry large inventories was eliminated by the introduction of the "just-in-time" production and delivery concept practised in Pacific Rim countries.

Quality control was improved by the introduction of statistical process control which gave production line employees responsibility for ensuring the quality of their own work. This enabled problems to be solved at the source instead of by backtracking. Quality agents trained production personnel and instilled the need to build quality into the product. Routine quality inspections continued but only as spot check audits. As a result, while production tripled and quality improved 62 per cent, the percentage ratio of inspectors to workers dropped from 15 to seven per cent.

Plant 1 became the fabrication centre responsible for the manufacture of all parts and all subcontract assembly. Aircraft assembly was consolidated at Plant 3. In 1994 Gagnon delegated the responsibility for running the plants to general managers Réal Gervais at Plant 1 and Joseph Ederhy at Plant 3.

In Plant 1, many antiquated machines were replaced by

When Canadair reorganized its plants in 1989, some exotic sights appeared on the highways between Cartierville and Dorval. Here a Regional Jet fatigue test article and a Challenger wing jig are on the go between plants. (CL)

new technology which produced better quality components at lower cost. The technology included numerically controlled sheet metal and machining equipment and environmentally friendly chemical surface treatment machines, plus upgraded bonding and composite capabilities.

To make optimum use of the Plant 3 floor space, a 930-m² (10,000-sq.-ft.) mezzanine was installed over the final line. This allowed assembly of Challenger and Regional Jet aircraft at two levels and freed sufficient floor space for the CL-415 waterbomber final line to be added.

A 3,200-m² (34,500-sq.-ft.) warehouse was built beside the final line. Designed to ensure just-in-time delivery of

Canadair had Dorval in its expansion plans since the 1950s. It did not locate there until 1979, when a new complex was built to manufacture the CL-215 and the aft fuselage section for the 767. In 1992 work started on the new Dorval administrative headquarters (right). (CL)

Modernization at Canadair since the mid-1980s included installation of such equipment as the Recoules computer-numerically-controlled machine (CNCM) shown at top. Located in P1, it rivets large fuselage sections for the Airbus A330/340 and the Boeing rear fuselage bulkhead panel. The second photo shows the giant Cincinnati Milacron CNCM that routs wing spars from solid aluminum blocks. (CL)

parts for assembly, it featured computerized stock management, automatically controlled carousels and specially guided electric vehicles and forklifts. The resulting improvements reduced Regional Jet aircraft production cycle time to 77 days, preflight positions to one and production test flights to one by 1994.

The overall effects of five years of change were dramatic. When in 1995 the disposal of Plants 2 and 4 and Buildings 114 and 115 has been completed, total production floor area will have been reduced by one-third while revenue will have tripled.

Acquisitions – Shorts

Between 1989 and 1992, Bombardier expanded by acquiring three diverse aircraft manufacturing companies. On October 4, 1989, Bombardier acquired Short Brothers PLC (Shorts) of Belfast, Northern Ireland, Europe's oldest aircraft manufacturer, with $500 million in annual revenue and a $2-billion order backlog, for $60 million Cdn.

Established in 1908, Shorts had a distinguished record in the design and manufacture of a wide range of aircraft including the C-Class Empire flying boats of the 1930s and Sunderland flying boats and Stirling heavy bombers of the Second World War. After the war, it produced Solent and Sealand flying boats, several research aircraft, Belfast freighters and a series of turboprop airliners ranging from the small Skyvan to the 36-passenger SD-360. Several types were built under licence, including the Canberra jet bomber, Britannia airliner, and Tucano turboprop military trainer. The company also designed, developed and manufactured major aircraft components for other manufacturers as well as surface-to-air missiles for British and foreign armed forces.

Bombardier found that Shorts, like Canadair, was undercapitalized. As a result of minimal investment during 46 years of government ownership, it had antiquated production facilities and was losing money, although it had an excellent skills base and was producing quality products. As part of its turnaround strategy, Shorts was provided with the £200 million needed to completely re-equip its plant, machinery and facilities.

In 1992, Shorts won the British Quality Award, the nation's top quality accolade. Since the acquisition, sales and exports have doubled, losses have turned into profits, new products have been developed, and manpower has increased as the company has won valuable new orders.

Shorts of Belfast manufactures various major components for the Regional Jet including the fuselage centre-section. (Shorts)

The first Canadair Regional Jet centre-fuselage is loaded onto a Belfast freighter for the transatlantic flight to Montreal in July 1990. (Shorts)

profitable, there was no money to develop new business jets. What Bombardier gained from the purchase was a product with an excellent reputation, a trademark, a fleet of about 1,500 aircraft in service and a strong presence in the United States. By combining Learjet's resources, skills and experience in engineering, marketing, product support and customer service with those of Canadair, Bombardier established a firmer position in the business jet market. The acquisition also gave Bombardier the most complete range of business jets in the world and provided a completion centre for Challenger interiors in Tucson, Arizona. In mid-1991 a new centre dedicated to the flight testing and development of all Bombardier aircraft opened at the Learjet facility at Wichita, Kansas. Its first customer, Canadair Regional Jet No. 7001, arrived on July 16.

Learjet

In mid-June 1990, only eight months after acquiring Shorts, Bombardier bought Learjet Corp. for $75 million US plus an assumption of liabilities associated with Learjet's ongoing operations. Founded in the late 1950s by William P. (Bill) Lear, Learjet had built more than 1,600 business aircraft for customers in 37 countries. It employed some 2,700 people in the production of three light jets–models 31, 35A and 36A–and one medium jet, Model 55. Another medium jet, Model 60, was under development. Soon after the acquisition by Bombardier, the Model 55 was dropped and the Model 60 went into production. A new jet, the Model 45, sized between the traditional light and medium categories, was later launched with de Havilland designing and manufacturing the wing and Shorts the fuselage.

Learjet was unlike either Canadair or Shorts. Its former parent company, Integrated Resources, had declared bankruptcy, and though the aircraft manufacturing segment was still

de Havilland

On March 9, 1992, de Havilland Canada formally joined the Bombardier family, bringing with it a 64-year heritage in aircraft design and manufacturing. A pioneer in the development of short takeoff and landing (STOL) aircraft, de Havilland manufactured nearly 3,000 aircraft during the Second World War, including over 1,000 Mosquito fighters and bombers. After the war it became a leader in the STOL field, producing over 3,500 Beavers, Otters, Twin Otters, Caribous, Buffaloes and Dash 7s. It

Employees at the complex in Wichita pose with a Learjet and the first Regional Jet. (CL)

was acquired by the Canadian government from its British owners, Hawker Siddeley, in 1974 and was sold to the Boeing Aircraft Co. of Seattle, Washington, in 1986. Since the early 1980s, de Havilland's main endeavor had been development of the Dash 8 series of turboprop regional airliners.

The de Havilland acquisition was made through a newly created company, de Havilland Inc., which had equity of $100 million Cdn, 51 per cent provided by Bombardier Inc. and 49 per cent by the Province of Ontario. The situation at de Havilland was different again from that at Canadair, Shorts and Learjet. In the six years it owned the company, Boeing had pumped close to a billion dollars into completely refurbishing the facilities to broaden its own product line to include commuter and regional aircraft. Now, with Dash 8 sales slumping as a result of a recession, Boeing decided to abandon its plan and divest itself of de Havilland.

By acquiring de Havilland, Bombardier became a leader in another growing market niche–regional airlines–and the only manufacturer to offer both jet and turboprop aircraft in the 50-passenger category. It gained instant credibility in the regional market and a ready-made regional airline product-support organization.

Bombardier's Commitment to Aerospace

The acquisitions enhanced Bombardier's position in the international aerospace community and underlined its commitment to employees, customers and shareholders. This commitment was endorsed by several substantial capital investments including a $400 million capital ex-

(Left) An Air BC de Havilland Dash 8-300 lands at Vancouver. (Larry Milberry)

(Below) The 50-56 seat Canadair Regional Jet on an early test flight. It took off for the first time on May 10, 1991. (CL)

Work progresses on the first two CL-215T water bombers in the spring of 1989. In the second photo, a Spanish Air Force CL-215T attacks a fire near Valencia. (CL, C72355-3)

penditure at Shorts; the five-year, $250 million expansion and modernization program at Canadair; similar investments in Learjet and de Havilland; and the flight test centre in Wichita.

In the summer of 1992, "Bombardier Aerospace Group – North America" was created to oversee the operations of Canadair, Learjet and de Havilland. Bob Brown was appointed president of both the Group and Canadair. At the end of 1994, the Group's senior executives reporting to Brown were Roland Gagnon, executive vice-president, manufacturing; John Holding, executive vice-president, engineering; Robert D. (Rob) Gillespie, vice-president, strategic planning and business development; James Gilmore, vice-president, finance; and Gilles Landry, vice-president, human resources.

The Group's management team offices were in a new administrative centre constructed beside Plant 3 at Dorval airport. Built between March 1992 and July 1993, the nine-storey facility provided 30,285 m² (326,000 sq. ft.) of net office space. Besides housing the management team, it consolidated the approximately 1,800 corporate and administrative personnel of Canadair and its Challenger, Regional Jet, Amphibious Aircraft and Manufacturing divisions, which had previously been spread through six different buildings in Saint-Laurent, Dorval and Laval. At the centre's inauguration on November 12, 1993, Bob

Brown remarked that "consolidating the management of the group's services in the new building is the culmination of our efforts to enhance our presence among our customers."

CL-215T Amphibian

Since the beginning of the CL-215 program, Canadair had searched for a suitable turboprop engine for the CL-215, but those available were underpowered or overweight, slow to accelerate and consumed too much fuel. In the early 1980s, however, a new generation of engines, built to power 30-passenger commuter aircraft, appeared on the market. One of these, the 2,380-shp Pratt & Whitney Canada PW123AF, was perfect for Canadair's waterbomber. On January 16, 1987, Bombardier announced development of the PW123AF-powered CL-215T amphibian.

For the CL-215T development phase, which included the construction of two prototypes, flight testing and certification, Canadair borrowed two new Series V aircraft from the Quebec government. Conversion was a big job. The wings had to be beefed up to take the extra power; slimmer nacelles designed to accept the smaller engines; and the engines, propellers and main electrical distribution panel moved forward to adjust the weight distribution. More efficient, four-bladed propellers were fitted and winglets added to improve lateral stability. A new electrical system, a revised cockpit, powered flight controls and pressure refuelling were installed.

In 1988, when Canadair was divisionalized, Andy Throner, vice-president and general manager, CL-215, assumed responsibility for all aspects of the CL-215T program, including engineering. He appointed Trevor Young, newly arrived from Pratt & Whitney Canada, as program manager, and Keith Rhodes, a recent recruit from England, director of engineering. Fern Richer became director, CL-215 assembly and pre-flight. Tony Guérin was vice-president of marketing, and Guy Charpentier and Ray Mathieu were marketing directors. Norm Forget was manager, contract administration.

Another 215 Record

Meanwhile, the piston-engined predecessor of the CL-215T set another record. In June 1987, at Wallace Lake in northern Manitoba, a provincial government aircraft, captained by George Cox, made over 70 drops in a little more than two hours to save 20 cottages from an advancing wall of flame 45 m (150 ft.) high. The homes were on a spit jutting into a lake so Cox set up a figure-of-eight

---

(Right) A Spanish CL-215T amphibian comes ashore after a day's flying. (CL C65741-27)

(Below) Although more than a half century separated the Canso (left) and CL-215T (right), both types were still fighting forest fires in 1995. In the background is a standard CL-215. (CL C51145-6)

pattern, scooping on alternate sides of the spit. The interval between drop and scoop was so short he had to delay starting each scooping run until he was sure the water tank doors had closed from the previous drop.

In 1988 Canadair put a leased Quebec water bomber at the disposal of four southeastern states: Virginia, North and South Carolina, and Florida. While demonstrating in North Carolina, Quebec pilot Robert Laliberté, climbing away after a balked scooping run, clipped the top of a tree. Feeling only a slight jar, he assumed he had just brushed the top branches but his composure was shattered when Ray Mathieu and John Reid of marketing later brought him a piece of 15-cm (6-in.) -diameter trunk bearing traces of distinctive yellow paint.

When Andy Throner retired in June 1989, Trevor Young assumed the title of vice-president and general

Terry Hill, vice-president, quality assurance and flight operations (left) presents certificates recognizing the hours flown in Canadair piston-engined aircraft by pilots Bill Casselman, Doug Adkins, Yves Mahaut and Ian McDonald. (CL)

manager, CL-215. The CL-215T made its maiden flight on June 8, 1989, at the hands of pilots Doug Adkins and Yves Mahaut, with Doug Ford, flight engineer, and Ted Squelch, flight test observer.

The early flights showed that the combined effect of the changes had affected control and stability. This required the addition of powered elevators and rudder, finlets on the tailplane, a bullet at the junction of the tailplane and the fin, and a slat on the tailplane inboard of the right finlet. Subsequent flight tests showed the turboprop engines and other changes had improved the aircraft's takeoff and climb performance and raised its top speed from 306 km/h (190 mph) to 378 km/h (235 mph). They had done nothing to improve its aesthetics.

The last production CL-215 was delivered to Greece in May 1990, bringing the total supplied to 124. Of these, 30 went to Spain; 19 to Quebec; 16 to Greece; 15 to France; nine to Ontario; five each to Italy, Manitoba and Yugoslavia; four each to Alberta, Newfoundland, Saskatchewan and Yukon/Northwest Territories, and two each to Thailand and Venezuela.

While fire-fighting in North Carolina in 1988 Quebec government pilot Bob Laliberté had a close encounter with some good-size branches. Here he displays part of the tree his CL-215 struck; then, a look at the damage done to the port wingtip. (John Reid)

Engineering divisionalization was reversed in 1990. Saul Bernstein became chief designer CL-215/415 reporting to director of design, Keith Miller. In early March 1991, the CL-215 division was renamed the amphibious aircraft division.

The CL-215T received Canadian restricted category type approval in March 1991, utility category type approval in December 1991, and U.S. FAA restricted category type certification in March 1993. Meanwhile, installation began of the first of 15 turboprop conversion kits ordered by Spain. Canadair delivered the first converted CL-215T to Spain in June 1991. In June 1992, CL-215T conversion was moved to de Havilland at Toronto. Altogether, Canadair completed eight Spanish 215T conversions and de Havilland five. Spain planned to complete the final pair itself.

CL-415

Quebec and France had long wanted turboprops in their CL-215s but the older series I and II aircraft were unsuitable for conversion so the two governments opted for a new production version, the CL-415 turboprop amphibian. CL-415 production was launched on October 16, 1991, based on an order from France for 12 aircraft and a pending order for eight from Quebec.

Though similar in appearance to the CL-215T, the CL-415 was more modern, more efficient and more productive. The principal difference between a CL-415 and a retrofitted CL-215T is in the firefighting system—the CL-415 has a four-tank, four-door system carrying 6,130 litres (1,350 imp. gal.) or 15 per cent more than the CL-215. In a three-hour mission, fighting a fire 18.5 km (11.5 mi.) from water, a CL-415 can make 18 drops, totalling 110,520 l (24,311 imp. gal.), 38 per cent more than the CL-215 and 15 per cent more than a CL-215T. A computer-controlled system provides a better selection of drop patterns. Flight crew efficiency and comfort are improved by the addition of an electronic flight instrument system (EFIS), more comfortable seats and cockpit air conditioning.

A foam chemical system is optional. When installed, it enables a foam concentrate to be injected automatically into each water load to increase effectiveness. Since 1985, when foam systems were first installed in two French and two Spanish CL-215 aircraft, the use of foam increased to a point where every CL-215 in Canada and most of those in Europe adopted foam. The concentrate is a liquid soap, which when mixed with the water load at a ratio of about 0.6 parts of foam to 99.4 parts of water, is three to five times more effective than plain water. The CL-215 system carries sufficient concentrate for up to 16 drops.

On May 15, 1992, Pierre-André Roy was appointed president of the amphibious aircraft division, replacing Trevor Young who had moved to the Global Express program. Roy had previously been vice-president, finance. On August 13, 1992, Quebec confirmed its order for eight CL-415 aircraft at a value of approximately $155 million.

Adkins, Mahaut, Ford and Squelch flew the CL-415 for the first time on December 6, 1993. Following a short shake-down period at Dorval, it was flown to Wichita for flight test and certification. In January 1994, Italy ordered four CL-415 waterbombers, bringing the total on order to 24.

On February 22, 1994, Pierre-André Roy became president of Bombardier Capital Group. His place as president of the amphibious aircraft group was taken by James C. Cherry, formerly president of Oerlikon Aerospace. Nick Perkins became project director and Dave Pelling manager, project engineering. The CL-415 received its Canadian type approval, in both restricted and utility categories, on June 24, 1994.

The CL-415T takes off for the first time on December 6, 1993. Early orders from France, Italy and Quebec totalled 24 and got the program off to a good start. (CL C68794)

Efforts initiated during the 1988 tour of the southeastern United States showed signs of coming to fruition in 1994. After five years of leasing CL-215 aircraft from Quebec and Newfoundland, North Carolina requested a price proposal from Canadair for the sale of three reconditioned CL-215 aircraft.

The disastrous California fires of October and November 1993 prompted California State Assemblyman Friedman to submit a new bill for an evaluation of the CL-215T. At the time of writing, this had been approved in principle for an evaluation during the 1995/96 fire season. Meanwhile, on August 23, 1994, the Los Angeles County board of supervisors approved a plan to lease a Quebec CL-215T for 60-90 days beginning in October 1994. The evaluation was underway in mid-December using two Quebec aircraft, one sponsored by L.A. County, the other by Canadair and the Personal Assurance Society of California.

CL-415M

In March 1993, the CL-215T prototype visited several Florida bases of U.S. Customs and the U.S. Special Forces to demonstrate the advantage of its amphibious abilities in roles such as drug interdiction, smuggling and other special missions. Since then, the division has been busy developing the CL-415M, a multi-mission variant.

In late 1994, the division was evaluating potential partners for a program to modify and install the equipment needed for roles such as search and rescue, drug interdiction, fisheries protection, disaster assistance, and passenger and cargo transportation. The equipment would include maritime surveillance radar, electro-optic sensors, precision navigation and communication equipment and an autopilot.

With CL-415 deliveries scheduled to start in October 1994, some early CL-215 aircraft became available for sale. France sold two, through Canadair, to Croatia and was ready to part with a further nine. Quebec leased two to Croatia and was prepared to sell six more. All were pis-

The second CL-415 water bomber banks over Lac St. François during a photo session in March 1994. It was later delivered to France. (CL)

ton-engined Series I and II versions delivered between 1969 and 1973. Although over 20 years old, none had flown more than 7,300 flight hours and all were in excellent condition.

Because of the length of the CL-215 program, few longtime Canadair employees can claim never to have been connected in some way with the CL-215. All the familiar engineering and manufacturing names were involved at one time or another with the development of an aircraft unique in its field and a program that may someday rival the DC-3 for longevity.

The Challenger Program

When Bombardier bought Canadair, Challenger production was running relatively smoothly. Sales, however, were suffering from a lack of credibility due to the pro-

longed uncertainty about Canadair's ownership, and operators' concerns over the cost of running the aircraft.

One of Bombardier's first moves was to revitalize marketing and give its sales personnel more freedom in dealing with customers. Carl Perry was appointed senior vice-president, Challenger marketing, Bryan Moss was in charge of North American marketing, and Ed van Dam was responsible for international marketing. Customer satisfaction was significantly improved by a "Smart Parts" program introduced by vice-president, customer services, Peter Ginocchio, which offered operators a cost-per-flight-hour replacement program for factory-installed components, and by a direct mail program targeted at CEOs and aviation directors.

Meanwhile, Challenger 601-3A flight testing and certification finished without a hitch. Canadian type approval

In April 1993, the Canadian Forces retired the second pre-production Challenger 600 and put it on display in the Air Command aviation heritage park at CFB Winnipeg. In nearly 15 years of service, it had logged 2,068 flight hours, mostly on test programs. (Jan Stroomenbergh)

ground; by contrast, the extended range provided by the tail cone fuel tank was in great demand.

In July 1992, the Challenger division was renamed the business aircraft division with Bryan Moss as president. Dave Orcutt succeeded Pete Ginocchio as vice-president, product support, when that function was moved to Montreal in 1993. By the end of 1992, 270 Challengers had been delivered—seven during October alone.

was granted on April 21, 1987, and U.S. type certification nine days later. The first -3A was delivered on May 6. Production of the 601, now referred to as the 601-1A, ended after 66 had been built. In October 1988, Challenger president Tony Edwards consolidated all Challenger marketing activities under Bryan Moss and appointed Keith Garner vice-president, North American Sales, reporting to Moss.

Engineering continued with improvements to the aircraft's range by designing a tail cone fuel tank holding 685 l (180 U.S. gal.), to replace the standard tail cone fairing. This gave the aircraft, designated the 601-1A/ER and 601-3A/ER, a range of 6,635 km (3,585 nm) or 220 km (119 nm) more than the standard aircraft. The first flight of a modified 601-3A/ER was on November 8, 1988. The first 601-1A/ER was delivered on March 17, 1989 and the first 601-3A/ER two days later. A record eight Challenger aircraft were delivered in December 1988, bringing deliveries for the year to 23. This was the first real indication that the Challenger had finally matured and earned a prominent position in the business jet market place.

601-S

On June 9, 1989, Tony Edwards announced the Challenger 601-S. This transcontinental version was intended to appeal to the operator who was willing to accept a shorter 5,550-km (3,000-nm) range, fewer avionics and a standard 12-passenger interior, in return for a price saving of almost $2 million. The shorter range 601-S never got off the

601-3R and 604

On May 10, 1993, Canadair announced the Challenger 601-3R. Powered by the same GE CF34-3A1 commercial engines as the new Canadair Regional Jet, it boasted the lowest hourly operating cost of any large business jet. Its maximum takeoff weight was 20,500 kg (45,100 lb.) and its high speed cruise was Mach 0.83. Equipped with a tail cone fuel tank as a standard, the 601-3R flew 6,635 km (3,585 nm) and cost the same as a Challenger 601-3A/ER. The first 601-3R was delivered on July 14, 1993.

One month later, Bryan Moss announced the Challenger 604, a longer range version able to fly non-stop London-Chicago, New York-Moscow and Riyadh-Singapore. Powered by new GE CF34-3B engines with three per cent lower fuel consumption than 3A engines, the 604 was to have a takeoff weight of 21,600 kg (47,600 lb.), a high speed cruise of Mach 0.83, a normal cruise of Mach 0.80 and a maximum range of 7,400 km (4,000 nm).

The 604 will feature a new cockpit incorporating a state-of-the-art avionics system, a new landing gear, larger wheels, an improved braking system, and a new wing-to-fuselage and underbelly fairing. It also will carry an additional 1,242 l (328 U.S. gal.) of fuel. Certification is scheduled for the third quarter of 1995.

The business aircraft division achieved a breakthrough in October 1993 when it sold a 601-3R to the U.S. FAA for flight inspection of airway navigation and airport approach and landing aids. This was the first time Canadair had sold an aircraft to a U.S. government agency since the Sabre in the early 1950s. The last 601-3A produced, No. 5134, was delivered on October 29, 1993.

Doug Adkins, Bruce Robinson and Ted Squelch flew the prototype 604 on September 18, 1994, and Don Stephen and Robinson took it to the National Business Aircraft Association convention at New Orleans after only 12 flight hours. There Bombardier announced that Challenger 604 pilot training, Challenger maintenance training and Regional Jet pilot and maintenance training would be conducted in-house in a new location.

By mid-December 1994, Challenger 601-3R aircraft were rolling off the line at a steady two per month, and 33 had been produced. At the time this book was published, well over 300 Challenger jets had been delivered to customers on every continent. Top in its class for versatility, value and passenger comfort, it was authorized for civil use in 28 countries and for military use in four. The once-maligned Challenger 600 had developed into a fine transcontinental aircraft. In late 1994, some used 600s were selling for more than their original price.

Final Salute

As the aircraft improved, so did its support. For several years, industry surveys consistently awarded the Canadair business aircraft division top marks for the best overall customer support in the business jet industry. Bryan Moss, president of the business aircraft division, a member of the Challenger sales team since 1979 and a key contributor to the success of the program, offered this tribute to those who brought it through its many trials:

"It was Pete Ginocchio, Tom Moffatt, Frank Barker and the field service representatives who were the glue that held the program together in the early days when we were having customer problems in White Plains, Houston and Los Angeles. The FSRs were the ones that got up in the middle of the night to fix somebody's airplane or drove to Bradley, grabbed a part and hand-delivered it to Teterboro or White Plains. They provided the crutch for the product until we could get the reliability to satisfy our very sophisticated, very demanding customers."

The first Challenger 601-3R nears completion in P3. It made its first flight on June 22, 1993 and was delivered to the J.C. Penney Company in Dallas, Texas. (CL)

The Canadair Challenger 604 cockpit has the Collins Pro Line 4 avionic system featuring six 7.25-inch (18.4 cm) square CRT displays. (CL)

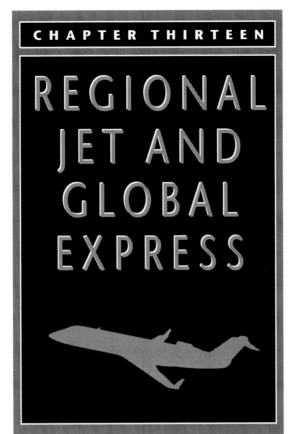

CHAPTER THIRTEEN

REGIONAL JET AND GLOBAL EXPRESS

During 1986 and 1987, Aviation Planning Services Ltd. (APS) of Montreal, at the request of Canadair, conducted a major survey of the potential market for a regional jetliner. Concurrently, an advanced design team of Trevor Hughes, Ken David and Ross Richardson made several conceptual studies to assist the preliminary costing and definition of a such an aircraft.

APS's market projections, derived from discussions with some 130 regional and major airlines, were based on the production of between 400 and 500 aircraft by the year 2001, at $13 million each. The preliminary concept, released in July 1987, was for a 48-seat aircraft with a range of 1,600 km (1,000 mi.) at a cruise speed of 785 km/h (488 mph). In October 1987, the Bombardier board of directors authorized the advanced design and development of a regional jetliner, the Canadair Regional Jet.

Shortly after this go-ahead, Don Lowe persuaded APS president Eric McConachie to rejoin Canadair and begin Regional Jet technical and marketing studies. McConachie was no stranger to Canadair: he had joined it in 1958 and had been general manager of marketing when he left in 1967 to start his own company.

A Lufthansa CityLine Regional Jet taxis past the CL-44-O Guppy during Canadair's 50th anniversary festivities in June 1994. CityLine's first Regional Jet entered service on November 2, 1992, and for its first month logged nearly 300 hours.(Larry Milberry)

People

Peter Clignett, an engineer formerly with Fokker of the Netherlands, was appointed director of Regional Jet advanced design. His team consisted of a talented group of senior engineers including Eric Haines, Trevor Hughes, Dave Miles, Colin Pond, Tony Read, Ross Richardson, John Taylor, Dave Turner and Hank Viger.

In February 1988, Laurent Beaudoin appointed Bob Wohl as executive vice-president, to lead the Regional Jet. Though a lawyer by profession, Wohl had, before joining Canadair in 1970, acquired considerable experience in program management and engineering development as project manager for General Dynamics on the Atlas ICBM missile and Mercury suborbital space flight programs of the late 1950s and early 1960s.

The team set up offices in a part of the former Menasco building on Côte Vertu Road in Saint-Laurent. It included Wohl, McConachie, Clignett, and directors Gitty Dowlat, procurement, Paul Francoeur, contracts, and Tom Keogh, marketing. Terry Brooks was appointed Regional Jet manufacturing team leader, and Jeremy Cartlidge the early customer support coordinator.

It soon became apparent that the Regional Jet would not go unchallenged. Short Brothers of Northern Ireland announced plans to built the FJX, a regional jet in the same

Don Lowe, Bob Wohl and Laurent Beaudoin at the March 1989 news conference announcing the Regional Jet go-ahead. (CL C44392-1)

class as the Regional Jet. Lowe, Wohl and McConachie visited Shorts in the spring of 1988 to try to get them to join the Regional Jet program but they refused. Later, Brazilian manufacturer Embraer unveiled its EMB 145 but it ran into design and funding problems and soon fell behind.

The first real show of marketplace interest in the aircraft came during the Farnborough (England) Air Show in

September 1988. After lengthy discussions at the show with Wohl, McConachie and Clignett, a spokesman for DLT Deutsche Luft Transport GmbH, now called Lufthansa CityLine, told an international aviation magazine that it aimed to be the Regional Jet launch customer.

Between September 1988 and January 1989, marketing and technical efforts were intensified and detailed cost estimating and financial assessments were run and rerun by Ron Broad, Marc Comiré and Mike Lacroix under the watchful eyes of vice-president finance Paul Larose. By early 1989, the team had a good estimate of the non-recurring and production costs, a good definition of the airplane and a good idea of what the customer wanted.

In February 1989, Wohl told the press that DLT had signed for six aircraft with options on another six. He also said that 50 launch orders was the magic number needed for board approval, and that the Regional Jet team had established a 50-seat configuration as standard.

Regional Jet Production Go-ahead

Bombardier launched the Regional Jet program on March 31, 1989, on the strength of 56 orders and six options, and it was an instant market success. Canadair secured 116 commitments in the nine weeks following go-ahead. They came from DLT and airlines in the United Kingdom, Australia, Italy, the United States and Canada.

During the summer of 1989, the organization was further refined. Eric Haines retired and Danny Lebeuf took over airframe design. Ian Montgomerie (electrics and avionics) and Ivan Vlatko (hydraulics and landing gear) joined the team. A program management office was created, and André Brais was brought on board as director after his successful role managing Bombardier's New York subway program. Terry Provence joined McConachie's organization as marketing director.

A new Regional Jet division was inaugurated on August 7, 1989, in leased accommodation at the corner of Cavendish Boulevard and Trans-Canada Highway in Saint-Laurent. Wohl was appointed president. Beside

McConachie, Francoeur (now vice-president, contracts) and Brais, Wohl had André Carrier (from Bombardier mass transit) as controller, and Larry Dugan (formerly with Douglas and American Airlines) as vice-president, customer support.

With the return of engineering centralization, the advanced design team was integrated back into the engineering division under the new vice-president of engineering, John Holding.

Bob McCall returned to Canadair after 13 years at de Havilland, to become special advisor to Wohl and Brais who had to build a whole new organization to design, manufacture, sell and support a product for a market that was completely new to Canadair. Dugan had to create, virtually from scratch, an entire customer support organization with a thorough knowledge of airline operations.

Some of the design engineers were transferred from Canadair's newest subcontract, under which the company was designing and building major components for Aerospatiale for the Airbus A330/340. Canadair, in particular the Regional Jet program, benefited greatly from its involvement with Airbus. It brought new approaches and ideas in dealing with the interface between engineering and manufacturing. It accelerated Canadair's development of computer-aided design and manufacturing (CADAM) procedures, including the use of CATIA, a three-dimensional CADAM process. It introduced Canadair stress engineers to more advanced computerized stress methods and procedures, and gave Canadair access to Aerospatiale's composite materials expertise.

Metal-cutting of the first Regional Jet production parts began in November 1989. The key people in manufacturing at this point were Roland Gagnon, Peter Kukovica, John Ballard and Tony Natlacen, all reporting to the president of manufacturing, Vince Ambrico. Ambrico retired in early 1990 and Gagnon became vice-president, manufacturing. Joe Ederhy became director of planning and later director of assembly; Réal Gervais became director of production, Plant 3; and Jacques Descarrega became final assembly manager.

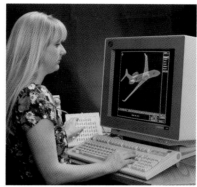

Canadair began using computers in the 1950s. The CL-600 project showed the potential of computers in design. The company committed fully to them when it became involved with Airbus Industrie, then moved ahead with the Regional Jet. By late 1994, more than 180 CATIA work stations were running at Canadair. (CL)

By mid-1990, the list of potential Regional Jet operators had grown. Canadair now held memoranda of agreements for 139 aircraft and options with nine airlines in seven countries. The Embraer EMB 145 was still a distant threat, though its development schedule had slipped considerably. Shorts' FJX had been dropped following Bombardier's purchase of the company the previous October. In fact, Shorts was already involved in the Regional Jet program as supplier of the 9.7-m (32-ft.) long centre fuselage and flight control surfaces. Shorts delivered the first fuselage section on July 20, 1990. It was mated with the wing on October 15.

Second Version

At the Farnborough Air Show on September 3, 1990, Canadair announced plans to certificate two versions of the Regional Jet simultaneously–the standard Series 100 and the extended range Series 100ER. The Series 100 would have a maximum gross weight of 21,546 kg (47,500 lb.) and a range of 1,561 km (970 mi.). The Series 100ER would have a gross weight of 23,134 kg (51,000 lb.) and a range of 2,620 km (1,630 mi.).

Though development and initial production were proceeding smoothly, the deepening economic recession, and its impact on the airlines, dampened sales. Marketing was unable to convert more of the initial commitments to orders.

On May 6, 1991, Prime Minister Brian Mulroney, Quebec Premier Robert Bourassa, Bombardier chairman Laurent Beaudoin and Canadair president Bob Brown joined 1,800 employees and guests to witness the Regional Jet rollout. Only four days later, on May 10, 1991, the aircraft flew, meeting a first-flight target date set more than three years earlier. At the controls were Doug Adkins and co-pilot Don Stephen.

In mid-May, the sales picture brightened when DLT increased its original commitment to 13 firm orders and 12 options. Three weeks later, another European customer ordered four with an option for a further two, and DLT asked that deliveries of its initial order be accelerated.

Flight Test and Certification

On July 16, 1991, Adkins ferried Regional Jet No. 7001 to the flight test centre at Wichita for flight test and certification. It was joined on August 26 by No. 7002 which had made its maiden flight on August 2. Certification was scheduled to take 12 months. John Taylor was appointed director of the flight test program and Bill Greening was manager, flight test.

Three aircraft took part in certification. No. 7001 was used for performance, stability and control development. No. 7002 was used for systems development and testing, electronic flight instrument system (EFIS) and engine instrumentation crew alert system (EICAS) evaluation, autopilot development, environmental control system analysis, and anti-ice testing. No. 7003 was used principally for function and reliability (F & R) testing and operations manual performance evaluation. F & R testing is a 150-flight-hour program which simulates typical airline operations.

No. 7002 had a completely new state-of-the-art digital avionics system. It was only the second aircraft (after the Boeing 747-400) to have an EICAS which enabled the pilots to see a display of the entire synoptics of any system by simply pressing a button. No. 7003 was the first Regional Jet with a complete airline interior. It flew for the first time on November 17, 1991.

In October 1991, Comair Inc., a Delta Connection carrier based in Cincinnati, became the first North American

The first Regional Jet has its engines installed, then is seen at the gala rollout ceremony held at Dorval in May 1991. (CL)

customer for the Regional Jet when it ordered 20 aircraft with an option for a further 20. The same month, the business aircraft division sold its first Corporate Jetliner to Xerox Corp. (The business aircraft division sells and supports the Corporate Jetliner.) The Corporate Jetliner is for corporations requiring airline-type service.

By April 1992, the three test aircraft had recorded more than 800 flying hours. Ground tests involving two test articles proceeded normally. During a wing upgust bending load test on the static test article, the wing tip had been successfully deflected upwards by 1.52 m (60 in.).

The CAE Electronics Ltd. Regional Jet simulator "flies" just like the real thing and trains pilots in all phases of flight operations, including Category III landings. In the simulator cockpit scene Werner Laatz of CityLine is having a session with Canadair training captain Jean Guimond. (CL)

Training

Early in the program, Canadair decided that Regional Jet pilot training would be done in-house. The first training centre was opened on April 2, 1992, in CAE facilities at Saint-Laurent. In December 1992, Bombardier, CAE and Lufthansa established a training facility at Schönefeld Airport, Berlin.

The Saint-Laurent centre, managed by Dayton Webb, director of customer training, featured a CAE full-motion flight simulator and a Rediffusion 150-degree wide-angle visual system providing the most realistic cockpit environment available.

By June 1992, flight tests indicated the Regional Jet burned less fuel, flew farther and climbed faster than previous estimates. Tom Appleton, executive vice-president, Regional Jet division, told customers this meant they would get up to 275 km (170 mi.) more range with 50 passengers. Appleton had come from de Havilland to replace McConachie, who returned to his consulting firm in July 1991. Appleton's staff included John Giraudy, vice-president, international sales; John Horvath, vice-president, domestic sales; and Douglas Campbell, manager, North American sales.

Regional Jet No. 7002 during water trough testing at Cartierville to determine the effect of water ingestion on engine performance. (CL)

No. 7002 is serviced overnight to be ready in the morning for more flight test work at Wichita. (CL C56883-12)

Bombardier Regional Aircraft Division

In March 1992, Bombardier completed acquisition of de Havilland, and immediately established a de Havilland/Canadair team to study possible areas of co-operation. The study determined there was sufficient in common between the Regional Jet and Dash 8 programs that they would benefit from being combined in certain functions. On July 7, Bombardier formed the Bombardier Regional Aircraft Division (BRAD) by combining Regional Jet and Dash 8 marketing, contracts and customer support functions in the de Havilland facility at Downsview, Ontario.

Bob Wohl was appointed president of BRAD. He moved his management team of Appleton, Francoeur and Dugan and approximately 50 Canadair staff to Toronto in August, and by October the Regional Jet team was fully integrated, with approximately 300 former de Havilland employees, into a single organization. The Regional Jet program management office, customer training and technical publications, though still part of the new division, remained in Montreal.

Certification

On July 31, 1992, following an intensive 14-month flight test and certification program, the Regional Jet received Canadian type approval. The first aircraft was delivered to Lufthansa CityLine in Berlin on October 19, 1992, and entered revenue service on November 2. CityLine's first four aircraft logged 1,237 flight hours in the first 100 days of service and achieved operational reliability of 99 per cent—a remarkable performance for a new airplane and a good start for Paul Massé, Canadair's field service representative at Lufthansa CityLine.

At the end of January 1993, Lufthansa CityLine co-managing director Helmut Horn remarked: "All performance guarantees have been met or exceeded, which is unusual for a new aircraft providing a new type of service." The aircraft were reported burning eight per cent less fuel than predicted, saving the airline about $100,000 per year per aircraft from its original cost predictions. It was also quiet. Tests conducted by Canadair and General Electric showed the Regional Jet to be the quietest jetliner in its category, operating well within the U.S. FAA's stringent Stage 3 noise requirements, significantly below competing turbofan aircraft, and below some similar size turboprops. Most gratifying was that the development program had achieved these results essentially on schedule and on budget.

European joint airworthiness type approval was received on January 15, 1993 and the U.S. type certificate on January 21. The first Corporate Jetliner was delivered to Xerox Corp. in January. Seating 30 passengers in business-class comfort, the Xerox aircraft had a range of 3,735 km (2,320 mi.). It entered shuttle service in June 1993, flying twice daily between White Plains and Rochester, New York. As of September 29, 1994, the aircraft had accumulated more than 1,400 flight hours with a dispatch reliability exceeding 99.2 per cent.

Loss of 7001

Tragedy struck the Regional Jet program on July 26, 1993, when No. 7001 crashed near Wichita, while conducting a test manoeuvre to extend the flight envelope. The crew of three were killed: David Martin, pilot; Robert Normand, co-pilot; and Roger Booth, flight test engineer. The accident occurred during steady-heading sideslip testing to verify lateral and directional stability. The test was being carried out with a new flap setting, at a lower speed and a higher angle of attack than had previously been tested. The crew lost control when the trailing wing stalled and were unable to recover before the aircraft crashed.

David Martin spent his entire 15-year Canadair career in flight operations, the first five years as a flight test engineer, followed by five years in a joint capacity as flight test engineer and pilot, then exclusively as a test pilot. He had transferred to Wichita for the Regional Jet flight test program in 1991. Robert Normand joined Canadair in 1991 following a distinguished eight-year career with the Canadian Forces. Roger Booth joined experimental engineering in 1979 before transferring to flight operations in 1983. He played a key role as flight test engineer in the Challenger 601, CL-215T and Regional Jet programs, and was a member of the Challenger 601 crew which set the non-stop Calgary-London world record in August 1983.

F-GNME was the first of two Regional Jets for Air Littoral, which operates them for Air France. (CL)

More Orders

The accident had no impact on Regional Jet sales. Only three weeks later, on August 16, Air Canada signed a letter of intent for 24 aircraft and 24 options. The next day, SkyWest Airlines, a Delta Connection airline based in St. George, Utah, ordered 10 with options on a further 10.

Air Canada's president, Hollis Harris, with Bob Brown while celebrating Air Canada's Regional Jet order. (CL C68868-12)

Bob Wohl retired on August 30 and his position as president of Bombardier Regional Aircraft Division was assumed by Pierre Lortie, formerly president of Bombardier Capital Group. In September, Lauda Air Luftfahrt of Vienna, Austria, ordered six Regional Jets and optioned six more. The first of two or-

Niki Lauda accepts "the key" to Lauda Air's first Regional Jet from Bob Brown and BRAD president Pierre Lortie. Looking on is Walter Lichem, the Austrian ambassador to Canada. (CL C69238-10)

Comair's first Regional Jet lifts off at Dorval. It was delivered on April 30, 1993. (CL)

The Regional Jet and CL-601 lines in P3. The two nearest aircraft were Regional Jets No. 7030 for SkyWest and No. 7031 for Comair. (CL C67517-3)

dered by Air Littoral of France was handed over on October 20. Air Canada confirmed its first order for 10 on December 10.

Regional Jet deliveries for the fiscal year ended January 31, 1994, totalled 23. Comair exercised five of its 20 options, bringing the total of firm orders to 64, of which 29 had been delivered.

LR Version

On February 22, 1994, Lortie announced a new long-range version, the LR. The LR option increased the maximum gross weight to 24,041 kg (53,000 lb.) and extended the range to more than 3,515 km (2,185 mi.). Lauda Air became the first LR customer by ordering the LR option applied to its order for six aircraft and six options.

The Regional Aircraft Division also announced further improvements to all Regional Jet versions including a modified wing leading edge to reduce takeoff distance by eight per cent; a new eight-degree flap setting to enable the aircraft to lift heavier payloads under "hot and high" conditions; new flight management and inertial reference systems to improve navigational capability, and a Category IIIa manual landing system with headup guidance display. (Cat. IIIa landing limitations stipulate a 15-m (50-

ft.) decision height and a 213-m (700-ft.) runway visual range.)

To December 16, 1994, Regional Jet aircraft deliveries totalled 49, leaving a backlog of 42. Production was to increase to three aircraft per month in early 1995. At the time of writing, studies were underway into potential stretched versions of both the Regional Jet and the Dash 8. Decisions were anticipated by early 1995.

Bombardier Global Express

The Global Express program began with a call from Bombardier chairman Laurent Beaudoin on his car phone to vice-president, engineering, John Holding, in early 1991. Beaudoin wanted Holding to start thinking about the next project. He did not want it to be just an improvement on what Canadair was building now, nor

something that would just equal the competition. He wanted Bombardier to become the leader by producing a top-of-the line product that would leapfrog the competition. He left it to Holding to decide what kind of aircraft it should be.

After discussions with Bryan Moss and Nick Perkins, Holding recommended the development of a new corporate aircraft for the 21st century: one with better range, comfort and performance than any previous corporate aircraft. He put Perkins and his advanced design team to work on a conceptual design. Avraham Ardman (system design), Peter Webb (structural design) and Kevin Hoffman (configuration definition) coordinated advanced design.

The product definition phase involved close collaboration between engineering and marketing, particularly re-

The image of things to come—the Global Express soars in the rendering at top, and the marketing mock-up "steals the show" at the 1994 National Business Aircraft Association convention in New Orleans. (CL)

garding the determination of the aircraft's range requirement. The competition was hinting that it was studying an aircraft with a range of 9,300 km (5,000 nm). An important west coast operator, on a visit to Canadair, identified a need for a range greater than 5,000 nm. Market studies indicated a minimum range of 10,400 km (5,600 nm).

During the product definition stage, Perkins's team worked closely with Peter Clignett's technical team and Keith Miller's design team led by Tony Barber and Danny Lebeuf and including George Chan, Roger Goudreau, Jim Moran, Ivan Vlatko and Bill Watson. The marketing input was provided by Ralph Aceti and Philippe Crevier.

In September 1991, Holding presented a proposal for the "Orient Express": a completely new corporate aircraft with a 10,400- to 10,550-km (5,600- to 5,700-nm) range at Mach 0.80 and 9,600-km (5,000-nm) at Mach 0.85. He told Beaudoin there would be no commonality between this aircraft and any previous product, and estimated its development cost at one billion dollars.

Beaudoin thought the concept was great but was not happy with the cost. He encouraged the trio to be as creative and innovative with the business plan as they were going to be with design. They decided that program-sharing—persuading one or more major suppliers to assume a share of the development cost—was the only way to make the program financially viable.

Program Is Announced

The National Business Aircraft Association convention at Houston, Texas, in October 1991 was the site for the announcement of the new project. By then the name *Orient Express* had been dropped in favor of the more appropriate *Global Express*. The range, with eight passengers and four crew, was 10,460 km (5,650 nm) at a long-range cruise speed of Mach 0.80. It would fly non-stop between such city pairs as Los Angeles-Tokyo, Tokyo-London, and London-Los Angeles, in about 12 hours, bettering the competition's best offering by over 1,110 km (600 nm).

Its gross weight would be 32,659 kg (72,000 lb.). It would have a new high technology transonic wing featuring an advanced airfoil section and leading edge slats. Its wing span of 28 m (92 ft.) would be 6.63 m (21 ft. 9 in.) wider than the Canadair Regional Jet. Power would be come from two new high-efficiency turbofans. And it would fly above the airlines at altitudes up to 15,500 m (51,000 ft.). Beaudoin had his wish—an airplane that was in every respect ahead of the competition.

The announcement of the project stimulated market interest in both Global Express and Challenger aircraft. It confirmed Bombardier's continuing commitment to corporate aviation and put an end to concern of a possible transfer of the corporation's attention to the regional airliner market.

In May 1992, a Global Express program office was established. Trevor Young became vice-president, Global Express program reporting to Bryan Moss, president, Challenger division.

A full-size mockup of the aircraft's fuselage, completed by Learjet, confirmed Canadair's claim that the Global Express had the largest cabin in corporate aviation: 14.6 m (48 ft.) long, 2.49 m (8 ft. 2 in.) wide at the centreline and 1.90 m (6 ft. 3 in.) in height. The mockup cabin was divided into three compartments: an office with a complete workstation and seating for four; a conference room with a convertible cocktail/dining table and seating for six, and a state room with a full-size fold out bed and two large chairs. A crew rest area was also provided.

Potential Global Express owners had a significant input into the layout of the mockup, as they had in all aspects of the evolution of the program. Not only was the initial concept based on clearly defined market requirements, the details were refined through a continuous sampling of input from prospective clients and the marketplace in general by Moss and his marketing and sales team lead by Aceti, Keith Garner and John Lawson. In the closing months of 1992, the marketing team took the mockup on a successful tour of 13 U.S. cities from Minneapolis to White Plains, New York, and south to Fort Lauderdale, Florida, before returning it to Montreal and a showing to Canadair employees.

A multiphase, 2,000-hour wind tunnel program began in February 1993 following 18 months of extensive computational fluid dynamics (CFD) development. CFD combines fluid dynamic theory, applied mathematics and powerful computers to simulate the motion of fluid around objects. It enables the aircraft designer to develop an aircraft shape that maximizes lift and drag characteristics without the need for expensive prototype aircraft. It also reduces the amount of wind tunnel testing required. CFD was one of the advances in aerodynamics which, together with parallel advances in structural materials and systems, made possible the Global Express's long range and high speed.

Engine

In mid-March 1993, following studies of offerings from six engine manufacturers, Canadair chose the BMW Rolls-Royce BR710-48-C2 turbofan, an ultra-quiet, environmentally friendly engine providing 65.34 kN (14,690 lb.) of thrust. BMW Rolls-Royce became a risk-sharing

participant responsible not only for the powerplant, including the engine, fuel controls, thrust reversers and the nacelle, but also for the powerplant's performance.

This performance accountability was an example of changes taking place in the industry. Bombardier now required suppliers to share the risk by providing performance guarantees as they relate to packaged and complete components. It no longer wanted to be an integrator of small pieces. When Bombardier asked for a power pack, for instance, it wanted a nacelle working with the engine in such a way as to perform to a certified level with spe-

BMW Rolls-Royce chairman Albert Schneider shakes hands with Bob Brown as David Evans of BMW Rolls-Royce looks on. They were viewing the Global Express mock-up following Bombardier's decision to select the BR710-48-C2 turbofan for the Global Express. (CL)

Experimental test engineer René Barakett and advanced aerodynamics section leader Dr. Fassi Kafyeke prepare a 7% Global Express scale model for testing in the NRC's low-speed wind tunnel in Ottawa. Wind-tunnel trials support the aerodynamic development of the aircraft and establish guaranteed performance figures needed by customers. Data gathered are analysed in a supercomputer. A final report provides specific conclusions and makes recommendations for improving design. Global Express wind-tunnel models were also tested at Rockwell in California and at the Aircraft Research Association in Bedford, UK. (CL C69364-18)

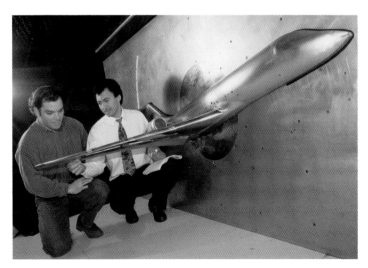

cific performance guarantees. This was effectively reducing the number of suppliers the corporation used.

Representatives of the engine manufacturer were present on April 2, 1993, when the 40 or so deposit holders were told the aircraft's range had again been increased, this time to 12,000 km (6,500 nm). This brought such city pairs as New York-Tokyo, Riyadh-Rio de Janeiro and London-Buenos Aires within non-stop range. Further changes were announced. The aircraft's length was now 29.51 m (96 ft. 10 in.); its span was 27.63 m (90 ft. 8 in.), and its maximum takeoff weight 41,278 kg (91,000 lb.).

Late in September, Mitsubishi Heavy Industries Ltd. of Tokyo joined the program as a risk-sharing participant responsible for developing and building the complete wing and centre fuselage sections.

Program Launch

Laurent Beaudoin launched the Bombardier Global Express program on December 20, 1993, on the basis of 30 firm orders and eight options at a firm price of $27.95 million in January 1994 U.S. dollars.

The announcement came a few days after Gulfstream Aerospace Corp. offered to double the value of $250,000 deposits on its G-V to any Global Express customers who would switch and order a G-V by December 31, 1993. No Global Express customer accepted the Gulfstream offer.

The Global Express program was unique in a number of ways. It was the first aerospace product to carry the Bombardier name, for rather than being the product of a single organization, it combined the technical skills of several members of the Bombardier family. Canadair, as overall project manager, system integrator and leader of the joint definition projects, would manage certification, flight testing, sales, marketing and support. Canadair and de Havilland would share engineering and planning. Meanwhile, Shorts was designing and building the engine nacelle and the composite horizontal tail. The remaining structural work was shared among all the Bombardier aerospace units. The flight test program was planned for Wichita.

Global Express was the first program to involve risk-sharing participants, and to have engineers from the participants, from other suppliers, and from other Bombardier groups, participating as a team in the early stages.

On February 1, 1994, engineers from Canadair, Mitsubishi, Shorts, de Havilland and BMW Rolls-Royce began the joint definition phase at Montreal. Teams from other leading systems and structural manufacturers joined as they become participants in the program.

In February 1994, Keith Miller was appointed engineering project director, business aircraft, responsible for the Global Express. Key engineering integrators at that time were Avraham Ardman, systems; Claude Boucher, technical and experimental; and Danny Lebeuf, structure.

By mid-1994 all major Global Express participants were on board and over 400 participant representatives were engaged in the program. First flight was expected in the third quarter of 1996 and certification for May 1998.

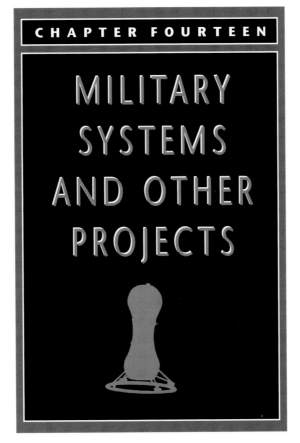

CHAPTER FOURTEEN

MILITARY SYSTEMS AND OTHER PROJECTS

At the time Bombardier acquired Canadair, Len Box was vice-president, surveillance systems. In May 1987 surveillance systems became part of a new military division with Laurent A. Bergeron as president, Jacques Cadieux as vice-president and general manager of surveillance systems, and Walter Niemy as vice-president and general manager for military aircraft.

Bergeron left in mid-1988, Box retired for good in July 1989, Yvan Lafortune became vice-president and general manager of surveillance systems and was later replaced by Bill Dawes. In February 1993, the surveillance systems division was absorbed into the defence systems division under Walter Niemy, a former Canadian Forces brigadier general. On October 3, 1994, Niemy was succeeded as president of the division by David Huddleston, formerly chief of Canadian Forces Air Command.

CL-289

Canadair won the largest export order in its history when, on November 25, 1987, Canada, West Germany and France signed a $411 million contract to provide the German and French armies with CL-289 systems consisting of drone air vehicles and launchers. It was also the largest defence export order ever won by a Canadian company.

The CL-289 production program was a joint effort between Canadair, Dornier GmbH of Germany and Société Anonyme de Télécommunications (SAT) of France. As prime contractor with overall responsibility as system manager, Canadair built and tested the aft portion of the drones, the wings and the launch pedestals. Dornier built the balance of the drone and elements of ground support

The first pre-production CL-289 drone and launcher with some of those involved in the project: Brian Anderson, Gordie Lloyd, a Dornier representative, Bob Ross, George Campbell and Robin Crawford. (CL 12763)

A pre-production CL-289 launches on an evaluation flight. (CL C19773-7)

At the time of the contract, Andrew Clark was director of engineering and Bill Chisholm was director, CL-289 program management. Stan Rose was appointed director of CL-289 production; Eric Lavender was program manager; John McGovern was director, product engineering; and Michel Charest was director, materiel. The division's sales effort was led by Rex Hynes based in Montreal and Mike Stacy in the United States.

Canadair shipped the first production CL-289 component, an aft drone section, to Dornier in December 1988. The entry of the system into service was preceded by a system validation test program which began in January 1990 at the Meppen test centre in northern Germany. Official entry into German Army service was celebrated on November 29, 1990, at Dornier's facility in Friedrichshafen. The CL-289, NATO designation AN/USD-502, thus became the first operational system to satisfy the upgraded requirements of NATO operations, and the first corps level system to enter service.

Between November 19 and December 5, 1991, the German Army conducted 10 successful flights at the Meppen test centre, including a record four successful flights in one day. In February 1992, it carried out more flights under simulated operational conditions at its Bergen-Hohne range. The first French flight trials occurred between November 1991 and January 1992. The French system, named "Piver," became operational in December 1992. Canadair completed its final CL-289 aft drone section on April 16, 1993. Follow-on sales had been expected from both operators and other potential customers, but these fell victim to a changed political/military environment. By late 1994 the division had completed delivery of an order

equipment and provided systems integration and testing for the German Army. (Aerospatiale, through its tactical missiles division, provided this service for the French Army.) SAT supplied the infrared linescan sensor and data link.

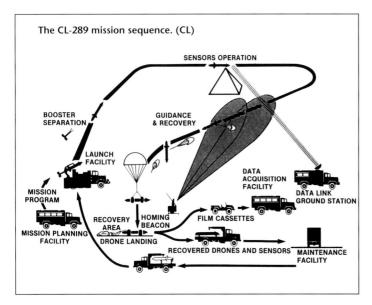

The CL-289 mission sequence. (CL)

for $8 million of spare parts ordered in 1991 and had started work on a follow-on spares contract.

The CL-89 and CL-289 were examples of international co-operation at its best. Both programs involved participation from government, the military and industry from four countries and it is to the credit of all involved that the programs were so successful.

CL-227

The CL-227 is a rotary-winged, unmanned air vehicle (UAV) for surveillance and target acquisition. Only 1.6 m (5.4 ft.) in height, it is powered by a 37-kw (50-hp) Williams International gas turbine engine. It can take off and land vertically, hover, reach speeds of up to 130 km/h (80 mph) and remain airborne for over 2.5 hours. Because of its shape it is affectionately known as the "Flying Peanut", though the official name, "Sentinel", was chosen in a competition among Canadair employees in February 1984.

The CL-227 upper sphere contains the engine and fuel tank; the centre "waist" houses the computer and control mechanisms for the rotors and rotor blades. The lower sphere is the payload module for up to 36 kg (80 lb.) of payload such as a forward-looking infrared (FLIR) system, a real-time video system, a radio communications relay, or an electronic warfare jamming and decoy system. The vehicle is remotely controlled by an operator in a ground station equipped with a TV monitor which displays what the payload is "seeing" as it flies or hovers.

A complete land-based CL-227 system consists of several UAVs, a mobile ground control station, a trailer-mounted ground data terminal and a launch/recovery vehicle. The UAV is designed to survive in a modern battlefield environment. Its small size, quietness, ability to fly as high as 3,000 m (10,000 ft.), and low radar and heat signatures, make it difficult to detect. It is also highly mobile and requires minimum support equipment.

How the Program Started

The origin of CL-227 dates to 1964 when John P. Kerr, then section chief, advanced design, missiles and systems division, was invited to evaluate the Periscopter. It was a battlefield surveillance project involving Canadian Westinghouse, CARDE and Servotec, the British company that designed and built the CL-84 tail rotors. The Periscopter was a tethered flying vehicle with electric mo-

An early flight of the CL-227 "Peanut". (CL C16162-4)

John Kerr inspects an early CL-227. He joined Canadair in 1952 in aircraft design, then moved to the Missiles and Systems Division where he worked on the Velvet Glove, Sparrow II and Black Brant. He next headed design of the CL-89 and in 1964 began the studies which led to the first flight of the Phase I CL-227 on August 25, 1978. (CL C10632)

The CL-227 system includes (from the top left): a ground position data link, generator (in trailer), 2 ¹/₂-ton truck with ground control station/recovery vehicle and take-off platform. (CL C42857-5)

tors driving a pair of rotors. Its purpose was to carry a low-light video sensor as high as 2,400 m (8,000 ft.).

Kerr had joined Canadair in 1952 as a systems analyst in advanced design. He transferred to the missiles and systems division in 1955 and worked on the Velvet Glove, Sparrow II, robot dispatch carrier and Black Brant rocket. When the Sparrow was cancelled, he played a key role in the initial design and development of the CL-89. After reviewing the Periscopter, Kerr recommended that a free-flying vehicle powered by an internal combustion engine would better suit the system's intended role, which was to provide short-range battlefield surveillance for the army brigade commander. He also suggested that technology used in the CL-84 tail rotor design would improve vehicle control.

CARDE subsequently dropped the Periscopter, but Kerr and a small team consisting of Peter Ghey, Marius Huvers, Denyse Parisien and Henry Szot continued design studies, supported partly by Canadair research and development and partly by the United Kingdom. The team's first concept (1965) was called the Dynacopter. Only 1 m (3 ft. 4 in.) high and weighing 40 kg (90 lb.), it had a nine-kilowatt (12-hp) rotary combustion engine, an endurance of one hour and a top speed of 110 km/h (70 mph). The next concept (1967) was 1.6 m (5 ft. 4 in.) high and had a rotary combustion engine driving two contra-rotating, twin-bladed rotors.

Between 1967 and 1977 further design studies were made, and a wind tunnel model and various rotors were built and tested. This showed that two-bladed rotor systems suffered from vibration problems, so three-bladed rotors were substituted.

Phase I

CL-227 development progressed in three phases. Phase I (proof of concept) began in 1977 with construction of two prototype air vehicles, each 1.5 m (5 ft.) high and powered, in the absence of a suitable gas turbine engine, by a 17-kilowatt (23-hp) Saurer GT15 rotary combustion engine. In 1978, Ottawa provided funds for technology development. The initial flight of a prototype took place on August 25, 1978, with the air vehicle flying for 10 minutes, tethered by a steel cable inside a 7.3-m (24-ft.) high cage.

On July 20, 1979, the vehicle flew for the first time in a larger test facility using a unique tether which allowed it limited vertical and lateral flight via a running tether attached to the top and bottom of the vehicle. By early 1981 the two prototypes had made some 300 tethered flights from the two facilities. The first free flight took place on March 19, 1980. Connected only by a 30-m (100-ft.) command and data transmission umbilical harness, the UAV took off and flew within a 20-m (66-ft.) square caged area. It landed on a patch of ice and skittered about like a hockey puck on a rink until the engine was turned off.

During 1980, 19 free flights totalling 45 minutes of air time, were made without incident. On the last (November 1980) Peter Ghey carried out three successful haul-down landings using a thin Kevlar line attached to the bottom of the UAV. From 1977 through 1981, the Phase I design, integration and flight test department numbered about a dozen people. In 1978, the core group consisted of Kerr's original team plus Andy Auld, Ron Eberts, Fred Horst, Gilbert Ouellette, Ernie Semple and Richard Théberge. In 1979, Auld, Eberts and Théberge left and were replaced by Andrew Clark, Guenther Goritschnig, Gareth Richardson and Bill Upton. Al Stone of experimental provided the composite skin and propeller blade design and built the blades.

Phase II

Design work on Phase II (technology demonstration) began in 1980 with the aim of demonstrating surveillance and target acquisition using a real-time video camera and a data link. By this time Derek Higton was director, surveillance systems programs, reporting to vice-president, engineering and technology, Len Box. Fred Agnew was CL-227 program manager, and Andrew Clark was section chief, CL-227 engineering.

Four Phase II vehicles were produced, each 1.7 m (5.5 ft.) high and powered by a 24-kw (32-hp) Williams International WR-34 series gas turbine engine. A mobile control station and takeoff platform were also built. The Phase II UAV's engine was designed as a lawn mower engine for the T. Eaton Co. of the United States, which had shelved it when the price of gasoline skyrocketed. Canadair obtained the rights and transferred them to Williams International which developed the engine.

The tether testing facility was again used for preliminary flight tests. The first flight was made on September 1, 1981. The first free flight was on December 3. Three more successful flights were made for representatives of the U.S. and Canadian armed forces on December 14, 15 and 16. A thin Kevlar line connected to the vehicle prevented it from escaping in case of a malfunction. Excellent sensor imagery was recorded, and station-keeping using the imagery was demonstrated. Kerr retired in 1981, but not before he received a Canadair Certificate of Invention and a cash award for his work on the CL-227.

During February and March 1982, eight free flights, each lasting from eight to over 20 minutes, were made at the Defence Research Establishment (DRE) near Suffield, Alberta. These demonstrated the ability of the vehicle to be controlled under all test conditions including hail, snow and bone-chilling cold. The maximum height achieved was 750 m (2,460 ft.) above sea level, 250 m (820 ft.) above the ground, and the maximum speed recorded was 25 m per second (56 mph).

In early May 1983, the flight test team of Clark, Goritschnig, Horst, Richardson, Semple and Upton augmented by Ben Grass, Don Lovegrove, Bill Low and Rupert McCoy, participated in an army exercise at Yakima, Washington, involving the U.S. Army's 9th Infantry Division. The night before the exercise, simulated enemy forces infiltrated the Sentinel area and made off with all the mechanical hardware spares. Luckily, a member of the team managed to recover enough parts to allow the exercise to go on.

The full-scale exercise, witnessed by senior officers

The CL-227 family: Phase I (1979-81), Phase II (1981-83) and Phase III (1986-) were displayed together for the first time at Canadair in June 1994. (Bill Upton)

Part of the CL-227 team. From the left: Stan Rose, Vincent Soccio, John Henry, Jean-Marie Leemars, Marc Comiré, Frank Lojko, Norbert Trutschnigg, Robert Deslauriers, Denis Maisonneuve, Dave Roe (behind), Earl Hooper, Andrew Leeming (behind), Gilles Charette, Ian Moody, Dave Cool, Ron Leblanc, Harry Hanlon. In front: Roger Geoffre, Samy Raspa. (CL C37010-9)

from all services, included attacks by F-111s, interdiction by F-16s, infiltrations by helicopter-borne soldiers and armament covered by helicopter gunships. The 227 and its test team earned high praise for their performance which included a post-attack reconnaissance of the battle area.

Following that successful demonstration, no more free flights were necessary. Phase II ended after 13 free flight missions and some 100 tethered flights. In 1984, Canadair decided to fund CL-227 Phase III (full scale engineering development).

In 1986, the Canadian government contributed $30 million toward completing development and production of 10 CL-227 air vehicles, two ground control stations and a series of look-down payloads. Phase III of this program was well underway at the time of the sale to Bombardier.

In the two years since the start of Phase III in 1984, the UAV had been totally re-engineered by a team led for the most part by Andrew Clark, John McGovern and Ray Atkins. The basic concept, principle of operation and vehicle shape remained unchanged from Phase II, but the engineering of the vehicle and the flight and support equipment were significantly re-engineered to military standards.

Fuel capacity was more than doubled to 50 l (11 imp. gal.). The UAV shape was cleaned up to improve aerodynamic drag characteristics and radar cross section. Engine power was increased from 24 to 37 kilowatts (32 to 50 hp) and larger rotor blades were installed. Navigation capability was improved significantly by the substitution of a digital computer and inertial measuring unit for the analogue autopilot and gyros.

The first tethered flight of the Phase III vehicle took place in June 1987. It was followed by 25 "flights" in a wind tunnel test program with the UAV suspended in the exhaust of the NRC tunnel at Ottawa. The first free flight was made at Cartierville on November 20, 1987.

The next step was a free flight test program which began in February 1988 at the DRE at Suffield. It established an initial flight envelope within a range of 10.0 km (6.2 mi.) of the ground station. Flight test priority then gave way to the development of a system for a naval demonstration program.

Sea Sentinel

Development of a maritime version of the CL-227, the Sea Sentinel, was prompted by a show of interest from

Germany and several other countries. The first Sea Sentinel made its maiden flight in August 1988. Almost the same as the land version, it had different legs and feet which, in conjunction with a 3.6-m (12-ft.) diameter landing grid and a mobile takeoff platform, called a traverser, enabled it to operate from the deck of a ship at sea.

The traverser moved the UAV to and from the launch area. Prior to launch, it provided electrical and pneumatic services to the engine and the vehicle's electronics. During landing, probes extending downward from the vehicle's legs operated butterfly locks on the legs to lock the vehicle on the grid after touchdown.

The first flight was unintentional. A planned full system ground test became a first flight when a switch was mistakenly selected during preflight checks and the vehicle took off. The operators quickly gained control of the errant UAV and landed it on the predesignated spot, only to find that support personnel and onlookers had disappeared!

In August and September 1989, the Sea Sentinel underwent extensive flight testing at the Pacific Missile Test Center in California. On August 24, 1989, a UAV lifted off the U.S. Army ship *Jan Tide* for the first of a series of nine VTOL operations to demonstrate the system's target-spotting capabilities in support of such missions as drug interdiction.

On one flight, the UAV was vectored to two 27-m (90-ft.) power boats simulating a drug run, including evasive manoeuvres. The UAV was vectored to the target boats by a radar-equipped balloon flying above the ship. Once over the targets, the UAV visually tracked them while remaining undetected. A trained observer on one of the boats never spotted the Sea Sentinel hovering quietly 700 m (2,300 ft.) above, even when told where to look. In contrast, the vehicle recorded every move of both boats and transmitted the information back to *Jan Tide*.

On another mission, the video imagery from the 227 was obscured by cloud. Navigation was entirely through the data link system until the UAV descended below cloud and spotted the ship's wake. This gave added confidence in the system's ability to operate in bad weather.

The project was not without its touch of light drama. While making a photographic record of the demonstration, Paul Sagala and Bill Upton were photographing the

In 1989 the first CL-227 shipboard flight trials were conducted aboard the *Jan Tide* off California. Included were joint trials with the US Army's radar-equipped Small Aerostat Surveillance System, a balloon tethered to the ship that provided the CL-227 with bearings to targets. Note the CL-227 resting on the *Jan Tide's* helicopter deck. The first shipboard flight of the CL-227 Sea Sentinel was on August 24, 1989. (CL)

In 1991 USS *Doyle* sailed on a six-month NATO cruise carrying a complete CL-227 system for operatonal evaluation. Here the CL-227 rests on its landing platform. Its recovery grid is behind. The recovery system was developed by Indal Technologies of Mississauga, Ontario. (CL C58631-3)

sign for the Headquarters Pacific Missile Test Center when they were surrounded by military and civil security guards and guard dogs. It appeared they were on the wrong side of the line dividing government and civilian property. They were allowed to leave when a state trooper pointed out that the dividing line hadn't yet been painted on the road.

Gareth Richardson, Mark Roe and Bill Upton had an opportunity to view a piece of Canadair history when, during October 1989, they took a UAV to Holloman AFB in New Mexico to determine its radar cross section. For a month, their daily travel route took them past a line of Canadair-built F-86 Sabres configured as QF-86 unmanned drones. On several occasions they watched a QF-86, still bearing faint signs of RCAF markings, trying to dodge a pursuing F-15 interceptor.

MAVUS

The level of system maturity demonstrated during these land- and ship-based programs generated increased support for the VTOL concept in the United States and other NATO countries. In May 1990, the U.S. UAV joint project office selected the Sea Sentinel for a six-month MAVUS (Maritimized vertical takeoff and landing unmanned aerial vehicle system) operational evaluation aboard the frigate USS *Doyle*. The main objective of MAVUS was to develop ship-based UAV systems. The contract called for the integration into the CL-227 system of many new components including a mission planning and control station, antenna and data link, and new payloads such as a communications relay, an electronic warfare package, a daylight TV and a FLIR (forward looking infra red). Denis Bouchard was appointed MAVUS program manager. Mike Hughes and Mike Stacy from the Washington office represented marketing.

Preliminary systems integration and flight safety clearance tests were conducted at the Naval Air Test Center, Patuxent River, Maryland, from May to September 1991. The 46 missions included autonomous (hands-off) preprogrammed missions and multiple flights in a single day. On one flight, a MAVUS vehicle with a FLIR payload flew more than 60 km (37 mi.).

Tracking the flights was frequently a problem. Chase helicopters, used on early flights in case the vehicle's tracking system malfunctioned, often lost sight of the vehicle because of its small size and rapid acceleration. This necessitated hovering the UAV while the helicopter was vectored to it. The UAV, meanwhile, constantly tracked the helicopter with its FLIR. On one occasion, a UAV trainee operator raised a few pulse rates by inadvertently directing the vehicle to veer suddenly toward the helicopter, and the chase helicopter became the chased!

Following the Patuxent River trials, a complete Sea Sentinel system was installed on *Doyle* at Den Helder, Holland. The system included three air vehicles, an integrated planning and control station, several sensor payloads, and takeoff and landing subsystems.

From October to December 1991, the UAV, flying from *Doyle*, took part in NATO exercises with Canadian, British, Dutch and U.S. ships. During the exercises, imagery generated by the vehicle's television and forward-looking infrared payloads was transmitted to *Doyle* and rebroadcast simultaneously to the other vessels.

The Sea Sentinel made seven flights, totalling 8.5 hours, aboard *Doyle*. The results confirmed that the vehicle had a range of 60 km (37 mi.), could land during 25-degree ship rolls, and operate concurrently with three helicopters. It also demonstrated that payloads could be changed in less than 30 minutes and that the system was capable of flying multiple sorties per day. U.S. Navy Commander Al Hutchins felt that the CL-227 was two or three generations ahead of anything else.

U.S./Canadian Evaluation

From July 1989 to April 1990, U.S. and Canadian military personnel conducted a thorough evaluation of the land-based Sentinel, first at Suffield, Alberta, and later at Holloman AFB and Fort Huachuca, Arizona. Canadian

Forces personnel operated the UAV throughout the evaluation, with Canadair providing logistical support.

Flights at Fort Huachuca used a vehicle finished with a radar-absorbent coating to improve its stealthiness, and a FLIR sensor payload. The evaluation resulted in a significant expansion of the flight and performance envelopes, with one flight reaching a target more than 40 km (25 mi.) from its launch point. Thirty-three flights were conducted in desert, prairie and mountain conditions, and the tests culminated with the system performing a mock airfield damage assessment, locating and identifying simulated runway damage and unexploded ordnance.

In September 1991, Bill Dawes announced the establishment of a facility for the final integration and flight testing of the CL-227 and the CL-289 at Lawton, Oklahoma, a site chosen for its good facilities and proximity to Fort Sill, home of the U.S. Army Artillery Center and School.

CARS

In July 1992, officials from the UAV joint project office watched as the CL-227 successfully completed the initial phase of another U.S. Navy contract by demonstrating five automatic landing recoveries at Fort Sill using Sierra Nevada Corp.'s common automatic recovery system (CARS). Further auto-land demonstrations were made in October and December 1992.

Effective February 1, 1993, the surveillance systems division combined with the former military aircraft division to become the defence systems division under Walter Niemy. Bill Dawes became executive vice-president responsible for the marketing of military aircraft and UAV systems. Gaston Lamarre was appointed vice-president, UAV operations.

MAVUS II

At the Paris Air Show in June 1993, Canadair announced a $10 million contract to evaluate Sea Sentinel automatic landing capabilities on a U.S. Navy guided missile frigate. The deployment, designated MAVUS II, would also assist the Navy to further test the effectiveness of a VTOL UAV with a small surface vessel. New functions of CARS were integrated into the UAV, and tethered proving flights with communications relay and electronic warfare payloads were done at Montreal before the system was shipped to Lawton for final validation.

MAVUS II was then installed on the USS *Vandegrift*. Between February and mid-June 1994, 37 days were spent off the Pacific coast. Conflicting ship priorities and technical problems hindered the trials, and only two missions were completed. Many CARS approaches were made, however, and sufficient data were generated to demonstrate that the auto-land system could successfully recover a CL-227 on this class of ship.

In September 1993, the Direction des Constructions Navales, France's naval engineering branch, contracted for a two-phase, 18-month study into using the CL-227 on French Navy ships. Phase 1 defined the study, Phase 2 included the provision of an automatic landing system.

Early in 1994, the division received a contract for an engine improvement program which covered the integration of an enhanced turboshaft engine and the demonstration of a three-hour endurance. It was scheduled for completion by March 1996. Planning began on the first phase of an avionics improvement program. At the end of 1994, the surveillance systems division was integrated into the operations at Mirabel and Lawton, Oklahoma, and the Plant 4 buildings were closed.

CF-18 System Engineering Support Program

The October 31, 1986 announcement that Ottawa had awarded the CF-18 system engineering support (SES) contract to the Canadair-CAE Electronics-Northwest Industries Ltd. (Edmonton) team put Canadair back in the news. Competition for the valuable contract had boiled down to a battle between this team and one led by Bristol

Aerospace of Winnipeg. When the award was announced, accusations flew. Bristol management claimed that the DND had said that Bristol would get the contract. The familiar cries of "favoritism" and "Quebec again" arose from segments of the industry and the public, but Canadair kept the contract.

Prime Minister Brian Mulroney, replying to a letter from Canadair retiree Jean-Paul Roy, wrote: "The government chose Canadair because it both builds and repairs aircraft. This is something its competitors do not do. Thus Canadair will be able to apply the expertise and state-of-the-art technology gained by repairing and maintaining the CF-18 to the production of aircraft in this country." The award made Canadair the first organization (other than the aircraft's manufacturer, McDonnell Douglas) to earn responsibility for the modification and maintenance of this sophisticated fighter. It also sparked a flurry of job applications from engineers and technicians keen to be associated with the CF-18. Canadair's personnel department received 3,500 applications for 255 vacancies.

The winning proposal had been prepared by a joint Canadair/CAE team led by Canadair director of product support, Peter Hargrove, and Ray Learmond of CAE. The SES contract called for the provision of complete support for the CF-18 weapon system including engineering, logistic and documentation support; aircraft sampling inspections; depot-level inspection repair; component repair; fly-in repairs; and mobile repair parties. Other major tasks included software design, technical analysis of

An aerial view of Canadair's Mirabel complex, then a 425 (Alouette) Squadron CF-18 from CFB Bagotville arriving for maintenance. (CL)

One of six CF-18s to be trucked to Mirabel from Plant 4 is loaded in May 1990. The move of the CF-18 group from Cartierville to Mirabel took place in April and involved some 400 employees. As well, about 100 from CAE moved from Montreal to Mirabel. The first CF-18 for the new MAD landed on May 17, 1990. When the CF-18 group left P4, Buildings 408 and 423 there were renovated for use by the newly integrated Surveillance Systems Division. Before this, its 290 employees had been scattered around P1. (CL C49173-6)

weapon systems, and adapting programs developed by other F/A-18 operators for the CF-18 weapon systems.

As prime contractor, Canadair was responsible for repair work on the airframe and associated systems and for overall program management. Principal subcontractor CAE Electronics handled avionics and computer software. Northwest Industries provided aircraft refinishing, mobile repair parties and fly-in repairs. The initial contract (it has since been renewed several times) ran from November 1, 1986 to March 31, 1990.

The SES program became the responsibility of the newly formed military aircraft division, headed by Walter Niemy. Hargrove became director and program manager, CF-18 SES, while Chris Masterman became director, military support responsible for engineering and logistics support to CF T-33s, CF-5s, Cosmopolitans and Tutors.

The first of 10 CF-18s designated for sampling inspection arrived at Canadair on July 14, 1987. Sampling involved non-destructive testing of all major parts of the aircraft,

with special attention to composite parts and areas subject to high loads and stresses. Any problems found were analysed and remedial actions were suggested to the DND. At the same time, Canadair installed manufacturer-suggested upgrade modifications.

In 1987 Ottawa awarded Canadair a contract for full-scale durability and damage tolerance testing to study the Northrop CF-5 service life and ways of extending it. Airframe testing was completed in August 1994. The aircraft was then taken apart for inspection and all structural components were analysed for signs of damage. This inspection was completed at the end of 1994.

Mirabel

MAD was initially located in Plants 2 and 4; however, it quickly became apparent that the SES program would outgrow its space. On June 28, 1988, plans were announced for a new facility at Montreal International Airport at Mirabel. It was to be the most capable integrated military support complex in Canada. Construction of the 18,600-m² (200,000-sq.-ft.) facility began on August 29, 1988. Personnel from the military aircraft division moved in during April and May 1990.

The facility included hangar space for 10 CF-18s and a 1,200-m² (13,000-sq.-ft.) TEMPEST area where mission computer software could be developed, integrated and tested in complete security.

In October 1988, following a two-year build-up of expertise and equipment, the Canadair team replaced CF-18 manufacturer McDonnell Douglas as direct supporter for the CF-18 system.

In 1991, the division received a contract for a durability and damage tolerance investigation of the CF-18 centre fuselage as part of the international follow-on structural test program (IFOSTP), a joint Canada/Australia study to establish the economic life of the F/A-18's structure. This entailed raising the ceiling of the repair and overhaul shop at Mirabel 3 m (10 ft.) to accommodate the large test rig the division designed and built to hold the

CAE's Ray Learmond (deputy program manager) and Canadair's Peter Hargrove (program manager) of the CF-18 System Engineering Support organization. On December 19, 1986, Canadair signed with Ottawa for stage one of the CF-18 maintenance contract. SES began life in temporary office space on Côte Vertu and maintenance facilities in P4. (CL 57037)

Walter Niemy of the Military Aircraft Division at Beech in Wichita where he accepted the first of eight C-90A King Airs for Bombardier. (CL 92014-4)

test aircraft. Under Jim Henry, three teams totalling 30 engineers and technicians set to work in September 1991. Physical testing began in September 1994 and was scheduled for completion in 1998. In late 1994, Gilles Saintonge was program manager and Jean Roussel the senior engineer on the program.

When the military aircraft and surveillance systems combined to form the defence systems division, Niemy was appointed president; Dawes was executive vice-president; Hargrove was vice-president, aircraft operations; and Lamarre was vice-president, UAV operations.

A new paint shop and paint stripping facility, a composite repair shop and an engine test house were added at Mirabel in December 1992. The paint stripping facility featured high technology plastic pellet blasting to strip paint without damaging delicate composite materials. In late 1994, a 7,000-m² (75,000-sq.-ft.) storage hangar for storing 20 CF-18s was added, and the paint/strip facility was expanded to 2,600 square m (28,000 sq. ft.). The divi-

Stripping a CF-18 at Mirabel. About 2,500 lb. of plastic globules (95% of which are recoverable) are used in the 800-hour process. Following stripping, the airframe is hand-washed, then receives three coats of paint and 800 stencils before return to the air force. (CL C66857-36)

sion was to begin painting Regional Jet aircraft in early 1995.

In June 1993, Lockheed Canada Inc. awarded the division a $26-million subcontract to modify three CF Challenger 600 aircraft for electronic support training (EST). These aircraft were used for training military electronic equipment operators by simulating enemy aircraft and jamming the trainees' electronics. EST modifications included the installation of electronic operator stations and equipment, a large number of additional antennas, two radomes, wingtip electronic measures pods, and chaff dispensers in the tail cone. The first aircraft was being modified at Mirabel late in 1994.

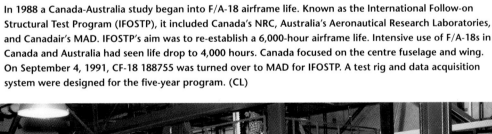

In 1988 a Canada-Australia study began into F/A-18 airframe life. Known as the International Follow-on Structural Test Program (IFOSTP), it included Canada's NRC, Australia's Aeronautical Research Laboratories, and Canadair's MAD. IFOSTP's aim was to re-establish a 6,000-hour airframe life. Intensive use of F/A-18s in Canada and Australia had seen life drop to 4,000 hours. Canada focused on the centre fuselage and wing. On September 4, 1991, CF-18 188755 was turned over to MAD for IFOSTP. A test rig and data acquisition system were designed for the five-year program. (CL)

Nine CF-18s in the hangar at Mirabel. (CL C49819-3)

In December 1993, Canadair became the first major Canadian aerospace manufacturer to adopt the standards of the Geneva-based International Organization for Standardization (ISO) when it was granted ISO 9001 approval, the world's most recognized quality standard.

When the Cosmopolitan was retired and its support was no longer required, the division began offering a customizing service ranging from minor modifications to the installation of full mission suites for Challenger, Regional Jet, CL-415 and Dash 8 aircraft.

Canadian Aviation Training Centre

In June 1990, the federal government decided to privatize military flying training and invited bids from industry for this cost-cutting scheme. Anticipating Ottawa's intentions, Niemy and Masterman laid the ground work for an eventual bid. These two together with Gary Bingham and pilot training consultant Dave Tate, who spearheaded the proposal team, were amply rewarded: in September 1991, the Canadair-led team of nine Canadian companies won a five-year, $165 million contract to provide a variety of flying training programs for the CF.

The contract covered primary, basic helicopter and multi-engine flying training at the Canadian Aviation Training Centre (CATC) at the former CFB Portage la Prairie, Manitoba. As prime contractor Canadair was responsible for project and contract management, primary flying training, training administration, and the acquisition of primary and multi-engine aircraft and a multi-engine operational procedures trainer. Team member Atlantis Aerospace of Toronto manufactured the simulator for the Beech King Air multi-engine trainers. Field Aviation of Toronto and Calgary was responsible for the maintenance and logistics for the aircraft and helicopters. Frontec Logistics Corp. of Edmonton was responsible for airfield operation and maintenance. Thompson-Hickling Aviation of Ottawa handled airspace management and air traffic control. Versa Services of Winnipeg took care of accommodation and food.

Dynamair Aviation (St-Jean-sur-Richelieu, Quebec), Kingston Flying Club (Kingston, Ontario) and Victoria Flying Club (Victoria, B.C.) provided the annual flying training each student needed to maintain proficiency while completing academic studies. Dynamair also provided pilot training for students attending language training.

CATC operated 14 Jet Rangers (on loan from the DND), 12 Slingsby Firefly primary trainers, eight King Airs and one multi-engine operation procedures trainer. Also on loan was one helicopter instrument procedures trainer. The first King Air was delivered on March 11, 1992, and operations began a month later. The first Firefly arrived in June, and primary training began in September. The training centre opened officially on July 2, 1992. Peter De Smedt, a former base commander at CFB Portage la Prairie, was appointed CATC director.

The program gave new students 27 hours primary flying training in the single-engined Firefly at CATC over a period of nine weeks. They then spent about two years completing military college, language training or military training, during which they completed 25 hours flying training annually at a local flying school and earned a private pilot's licence.

Students then moved to Moose Jaw for 140 hours basic flying training in the Tutor. Those heading for basic helicopter or multi-engine training then returned to CATC, while those for advanced jet flying training continued at Moose Jaw for a further 60 hours in the Tutor. At CATC, helicopter students completed 90 hours in the Jet Ranger over a 16-week period. Multi-engine students

Ken Carr banks away from his wingman during a formation training flight of January 6, 1993. (Larry Milberry)

Slingsby trainers in the CATC hangar at Portage la Prairie. (Larry Milberry)

The flightline at the CATC at Portage la Prairie and (left) King Air's 902 and 907 ready for work on a frigid morning in January 1993. (CL, Larry Milberry)

A typical classroom scene at the CATC as Canadian Forces and foreign exchange student pilots attend a lecture. (Larry Milberry)

pean-Japanese space station scheduled for launch in 1996. Canada was to supply the mobile servicing system which will help build the station, repair it and clean its exterior.

The team was to determine how to control a highly dexterous two-arm robot on the end of a 17-m (56-ft.) version of the space shuttle's Canadarm. The robot would be capable of simple tasks like screwing nuts and bolts together and cleaning windows and solar panels. This meant being able to have the hands apply pressure in one direction while moving in another, and ensuring the arms would not collide with the structure nor each other.

Canadair planned to demonstrate some initial techniques for controlling a single-arm robot to representatives of the Canadian Space Agency in late December 1994. The next tests would be for controlling a two-arm robot to perform simple tasks such as picking up a strut.

flew 80 hours in the King Air in 14 weeks. All graduates then received their wings.

In early September 1993, work began on a $500,000 CATC upgrade to accommodate some 40 employees and 84 students daily. Ken Carr replaced De Smedt as director of CATC, Greg McQuaid was chief instructor and Gary Dolski was administrative manager. By December 2, 1994, 263 primary, 183 helicopter and 155 multi-engine students had graduated from the centre.

Canadair and Space

In January 1991, a small defence systems division team of Alan Robins, Claude Tessier and Bernard Langlois began work on a Canadian Space Agency (CSA) contract connected with "Freedom," the joint U.S-Canadian-Euro-

Subcontracts: 1987 to the Present

Subcontracts continued uninterrupted throughout the period under the direction of Peter Candfield, and later Joe Guglielmi and T.K. Raghunathan. Joe Ederhy was the director in charge of subcontract assembly; he was succeeded later by Michel Fortin.

The Lockheed P-3 provided a great deal of work at Canadair. This version is a Canadian Forces CP-140 Aurora. (CL C-17995)

Workers from the P-3 line cheer as they send off the last P-3 wing in September 1990. (CL C51642)

The subcontract under which Canadair machined bulkheads and frames for the McDonnell Douglas F-15 Eagle ended in 1988 after approximately 17,000 items had been delivered.

Production of components for the Lockheed P-3C (CL-281) continued until September 1990 when the last of some 160 shipsets of outer wing boxes, stub wings, aft fuselages, forward and aft radomes and main electrical load centres was shipped.

In 1989, Canadair bid to supply components for the Lockheed P-7 long range anti-submarine warfare aircraft (LRAACA), which was to replace the P-3C. The program never materialized.

In 1992, it received a contract to supply eight shipsets of P-3C stub wings, nose and aft radomes and main electrical load centres and aft fuselages to Lockheed for South Korea. The contract, which was carried out at de Havilland and Canadair, was scheduled for completion in December 1994.

Production of the Boeing 767 rear fuselage section (CL-282) continued throughout the period. A further contract, awarded in September 1992, allows Canadair to continue deliveries until 1996. In 1989, Boeing awarded Canadair its Pride in Excellence award for the sixth consecutive time in recognition of its performance on this contract. Less than one per cent of Boeing's 3,000 suppli-

ers have ever received the award and only two other 767 subcontractors have received it more than five times in a row. To November 30, 1994, Boeing had delivered 567 of its 767s, and had a backlog of 110 orders.

McDonnell Douglas F/A-18 fuselage nose barrels (CL-274) continued to be supplied at two per month through 1994. A total of 531 had been supplied to November 30, 1994. Total program orders were for 583.

On September 23, 1988, Bombardier and Aerospatiale of France signed a $1.2 billion contract covering the supply by Canadair of 607 shipsets (7 test, 600 production) of six major components (CL-330) for the Airbus A330 and A340 jetliners. This was the largest subcontract in Canadair history.

This Boeing Stratocruiser "Guppy" was used to airlift P-3 outer wing sets from Canadair to Burbank, California. (CL C10459)

The 500th 767 shipset ready to leave Canadair (March 1993). Inset is a typical shipset on the floor at Boeing in Seattle with Air Canada 767s on the final line. (CL 62199, Boeing H45665)

The components were: centre fuselage keel beam, pressurized lateral floor, aft pressure bulkhead, nose bottom fuselage, nose gear doors, floor structure and lateral shell frames. Canadair had a risk-sharing role in the program and was responsible for the design, manufacturing engineering, research and development as well as manufacturing. Peter Candfield was the early program manager.

The CL-330 plan called for development of the design to an advanced layout level to be carried out jointly by Aerospatiale and Canadair at Toulouse, France. With divisionalization in effect, the Canadair Airbus division had its own design team in Toulouse. Once the preliminary design work was completed, the team moved into leased office space in Chomedey (Plexus) for detailed design. It took months of concentrated effort but the first components were delivered on schedule on October 5, 1989. As of November 30, 1994 Canadair had despatched 114 shipsets of A330/340 components.

On November 12, 1988, British Aerospace awarded Canadair a $400 million contract to supply 607 shipsets of inboard fixed leading edge assemblies (CL-350) for Airbus A330 and A340 wings. The contract was formally signed on April 11, 1989.

The 10-m (33-ft.) long assemblies were designed to very close tolerances to match the wing design. Each assembly was built on a one-piece aluminum spar machined from a solid billet. Each also incorporated sophisticated composite materials and aluminum lithium, a new alloy developed to compete with nonmetallic composites. Stronger

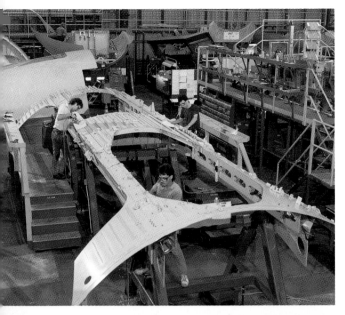

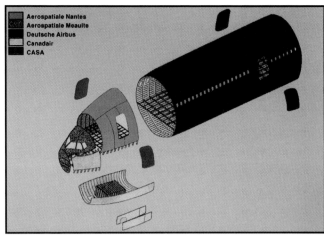

The diagram shows the A330/340 components designed and manufactured by Canadair under the Aerospatiale contract. At left A330/340 components are being manufactured at Cartierville. (CL)

and lighter than conventional aluminum alloys, it cost eight times as much.

The first shipset was delivered in December 1989. A total of 121 sets had been delivered by November 30, 1994. However, due to lack of work at British Aerospace, production has been repatriated to the United Kingdom.

In September 1994, the Boeing Commercial Airplane Group contracted for the supply of support structures for the wing fixed trailing edge of the Boeing 737-500X, -700 and -800 family of airliners. Deliveries were to begin in the fourth quarter of 1995 and continue until late 2002.

US Navy F/A-18 nose barrels being finished in newly modernized P1. More than 500 units had been delivered by early 1995. (CL)

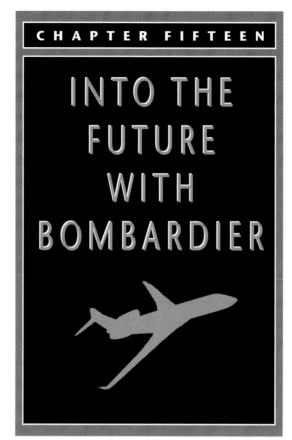

CHAPTER FIFTEEN

INTO THE FUTURE WITH BOMBARDIER

The 1986 acquisition of Canadair was a major step on Bombardier's path toward industrial diversification, adding a third segment to those of motorized consumer products and rail transportation equipment. It launched a period of unprecedented expansion, with six more acquisitions in the next five years.

Bombardier deliberately chose acquisition as the way to gain access quickly to the technology it needed to ensure growth. The tactic was successful: in the next seven years Bombardier's revenues increased eightfold and its net income grew elevenfold. Bombardier now has manufacturing operations in eight countries, markets in more than 60 and a labor force which has mushroomed from 12,000 in 1986 to 37,000 in 1995.

First in Rail Transportation

In recent years, Bombardier has gone to the forefront in several international transportation markets. The corporation's industrial presence in the three North American Free Trade Agreement countries (United States, Canada and Mexico) and in five member countries of the European Union makes it the world's most geographically diversified manufacturer of passenger-rail transportation equipment.

In this segment, activities involve the development, production and support of high technology subway, commuter and intercity rail cars and light rail vehicles for the North American and European markets. A major recent achievement was the design and production of the huge stainless steel shuttle-train cars for the English Channel

The graceful A340 first flew in October 1991. Canadair is a key subcontractor on this long-term venture. (Airbus)

Two proposed types from the Bombardier family of commuter aircraft. An artist's impression of the proposed Canadair CRJ-X, aimed at the 70-76-passenger market. In the spring of 1995 the Dash 8-400 concept awaited the green light for development to the prototype stage. (CL, de Havilland)

tunnel. In North America, Bombardier leads the rail transit market where it has delivered more than 2,500 vehicles to most of the major transportation authorities over the past 20 years. It controls the technologies related to all types of passenger-rail transportation—urban, suburban and intercity—and owns the North American marketing and manufacturing rights to the French TGV high-speed train.

In the European Union countries, Bombardier's acquisitions in Belgium, France and England have strengthened the corporation's strategic position in these three domestic markets. Bombardier Eurorail, with five plants in four countries, is in first place in the Benelux countries (Belgium, the Netherlands and Luxembourg), and in second place in France and Austria at the beginning of 1995. The future of the rail transportation segment is guaranteed by Bombardier's investments in the development of products suited to the evolving needs of the operating authorities, including prototypes for new-generation subway cars, low-floor tramways, and of a bimodal transit system which combines the characteristics of a tire-equipped tramway with the autonomy of an articulated bus. At the end of 1994, Bombardier's backlog in the transportation equipment segment totalled $4 billion.

In the motorized consumer products segment, the Ski-Doo line of snowmobiles has been completely renewed. Ski-Doo snowmobiles, already the leaders in Canada, are gradually strengthening their position in the North American market, where they have a market share of approximately 25 per cent. The Sea-Doo line of watercraft,

bolstered by the addition of the Speedster—a four-seat jet boat powered by twin Bombardier-Rotax engines—is now clearly in first place with 40 per cent of the North American market in sit-down personal watercraft. Bombardier snow grooming vehicles rank first in North America and second in Japan.

World Leader in Aerospace

While many aerospace companies struggle to survive, Bombardier's diversity of products and markets has enabled the company to weather the recent economic downturn and remain profitable while becoming the sixth largest civil aviation company in the world.

The aerospace sector including defence contributes more than 50 per cent of the corporation's revenue. By 1995, the four aerospace units—Canadair, Shorts, Learjet and de Havilland—delivered well over 100 aircraft and 1,000 airframe shipsets and had a backlog totalling more than $5 billion.

Bombardier is now firmly established as a world leader in two niche markets, business aircraft and regional aircraft. It has a modest but stable defence business, a well diversified subcontract business, and the CL-415 firefighting aircraft, a niche within a niche.

Under Bombardier, the fortunes of Shorts, Learjet, de Havilland and Canadair have improved immeasurably. In the past three years, Shorts sales have doubled and losses have turned to profits. Shorts has joined Hurel-Dubois of France to form International Nacelle Systems which offers a complete engine nacelle design and manufacturing capability. Shorts and Thompson-CSF of France have formed Short Missile Systems Ltd. to supply air defence missile systems to the United Kingdom and overseas. In November 1993, Shorts bought Airwork Ltd. of England and created a support services division to integrate the civil and military aviation support activities of the two companies. Shorts is converting civil SD-360 airliners to military C-23 Sherpa transports for the USAF and U.S. Air National Guard, and is also producing components for Fokker and Boeing. Its labor force, including Airwork, totals some 9,500 people.

With Bombardier's support, Learjet has introduced new products and its aircraft sales are climbing. In 1994, 36 aircraft were delivered, including the Learjet 60, now the bestselling mid-size business aircraft. The company's labor force of 3,700 also produces for the U.S. space shuttle and for other major aerospace firms.

de Havilland is actively diversifying its business base. It continues to deliver and support the 37-passenger Dash 8-100 and 50-passenger Dash 8-300 and plans to deliver the first Dash 8-200, developed since the Bombardier acquisition, in the spring of 1995. A 70-passenger Dash 8-400 is also being considered. de Havilland currently employs 2,900 people.

Since its purchase of Canadair, Bombardier has introduced the CL-215T, CL-415, Challenger 601-3R, Chal-

The eight-passenger Learjet 45 is the first of the Lear family of business jets developed under Bombardier. The fuselage is manufactured by Shorts in Belfast, the wings by de Havilland. (Shorts)

In the photo above, taken October 21, 1994, the first Learjet 45 fuselage arrives at the Learjet plant in Wichita, where final assembly takes place. First flight of the Learjet 45 is scheduled for summer 1995. (Learjet)

An overall view at Dorval of Plant 3 looking towards the west. The new administration centre is to the right, then the main plant extends almost to the big Air Canada maintenance base. These complexes lie between Dorval's two main east-west runways. (CL 71147)

lenger 604, Canadair Regional Jet and Bombardier Global Express aircraft and is working on the preliminary design of a 70-passenger regional jet. Bombardier has revolutionized the manufacturing process, tripled the production rate, and reduced the floor space required for production by nearly 30 per cent. Current employment is approximately 8,000.

Benefits of Synergy

"Synergy" is a popular corporate buzzword meaning the working together of two entities to produce an effect greater than the sum of their individual effects.

The Bombardier organization has benefited significantly from the synergistic results of its acquisition policy. All member groups of the corporation have taken advan-

tage of the resources, capabilities and technologies of other members. By consolidating purchasing power and standardizing engineering and manufacturing systems, Bombardier has improved the quality of its products, reduced costs and gained a sharper competitive edge in the international market.

Challenger and Learjet, for example, though serving different areas of the business jet market, have exchanged technology, improved customer-supplier relationships and taken advantage of market synergies to enable them to consolidate their leadership in their markets. Combining the Learjet/Challenger service centre network has provided expanded service centre capabilities to operators, and enhanced Bombardier's reputation as the industry

leader in customer service.

The Regional Jet and Dash 8 aircraft also have much in common in terms of marketing and product support because their products appeal to the same customer base. Bombardier, through its regional aircraft division, is the only company in the world able to offer both jet and turboprop airliners in the 50-passenger category.

The benefits of synergy are readily apparent in the engineering and manufacturing functions. Shorts designs and produces the complete Learjet 45 fuselage and components, and nacelles for the Regional Jet and Global Express aircraft. de Havilland builds wings for the Learjet 45, and is finishing the interiors of and painting Regional Jet aircraft. Learjet provides its test centre facility to the other units and is finishing the interiors of and painting Challenger aircraft.

Building on its success at Canadair, Bombardier is extending its manufacturing system to de Havilland and Learjet. Roland Gagnon has installed two key people—Serge Perron and Ghislain Bourque—as vice-president, operations at de Havilland and Learjet, respectively, to oversee the changes. Perron was previously vice-president, production at Canadair; Bourque was director of methods. Both had come to Canadair from other Bombardier divisions.

Challenger executive jets and Regional Jets in the preflight hangar at Plant 3. (CL 67526-9)

Changes at Cartierville. These views taken in June 1994 show the airport since it closed. The wide view looks westerly down Runway 28-10, now a huge housing development. You can see Plant 2 across the field, and Plant 4 at Cartierville's northeast corner. Compare this aerial with others in the book to see how things have changed over the years. The second aerial is a detail of the housing complex. (CL 71151, '154)

(Below) The old Curtiss-Reid building in Plant 4 was closed by 1995. The historic name still hung over the front door. (CL 73376-3)

A typical cabin arrangement in the Global Express mock-up.
(CL C63513-15)

(Inset) One of the employees at the Learjet completion centre in Tucson readies furnishings for a new Challenger jet.
(CL C-72955-3)

Bombardier's Strategy for the Future

The worldwide economic recession of the past few years has created an increasingly competitive environment in the aerospace industry. Trade barriers have shifted significantly. Today Canadair is up against foreign competitors whose markets and interests were essentially regional only a few years ago. Now these competitors are entering the global scene with proven products and aggressive marketing strategies. Competition is coming from new products, from Asia-Pacific manufacturing companies, and from defence contractors converting to commercial business. At the same time, government funding and military budgets are shrinking.

The challenge facing Bombardier's finance, marketing and sales personnel, is to find creative ways to achieve customer satisfaction. Innovative and cost effective solutions are required from engineering, purchasing and manufacturing personnel to enable the corporation to continue offering superior products and services at a competitive price. The only way to sustain leadership in this competitive environment is by continuing to improve overall performance.

While growth has always been one of Bombardier's objectives, another underlying principle of the corporation's strategy is balanced diversification of both industrial segments and geographic markets. With balanced diversification, the effects of a downturn in one market are generally offset by an upswing in another.

Basic to Bombardier's future well-being is a policy to continue to operate in specific market niches where it can be a leader in the world. Unlike those companies which rely on defence sales for a large share of their revenue, Bombardier will try to maintain its defence business at around eight per cent of its aerospace sector. As the corporation intends to control its own destiny, it will limit subcontract component manufacturing to 10 to 15 per cent.

This sector will continue to maintain and build on the technology it has acquired and to acquire new technologies. It will strive to remain competitive and maintain a leadership position by joining with other companies in risk-sharing arrangements which will allow it to minimize costs and risks, yet pursue its development goals.

Decisions about new production programs, such as the proposed 70-passenger versions of the Regional Jet and Dash 8 aircraft, will depend on management's confidence that it will be able to meet the customers' requirements, using the available resources, and make a profit.

Similarly, the use of the name Bombardier in the title of any future product will depend on whether its use helps sell the product. According to Bob Brown, Bombardier management has great confidence in the credibility and reputation of the names Canadair, de Havilland, Learjet and Shorts. "There is a value added by the name Bombardier that will be assessed as products are developed," he said.

"We used Bombardier for the Global Express essentially because it is a project that involves everybody in the group. The only criteria to determine what we do in the future is what will give us an advantage in the marketplace."

A most important factor in Bombardier's future is management's relationship with employees. The corporation's management strives to establish an environment where employees feel good about their work and are proud of their company. Being fair in dealings with employees and with suppliers is an investment in the future that will reinforce a strong organization.

Promise and Challenge

In an address to Bombardier shareholders in June 1994, Laurent Beaudoin said: "I am firmly convinced that the decisions we have made in keeping with our strategic choices over the past few years will enable Bombardier to continue on the path of growth and profitability. The corporation's diversification in terms of both products and geography, together with its investments in products that hold promise, bode well for the future, a future that will also present new challenges."

A few months later Bombardier's financial results for the first nine months of fiscal 1994-95 showed that revenue had risen 13 per cent over the same period in 1993-1994 and profits had increased 40 per cent, and as this book went to press the corporation was heading toward the $6 billion mark in sales. These numbers offer proof that Bombardier is travelling along the path to continuing success, a path made straighter and smoother by the efforts of those who created and fostered a major contributor to this remarkable Canadian success story–the people of Canadair.

CANADAIR SCENES
PAST
AND PRESENT

(Top) This perfect replica of a Canadian Vickers Vedette was built over several years by members of the Western Canada Aviation Museum. The team included some craftsmen who had worked on the Vedette in the 1920s. The Vedette was nearing completion in 1995. (Jan Stroomenburgh)

(Above) More history. In 1993 CL-84 No. 402 went to Peterborough for restoration by Airtech Canada. On November 9, 1994, the famous Canadair VTOL was returned to Ottawa for display in the National Aviation Museum. (Larry Milberry)

Al Lilly, one of Canadair's Aviation Hall of Fame members, shows off a model of the prototype Sabre which he took on its first flight in 1950. Al retired in 1970 as director of public relations and in 1995 was living in Moncton. (Moncton Telegraph Journal)

Models and replicas. The first photo here shows the participants in a Canadair model contest. On a less serious note is the "Snow Bomber" made by some of the employees in engineering and "test flown" on the ski slopes during the Starlight Foundation Snowbox Derby in the Laurentians, March 1994; then a CL-89 cartoon that appeared in the *Canadair News*.

The little leagues and the big leagues. Canadair employees take part in a charity go-cart race put on by Regional Jet customer Comair; then Bryan Moss, president of the business aircraft division, with Indy car driver John Andretti at the 1994 Indianapolis 500. After completing the "500", Andretti flew with Moss in a Challenger jet to Charlotte, N.C. There he completed in the Coca-Cola NASCAR race the same day.

Many Canadair employees help keep fit by using the gym facilities in the Canadair Building. (CL C69294)

Canadair participates in all sorts of community activities. Here are some of its basketball players greeting a team of wheelchair competitors. (CL)

Scenes from Canadair's gala 50th anniversary open house in June 1994. Crowds view the company's products from the 1944 Canso to the 1994 Regional Jet, including the world's last flying CL-44, and tour the assembly line. (Below) VIPs and retirees on the podium, with Bob Brown speaking. The others, from the left, are Jim Moffatt, George Moffatt, Laurent Beaudoin, Normand Cherry, Sam Joffre and Fernand Gendron. (CL)

The awards continue year by year at Canadair. In this 1981 event, J.D.F. McNaughton is presenting Doug Adkins with Canada's premier annual aviation award, the McKee Trans-Canada Trophy. (CL C20423-6)

Canadair has many other interesting "people" connections. In this case, Canadair pilot Bob Flynn and his son Bill. Bob flew Sabres in the RCAF before joining Canadair. Bill became a CF-18 pilot, spent a season as the CF-18 demonstration pilot in Europe, then attended the USAF Test Pilot School at Edwards Air Force Base in California. While Bob was flying Challenger business jets, Bill spent five years at Edwards flying many exotic experimental planes. (CL)

Gerry LaGrave, seen throughout this book, has had an aviation career spanning eight decades. In 1994, when Gerry was 92, the air force took him for a flight in the CF-18 Hornet, and that June he posed for this photo with BGen Jeff Brace, Commander of Air Transport Group. Gerry had known Jeff Brace when he was an Air Cadet at Canadair in the 1950s. Both of Brace's parents worked at Canadair. (Larry Milberry)

(Right) In recent years many Canadair "old timers" have returned to the company to serve as guides for plant tours. This group includes Jim Moffatt, Pauline Simard, George Moffatt, Sam Joffre, Georgette Bérubé (public relations), Adrien Lemieux, Eugène Littner and Fernand Gendron. Behind them is a Boeing 767 pressure bulkhead in its jig. (CL C66478-4)

The retirees often gather at regular lunch meetings, but also meet informally to renew acquaintances. This group met in Vero Beach, Florida, in 1993 to share some memories with Ron Pickler: Joe MacBrien, Jim Taylor, Dick Richmond, Peter Aird, Bud Sager, George Turek, Bill Jolliffe, Bob Raven, John Smith, Andy Throner and Len Box. (Ron Pickler)

The photography department has been a key element at Canadair since 1944. It is called upon regularly to do a variety of tasks, from taking simple passport photos, to shooting on the final line or doing aerial work. In 1995 the staff included Paul Sagala, Gordon K. Tottle, Garth Dingman, John Wulfraat, Lucio Anodal, Alain Girard and Cliff Symons. (CL C73217-6)

(Below) The photography department at work shooting plant aerials from a Bell Jet Ranger in June 1994. (CL C71493-35)

The *Canadair News* ran this cartoon in 1989.

(Left) The night shift. Lucio Anodal, Garth Dingman and Joe DeFranco take a 4:00 a.m. break during a shoot with the Xerox Corporate Jetliner. An array of lights shines through filters on the windows, giving even lighting for interior photography. (CL65829-1)

GLOSSARY

AC	alternating current
ACV	air cushion vehicle
AECL	Atomic Energy of Canada Ltd.
ASW	anti-submarine warfare
B	building (as in B106)
BOAC	British Overseas Airways Corporation
BRAD	Bombardier Regional Aircraft Division
CADAM	computer-aided design and manufacturing
CAF	Canadian Air Force
CAIR	calendar aircraft inspection and repair
CAMRA	Canadian Multi-Role Aircraft
Canarch	Canadair Architectural
CARDE	Canadian Armament Research and Development Establishment
CARS	common automatic recovery system
CC	Canadian military designation for cargo aircraft
CCF	Canadian Car & Foundry
CDIC	Canada Development Investment Corp.
CEPE	Central Experimental and Proving Establishment
CERA	Canadair Employees Recreational Association
CF	Canadian military designation for fighter aircraft
CFB	Canadian Forces Base
CFD	computational fluid dynamics
CL	Canadair Limited
cm	centimetre
CNCM	computer numerically-controlled machine
CNR	Canadian National Railways
"Cosmo"	CL-66 Cosmopolitan
CP&W	Canadian Pratt & Whitney
CPA	Canadian Pacific Airlines
CRT	cathode ray tube
cu. ft.	cubic foot
CV	Canadian Vickers
DC	direct current
DDP	Department of Defence Production
DFC	Distinguished Flying Cross
DHC	de Havilland Canada
DLT	Deutche Luft Transport GmbH
DND	Department of National Defence
DOT	Department of Transport
DRB	Defence Research Board
DRE	Defence Research Establishment
EFIS	electronic flight instrument system
EICAS	engine instrumentation crew alert system
f/f	first flight
F/O	flying officer
FAA	Federal Aviation Administration
FAI	Fédération Aéronautique Internationale
FLIR	forward-looking infrared
FSR	field service representative
FTL	Flying Tiger Line
GD	General Dynamics
GE	General Electric
hp	horsepower
ICTS	Intermediate Capacity Transit System
IFOSTP	international follow-on structural test program
imp. gal.	Imperial gallon
in.	inch
kg	kilogram
km	kilometre
km/h	kilometres per hour
kN	kilonewton
l	litre
lb.	pound
LIM	linear induction motor
LRC	Light, Rapid, Comfortable
LRPA	long-range patrol aircraft
LTV	Ling-Temco-Vought
m	metre
m²	square metre
MAD	Military Aircraft Division
MATS	Military Air Transport Service
mi.	statute miles
MIT	Massachusetts Institute of Technology
mm	millimetre
"mod"	modification
mph	miles per hour
MRCA	multi-role combat aircraft
MRP	mobile repair party
NAE	National Aeronautical Establishment
NASA	National Aeronautical and Space Administration
NATO	North Atlantic Treaty Organization
NBAA	National Business Aircraft Association
NF-5	Netherlands version of CF-5
nm	nautical miles
NRC	National Research Council
OBE	Order of the British Empire
P&W	Pratt & Whitney
P1 to P4	Plant 1 to Plant 4
RAF	Royal Air Force
RAT	Remote Articulated Track
RCAF	Royal Canadian Air Force
R-R	Rolls-Royce
s/n	serial number
shp	shaft horsepower
SES	system engineering support
STOL	short takeoff and landing
"T-bird"	CL-30 Silver Star, T-33
TC	Transport Canada
TCA	Trans-Canada Air Lines
tech rep	technical representative
UAV	unmanned air vehicle
USAAF	United States Army Air Force
USAF	United States Air Force
USN	United States Navy
USS	United States Ship (as in USS *Guam*)
UTDC	Urban Transportation Development Corp.
V/STOL	vertical/short takeoff and landing
VTOL	vertical takeoff and landing
WWII	World War II

APPENDICES

THREE-VIEWS OF CANADAIR AIRCRAFT

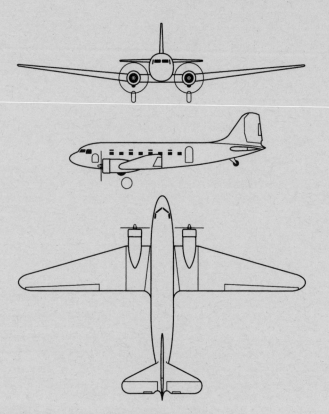

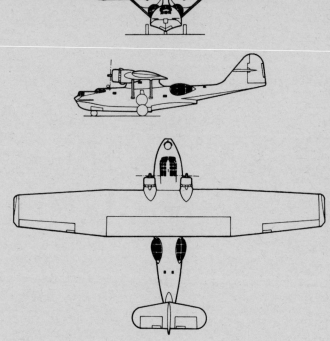

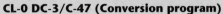

CL-0 DC-3/C-47 (Conversion program)

Engine
Two Pratt & Whitney R-1830 "Twin Wasp" radial (each 1200 hp)
Three-blade Hamilton Standard constant-speed propeller

External Dimensions

Wing span	95 ft.	28.9 m
Length	64 ft. 5 1/2 in.	19.63 m
Height	16 ft. 11 1/8 in.	5.2 m

Internal Dimensions

Cabin length	27 ft. 8 in.	8.44 m
Max. width	7 ft. 8 in.	2.34 m
Max. height	6 ft. 6 in.	1.98 m

Weights

Empty weight	16970 lb.	7750 kg
Loaded weight	26000 lb.	11805 kg

Performance

Stall speed	67 mph	108 km/h
Cruise speed	207 mph	331 km/h
Max. speed (8500 ft./2590 m)	230 mph	368 km/h
Range	2125 mi.	3400 km
Ceiling	23200 ft.	7076 m

CL-1 PBY-5A Canso, OA-10A

Engine
Two Pratt & Whitney R-1830 "Twin Wasp" radial (each 1200 hp)
Three-blade Hamilton Standard full-feathering propeller

External Dimensions

Wing span	104 ft.	31.72 m
Length	65 ft. 1 in.	19.83 m
Height	18 ft. 6 in.	5.64 m

Weights

Empty weight	17564 lb.	7974 kg
Loaded weight	34000 lb.	15436 kg

Performance

Stall speed	70 mph	112 km/h
Cruise speed	117 mph	188 km/h
Max. speed (10500 ft./3200 m)	190 mph	304 km/h
Range	4000 mi.	6400 km
Ceiling	21900 ft.	6680 m

CL-2 North Star, CL-4 Argonaut, C-5

Engine

CL-2 (C-54GM/DC-4M-1)
Four Rolls-Royce Merlin 620 or 622 in-line (each 1760 hp)
Three-blade Hamilton Standard constant-speed reversible propeller

CL-2 (DC-4M-2)
Four Rolls-Royce Merlin 620, 624, 722, or 724 in-line (each 1760 hp)
Three- or four-blade Hamilton Standard constant-speed reversible propeller

CL-4 (C-4)
Four Rolls-Royce Merlin 624 or 724-1 in-line (each 1760 hp)
Three-blade Hamilton Standard constant-speed reversible propeller

CL-5 (C-5)
Four Pratt & Whitney R-2800 "Double Wasp" radial (each 2100 hp)
Three-blade Hamilton Standard constant-speed reversible propeller

External Dimensions

CL-2 & CL-4

Wing span	117 ft. 6 in.	35.8 m
Length	93 ft. 7 ^{1}/$_2$ in.	28.6 m
Height	27 ft. 6 ^{5}/$_{16}$ in.	8.4 m

CL-5

Wing span	117 ft. 6 in.	35.8 m
Length	93 ft. 7 ^{1}/$_2$ in.	28.6 m
Height	29 ft.	8.8 m

Internal Dimensions

Cabin length	46 ft. 6 in.	14.17 m
Max. width	8 ft. 8 in.	2.64 m
Max. height	7 ft. 0 in.	2.13 m

Weights

CL-2 (C54GM/DC-4M-1)

Empty weight	44000 lb.	19958 kg
Max. takeoff weight	78000 lb.	35380 kg

CL-2 (DC-4M-2)

Empty weight	50955 lb.	23113 kg
Max. takeoff weight	79850 lb.	36219 kg

CL-4

Empty weight	45654 lb.	20709 kg
Max. takeoff weight	80200 lb.	36378 kg

CL-5

Empty weight	49475 lb.	22442 kg
Max. takeoff weight	86000 lb.	39009 kg

Performance

CL-2 (DC-4-M2)

Stall speed	89 mph	143 km/h
Cruise speed	238 mph	383 km/h
Max. speed (20000 ft./6096 m)	382 mph	616 km/h
Range	3060 mi.	4924 km
Ceiling	26700 ft.	8138 m

CL-4

Stall speed	89 mph	143 km/h
Cruise speed	302 mph	485 km/h
Max. speed (20000 ft./6096 m)	382 mph	616 km/h
Range	3880 mi.	6240 km
Ceiling	29500 ft.	9000 m

CL-5

Stall speed	89 mph	143 km/h
Cruise speed	303 mph	485 km/h
Max. speed (20000 ft./6096 m)	382 mph	616 km/h
Range	3985 mi.	6376 km
Ceiling	29500 ft.	9000 m

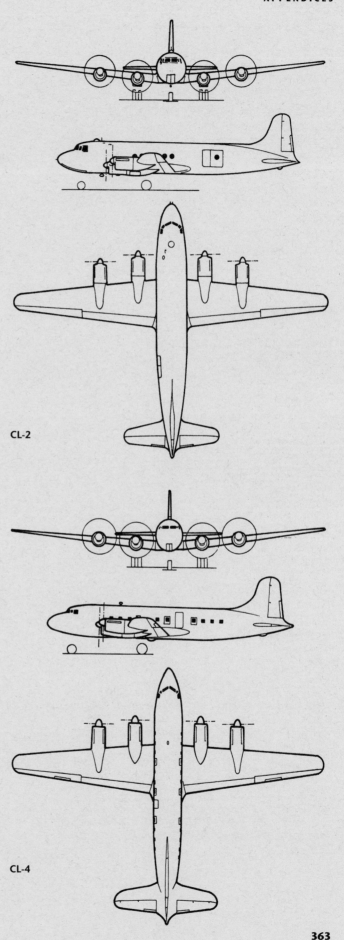

CL-2

CL-4

CL-13 Sabre Marks 1 to 6 (F-86)

Engine

Mark 1
One General Electric J47-GE-13 turbojet (5200 lb. thrust)

Mark 2
One General Electric J47-GE-13 turbojet (5200 lb. thrust)

Mark 3
One Orenda 3 turbojet (6000 lb. thrust)

Mark 4
One General Electric J47-GE-13 turbojet (5200 lb. thrust)

Mark 5
One Orenda 10 turbojet (6500 lb. thrust)

Mark 6
One Orenda 14 turbojet (7440 lb. thrust)

External Dimensions

Wing span	37 ft. 1 1/2 in.	11.32 m
Length	37 ft 6 in.	11.43 m
Height	14 ft. 9 in.	4.49 m

Weights

Mark 1
Empty weight	10093 lb.	4578 kg
Max. weight	15876 lb.	7201 kg

Mark 2
Empty weight	10434 lb.	4732 kg
Max. weight	17750 lb.	8051 kg

Mark 3
Empty weight (approx.)	11000 lb.	4990 kg
Max. weight (approx.)	17000 lb.	7711 kg

Mark 4
Empty weight	11000 lb.	4990 kg
Max. weight	17750 lb.	8051 kg

Mark 5
Empty weight	10662 lb.	4836 kg
Max. weight	17581 lb.	7975 kg

Mark 6
Empty weight	10638 lb.	4825 kg
Max. weight	17560 lb.	7965 kg

Performance

Mark 1
Cruise speed	533 mph	858 km/h
Max. speed (sea level)	679 mph	1093 km/h
Range	1052 mi.	1693 km
Ceiling	48000 ft.	14630 m

Mark 5
Cruise speed	552 mph	888 km/h
Max. speed (sea level)	696 mph	1120 km/h
Range	1220 mi.	1933 km
Ceiling	50700 ft.	15453 m

Mark 6
Cruise speed	552 mph	888 km/h
Max. speed (sea level)	698 mph	1123 km/h
Range	1486 mi.	2391 km
Ceiling	54100 ft.	16490 m

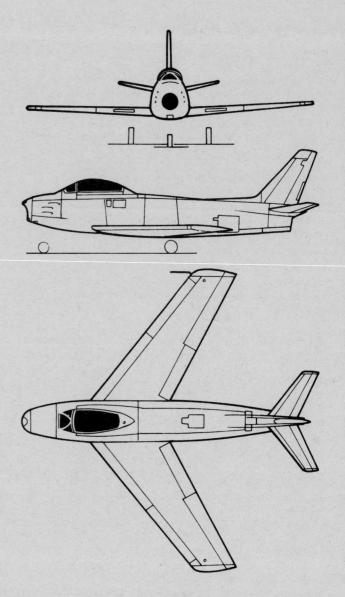

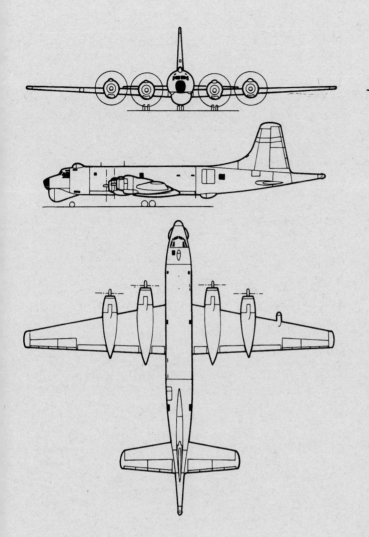

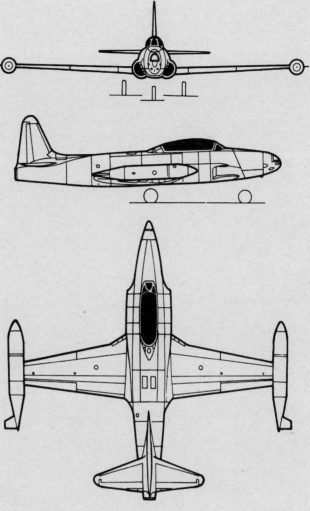

CL-28 Argus

Engine
Four Wright R-3350 turbo-compound (each 3700 hp)
Three-blade Curtis-Wright Electric propeller

External Dimensions

Wing span	142 ft. 3 $^1/_2$ in.	43.38 m
Length	128 ft. 3 in.	39.09 m
Height	36 ft. 8 $^1/_2$ in.	11.19 m

Weights

Empty weight	81000 lb.	36742 kg
Max. takeoff weight	148000 lb.	67133 kg

Performance

Stall speed	96 mph	154 km/h
Cruise speed	207 mph	333 km/h
Max. speed	290 mph	467 km/h
Range	4000 mi.	6440 km
Ceiling	24200 ft.	7376 m

CL-30 T-33 Silver Star

Engine
One Rolls-Royce Nene 10 turbojet (5100 lb. thrust)

External Dimensions

Wing span	42 ft. 5 in.	12.93 m
Length	37 ft. 8 in.	11.48 m
Height	11 ft. 8 in.	3.55 m

Weights

Empty weight	8440 lb.	3832 kg
Max. takeoff weight	16800 lb.	7627 kg

Performance

Cruise speed	190 mph	306 km/h
Max. speed	570 mph	917 km/h
Stall (without flaps)	113 mph	182 km/h
Ceiling	47000 ft.	14325 m

CL-41 Tutor

Engine

One General Electric J85-CAN-40 turbojet (2950 lb. thrust)

External Dimensions

CL-41A, G

Wing span	36 ft. 6 in.	11.13 m
Length	32 ft.	9.75 m
Height	9 ft. 4 in.	2.84 m

CL-41R

Wing span	36 ft. 6 in.	11.13 m
Length	42 ft. 2 in.	12.85 m
Height	9 ft. 4 in.	2.84 m

Weights

CL-41A

Empty weight	4895 lb.	2220 kg
Max. takeoff weight	7397 lb.	3355 kg

CL-41G

Empty weight	5296 lb.	2402 kg
Max. takeoff weight	11288 lb.	5120 kg

CL-41R

Empty weight	4895 lb.	2220 kg
Max. takeoff weight	8300 lb.	3765 kg

Performance

CL-41A

Stall speed	81 mph	130 km/h
Max. level speed	498 mph	801 km/h
Max. diving speed	575 mph	926 km/h
Ceiling	43000 ft.	13106 m

CL-41G

Stall speed	83 mph	133 km/h
Max. level speed	470 mph	755 km/h
Max. diving speed	550 mph	885 km/h
Ceiling	42200 ft.	12863 m

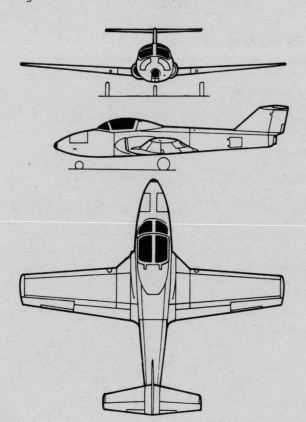

CL-66 Cosmopolitan

Engine

Original

Two Napier Eland 504A turboprop (each 3500 bhp)
Four-blade de Havilland constant-speed feathering propeller

Later conversion

Two Allison T56 turboprop (each 4300 bhp)
Four-blade propeller

External Dimensions

Wing span	105 ft. 4 in.	32.12 m
Length	81 ft. 6 in.	24.84 m
Height	28 ft. 2 in.	8.49 m

Internal Dimensions

Cabin length	54 ft. 10 in.	16.7 m
Max. width	8 ft. 11 in.	2.72 m
Max. height	6 ft. 7 in.	2.0 m

Weights

Empty weight	32333 lb.	14666 kg
Max. takeoff weight	53200 lb.	24130 kg

Performance

Stall speed	92 mph	148 km/h
Cruise speed (20000 ft./6096 m)	322 mph	518 km/h
Max. speed	340 mph	574 km/h
Range	2275 mi.	3660 km
Ceiling	25000 ft.	7620 m

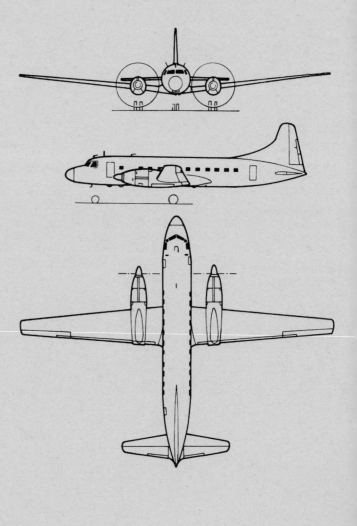

CL-44-6 Yukon, CL-44D4 Swingtail, CL-44J

Engine

CL-44-6 Yukon
Four Rolls-Royce Tyne II turboprop (each 5500 shp)
Four-blade de Havilland Hydromatic 4/7000/6 fully-reversing propeller

CL-44D4 & CL-44J
Four Rolls-Royce Tyne R.Ty.12 turboprop (each 5730 shp)
Four-blade Hawker-Siddeley Dynamics Hydromatic 4/7000/6 fully-reversing propeller

External Dimensions

CL-44-6 & CL-44D4

Wing span	142 ft. 3 1/2 in.	43.37 m
Length	136 ft. 10 in.	41.7 m
Height	38 ft. 8 in.	11.8 m

CL-44J

Wing span	142 ft. 3 1/2 in.	43.37 m
Length	151 ft. 10 in.	46.28 m
Height	38 ft. 8 in.	11.8 m

Internal Dimensions

CL-44-6 & CL-44D4

Cabin length	98 ft. 7 in.	30.04 m
Max. width	11 ft. 0 in.	3.35 m
Max. height	6 ft. 9 in.	2.06 m

CL-44J

Cabin length	113 ft. 3 in.	34.52 m
Max. width	11 ft. 0 in.	3.35 m
Max. height	6 ft. 9 in.	2.06 m

Weights

CL-44-6

Empty weight	91000 lb.	41314 kg
Max. takeoff weight	205000 lb.	93075 kg

CL-44D4

Empty weight	88952 lb.	40348 kg
Max. takeoff weight	210000 lb.	95250 kg

CL-44J

Empty weight	114315 lb.	51853 kg
Max. takeoff weight	210000 lb.	95250 kg

Performance

CL-44-6 & CL-44D4

Cruise speed (20000 ft./6096 m)	386 mph	621 km/h
Range	5587 mi.	8990 km
Ceiling	30000 ft.	9144 m

CL-44J
Speed

Cruise speed (20000 ft./6096 m)	380 mph	612 km/h
Range	5260 mi.	8460 km
Ceiling	30000 ft.	9144 m

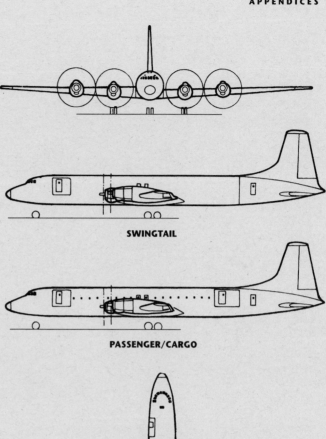

SWINGTAIL

PASSENGER/CARGO

CL-90/CL-201 CF-104 Starfighter

Engine
One Orenda-built General Electric J-79 turbojet (15800 lb. thrust
with afterburner)

External Dimensions
Wing span	21 ft. 11 in.	6.39 m
Length	54 ft. 9 in.	16.69 m
Height	13 ft. 6 in.	4.11 m

Weights
Empty weight	13909 lb.	6309 kg
Max. takeoff weight	26800 lb.	12156 kg

Performance
Max. speed (35000 ft./10668 m)	Mach 2	
Radius of action	690 mi.	110 km
Ceiling	55000 ft.	16764 m

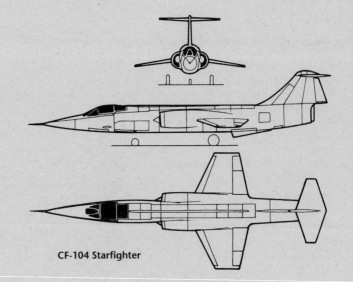

CF-104 Starfighter

CL-84 Dynavert

Engine
Two Lycoming T53 turboshaft (each 1500 shp)
Four-blade Curtiss-Wright lightweight propeller
Four-blade contra-rotating horizontal Servotec tail propeller

External Dimensions
Wing span	33 ft. 4 in.	10.16 m
Span over propeller tips	34 ft. 8 in.	10.56 m
Length	47 ft. 3 $^1/_2$ in.	14.41 m
Height – wing at 0⁰ tilt	14 ft. 2 $^3/_4$ in.	4.34 m
Height – wing at 90⁰ tilt	17 ft. 1 $^1/_2$ in.	5.22 m

Weights
Empty weight	8437 lb.	3827 kg
Max. takeoff weight (VTOL)	12600 lb.	5715 kg
Max. takeoff weight (STOL)	14500 lb.	6577 kg

Performance
Max. level (10000 ft./3050 m)	321 mph	517 km/h
Max. cruising	309 mph	497 km/h
Max. speed	415 mph	667 km/h
Range	421 mi.	677 km

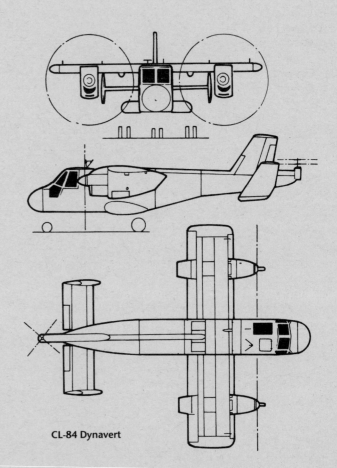

CL-84 Dynavert

CL-89

Engine
Launch: One PERME Wagtail booster rocket (5000 lb. thrust)
Flight: One Williams International WR2-6 turbojet (125 lb. thrust)

External Dimensions
Wing span	3 ft. 1 in.	0.94 m
Foreplane span	1 ft. 7 in.	0.48 m
Length (with booster)	12 ft. 3 in.	3.73 m
Length (without booster)	8 ft. 6 $^1/_2$ in.	2.6 m
Body diameter	1 ft. 1 in.	0.33 m

Weights
Dry weight	172.4 lb.	78.2 kg
Max. launch (with booster)	343 lb.	156 kg
Max. launch (without booster)	238 lb.	108 kg

Performance
Max. speed	460 mph	741 km/h
Range (standard)	74 mi.	120 km
Range (extra fuel tank)	87 mi.	140 km
Ceiling	10000 ft.	3050 m

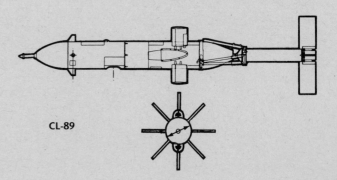

CL-89

CL-215

Engine
Two Pratt & Whitney R-2800 radial (each 2100 bhp)
Three-blade Hamilton Standard Hydromatic constant-speed
feathering propeller

External Dimensions

Wing span	93 ft. 10 in.	28.6 m
Length	65 ft. 0 $^1/_2$ in.	19.82 m
Height	29 ft. 5 $^1/_2$ in.	8.98 m

Internal Dimensions

Cabin length	30 ft. 9 $^1/_2$ in.	9.38 m
Max. width	7 ft. 10 in.	2.39 m
Max. height	6 ft. 3 in.	1.90 m

Weights

Empty weight	28340 lb.	12855 kg
Max. takeoff weight (land)	43500 lb.	19731 kg
Max. takeoff weight (water)	37700 lb.	17100 kg

Performance

Stall speed	76 mph	123 km/h
Cruise speed (10000 ft./3050 m)	181 mph	291 km/h
Max. speed	189 mph	304 km/h
Ferry range	1720 mi.	2750 km.
Productivity	5500 gal/h	25000 l/h
Ceiling	20000 ft.	6048 m

CL-219/CL-226 CF-5/NF-5 Freedom Fighter

Engine
Two Orenda-built General Electric J85-15 turbojet (each 4300 lb.
thrust with afterburner)

External Dimensions

Wing span (no tip tanks)	25 ft. 3 in.	7.7 m
Wing span (tip tanks)	25 ft. 9 in.	7.85 m
Length	47 ft. 2 in.	14.38 m
Height	13 ft. 2 in.	4.01 m

Weights

Empty weight	8681 lb.	3938 kg
Max. takeoff weight	20390 lb.	9249 kg

Performance

Stall speed	148 mph	239 km/h
Max. speed (36000 ft./10970 m)	Mach 1.48	
Radius of action	195 mi.	314 km
Ceiling	50000 ft.	15240 m

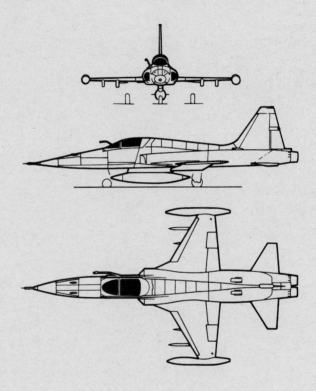

CL-227 Sentinel

Engine

Phase 1
One Wankel-type rotary (20 hp)
Two sets of horizontal contra-rotating three-blade Canadair rotors

Phase 2
One Williams International WR34-15-2 turboshaft (32 hp)
Two sets of horizontal contra-rotating three-blade Canadair rotors

Phase 3
One Williams International WTS-34 or WTS-37 turboshaft (50 hp)
Two sets of horizontal contra-rotating three-blade Canadair rotors

External Dimensions

Phase 1

Height	5 ft. 0 in.	1.52 m
Rotor Diameter	8 ft. 4 in.	2.54 m
Body Diameter	2 ft. 1 in.	0.64 m

Phase 2

Height	5 ft. 6 in.	1.67 m
Rotor Diameter	8 ft. 5 in.	2.57 m
Body Diameter	2 ft. 1 in.	0.64 m

Phase 3

Height (land legs)	5 ft. 10 in.	1.77 m
Height (sea legs)	6 ft. 3 in.	1.91 m
Rotor Diameter	9 ft. 2 $\frac{1}{4}$ in.	2.80 m
Body Diameter	2 ft. 1 in.	0.64 m

Weights

Phase 3

Dry weight	225 lb.	102 kg
Max. takeoff weight	419 lb.	190 kg

Performance

Phase 3

Max. level speed	81 mph	130 km/h
Operating radius (typical)	37 mi.	60 km
Ceiling	10000 ft.	3050 m

CL-289

Engine

Launch
One Bristol Aerospace booster rocket (7200 lb. thrust)

Flight
One KHD T117 turbojet (240 lb. thrust)

External Dimensions

Wing span	4 ft. 4 in.	1.32 m
Length (with booster)	16 ft. 4 in.	4.98 m
Length (without booster)	11 ft. 6 $\frac{1}{2}$ in.	3.52 m
Body diameter	1 ft. 3 in.	0.38 m

Weights
Classified

Performance

Max. speed	High subsonic
Range	Classified
Ceiling	Classified

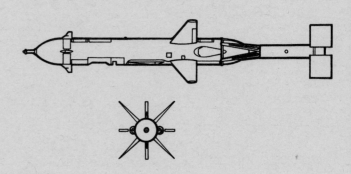

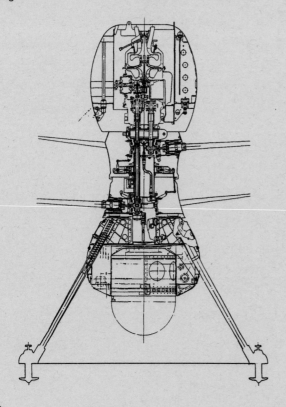

CL-415

Engine
Two Pratt & Whitney PW123AF turboprop (each 2380 shp)
Four-blade Hamilton Standard 14SF-19 constant speed reversible propeller

External Dimensions
Wing span	93 ft. 11 in.	28.63 m
Length	65 ft. 0 ½ in.	19.82 m
Height	29 ft. 5 ½ in.	8.98 m

Internal Dimensions
Cabin length	30 ft. 9 ½ in.	9.38 m
Max. width	7 ft. 10 in.	2.39 m
Max. height	6 ft. 3 in.	1.90 m

Weights
Empty weight	28353 lb.	12861 kg
Max. takeoff weight (land)	43850 lb.	19890 kg
Max. takeoff weight (water)	37850 lb.	17168 kg

Performance
Stall speed	79 mph	126 km/h
Cruise speed (10000 ft./3050 m)	234 mph	376 km/h
Max. speed	247 mph	398 km/h
Ferry range	1508 mi.	2428 km.
Productivity	7700 gal/h	35000 l/h
Ceiling	20000 ft.	6048 m

Challenger 600

Engine
Two Avco Lycoming ALF 502-L2 or L2-C turbofan (each 7500 lb. thrust)

External Dimensions
Wing span	61 ft. 10 in.	18.85 m
Wing span (winglets)	64 ft. 4 in.	19.61 m
Length	68 ft. 5 in.	20.85 m
Height	20 ft. 8 in.	6.3 m

Internal Dimensions
Cabin length	28 ft. 3 in.	8.61 m
Max. width	8 ft. 2 in.	2.49 m
Max. height	6 ft. 1 in.	1.85 m

Weights
Empty weight	23650 lb.	10728 kg
Max. takeoff weight	41250 lb.	18711 kg

Performance
Normal cruise speed	509 mph	819 km/h	442 kt
Max. cruise speed	529 mph	850 km/h	459 kt
Long-range cruise speed	463 mph	744 km/h	402 kt
Range	3435 mi.	5528 km	2985 nm
Ceiling	41000 ft.	12500 m	

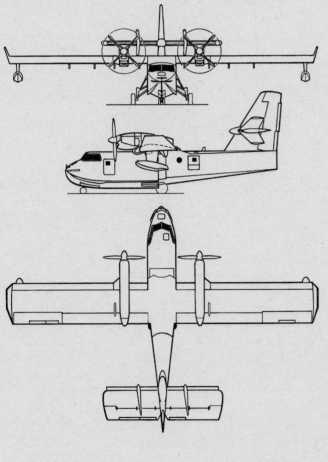

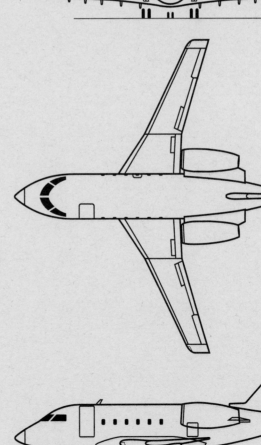

Challenger 601-1A, 3A (no tail tank)

Engine

Challenger 601-1A
Two General Electric CF34-1A turbofan (each 8650 lb. thrust)

Challenger 601-3A
Two General Electric CF34-3A turbofan (each 8729 lb. thrust)

External Dimensions

Wing span	64 ft. 4 in.	19.61 m
Length	68 ft. 5 in.	20.85 m
Height	20 ft. 8 in.	6.3 m

Internal Dimensions

Cabin length	28 ft. 3 in.	8.61 m
Max. width	8 ft. 2 in.	2.49 m
Max. height	6 ft. 1 in.	1.85 m

Weights

Challenger 601-1A

Empty weight	25400 lb.	11521 kg
Max. takeoff weight	43100 lb.	19550 kg

Challenger 601-3A

Empty weight	25500 lb.	11567 kg
Max. takeoff weight	43100 lb.	19550 kg

Performance

Normal cruise speed	528 mph	850 km/h	459 kt
Max. cruise speed	548 mph	882 km/h	476 kt
Long-range cruise speed	489 mph	787 km/h	425 kt
Range	3872 mi.	6232 km	3365 nm
Ceiling	41000 ft.	12500 m	

Challenger 601-3A/ER, 3R (with tail tank)

Engine

Challenger 601-3A/ER
Two General Electric CF34-3A turbofan (each 8729 lb. thrust)

Challenger 601-3R
Two General Electric CF34-3A1 turbofan (each 8729 lb. thrust)

External Dimensions

Wing span	64 ft. 4 in.	19.61 m
Length	68 ft. 5 in.	20.85 m
Height	20 ft. 8 in.	6.3 m

Internal Dimensions

Cabin length	28 ft. 3 in.	8.61 m
Max. width	8 ft. 2 in.	2.49 m
Max. height	6 ft. 1 in.	1.85 m

Weights

Challenger 601-3A/ER

Empty weight	25760 lb.	11685 kg
Max. takeoff weight	44600 lb.	20230 kg

Challenger 601-3R

Empty weight	25760 lb.	11685 kg
Max. takeoff weight	45100 lb.	20457 kg

Performance

Normal cruise speed	528 mph	850 km/h	459 kt
Max. cruise speed	548 mph	882 km/h	476 kt
Long range cruise speed	489 mph	787 km/h	425 kt
Range	4126 mi.	6639 km	3585 nm
Ceiling	41000 ft.	12500 m	

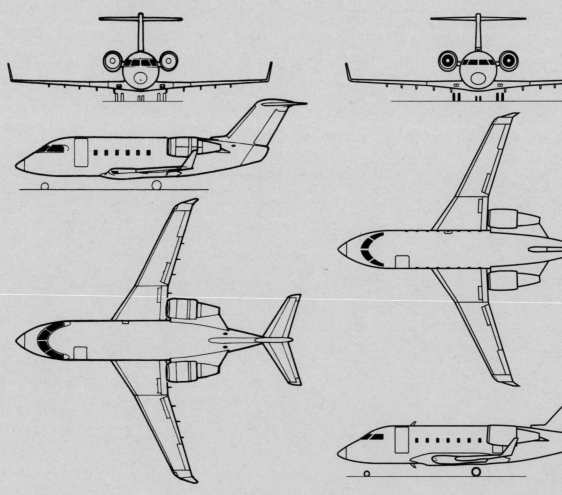

Canadair Regional Jet

Engine
Two General Electric CF34-3A-1 turbofan (each 8729 lb. thrust)

External Dimensions
Wing span	69 ft. 7 in.	21.21 m
Length	87 ft. 10 in.	26.77 m
Height	20 ft. 5 in.	6.22 m

Internal Dimensions
Cabin length	48 ft. 5 in.	14.76 m
Max. width	8 ft. 5 in.	2.57 m
Max. height	6 ft. 1.5 in.	1.87 m

Weights

100
Empty weight	30100 lb.	13653 kg
Max. takeoff weight	47450 lb.	21523 kg

100ER
Empty weight	30122 lb.	13663 kg
Max. takeoff weight	51000 lb.	23133 kg

100LR
Empty weight	30122 lb.	13663 kg
Max. takeoff weight	53000 lb.	24040 kg

Performance

100
Normal cruise speed	488 mph	786 km/h	424 kt
Max. cruise speed	528 mph	850 km/h	459 kt
Range	1130 mi.	1815 km	980 nm
Ceiling	41000 ft.	12496 m	

100ER
Normal cruise speed	488 mph	786 km/h	424 kt
Max. cruise speed	529 mph	851 km/h	459 kt
Range	1864 mi.	3000 km	1620 nm
Ceiling	41000 ft.	12496 m	

100LR
Normal cruise speed	488 mph	786 km/h	424 kt
Max. cruise speed	529 mph	851 km/h	459 kt
Range	2270 mi.	3650 km	1970 nm
Ceiling	41000 ft.	12496 m	

Bombardier Global Express

Engine
Two BMW Rolls-Royce BR710-48-C2 turbofan (each 14690 lb. thrust)

External Dimensions
Wing span	93 ft. 6 in.	28.50 m
Length	99 ft. 5 in.	30.30 m
Height	24 ft. 6 in.	7.47 m

Internal Dimensions
Cabin length	48 ft. 0 in.	14.63 m
Max. width	8 ft. 2 in.	2.49 m
Max. height	6 ft. 3 in.	1.91 m

Weights
Empty weight	48500 lb.	22000 kg
Max. takeoff weight	91000 lb.	41277 kg

Performance
Normal cruise speed	562 mph	904 km/h	488 kt
Max. cruise speed	581 mph	935 km/h	505 kt
Long-range cruise speed	528 mph	850 km/h	459 kt
Range (at LRC)	7480 mi.	12038 km	6500 nm
Ceiling	51000 ft.	15545 m	

NOTE: All figures for the Bombardier Global Express are based on preliminary engineering specifications and are subject to change pending final design configuration and flight test confirmation.

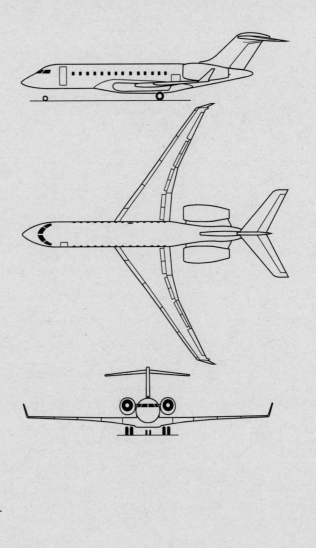

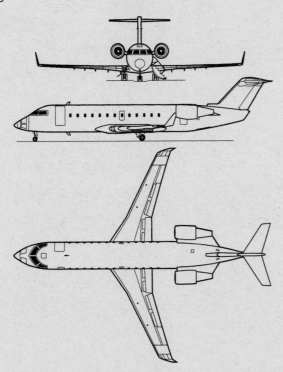

CANADAIR MODEL DESIGNATIONS

Model	Version	Description	Date**	Engines
CL-0		DC-3,C-47 conversions	1945	P&W R-1830 or Wright R-1820
CL-1	PBY-5A	Canso	1944	P&W R-1830
	OA-10A		1944	P&W R-1830
CL-2	C-54GM	North Star (RCAF unpressurized)	1944	R-R Merlin
	DC-4M-1	North Star (TCA unpressurized)	1944	R-R Merlin
	DC-4M-2	North Star (TCA pressurized)	1946	R-R Merlin
CL-3*	C-125	Northrop Raider (became CL-12)	1949	Wright R-1820
CL-4	C-4	Argonaut (BOAC)	1948	R-R Merlin
	C-4-1	North Star (CPA)	1948	R-R Merlin
	Plus two other versions not built			
CL-5	C-5	VIP Transport	1949	P&W R-2800
CL-6		Not assigned		
CL-7*	C-7	Transport	1950	P&W R-2800
CL-8 to CL-10		Not assigned		
CL-11*		VIP Transport		
CL-12*	C-125	Northrop Raider	1949	Wright R-1820
CL-13		F-86A Sabre 1	1949	GE J47
		F-86E Sabre 2	1950	GE-J47
		F-86E Sabre 3	1952	Orenda 3
		F-86E Sabre 4	1952	GE J47
	CL-13A	F-86E Sabre 5	1953	Orenda 10
	CL-13B	F-86E Sabre 6	1954	Orenda 14
	CL-13C	F-86E Sabre 6	1953	Orenda 14 with afterburner
	CL-13D*	F-86E Sabre 6		Orenda 14 with Snarler rocket
	CL-13E	F-86E Sabre 5		Orenda 10, area rule fuselage
	Plus five other versions not built			
CL-14*		Military jet trainer	1950	
CL-15*		T-36 USAF crew trainer	1951	Wright R-1820
	CL-15A*	Twin engine pilot trainer	1951	Amstrong-Siddeley (AS) Mamba
CL-16*		Pilot trainer	1951	P&W R-2800
	Four other versions. None built			
CL-17*		Twin engine 15-seat local transport	1951	Wright C7B6
CL-18*		27-seat local transport	1951	Wright 959, C98EI
	Plus 24-seat version, not built			
CL-19*		32-seat twin engine inter-city transport	1951	Napier Eland
	Plus three other versions, not built			
CL-20		Velvet Glove missile	1951	Rocket motor
CL-21*		Twin-engine 32-seat local transport	1952	Wright Cyclone C9HE
	Plus two other versions, not built			
CL-22*		Twin engine 32-seat intercity transport	1951	Double AS Mamba
CL-23*		Twin engine 21-seat local transport	1951	Single AS Mamba
CL-24*		Royal Canadian Navy SAR aircraft	1951	
CL-25*		Twin engine 32-seat local transport	1952	Single AS Mamba (1952 Rating)
CL-26*		32/36-seat twin engine local transport	1952	P&W R-2180
	Plus three versions, high- or low-wing. None built			
CL-27*		60 to 84-seat intercity transport	1951/2	4 Allison T38
	Plus three versions, not built			
CL-28		Maritime reconnaissance aircraft	1952	4 Wright R-3350-85
	CL-28-1	Argus Mk.1 maritime recon. aircraft	1954	4 Wright 981-TC-18EAI
	CL-28-2	Argus Mk.2 maritime recon. aircraft		4 Wright 981-TC-18EAI
	Plus 18 other versions, none built			
CL-29*		Maritime reconnaissance aircraft	1953	Wright R-3350-85
CL-30		Lockheed T-33 jet trainer	1952	R-R Nene Mk. 10
CL-31*		Four engine maritime recon aircraft	1953	Wright R-3350-85
CL-32*		Americanized Bristol Britannia	1953	
CL-33*		Maritime reconnaissance aircraft	1953	Wright R-3350-32W (34FS)
CL-34*		Velvet Glove airframe trainer	1954	
CL-35*		DC-4M-2/3 conversion for TCA	1953	R-R Dart R.DA-5
CL-36*		Target drone, ground /air launched	1953	R-R Soar
	Plus three other versions, not built			
CL-37*		Four engine military a/c based on CL-5	1953	P&W R-2800
	Plus three other versions, not built			

* Not built.

** Date model number allocated

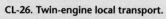

CL-26. Twin-engine local transport.

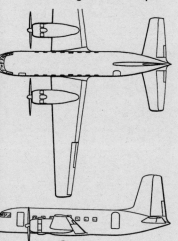

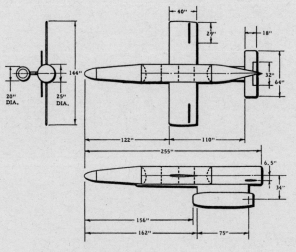

CL-36. Target drone.

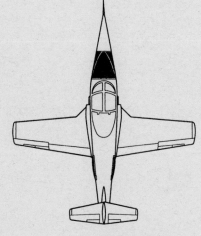

CL-41R. NASARR trainer for CF-104.

Model	Version	Description	Date	Engines
CL-38*		Cargo/pass/ambulance transport	1953	Wright R-3350-32 (34FS)
CL-39*		Four engine turboprop airliner	1953	Wright T49
CL-40*		68 to 116-seat turboprop airliner	1953	4 Bristol BE-25
CL-41		Side-by-side jet trainer	1954	Viper*
	CL-41A	Tutor basic pilot trainer	1959	GE CJ-610-1B in prototype, replaced by J85-CAN-40 prodn.
	CL-41C	Basic Trainer	1960	P&W JT12A-5
	CL-41G	Ground support tactical a/c	1961	J85-CAN-40 (prototype only)
	CL-41G-5	Ground support tactical a/c (Tebuan)	1964	GE J85/J4
	CL-41R	NASARR trainer for CF-104	1960	GE CJ-610-1B (prototype only)
	Plus 28 other versions, not built			
CL-42*		Twin engine executive aircraft	1954	P&W R-2800-CB-17
CL-43*		Twin engine logistic supply transport	1954	P&W R-1340
CL-44		Four engine military transport	1954	Wright 981*
	CL-44-6	Yukon four engine military transport	1958	R-R Tyne 11
	CL-44D4	Commercial cargo transport, tail loading	1959	R-R Tyne 12
	CL-44D4-1	Seaboard & Western	1959	R-R Tyne 12
	CL-44D4-2	Flying Tiger Line	1959	R-R Tyne 12
	CL-44D4-6	Slick Airways	1960	R-R Tyne 12
	CL-44J	Long range cargo, extended fuselage	1963	R-R Tyne 12
	Plus 50 other versions, not built			
CL-45*		ASW helicopter for RCN (with Hiller)	1954	3 GE T38-GE2
CL-46		Prototype control rod, nuclear reactor	1957	
CL-47		Tracked vehicle suspension bar	1955	
CL-48*		RCN DNG-1 anti-aircraft guided missile	1955	Rocket
CN-49		Pool test reactor for AECL	1955	
CL-50*		Turboprop airliner, single/double deck, high/low wing, straight-/swept-wing	1955	4 Bristol BE-25
	CL-50A*	Jetliner: 4/5 engines underwing or in pods on rear fuselage	1951	AS Sapphire, P&W J57 or R-R Conway
CL-51*		Tartar anti-aircraft missile for USN	1955	
CL-52		B-47 flying test bed for Iroquois engine	1956	Orenda PS-13 (test installation)
CL-53*		USAF crew readiness trainer/bizjet	1956	3 Fairchild J83, R-R RB-108
CL-54		Sparrow guided missile for RCAF	1956	Rocket
CN-55		Beta ray spectrometer for AECL	1956	
CN-56		Research reactor: University of Toronto	1956	
CN-57*		Control rods/control rod system	1957	
CN-58*		Dielectric heating process: pulp digestion	1957	
CN-59*		Tank nuclear reactor	1958	
CL-60		T-36 trainer for USAF (as per CL-42)	1951	2 P&W R-2800

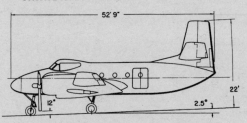

CL-42. Twin-engine business aircraft.

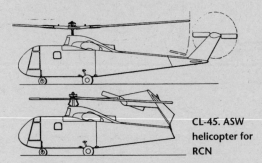

CL-45. ASW helicopter for RCN

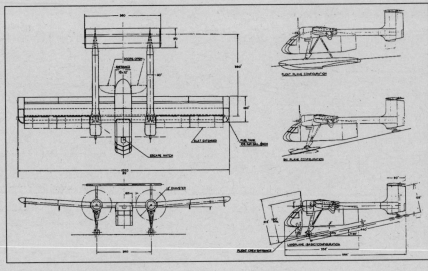

CL-43. Twin-engine transport.

Model	Version	Description	Date	Engines
CL-61		Articulated light snowmobile (RAT)	1956	Volkswagen 35 hp
CL-62*		VTOL tiltwing transport		
	Nine other versions, none built			
CN-63*		Subcritical nuclear reactor	1957	
CN-64*		Fuel charge and discharge gear for nuclear reactor	1957	
CL-65*		Towed target (towed by F-86,T-33)	1957	
CL-66		Twin engine airliner	1958	Napier Eland or Allison
	CL-66B-1	Military transport, cargo/VIP	1958	Eland
	CL-66C-1	Airliner for Quebecair	1960	Eland
	Plus 15 other versions, not built			
CL-67*		Four engine maritime patrol aircraft	1958	R-R Tyne or AS Mamba 10
CL-68*		Special Weapons anti-missile missile	1958	
CL-69*		Twin engine utility/executive transport	1958	
	Four versions. none built			
CL-70		Production version of CL-61 RAT	1957	Volkswagen 35 hp
CL-71*		One-ton tracked cargo carrier	1957	Porsche 1600 70 hp
CL-72*		Four engine VTOL strike/recon aircraft	1958	Orenda PS-16
CL-73*		VTOL tilt wing reconnaissance aircraft	1958	GE T58
	Ten versions, none built			
CL-74*		Twin engine VTOL army liaison a/c.	1958	
	Two versions, not built			
CN-75*		Z-2 research nuclear reactor	1958	
CL-76*		Twin engine, low-level tactical bomber	1958	
	Three versions, none built			
CL-77		Automatic mail sorter	1959	
CN-78		Magnetic coils: Beta-ray spectrometer	1959	
CL-79		Bomarc valves	1959	
CL-80		Convair Astronautics test equipment	1959	
CL-81*		Four engine short/medium range 70-90-seat jetliner for TCA:GW 80,000 lb.	1959	GE, P&W or R-R
CL-82*		Place Ville Marie curtain wall	1959	
CL-83		Snow Goose high altitude test vehicle (later re-named Black Brant)	1959	Supplied by CARDE
CL-84		Twin engine V/STOL recon. prototype (growth version of CL-73)	1959	P&W C PT6*
	CL-84-1	Operational evaluation aircraft (CX-84)	1965	Lycoming 1K-4C
	CL-84-1A	Sea Control Ship eval. a/c (CL-84-1)	1972	Lycoming LTCIK-4J
	Plus 51 other versions, not built			
CL-85*		Robot dispatch carrier		
CL-86		Not assigned		
CL-87*		Army logistic missile system	1960	

Model	Version	Description	Date	Engines
CL-88*		Medium range jet transport based on Convair 880 to meet TCA enquiry	1960	R-R or Allison
CL-89		Short range reconnaissance drone sys.	1960	Williams Research WR-2-1
		Plus four versions with WR-2-2, 2-5 and 2-6 engines		
CL-90		Strike recon. aircraft (Lockheed F-104)	1959	GE J79-GE-7
CL-91		XM-571 Dynatrac tracked cargo carrier	1961	GM Corvair modified R-10
CL-92		CIL House curtain wall	1960	
CL-93	CL-93A	CF-104 flight simulator RCAF	1960	
	CL-93-B	F-104G flight simulator	1960	
CL-94		Malton Airport Aeroquay curtain wall	1961	
CL-95*		Twin engine turboprop executive a/c	1961	P&W C PT6A
		Four versions, high and low wing, 6/8 passengers: none built		
CL-96*		Convair high altitude probe (Black Brant II)	1961	Rocket
CL-97*		6 to 8 seat version of CL-95 for military	1961	Orenda PS-25C turbofan
CL-98*		Medium range rear-loading transport for RCAF	1961	GE T64
CL-99*		Cargo transport with multiple mechanized cargo compartments, GW 400,000 lb. (Same category as Lockheed C-5)	1961	P&W JT3D-14 turbofans
CL-100 to CL-199		Not used to avoid confusion with military aircraft designations		
CL-200	1 A10*	Six engine all-wing (325' span) cargo a/c, laminar flow control, hinged wingtips, GW 1,000,000 lb.	1961	P&W JT3D
CL 201	1A10	F-104G (MAP) fighter-bomber	1961	GE J79-GE-11A w/afterburner
CL-202*		Handley Page Herald military tactical transport or nav/rad trainer (2 variants)	1962	R-R Dart R Da 542-10
CL-203*		Short/medium range cargo/pass a/c for RCAF, GW 50,000 lb.	1962	R-R Spey turbo jets or fans
CL-204*		Firefighting aircraft	1962	P&W R-2800-B
		Two versions: GW 38,000 and 43,000 lb. None built		
CL-205	1A10	Sikorsky CH-53A components	1963	
CL-206*		NAA Sabreliner	1963	
		Two versions. None built		
CL-207	1A10	F-111 fin, rudder and steel parts prog.	1963	
CL-208	1A10	Lance missile launcher	1963	
CL-209*		Overseas licensed CL-41 manufacture	1963	
CL-210	1A10	Tracking antenna for Northern Electric	1964	
	1A11*	Similar for India, not built		
CL-211		Avian Gyroplane assessment	1964	Lycoming 0-360A1D
CL-212	1A10	Air cushion vehicle: Three engine	1964	2 Mercury 100 outboards & 1 McCullough 4318E
	1A11	Air cushion vehicle: Two engine	1964	Ford Mustang 289 cu.in.
CL-213	1A10	Fisher off-road wheeled vehicle	1964	250cc 9 hp Rotax
CL-214*		Light close support aircraft	1964	

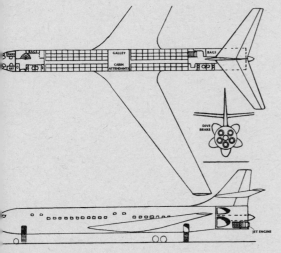

CL-50. Jet airliner.

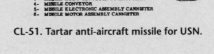

CL-51. Tartar anti-aircraft missile for USN.

1- SLIDING HATCH
2- BLAST SCREEN
3- MISSILE HOIST-CONVEYOR TO LAUNCHER
4- MISSILE CONVEYOR
5- MISSILE ELECTRONIC ASSEMBLY CANNISTER
6- MISSILE MOTOR ASSEMBLY CANNISTER

CL-53. USAF crew readiness trainer/business jet.

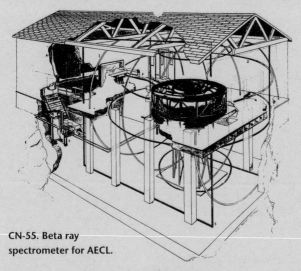

CN-55. Beta ray
spectrometer for AECL.

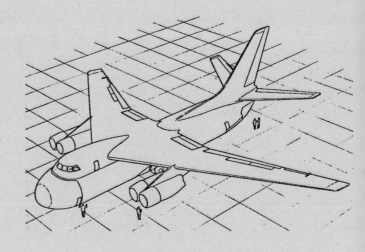

CL-99. Heavy transport. A twin-tail version was also investigated.

Model	Version	Description	Date	Engines
CL-215		Twin engine multi-purpose amphibian	1964	P&W R-2800
	1A27	Waterbomber variant	1966	P&W R-2800
	6B11	Turboprop conversion (CL-215T)	1987	P&W C 123A
	Plus 35 other versions, some with Allison 501, R-R, Dart, GE T64 and			
	Wright R-3350 engines and gross weights to 65,500 lb. None built.			
CL-216*	1A10	Air Cushion vehicle: 20-passenger	1965	
CL-217		Cable car for Hydro Quebec	1965	B&D electric motors
CL-218	1A10	Urban transit bus	1965	GM Detroit Diesel
CL-219	1A10	CF-5A single seat fighter	1965	2 GE J85-CAN-15
	1A17	CF-5D two-seat aircraft	1965	2 GE J85-CAN-15
	1A12 to 1A16 covering Norair F-5A/B, F-5AG/BG and T-38 components			
CL-220	1A13	Lockheed C-5A components	1966	
	1B10	Lockheed C-5B components	1983	
	1A10 thru 1A12 covering proposals to Lockheed and Boeing			
CL-221*	1A10	4-5 -seat air cushion vehicle	1965	Ford 289 cu.in.
CL-222*		Twin engine multi-purpose landplane	1965	
	Three versions.None built			
CL-223	1A10	Flxette 21 ft. transit coach	1965	Ford 300 cu. in.
CL-224*	1A10	Cable car for Ontario Hydro	1965	
CL-225	1A10	45-ft. antenna for Northern Electric	1966	
	1A11	30-ft. antenna for Northern Electric	1967	
CL-226	1A10	NF-5A for Royal Netherlands Air Force	1967	2 J85-CAN-15
	1A11	NF-5B for Royal Netherlands Air Force	1967	2 J85-CAN-15
CL-227	1A10	Short range real-time surveillance system.	1967	Saurer GT-15
		Prototype Sentinel UAV. Phase II vehicle had Williams		
		WR-34 engine, Phase III had Williams WTS-34.		
CL-228*		R&D high lift systems study	1967	
	Three wind tunnel models			
CL-229*	1A10	Polar mount 30-ft. diameter antenna	1968	
		Norther Electric Mid-Canada Microwave		
CL-230*	1A10	Turboprop SAR amphibian	1967	
CL-231	1A10	Air Traffic Control tower cab (66 sq.ft.)	1967	
CL-232	1A10	Mobile transportable tower cab	1967	
CL-233	1A10	Air Traffic Control tower cab (275 sq.ft.)	1967	
CL-234*	1A10	Canadian domestic communications	1968	
		satellite (structure & power systems)		
CL-235	1A10	Prototype television receive-only	1968	
		antenna(25-ft diam. for Northern Electric)		
CL-236*	1A10	Advanced multi-role aircraft (AMRA)	1968	
CL-237*	1A10	Tactical aircraft guidance system (CAE)	1968	
CL-238*	1A10	Two-seat trainer, tandem	1969	
CL-239	1A10	Lockheed 1011 production contracts	1969	

Model	Version	Description	Date	Engines
CL-240	1A10	Advanced V/STOL propeller program	1969	
CL-241*		Multi-role transport,/ASW	1969	
CL-242*	1A10	Airliner, high wing, deflected thrust, 20-26 passengers	1969	
CL-243*	1A10	Airliner, high wing, deflected thrust, 40-56 passengers	1969	
CL-244*	1A10	Proposed swing tail kit for Boeing 707	1969	
CL-245*		Replaced by CL-260		
CL-246*	1A10	Four engine commercial STOL 48-passenger (American Airlines RFP)	1970	T53-19A
	Plus 60-, 65-, 70-	passenger versions		
CL-247	1A10	Mercure II skins (pre-production)	1970	
CL-248	1A10	Falcon 10 wing panels	1971	
CL-249		Advanced materials	1971	
CL-250		Wastewater treatment package plant	1971	
CL-251	1A10	Mercure II components	1972	
CL-252	1A10	Electra 188C, ice recon. conversion	1972	
CL-253	1A10	DIR proposal 1006, Aerodynamic characteristics of counter-rotating rotors	1972	
CL-254	1A10	Oil collection system	1972	
CL-255		Aerodynamics prediction methods for propeller-wing-flap systems	1973	
CL-256		Radome: United Aircraft of Canada	1973	
CL-257	1A10	747 SP component subcontract	1973	
CL-258	1A10	Metro cars:Joint CL/MLW proposal	1973	
CL-259*		B-1 fin composite structure (USAF)	1974	
CL-260*	1A10	Single engine utility aircraft - Otter replacement	1970	P&W C PT6A-27
	1B11	As 1A10 but smaller wing and tail, retractable tricycle undercarriage	1970	P&W C PT6A-27
CL-261		Stores clearance definition program	1974	
CL-262		Fisheries control study	1974	
CL-263		Multi-purpose van bodies	1974	
CL-264	1A10	Proposal for Convair 580 to remote sensing role	1974	
CL-265*	1A10	VTOL RPV technology development	1974	
CL-266*		Twin PT6 medium utility aircraft	1975	P&W C PT6-A45
CL-267*	1A10	High-speed passenger train: proposal based on UAC Turbo train	1976	P&W C Turboshaft engines
CL-268*		Aerocrane	1977	4 P&W C PT6
CL-269*		Study of vertical axis wind turbine sub-contract to Shawinigan Engineering Co.	1978	
CL-270*	1A10	Light twin engine commercial aircraft		Allison 250-B17
CL-271	1A10	Grumman EF-111A, vertical stabilizer	1975	
CL-272	1A10	Grumman E2C: wet outer wing proposal	1975	
CL-273	1A10	Comparative study of wind turbine gen-erators (subcontract for Hydro Quebec)	1978	
CL-274	1A10	F-18A Serial No. 247	1981	
CL-275 to 279		Not assigned		
CL-280*	1A10	Long range patrol a/c(LRPA), Boeing	1974	
CL-281	1A10	LRPA, Lockheed version (CP-140)	1974	
CL-282	1A10	Boeing 767, Section 48	1979	
CL-283	1A10	Grumman subcontract B 767 parts	1980	
CL-284*		Tilt-wing V/STOL light intra-theatre transport (LIT)	1968	
	1A10	LIT, 4 propellers, parallel chord wing	1968	
	1A11	LIT, 4 propellers, tapered wing		
CL-285*	1A10	Energy efficient aircraft wing	1980	GE CF34
	2B11	Energy efficient aircraft Phase III	1981	
CL-286*	1A10	Primary training aircraft	1981	P&W C PT6A
CL-287 & 288		Not assigned		
CL-289	1A10	Intermediate range surveillance drone	1971	
CL-290		Intermediate capacity transit system	1975	
CL-291		Locomotive steerable axle truck	1978/9	
CL-292		Buffalo a/c: accelerometer data	1981	
CL-293		Falcon a/c: accelerometer data	1981	
CL-294		Hercules a/c: accelerometer data	1981	
CL-295		Musketeer a/c: accelerometer data	1981	

CL-200. All-wing cargo aircraft.

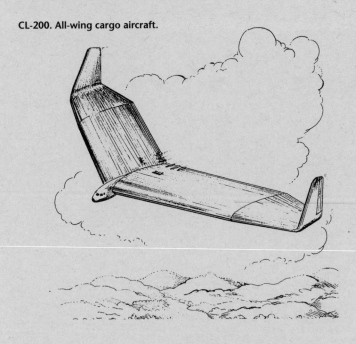

CL-202. Military close-support aircraft and nav/rad trainer based on Handley-Page Herald modified for RCAF.

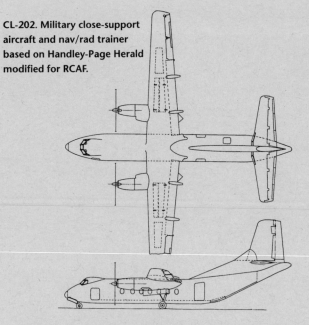

Model	Version	Description	Date	Engines
CL-296		Tracker a/c: accelerometer data	1981	
CL-297		Gulfstream II a/c: accelerometer data	1984	
CL-298		Constellation a/c: accelerometer data	1984	
CL-299		Northrop T-38 trainer aircraft	1984	
CL-300		Bell Helicopter Textron 400, tooling	1985	
CL-301		C-131H (USN): electrical load survey	1986	
CL-302 to 317		Not assigned		
CL-318		CF-18 systems engineering support	1986	
CL-319 to 326		Not assigned		
CL-327		Reserved for future upgrade of CL-227	1991	
CL-328 & 329		Not assigned		
CL-330		Airbus A330/340 (Aerospatiale)	1988	
CL-331-349		Not assigned		
CL-350		Airbus A330/340 (British Aerospace)	1988	
CL-351 to 399		Reserved for Defence Systems Div.	1993	
CL-400 to 599		Not assigned except as follows:		
CL-415		Marketing title for CL-215-6B11	1991	
CL-427 & CL-527		Reserved for future upgrade of CL-227	1991	
CL-600	1A10	Challenger twin-engine business jet	1976	Lycoming ALF-502L
CL-601				
CL-601-1A		Challenger twin-engine business jet	1981	GE CF34-1A
CL-601-3A		Challenger twin-engine business jet	1985	GE CF34-3A
CL601-3R		Challenger twin-engine business jet	1993	GE CF34-3A1
CL-604		Challenger twin-engine business jet	1993	GE CF34-3B
CRJ		Canadair Regional Jet 50-seat airliner	1987	GE CF34-3A1
CL-645	2B21	EST Challenger, Defence Systems Div.	1993	Lycoming ALF-502L
CL-646	2B22	Coastal patrol, Defence Systems Div.	1992	Lycoming ALF-502L
CL-700	1A10	Global Express twin-engine business jet	1993	BMW R-R BR710-48-C2

AIRCRAFT PROGRAMS
(Quantity as of 16 December 1994)

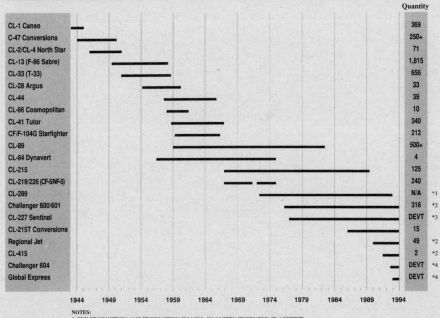

	Quantity
CL-1 Canso	369
C-47 Conversions	250+
CL-2/CL-4 North Star	71
CL-13 (F-86 Sabre)	1,815
CL-33 (T-33)	656
CL-28 Argus	33
CL-44	39
CL-66 Cosmopolitan	10
CL-41 Tutor	340
CF/F-104G Starfighter	212
CL-89	500+
CL-84 Dynavert	4
CL-215	125
CL-219/226 (CF-5NF-5)	240
CL-289	N/A *1
Challenger 600/601	316 *2
CL-227 Sentinel	DEVT *3
CL-215T Conversions	15
Regional Jet	49 *2
CL-415	2 *2
Challenger 604	DEVT *4
Global Express	DEVT *4

1944 1949 1954 1959 1964 1969 1974 1979 1984 1989 1994

NOTES:
1. PRE-PRODUCTION AND PRODUCTION PHASES. QUANTITY PRODUCED CLASSIFIED.
2. IN PRODUCTION AS OF 30 JUNE 1994.
3. INCLUDES 2 PHASE 1, 4 PHASE 2, AND 12 PHASE 3 AIR VEHICLES.
4. IN DEVELOPMENT

SUBCONTRACT PROGRAMS
(Shipsets as of 30 June 1994)

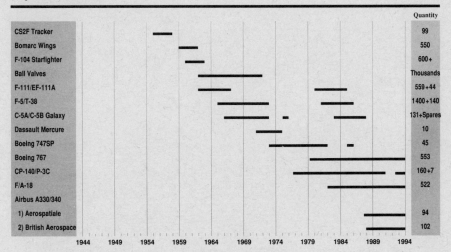

	Quantity
CS2F Tracker	99
Bomarc Wings	550
F-104 Starfighter	600+
Ball Valves	Thousands
F-111/EF-111A	559+44
F-5/T-38	1400+140
C-5A/C-5B Galaxy	131+Spares
Dassault Mercure	10
Boeing 747SP	45
Boeing 767	553
CP-140/P-3C	160+7
F/A-18	522
Airbus A330/340	
1) Aerospatiale	94
2) British Aerospace	102

1944 1949 1954 1959 1964 1969 1974 1979 1984 1989 1994

AVERAGE ANNUAL EMPLOYMENT LEVEL

12,000
11,000
10,000
9,000
8,000
7,000
6,000
5,000
4,000
3,000
2,000
1,000

1944 1949 1954 1959 1964 1969 1974 1979 1984 1989 1994

CANADAIR FIRST FLIGHTS

CL-1 Canso: December 5,1942. E.C. Dobbin, St. Hubert (a/c manufactured from US-supplied parts)

CL-2 North Star: July 15,1946. Bob Brush (Douglas), Al Lilly, Smokey Harris, Clayton Glenn (TCA)

C-4 Argonaut: March 6,1949. Lilly, Bill Longhurst

C-4-1 (CPA): April 22,1949 Lilly, Bud Scouten

C-5: May 15,1950. Lilly, Longhurst

CL-13 (F-86A): August 8,1950. Lilly

CL-13 (Sabre 2): January 31,1951. Longhurst

CL13 (Sabre 3): September 25,1952. Longhurst. (Also flown as Sabre 2: No. 19200: with J47 engine, June 14,1952 Glen Lynes.)

CL-13 (Sabre 4): August 28,1952. Hedley Everard

CL-13A (Sabre 5): July 30,1953. Longhurst

CL-13B (Sabre 6): October 19,1954. Longhurst

CL-30 (T-33ANX No. 14695 prototype Nene installation): October 28,1952. Everard

CL-30 (T-33AN production): December 22,1952. Longhurst

CL-28 (Argus Mk.1): March 28,1957. Longhurst, G.T. (Scotty) McLean, Harris, George MacFarlane, Peter Wreford Bush

CL-28 (Argus Mk. 2): August 27,1958. Bill Kidd, Bill Clark, Paul Del Rizzo, Bill Knibbs

CL-44-6 (Yukon): November 15,1959. Longhurst, McLean

CL-44D4 (Forty Four): November 16,1960. Longhurst, McLean, Harris, MacFarlane

CL-44J: November 8,1965. Longhurst (previously flown as a CL-44D4 March 17,1965)

CL-66C (Canadair 540): February 2,1959. Longhurst, McLean

CL-66B (CC-109 Cosmopolitan): January 7,1960. McLean, Ian MacTavish, Vern Groves, MacFarlane

CL-41 (JT-12 engine): January 13,1960. MacTavish

CL-41 (GE J85GE-7 engine): November 26,1962. MacTavish

CL-41 (Tutor GE J85 CAN-40 engine): October 31,1963. MacTavish

CL-41G (No. 26015 modified): June 9,1964. MacTavish

CL-41G (Tebuan): April 3,1967. MacTavish

CL-41R (NASARR trainer): July 13,1962. MacTavish

CL-90 (CF-104 Starfighter): May 26,1961, Palmdale, California, Glen (Snake) Reaves of Lockheed; August 14,1961, at Cartierville, No. 12703, Kidd, and No. 12704, Reaves

CL-89 (drone): March 1964

CL-84 (V/STOL): May 7,1965. Vertical flight only, Longhurst

CL-84: December 6,1965. Conventional flight only, Longhurst

CL-84: January 16,1966. Transition, Longhurst

CL-215: October 23, 1967. Longhurst, Doug Adkins, Harris

CL-219 (CF-5 Freedom Fighter): May 10, 1968. H. Chouteau (Northrop), at Edwards AFB, California

CL-219 (CF-5D): August 28,1968. Longhurst, Chouteau

CL-226 (NF-5): March 24,1969. Longhurst

CL-226 (NF-5D): July 7,1969. Seth Grossmith

CL-84-1: February 19,1970. Longhurst

CL-252 (Electra ice reconnaissance a/c): December 4,1972. Kiser (Nordair), Adkins, Colin Harcourt, Williams, Golze

CL-227 (UAV): Phase I, tethered August 25,1978; free March 19,1980

CL-289 (drone): March 3,1980.

CL-227: Phase II, tethered December 3,1981; free December 14,1981

CL-227: Phase III Sentinel, November 20,1987.

CL-600 (Challenger 600 business jet): November 8,1978. Adkins, Norm Ronaasen, Jim Martin, Bill Greening

Challenger 601 (CL-600 s/n 1003 with new aft fuselage and GE engines, redesignated s/n 3991): April 10,1982. Adkins, Jamie Sutherland

Challenger 601 (first production): September 17,1982. Adkins, Ian McDonald

Challenger 601-3A: September 28,1986. Adkins, Malcolm MacGregor, Greening

CL-227 (Sea Sentinel): August 1988

Regional Jet: May 10,1991. Adkins, Don Stephen

CL-215T: June 8,1989. Adkins, Yves Mahaut, Doug Ford, Ted Squelch

CL-415: December 6,1993. Adkins, Mahaut, Ford, Squelch

Challenger 604 (Challenger No. 3991 with uprated GE engines, redesignated No. 5991): September 18, 1994. Adkins, Bruce Robinson, Squelch

RESEARCH AND DEVELOPMENT

Over the years, the depth of Canadair research and development (R&D) depended largely on the attitude of the government of the day towards R&D and hence the availability of funds. Nevertheless, the R&D department took part in a wide variety of studies and application programs, some subcontracted, others company-funded. The following is a sampling of projects. The first four were part of "Project Save our Souls", the effort to retain the engineers idled by the loss of the Sparrow II contract.

CF-104 Vulnerability Study

In 1960-61, Canadair studied, for the Defence Research Board, the probability of a CF-104 being destroyed or damaged by fragments from an exploding enemy warhead. Operations Research personnel, Bob Deans, Maurice Deplanty, Stuart Geddes, John Kettle and Bob Price, made a miniature skeleton model of a CF-104 and sprayed it with tiny beams of light, simulating fragments of a warhead, emitted from a light source which simulated the exploding warhead. Whenever a light beam struck the aircraft it was assumed to have caused damage. The extent and effect of the damage depended on the size and weight of the fragment, the distance from the exploding warhead to the aircraft and the place where the fragment struck, be it the cockpit, fuel tanks, electronics or vital structure.

Battlefield Survivability Study

In 1962, Operations Research personnel, including Albert Brown, Bob Deans, Stuart Geddes, Nick Kurdyla, John Martin, Roy Nishizaki, Bob Price and Len Stachtchenko, conducted a study for the US Army to determine the probability of a reconnaissance aircraft surviving a mission into Soviet-held territory.

A terrain model, approximately 6 m long and 3 m wide (20 ft. x 10 ft.) was constructed. Soviet antiaircraft guns and missile launchers, simulated by light receptors, were positioned strategically throughout the model. The reconnaissance aircraft was simulated by a moving pinpoint of light. The researchers attempted to move the simulated aircraft through the terrain, using terrain-masking, nap-of-the-earth navigation techniques, without it being spotted by a gun. If a gun picked up the light it was assumed it could engage the aircraft at a certain distance and altitude. The study concluded that manned aircraft had little hope of surviving Soviet defences. To survive, the reconnaissance vehicle must be so small it couldn't be seen, heard or discerned by electronic means. Canadair marketing personnel made good use of these findings in their sales presentations for the CL-89 surveillance drone.

Escape Systems for Space Vehicles

A team of Fotis Mavriplis, Roy Nishizaki and Henry Szot carried out two study contracts concerning crew escape from space vehicles for the USAF. The first considered escape from three-person crew vehicles orbiting at altitudes ranging from 370 km (230 mi.) to 35,800 km (22,250 mi.). An evaluation of three alternative concepts concluded that a separable crew re-entry capsule offered the best chance of survival. The second study investigated escape capsules in 5- to 20-person vehicles orbiting at 370 km (230 mi.)

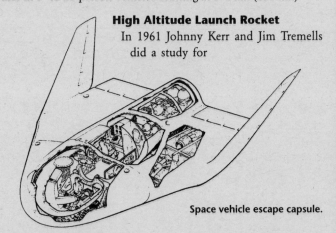

High Altitude Launch Rocket
In 1961 Johnny Kerr and Jim Tremells did a study for

Space vehicle escape capsule.

the USAF systems command at Dayton, Ohio, of the feasibility of launching a rocket into the stratosphere from an F-86 Sabre flying at maximum altitude. Many years later, the USAF conducted just such a test using a high-flying F-15 to launch a rocket and hit a satellite.

Propeller Static Thrust

The CL-84 presented the engineers with several unique problems, one of which was how to design a propeller that functioned while the aircraft was standing still in the air, or hovering. During the CL-84 advanced design phase, Odd Michaelsen and others conducted considerable research into ways of improving a propeller's static thrust so as to make it operate more efficiently when the aircraft was stationary.

With the aid of a test rig powered by a 425-hp Chevrolet truck engine driving a series of 2.13-m (7 ft.) diameter propellers, they studied the flow of air through and around the propeller. The data they gained helped develop propeller blade designs with substantially higher static thrust than any other V/STOL propeller and made Canadair a world leader in this method of increasing VTOL lift.

Aerodynamic Research on High Lift Systems

In the late 1960s, Fotis Mavriplis carried out lengthy research into aircraft high lift systems as part of an overall effort to develop technology for the design of advanced aircraft. He was able to apply his results to the design of the airfoils of the Challenger, Regional Jet and Global Express aircraft.

Wind Energy Program (CL-269)

Canadair became interested in wind energy in 1977 when the technology of producing electrical power without fuel costs began to show commercial potential. In 1978, it conducted a feasibility study of large vertical-axis wind turbines (VAWT) for the National Research Council of Canada (NRC). This led to further engineering and cost studies for NRC and Hydro Québec and, eventually, to Projet Éole.

Projet Éole was a cost-shared undertaking by NRC and Hydro Québec to create a prototype commercially viable VAWT. Hydro Québec already had a small VAWT operating on the Îles de la Madeleine in the Gulf of St. Lawrence but Projet Éole's turbine would have a rotor 108 m (354 ft.) high. It would consist of two curved airfoil-shaped blades forming a troposhein (the shape taken by a rotating skipping rope). The blades would have a chord of 2.4 m (7 ft. 10 in.) and be 64 m (210 ft.) apart at the centre. The turbine would drive an electric generator to produce about four megawatts of electricity. Installation of the turbine was scheduled for August 1985.

Lawrence Rowley was program manager. His design team included Ed Cheng, Brian Elmer, Ken Goodall, John Ho, Ken Kimber, Jim Smith and Len Stachtchenko, with Jack Waller, chief of materials and processes, as the composites expert. Their proposal was based on the use of composite materials and priced at traditional aviation industry costs, which proved too expensive for Hydro Québec.

Lawrence Rowley and Jack Waller were awarded Canadair certificates of invention and cash awards for their work in proposing the geometric arrangement of blade elements used in the CL-269. Canadair interest in wind turbines declined, however, and the CL-269 program office was disbanded.

Heavy Lift Aircraft—Aerocrane (CL-268)

In 1980, NRC asked Canadair to investigate the feasibility of a number of concepts for air vehicles capable of lifting very heavy loads such as huge logs from British Columbia forests. The concepts were basically controllable blimps consisting of a hybrid of a helium-filled bag, which provided most of the lift, and conventional wings or helicopter rotors which provided control and some additional lift. Phase I of the study, involving investigation of 24 different concepts and the selection of the seven most feasible, was conducted by an R&D team led by Art Jackes reporting to manager, advanced design and technology, Jeff Harwood, and director of R&D, Fred Phillips. This study favored the Cyclocrane, a product of an American company, Aerolift Inc.

The Cyclocrane was a form of blimp with four airfoil surfaces or "wings" projecting from around the centreline. A small turboprop engine was mounted at the end of each wing and the entire arrangement—blimp, wings and engines—rotated. The pilot and payload winch were carried in a suspended cupola held by cables attached from the blimp's nose and tail.

Phase II was intended to narrow the list of concepts to four. Phillips had retired and Roy Swanson had become director of R&D. Now Jackes' team concluded that none of the proposed concepts would work and instead suggested a concept of its own consisting of a cigar-shaped bag with a shaft running through its centre from nose to tail. Attached to each end of the shaft was an assembly of four wings in a cruciform arrangement like a waterwheel. Each wing had a span of 2.43 m (8 ft.), a chord of 0.9 m (3 ft.) and carried a small turboprop engine. The "waterwheels" rotated but the blimp did not. The pilot and winching apparatus were carried in a suspended cupola.

The findings of both studies were submitted to NRC which took no further action. Canadair, however, retained Phillips as a consultant for a year to maintain liaison with Aerolift Inc., which continued to develop the Cyclocrane and flew a prototype with a two-ton payload, but the company eventually ran out of funds and folded. Jackes was awarded a Canadair certificate of invention and a cash award for his design for airship buoyancy controls.

INVENTIONS/PATENTS

The Canadair Employee Inventions Plan has existed since 1955 to protect and reward patentable inventions or technical innovations conceived by employees. Under the plan, which was administered for many years by Tony Lebrun, employees whose inventions are accepted and patented by Canadair receive cash awards and certificates.

Recipients of Canadair Certificates of Invention:

Glen Adams	Blade angle scheduling mechanism
Saul Bernstein	Airborne mixing system (with Oakes & Richardson)
Garry Brooks	Noise reduction vacuum pad
J.J. André Brunel	Variable induced field compensator
	Automatic compensator
James E. Chatfield	Waste water treatment plant
Nat Eycken	Transportable control tower
Lawrence Gray	Skin welded joint (ICTS)
Marius Huvers	Gyroscopic North sensor device
	Stereoscopic viewer
	Suspension for gyroscopic viewer
	Yaw control system (CL-227)
Karl Irbitis	Gun blast deflector
	Propeller drive
	VTOL control mixing unit (CL-84)

Art Jackes	Airship buoyancy controls
	Propulsion and buoyancy control for an airship
Derek Jones	Flexible skirt for a ground effect machine (with A. Stone)
John P. Kerr	Unmanned airborne surveillance system (CL-89)
	Unmanned remotely piloted aircraft (CL–227)
Joseph Knap	Cant rail and cover combination (ICTS)
	Door closure and hanger system
	Passenger door system
	Sliding doors and seals system
William Kowal	Co-cured skin stiffeners system
Nick Kurdyla	Magnetometer
Paul Lamoureux	Composite fuel tank access door
Harold List	Railway truck
Harry Oakes	Airborne mixing system (with Bernstein & Richardson)
A. George Parker	Thrust reverser and noise suppressor (Challenger)
W. Ross Richardson	Airborne mixing system (with Bernstein and Oakes)
Lawrence P. Rowley	Blade construction for vertical axis windmill (with J. Waller)
Jorge Sobolewski	Pivotal connection (ICTS)
	Railway truck
	Suspension for LIM propulsion assembly
Alfred W. Stone	Flexible skirt for ground machine (with D. Jones)
Avo Sunne	Venous blood pressure recording device
Ian A. Thomas	Articulated joint assembly (CL-91)
Jason Waller	Blade construction for vertical axis windmill (with L. Rowley)
B.D.W. White	Method for measurement of crack propagation.

CANADAIR PLANTS

Plants 1, 2, & 4

When Canadair was formed it took over the 148,640-m² (1.6-million-sq.ft) former Canadian Vickers plant on Montée St. Laurent (later named Laurentian Boulevard, then Marcel Laurin Boulevard) in Saint-Laurent and designated it Plant 1. The main building was constructed in 1942 and 1943. Because of a wartime shortage of structural steel, it was built mainly of wood. In January 1946 Canadair leased and later purchased the former Noorduyn plant on the old Bois Franc Road. It became Plant 2.

In 1949, 200,000 sq. ft. was added to P1 as Building 103 at the south end of the main building, B102. The preflight hangar (B117); B114 and B115 on the east side of Montée St. Laurent and a tunnel under the highway linking B114 and B115 to P1, were added in 1952 and 53.

On March 1, 1950, with Canadair building the Sabre jet fighter,

a security classified program, Cartierville airfield was closed to the general public, except for access to the flying clubs. It remained closed, except for special events, until phased out of existence.

During the late 1940s and early 1950s, a shortage of office space at Cartierville forced Canadair to locate some activities in other Montreal sites. Certain engineering activities were located at the corner of Côte de Neiges and Queen Mary Road in the building that later became the Montreal Waxworks. Others were located in a former Safeway store on Côte de Neiges. Some sales and service personnel were located for a time in offices above the stores in the Norgate Shopping Centre in Saint-Laurent.

During the summer of 1952, Canadair took over the 39,020-m² (420,000-sq. ft.) former Canadian Car & Foundry plant at the corner of Montée St. Laurent and Bois Franc Road and this became Plant 4 (P3 was, at that time, a storage depot at Dorval).

At the end of 1959 and into 1960, Cartierville's main runway was extended from 1,935 m (6,350 ft.) to 2,682 m (8,800 ft.). This required Bois Franc Road to be diverted around the runway extension. Landing arrestor cables were installed in 1961 in preparation for CF-104 operations. In 1967, Cartierville was Canada's busiest airport but, on November 22,1968, it was closed to all flying except that of Canadair.

The short runway (R06/24) was grassed over in the mid-1970s after it had been mistaken for Dorval's R06/24 runway by pilots of BOAC, TCA, SAS, KLM and Air France transatlantic flights. Several aircraft actually landed at Cartierville; the pilots of others realized their error in time to overshoot and continue on to Dorval.

During the lean early 1970s, some of the P2 buildings were demolished and 65,030 m² (700,000 sq. ft.) of land, formerly occupied by the CERA sports field and a car park on the east side of Laurentian Boulevard, were sold for $23/m² ($2.15/sq. ft.). It became the site of Les Galeries Saint-Laurent.

Canadair had an arrangement with Transport Canada which allowed the use of Cartierville airport in return for $406,000 per year. Ownership of the airport was transferred from the Government of Canada to Bombardier as part of the sale of Canadair. At the time of the sale, Canadair owned 622,337 m² (6,699,000 sq. ft.) of land at Cartierville Airport. Canadair also owned 163,411 m² (1,759,000 sq. ft.) of vacant land (known as the "Cabbage Patch") adjacent to Dorval Airport. This was where the CL-44 assembly plant would have been built had the MATS program gone ahead. Considered unsuitable for aircraft manufacturing purposes, it was sold in 1982.

Following the opening of the new administrative building at Dorval in 1993 and the cessation of flying at Cartierville, land developers moved in and began to prepare the airport land for commercial development. Plants 2 and 4 and B114 and B115 on the east side of Marcel Laurin Boulevard were to be vacated in 1995 and the land used to build about 1000 homes. P1 was modernized between 1990 and 1995 as the Bombardier centre of excellence in aerospace machining for large aluminum components.

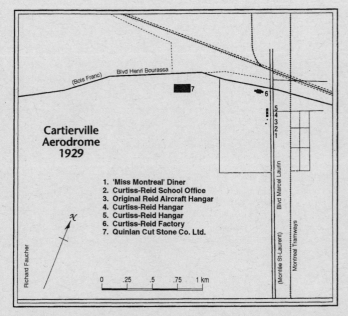

Cartierville Aerodrome 1929

1. 'Miss Montreal' Diner
2. Curtiss-Reid School Office
3. Original Reid Aircraft Hangar
4. Curtiss-Reid Hangar
5. Curtiss-Reid Hangar
6. Curtiss-Reid Factory
7. Quinlan Cut Stone Co. Ltd.

0   .25   .5   .75   1 km

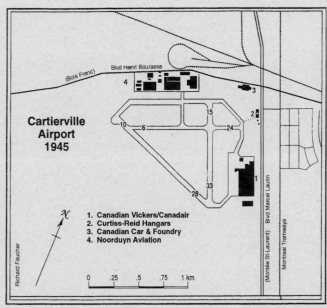

Cartierville Airport 1945

1. Canadian Vickers/Canadair
2. Curtiss-Reid Hangars
3. Canadian Car & Foundry
4. Noorduyn Aviation

0   .25   .5   .75   1 km

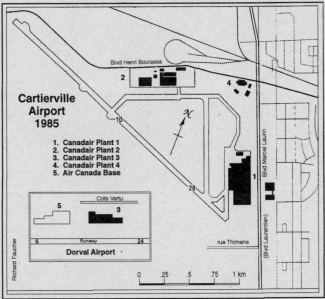

Cartierville Airport 1985

1. Canadair Plant 1
2. Canadair Plant 2
3. Canadair Plant 3
4. Canadair Plant 4
5. Air Canada Base

Cote Vertu

Runway

Dorval Airport

0   .25   .5   .75   1 km

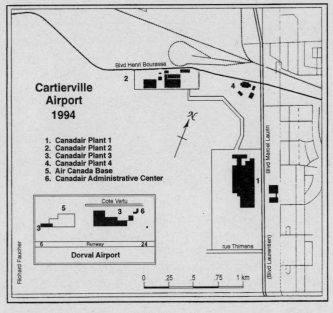

Cartierville Airport 1994

1. Canadair Plant 1
2. Canadair Plant 2
3. Canadair Plant 3
4. Canadair Plant 4
5. Air Canada Base
6. Canadair Administrative Center

Cote Vertu

Runway

Dorval Airport

0   .25   .5   .75   1 km

Plant 3

Construction of a new 28,870-m² (300,000-sq. ft.) plant at Dorval Airport began in October 1979 on land leased from the Government of Canada. Designated Plant 3, it initially housed CL-215 final assembly, and the Boeing 767 and McDonnell F/A-18 subcontracts. The first employees moved in on August 4,1980. A 3,530-m² (38,000-sq. ft.) plant extension and preflight hangar were added in 1988, bringing the covered area to 33,720 m² (363,000 sq. ft.). Challenger final assembly was transferred to P3 in the summer of 1989 and the first Challenger completed there rolled out in February 1990. A 950-m² (10,000-sq. ft.) mezzanine and a 3,200-m² (34,445-sq. ft.) warehouse were added later. In 1995 P3 housed all subassembly and final assembly for the Challenger, Regional Jet and CL-415 aircraft.

The lease of the land was to expire in 1999, however Bombardier retained the right to renew for a further 20 years. Bombardier also had the right of first refusal to lease a further 119,942 m² (1,291,090 sq. ft.) of adjacent land. It is on this land that the new Administrative building was erected.

The New Administrative Building

In March 1992, Bombardier announced that, as part of a five-year expansion and modernization program, a new administrative office building would be built at Dorval Airport. The $40-million, nine-storey, 38,340-m² (426,000-sq. ft.) building was completed on schedule and most of its 1,800 occupants moved in between early July and August 9,1993. They included those employees who had been housed in leased facilities on Cavendish Blvd. in Saint-

Laurent and in the Plexus building in Laval, Quebec. The new building was officially inaugurated on November 12,1993.

Mirabel
Plans to build a new plant at Mirabel Airport for the CF-18 System Engineering Support program and other military aircraft services, were announced on June 28, 1988. Construction of the 20,000-m² (200,000 sq. ft.) complex began on August 29,1988 and Military Aircraft Division personnel had moved in by May 21,1990. A 2,120-m² (22,826 sq. ft.) paint shop and paint stripping facility, a composite repair shop, and an engine test house were added in December 1992. In 1994, the paint facility was enlarged to 2,585 m² (27,826 sq. ft) and a 6,968-m² (75,000 -sq. ft.) storage hangar capable of storing 20 CF-18s was added.

THE UNIONS

Canadair's unionized employees are members of three lodges of the International Association of Machinists and Aerospace Workers. Shop workers are members of Lodge 712; security and fire prevention personnel are members of Lodge 2235; and cafeteria workers belong to Lodge 987. A small group of stationary enginemen are members of the Canadian Marine Officers Union. The total number of union members varied between approximately 8,000 in 1953 to a low of about 700 in 1975. In October 1994 the total stood at 4,100.

The relationship between the company and its unions has generally been excellent thanks to company negotiators like Bill Shuttleworth, Jacques Ouellet, Bernie Langlois and Gilles Landry, supported by Guy Baribeau, Bill Crowshaw, Guy Lapointe, Alec Wright, Gerry Verreault, Jacques Régimbald and many others. Also to Union business agent directors like Louis Laberge, Charlie Phillips, Normand Cherry, Jean Léo Côté and Claude Boisvert. Nevertheless, the accord was strained on a couple of occasions.

In October 1949 negotiations between the company and Lodge 712 were submitted to arbitration. Canadair refused the arbitration board award because it was "made on the basis of a meeting between the chairman of the arbitration board and the union representative at which no company representative was present. The company representative didn't know the meeting was being held; no draft copy of the award was issued to the company and the award falsely stated the position of the company representative."

Canadair president Oliver West told the board of directors that he felt the company's position was strong because Canadair's pay scale was the highest in the area. On that note, he addressed union members from the stand surrounding the partially-assembled C-5, advising them to forget about striking and get back to work. However, West was forced to back down when it came to light that Canadian Car & Foundry had just raised its pay scale above Canadair's.

The company experienced its first and only strike in 1965. It lasted from April 7 to June 7. The strike was marked, initially, by several unpleasant incidents involving damage to employee cars and harassment of employees attempting to enter the plant. Joey Wilkinson, then a foreman in production, recalls, however, that the strike was not all bad since supervisors and staff from engineering, planning and other departments were called upon to help out in production. This gave them a better insight into the workings of the production department.

Two union business agents achieved recognition in provincial labor relations: Louis Laberge, an early Lodge 712 business agent, went on to become a powerful force on the Quebec labor scene as president of the Quebec Federation of Labour. Normand Cherry, a Canadair employee for 36 years, spent 27 years as 712's business agent before being elected a Member of Quebec's National Assembly. Appointed Minister of Cultural Communities in the Liberal government of Robert Bourassa, he later became Minister of Labor and then Minister of Transport of Quebec. Other long-term union officers include Henry Bonani, Aldo Caluori, Mario Clermont, Charlemagne Desrochers, Serge Gariépy, Gilles Lacroix, Robert Lavoie, Maurice Litalien, René Michon, Michel Robichaud and Richard Rochon.

LANGUAGE POLICY

From its founding in 1944 until the early 1970s, Canadair management was predominantly English-speaking. Although French was widely used on the shop floor, company business was conducted almost exclusively in English. The federal government's efforts to promote bilingualism prompted a similar action at Canadair but it was not until the provincial government introduced its francization policy in 1977 that French was adopted as the normal and usual language in the workplace, for communications and business dealings.

A linguistics department was established in 1979 under manager Michelle Riopel and Canadair's francization program was officially approved in February 1981. A linguistics policy became part of Canadair's policy manual in 1989. Its objective was to promote French at all levels, acknowledging the language of the majority of the employees in manufacturing and resources who are covered by the francization program and taking into consideration the linguistic requirements of customers in and outside Quebec.

Canadair was divided into three groups: head office, engineering, and fabrication and human resources. The first two were covered by a special agreement allowing the use of languages other than French. While all groups were part of the francization process, it was especially aimed at the third group which included materiel, procurement, plant engineering, company services, human resources, assembly, manufacturing and preflight. New employees in these departments required a prescribed level of knowledge of French and English.

LONG-SERVICE EMPLOYEES

The following are Canadair employees with 45 or more years of service as of October 31, 1994:

Frank Reynolds	50 years
Joey Wilkinson	49
Saul Bernstein*	48
Claire Teasdale	48
Gerry Coleman	47
Henry Viger Jr. (Hank)	47

Jean-Paul Brazeau	46
Floyd Colligan	46
Roland Godin	46
Gilbert Ouellette	46
May Squires	46
Viateur Tessier*	46
Luc Bernier	45
J-P. Bouthillier	45
Roger Côté	45
Gaston Cyr	45
C. Desjardins	45
Dick Faucher	45
Robert Harris	45
Reg Hatter	45
Joseph Kokiw	45
Jim Murphy	45
Joe Pasquarelli	45
J.C. Thomson	45

* Still employed on October 31,1994

AWARDS

The following are awards received by Canadair employees:

1946: J. Geoffrey Notman: Order of the British Empire for services rendered during the Second World War.

1950: Peter H. Redpath: Royal Order of the Knight of the Danebrog (Norway) in appreciation of five years work as executive vice-president and vice-president, operations for the Scandinavian Airlines System

1962: W. Ken Ebel: McCurdy Award of the Canadian Aeronautics and Space Institute: the premier Canadian distinction in scientific and engineering fields of aeronautics and space.

1964: Edward H. Higgins: McCurdy Award

1970: Fredrick C. Phillips: McCurdy Award

1976: Richard L. Faucher: Canadian Plant Engineer of the Year Award of the American Institute of Plant Engineers

1979: Robert D. Richmond: C.D. Howe Award of the Canadian Aeronautics and Space Institute; awarded for achievement in the fields of planning, policy making and overall leadership in Canadian aeronautics or space activities.

1980: Harry Halton: ORT (Organization for Rehabilitation and Training) Centennial Medal for his outstanding contributions to aviation industry and training in Canada.

1981: Frederick R. Kearns: C.D. Howe Award

1981: F. Douglas Adkins: McKee Trans Canada Trophy of the Canadian Aeronautics and Space Institute: awarded for outstanding achievement in the field of air operations.

1981: Harry Halton: Gordon R. McGregor Memorial Trophy of the Royal Canadian Air Force Association: awarded in recognition of outstanding and meritorious achievement by Canadians in the field of air transportation.

1984: Alexander J. Lilly: Inducted into Canada's Aviation Hall of Fame.

1984: Harry Halton: Inducted into Canada's Aviation Hall of Fame.

1986: Michael B. Holliday: Medal of Bravery for rescuing the pilot of a crashed CL-215.

1989: Canadair: Government of Canada Export Award for outstanding achievement in global trade.

1994: Robert D. Richmond: Inducted into Canada's Aviation Hall of Fame.

PRESIDENTS OF CANADAIR

Benjamin W. Franklin	1944-46
H. Oliver West	1947-51
John J. Hopkins	1951-52
J. Geoffrey Notman	1952-65
Frederick R. Kearns	1965-83
Gilbert S. Bennett	1983-85
Pierre Des Marais II	1985-86
Donald C. Lowe	1986-90
Robert E. Brown	1990 to date

BOARD OF DIRECTORS

LIST OF CANADAIR BOARD CHAIRMEN

John J. Hopkins (GD)	1948-1957
Frank Pace Jr. (GD)	1957-1962
Roger Lewis (GD)	1962-1971
David Lewis (GD)	1971-1972
Gorden E. MacDonald (GD)	1972-1975
James M. Beggs (GD)	1975-1976
Leo Lavoie	1976-1981
Guy Desmarais	1981-1985
Pierre Des Marais II	1985-1986

BOARD OF DIRECTORS (as of Nov. 28, 1944)

This is the board of directors at the formation of the company:

Benjamin W. Franklin
John E.L. Duquet
Clayton F. Elderkin
Ralph G. Stopps
Walter H. Meacher

BOARD OF DIRECTORS (as of October 20, 1947)

This is the board shortly after the takeover by Electric Boat:

Douglas W. Ambridge, C.B.E.	Toronto
Sen. the Hon. G. Peter Campbell, K.C.	Toronto
J.P. Émile Collette	Montreal
Benjamin W. Franklin	Montreal
John Jay Hopkins (chairman)	New York
Joseph H. Himes (director, Electric Boat)	Washington
Henry M. Marx	New York
AVM Frank S. McGill, C.B.	Montreal
Otto Marx (director, Electric Boat)	New York
T. Rodgie McLagan, O.B.E.	Montreal
LCol W. Eric Phillips, C.B.E., D.S.O., M.C.	Toronto
AVM Adelard Raymond, C.B.E.	Montreal
Lawrence Y. Spear (chairman, Electric Boat)	Groton, Conn.
Henry R. Sutphen (director, Electric Boat)	New York
H. Oliver West (president)	Montreal

LIST OF CANADAIR DIRECTORS

Douglas W. Ambridge	1947-1962
Louis P. Beaubien	1960-1975 (as Advisory Director 1975-1976)
Gene K. Beare	1973-1976
James M. Beggs	1974-1976
Joel I. Bell	1983-1984
Gilbert S. Bennett	1983-1985
William P. Blundell	1984-1986
Micheline Bouchard	1985-1986
Jack L. Bowers	1969-1973
Thomas Murdoff Burns	1976-1976
G. Peter Campbell, KC and QC	1947-1964
Michael F.K. Carter	1985-1986
George W. Codrington	1951-1958
J.P. Émile Collette	1947-1963
Gordon Cowperthwaite	1984-1986
David M. Culver	1979-1984
Frank W. Davis	1963-1976
Bernard-M. Deschenes, QC	1976-1984
Guy J. Desmarais	1976-1985
Pierre Des Marais II	1984-1986
John A. Dundas	1963-1968
John E. L. Duquet, KC and QC	1944-1947, 1950-1979
Clayton F. Elderkin	1944-1945
Theodore J. Emmert	1948-1952
Ronald J. Farano, Q.C.	1985-1986
John P. Fisher	1982-1985
Claude Fontaine	1985-1986

Benjamin W. Franklin	1944-1948
Jean-Pierre Goyer, QC	1979-1985
Anthony Morris Guerin	1976-1981
W.P. Gullander	1962-1962
Milton E. Harris	1982-1985
M. Ogden Haskell	1945-1946
Joseph H. Himes	1947-1953
John Jay Hopkins	1946-1957
Earl D. Johnson	1955-1963
Edgar Kaiser	1984-1986
Frederick R. Kearns	1961-1983
Alexander S. Konigsberg	1985-1986
André Lachapelle	1985-1986
Guy Lavigueur	1976-1981
Léo Lavoie	1972-1984
Roger Lewis	1962-1972
Donald C. Lowe	1982-1985
J. Paul Marion	1982-1983
Henry M. Marx	1947-1971
Otto Marx	1947-1963
Gorden E. MacDonald	1971-1976
D.H. MacFarlane	1946-1947
AVM Frank S. McGill, C.B.	1947-1974 (as Advisory Director 1974-1976)
T. Rodgie McLagan, O.B.E.	1947-1972
Walter H. Meacher	1944-1946
Clifton M. Miller	1949-1968
Earle W. Mills	1951-1952
Roy T. Moore	1985-1986
J. Geoffrey Notman, O.B.E.	1950-1974
Frank Pace, Jr.	1953-1962

Hilliard W. Paige	1971-1973
John J. Pepper, QC	1979-1984
LCol W. Eric Phillips, C.B.E., D.S.O., M.C.	1947-1959
Charles I. Rathgeb, Jr.	1968-1986
AVM Adelard Raymond, C.B.E.	1947-1962
Dr. Gail Regan	1984-1985
Lawrence B. Richardson	1952-1960
Gordon R. Ritchie	1982-1982
O. Pomeroy Robinson, Jr.	1946-1947, 1954-1956
John A. Sargent	1964-1970
Guylaine Saucier	1984-1985
Thomas A. Scott	1947-1947
Leslie E. Simon	1956-1963
C. Roy Slemon	1964-1976
David D. Smith	1985-1986
Lawrence Y. Spear	1947-1949
Oliver Gerald Stoner	1976-1976
Ralph G. Stopps	1944-1946
John P. Sullivan	1981-1985
Henry R. Sutphen	1947-1950
William R. Teschke	1981-1982
Peter Morrow Troop, QC	1976-1976
Frederic Campbell Wallace	1959-1974 (as Advisory Director 1974-1976)
Walter G. Ward	1976-1982
Donald Watson	1976-1981
H. Oliver West	1947-1950
Robert H. Winters	1964-1966, 1968-1969

BOARD OF DIRECTORS OF BOMBARDIER INC. (as of December 14, 1994)

Philippe de Gaspé Beaubien
Chairman and Chief Executive Officer, Télémédia Corporation

Laurent Beaudoin, C.C., FCA
Chairman and Chief Executive Officer, Bombardier Inc.

J.R. André Bombardier
Vice-Chairman, Bombardier Inc.

Janine Bombardier
President and Governor, J. Armand Bombardier Foundation

Pierre Côté, C.M.
Chairman, Celanese Canada Inc.

André Desmarais
President and Chief Operating Officer, Power Corporation of Canada

Jean-Louis Fontaine
Vice-Chairman, Bombardier Inc.

Hon. Jean-Pierre Goyer, P.C., Q.C.
Lawyer and Corporate Director

Pierre Legrand, Q.C.
Senior Partner, Ogilvy Renault

Hon. Peter Lougheed, P.C., C.C., Q.C.
Senior Partner, Bennett Jones Verchere

Donald C. Lowe
Chairman, Sedgwick James, Inc.

Raymond Royer, O.C., FCA
President and Chief Operating Officer, Bombardier Inc.

J. Michael G. Scott
President, JM Scott Investments Inc.

William I.M. Turner, Jr., C.M.
Chairman and Chief Executive Officer, Exsultate Inc.

Hugo Uyterhoeven
Timken Professor of Business Administration, Graduate School of Business Administration, Harvard University

CANADAIR

circa 1952

1944

circa 1977

1986

1989

INDEX

DANIEL MARQUIS • FRANCIS MARQUIS • ALBERT MARRAS • CIPRIANO MARRAS • ANTONIO MARRICCO • LEOPOLD MARRIOTT • SERGIO MARRONE • GIUSEPPE MARSALA • STEPHANE MARSOLAIS • JOSEE MARTEL • ROBERT MARTEL • SYLVAIN MARTEL • REINE MARTEL • NORMAND MARTEL • JACQUES MARTEL • Y
YVON MARTEL • YVAN MARTEL • YVON MARTEL • ALAIN MARTEL • NICOLE MARTEL • LISE MARTEL • CLAUDE MARTEL • ANGELO MARTELLINO • FRANCOIS MARTIN • HELENE MARTIN • DANIEL MARTIN • ANDRE MARTIN • WESLEY MARTIN • RICHARD MARTIN • BRUNO MARTIN •
PHILIP JOHN MARTIN • JEAN MARTIN • PATRICK MARTIN • JEAN MARTIN • STEPHANE MARTIN • CHANTAL MARTIN • RAYNALD MARTIN • JEAN MARTIN • BRIGITTE MARTIN • GENEVIEVE MARTIN • LEOPOLD MARTIN • PIERRE MARTINEAU • JEAN PIERRE MARTINEAU • JACQUES MARTINEAU • DOMINIC MARTINEAU • ROSAIRE MARTINEAU • FRANC
MARCEL MARTONNE • FERNAND MARTINEAU • JEAN GUY MARTINEAU • DENIS MARTINEAU • SYLVIE MARTINEAU • YVES MARTINEAU • SYLVAIN MARTINET • JEAN MARTINEZ • PILAR MARTINEZ • MARIO CASTRO MARTINEZ • MICHEL MARTINEZ • JEAN MARTINEZ • JAIME MARTINS • LUIS MARTINS • ABILIO MARTINS • ISTVAN MARTON • FRA
TAOUFIK MARZOUGUI • GINO MASCOLO • JOHN MASON • GHYSLAINE MASSE • LOUISE MASSE • DANIEL MASSE • MARIO MASSE • GERALD MASSE • JEAN YVES MASSE • PIERRE MASSE • LUC MASSE • SERGE MASSE • JOHN LAWRENC MASSEY • SYLVAIN MASSICOTTE • GUILLAUME MASSICOTTE • JACQUES MASSON • PIERRE MASSON • PIE
MICHAEL MASTROGUISEPPI • MARIA MASTROMONACO • ROBERTO MASTROPIETRO • DOLORES MASTROSTEFANO • VICTORIANO MATE • LARRY MATEAU • GEORGE MATHEW • NATHALIE MATHIEU • DANIEL MATHIEU • MICHEL MATHIEU • RAYMOND MATHIEU • JEAN MATHIEU • GILLES MATHIEU • RAYMOND MATHIEU • NAVEEN MATHUR • MARY
DANIEL MATTE • JEAN MATTE • MARCEL MATTE • CHRISTIAN MATTEAU • ROBERT MATTEAU • JEAN MATTEAU • DAVID MATTEAU • TODD MATTHEWS • FILIPPO MATTIOLI • MAURO MAULA • PHILIP MAUNDER • ERIC MAURA • LOUIS MAURAIS • RONALD MAURICE • LAURENT MAURICE • DARIUS MAVALWALA • FOTIOS MAVRIPLIS • D
RAYMOND MAYER • THOMAS MAYER • PIERRE MAYER • ERIC MAYNARD • DANIEL MAYNARD • JEAN FRANCOI MAYOR • PIERRE YVES MAYOR • JEAN LOUIS MAZEROLLE • BRENDA MAZEROLLE • PETER MAZIAR • JIM MAZZONI • MARCO MAZZONI • DANIEL MC CAUGHEY • COLIN MC FARLANE • JOHN MC GOW • DANIEL MCALEAR • LOU
DONALD MCARTHUR • HEATHER MCARTHUR • DEAN MCBRIDE • BLAINE MCCARTHY • JEAN MCCARTHY • KEVIN MCCARTNEY • BILL MCCLEERY • ARTHUR MCCLEMENTS • DAVE MCCOMB • NORMAND MCCORMICK • MARK MCCORMICK • JAMES MCCOY • EMMETT MCCOY • JAMES MCCULLOGH • DAVID MCDUFF • CATHERINE MCENTEE • ROG
LAWRENCE MCFADZEN • DAVID MCFARLANE • ANDREW MCGARRELL • BARRY MCGILL • CHARLES MCGIVERN • JEAN MCGRAW • RICKY MCHARG • LOUISE MCINNES • MICHAEL MCINTYRE • JIM DAVID MCINTYRE • RAYMOND MCKAY • DAVID MCKEE • DIANE MCKENNA • FRANCIS MCKENVEN • KEITH MCKIBBEN • GARY
MICHAEL MCKINNON • MICHAEL MCKINNON • MELVIN MCLAUGHLIN • HAROLD MCLEAN • KEVEN MCLELLAN • DONALD MCLEOD • TIMOTHY MCNAMARA • KELLY ANN MCNAMARA • DONALD MCNICOLL • RICHARD GREG MCQUAID • STEVE MCWALTER • GILBERTO MEDEIROS • SUSANA MEDEIROS • ROBERTO MEI • ALAN MEINDERSMAN • BENC
JOACHIM MEISTER • SYLVAIN MELANCON • MARCEL MELAVEN • HENRYK MELCER • JUNE MELDRUM • EDUARDO MELO • LUIS MELO • ANDRE MELOCHE • LOUISE MELOCHE • GILLES MELOCHE • CHRISTIAN MELOCHE • ROBERT MELOCHE • JEAN MARC MELOCHE • JEAN MENARD • SYLVAIN MENARD • DANIEL MENARD • MARTIN MENARD • AN
LUC MENARD • JEAN LUC MENARD • MICHEL MENARD • LUC MENARD • MARC MENARD • LUC MENARD • STEPHANE MENARD • RENE MENARD • CLAUDE MENARD • ELISABETH MENARD • ZEFERINO MENDES • CARMINE MENDICINO • REY MENDOZA • DOMINIQUE MERCEUS • GILLES MERCIER • GERALD MERCIER • BRUNO MERCIER • AN
GINETTE MERCIER • CHANTAL MERCIER • JEAN CLAUDE MERCIER • ROSA MERCURI • JEAN CLAUDE MEREL • ZOUBIR MERKHI • ISAAC MESSALEM • DIANE MESSIER • LEAC MESSIER • MARCET METHOT • ANDRE METHOT • DENIS METHOT • MICHEL METHOT • PIERRE METIVIER • ANDRE METIVIER • DORIC METIVIER • CLAUDE MEUNIER • AN
ALAIN MEUNIER • JACQUES MEUNIER • SERGE MEUNIER • JACQUES MEUNIER • THOMAS MEUNIER • GILLES MEUNIER • DOMINIQUE MEZZANGO • EMANUELA MEZZAGNO POTVIN • CARMEN MIC • CONSTANTINE MICHAEL • JOANNE MICHAEL • ERICK MICHAUD • RICHARD MICHAUD • ALAIN MICHAUD • MARIO MICHAUD • YVON MICHAUD • CAR
HENRI PAUL MICHAUD • BERNARD MICHAUD • ANDRE MICHAUD • ERIC MICHAUD • JEAN PIERRE MICHAUD • FRANCESCO MICHETTI • IRENE MICHON • DIMITRIOS MICHOS • MARIO MIGNACCA • CHARLES MIGNAULT • VICTORIC MIGNEAULT • NUNO MIGUEL • CONSTANTIN MIHAI • SLOBODAN
VOJKO MIHAJLEVIC • ZVONIMIR MIHAJLI • HENRY MILCZEWSKI • MILENKO MILEKIC • DAVID MILES • LISE MILETTE • MARIAN MILEWSKI • NADA MILJKOVIC • TERRY MILLER • ALFRED KEITH MILLER • RONALD MILLER • STEEVE MILLER • YVES LOUIS MILLER • GUY MILLET • LEO MILLETTE • MARCEL MILLIARD • BRIAN MILLS • JOHN MILLS •
MARSHALL MILLS • MICHEL MILORD • KENNETH MINCHAU • DALE MINCHINTON • PATRICK MINOGUE • MARIO MINUCCI • FRANCIS MINVILLE • FERNANDO MIRANDA • MARZIALE MIRANDI • ROBERT MIREAULT • MANON MIRON • ANNE MIRONDETTE • VITO MISURACA • IAN MITCHELL • MICHAEL MITCHELL • JEAN MITKO • SIMON MIVILLE •
GLENN MOCKLER • MICHEL MODERIE • LUC MODERIE • SERGE MOFFAT • CHANTAL MOFFET • MAMDOUH MOHAMED • RENOCAR MOHAMMED • JAMES ROBERT MOINARD • MARYSE MOINEAU • LUC MOISAN • SERGE MOISAN • ROBERT MOISAN • SYLVIE MOISAN • JEAN CLAUDE MOIZARD • FARZAD MOKHTARIAN • DAVID MOLLOY • SUZA
ROBERT MOMBLEAU • MIKAEL MONCHAMP • NATHALIE MONETTE • PIERRE MONETTE • FRANCOIS MONGRAIN • DANIEL MONGRAIN • KEITH MONK • MANUEL MONTECATINE RODRIGUEZ • FREDERIC MONTEIL • MARYSE MONTEMAGNO • AUGUSTIN MONTERO • VINICIO MONTESI • DANIEL MONTFILS • IAN MONTGOMERIE • MARC MONTMARQUET • F
RENE MONTMINY • DANIEL MONTOUR • STEPHANE MONTOUR • JEAN ROBERT MONTPETIT • MARC ROBERT MONTPETIT • LORI MONTPETIT • GUY MONTPETIT • ROBERT MONTPLAISIR • MARIE FRANCE MONTY • IAN MOODY • WILLIAM MOODY • EDDISON MOORE • WILTON MOORE • JOSE MANUEL MORA VARGAS • PIERRE MORACHE • FA
JAMES MORAN • JOHN RICHARD MORAN • ANGELIE MORARESH • LISE MORARESH • ROBERT MORASSE • IRENE MORE • ALAIN MOREAU • FRANCOIS MOREAU • MARC MOREAU • JEAN CLAUDE MOREL • JERRY MOREL • JOSEPH MOREL • SERGE MOREL • RICHARD MOREL • PATRICK MORENCY • MARC MORENCY • SYLVAIN MORENCY • LAUR
JEAN PAUL MORENCY • DOMINIQUE MORENCY • RAYMOND MORENCY • MARIO MORETTI • LYNDA MORGAN-MARRONE • PIERRE MORIN • GUY MORIN • LORRAINE MORIN • GILLES MORIN • GILBERT MORIN • PIERRE YVES MORIN • ANDRE MORIN • BRUNO MORIN • CLAUDE MORIN • GHISLAIN MORIN • KENNETH MORIN • ANDRE MORIN •
STEPHAN MORIN • JULES MORIN • JEAN MORIN • ROCK MORIN • REGINE MORIN • CLAUDE MORIN • DANIEL MORIN • LOUIS MORIN • JOCELYN MORIN • SYLVAIN MORIN • CLAUDE MORIN • GUY MORIN • JEAN PHILIPP MORIN • CLAUDE MORIN • NICOLAS MORIN • FRANCINE MORIN • DENIS PAUL MORISSET • REJEAN
PIERRE MORISSETTE • ANDRE MORISSETTE • GUYLAINE MORISSETTE • DANIEL MORISSETTE • PHILIPE MORNEAU • LUC MORNEAU • FRANCO MOROSO • ALAN MORRISON • RAYMONDE MORRISSETTE • NORMAND MORRITT • JOHN MORYAS • NICOLE MOSCATO • ARTHUR MOSES • NABIL MOUNAYER • CARO
HENRY GEORGE MUNN • CATHERINE MUNRO • LYALL JESSE MUNRO • JOSEF MUNTIGL • DIANE MURDOCK • MARTIN MURPHY • JOHN MURPHY • MICHAEL MURPHY • THOMAS MURPHY • LAURA MURRAY • PIERRE MURRAY • BENOIT MURRAY • SLAWOMIR MUSIAL • CAROL MUSTILL • ESTHER MVENG • NICHOLAS MYJ
PIERRE MYRE • DAGFINN MYRVANG • YOUSSEF NACEF • LUDVIK NACHLINGER • CHARLES NADEAU • GAETAN NADEAU • JULES NADEAU • JACQUES NADEAU • GUY NADEAU • RAYMOND NADEAU • MARTIN NADEAU • ROSAIRE NADEAU • DIANE NADON • ALAIN NADON • JESSE NADON • ANDRE NADON • DANIEL NADON • MOHAMED NAGI •
JOHN NAGY • MICHEL NAIL • ALI NAILI • VENUGOPALAN NAIR • ANDRE NAKASHIMA • ROCCO NALLI • JEAN FRANCOI NANTEL • DENIS NANTEL • JEAN MARC NANTEL • ROCCO NAPOLETANO • ALAIN NAREAU • TERRENCE NASH • SAMY NASRY • NIKOLAY NATCHEV • GILLES NAULT • BARTHOLOMEW NAVARRO • GERALDINE NAZARETH • NA
VIJAY NEHRA • ANGIE NELLIS • ELIO NERI • MARISA NERO • GISELE NERON • RAYMOND NEW • ALICE NEW CAMPBELL • PHILIP NEWMAN • MOE NEWMAN • CHEONG PAK NG • CHUI-CHU NG • CHEONG FAT NG • CAROLE NG WONG • PAULINE NGHIEM • WEI HSIUNG NGO • TUYET PHUONG NGUYEN • THANH XUAN NGUYEN • HUU LUONG NGUYEN •
KIM LOAN NGUYEN • VAN NHUT NGUYEN • VAN HOANG NGUYEN • PHUC-LOC NGUYEN • TUYET ANH NGUYEN • TANG MY HANH NGUYEN • THANH SON NGUYEN • HONG PHUC NGUYEN • HUU NGUYEN • XUAN KHANH NGUYEN LE • TRIET NGUYEN QUANG • CATHY NGUYEN QUOC • NGHIA NGUYEN TRONG • SPILIOS NICOLOPOULOS • W
THEODORE NIKOLOPOULOS • GITA NISEL • LORENZO NITTOLO • KENNETH NIXON • GARY NIXON • DOROTHY NIXON • COLIN NIXON • ROBERT NIXON • FRANK NIXON • MYLENE NOCITI • CLAUDE NOEL • ROBERT NOEL • ANDRE NOEL • MARCEL NOEL • DENIS NOEL • GORDON NOEL • NORMAND NOEL • ROBERT NOISEUX • MARIO NOLET •
SYLVIE NOLIN • ALAIN NOLIN • CLAUDE HERGET NORMAND • PASCALE NORMANDEAU • JEAN GUY NORMANDEAU • DANIEL NORMANDIN • GLEN GORDON NORRIS • TERRENCE NORRIS • ROBERT NORRISH • MARTIN NORTHRUP • JANICE NORTON O'NEIL • PASCAL NOURI • AZIZ NOURY • AUREL NOVAC • NADSIKA NOVE • PET
PHILLIP NOWER • JACK NUDEL • LENITA NUNES • THOMAS O'BRIEN • GUY O'BRIEN • ROBERT O'BRIEN • KEITH O'BRIEN • BRIAN O'CONNELL • DANIEL O'DONNELL • PATRICK O'DONNELL • GARY O'DONNELL • ROBERT O'HARA • MICHAEL O'NEIL • TOM O'NEIL • MICHAEL O'NEIL • DIARMUID O'NEIL • CHRISTOPHER O'NEILL • MOIRA O'REILLY • N
ROGER O'SHAUGHNESSEY • SYLVIA OBERNDORFINGER • ANDREW OBERTI • PETER OGDEN • MARCO OHAYON • WAYNE OLDFORD • RICHARD OLENDER • JOSE OLIVEIRA • FERNANDO OLIVEIRA DE SOUSA • PAUL OLIVER • DANIEL OLIVIER • ARNETTE OLLIVIERRE • AUGUSTINUS OLSTHOORN • ANN ONDRECHAK • EMIL
DOMENICO ONORATI • DAVE ORCUTT • JESUS JR ORDEN • JESUS ORDEN • JOHN ORDILLAS • ANDRAS ORDOGH • STEPHEN ORE • WILLIAM OROZCO • GARY ORR • SANDRA ORR • BRUCE ORR • STEPHEN ORR • DANIEL ORSINI • ANDY ORTAASLAN • JEAN CLAUDE OSSE • BOGUSLAW OSTROWICZ • JACK PETER OSTROWICZ • CHRIS
STEPHANE OTIS • REAL OUELLET • DANY OUELLET • JACQUES OUELLET • RAYMOND OUELLET • CHANTALE OUELLET • ERICK OUELLET • MARY OUELLET • MARTIN OUELLETTE • JEAN GUY OUELLET • FRANCIS OUELLET • NORMY OUELLET • YVON OUELLETTE • SYLVAIN OUELLETTE • ROGER OUELLETTE • SERGE OUELLETTE •
GILLES OUELLETTE • MARC OUELLETTE • CHRISTIAN OUELLETTE • NORMAND OUELLETTE • BENOIT OUELLETTE • YVON OUELLET • MICHEL OUELLETTE • MARTIN OUELLETTE • PIERRE OUELLETTE • MICHEL OUELLETTE • GERARD OUELLETTE • RONALD OUELLETTE • MARC OUELLETTE • CHANTAL OUELLETTE • RAYMOND OUIMET •
SAVATH OUNNARATH • KENNETH OVERBURY • DIOGA OVIEDO • JOHN OWCHAR • GARY OWENS • JAMES OYAMA • PIERO PACE • HERMOGENES PACULAN • JEAN PAGE • ROBERT PAGE • CLEMENT PAGE • SIMON PIERRE PAGE • ERIC PAGE CHAVARIE • PATRICK PAGEAU • PETER PAGLIAVULJ • P
ERIC PAIEMENT • PIERRE ANDRE PAIEMENT • YVON PAIEMENT • RAYMONDE PAIEMENT • DENIS PAIEMENT • NATHALIE PAILLE • LISETTE PAINCHAUD • DANIEL PAINCHAUD • SYLVAIN PAINCHAUD • CYRILLE PAINCHAUD • STEVEN PETER PAK • CHITTA PAL • JOHN PALAMAR • ARA PALANDJIAN • FRANCESCO PALAZZESE • MICHAEL PALERMO • S
• MARY PALINKAS • JOHN JR PALKA • DAVID PALLADINI • JOSEPH PALMORINO • TERESA PALUMBO • MONIQUE PAMPEL • PETRU PANAITE • MIHAI PANAITE • MICHAEL PANASSIK • ANDRE PANASSENKO • NGUON THAY PANG • NIKOLA PANIC • UGO PANICONI • MARC PANNETON • TERRY PANOPALIS • BRUCE PANTON • JOSEPH PANTON • G
KOSMAS PAPACONSTANTINOU • PETER PAPADATOS • SYLVAIN PAPILLON • LOUIS PHILIP PAPIN • JEAN GUY PAPIN • CLAUDE PAPIN • ANDRE PAPINEAU • MARCO PAPINI • DIANE PAQUET • MARIE FRANCE PAQUET • RENALD PAQUET • MICHEL PAQUETTE • SYLVAIN PAQUETTE • NORMAN PAQUETTE • DANIEL PAQUETTE • LYNE PAQUETTE • MICHE
ALAIN PAQUETTE • SYLVAIN PAQUETTE • STEPHANE PAQUETTE • JEAN PAQUETTE • GUY PAQUETTE • CLAUDE PAQUETTE • GILBERT PAQUETTE • PIERRE PAQUETTE • MARCEL PAQUETTE • BENOIT PAQUETTE • GINETTE PAQUETTE • RICHARD PAQUETTE • JACQUES PAQUETTE • MICHEL PAQUETTE • REJEAN PAQUETTE • JAMI
ANDRE PAQUETTE • PIERRE PAQUETTE • WILLIAM PAQUIN • ALAIN PAQUIN • SERGE PAQUIN • FRANCOIS PAQUIN • JOSEE PAQUIN • ARMAND PAQUIN • JEAN GUY PAQUIN • BENOIT PARADIS • MARIO PARADIS • MARIE CHRIST PARADIS • MARTIN PARADIS • RICHARD PARADIS • LUC PARADIS • ERIC PARADIS •
• DIANE PARADIS • YVAN PARADIS • SYLVAIN PARANT • DANIL PARASCHIVOIU • HENRY PARDIAK • EDUARDO PARDO • VICTOR PARE • STEPHANE PARE • NICOLE PARE JACQUES • MARC PARENT • CLAUDETTE PARENT • CONRAD PARENT • JACQUES PARENT • YVES PARENT • PIERROT PARENT • MICHEL PARENT • MARC PARENT • NATH
CHRISTIAN PARENTEAU • MARTIN PARINO • CAROLINE PARIS • GHISLAIN PARISE • RICHARD PARISELLA • MICHEL PARISELLA • DENYSE PARISIEN • CAROL PARKE • JEAN CLAUDE PARKER • TINA PARKER • FRANK PARODO • PAUL PARODY • MARIO PARRA • BRIAN PARRACK • MICHEL PARSLOW • PATRICIA PARSONS • JEAN PARTISAN • FRA
JOSE PASCUAL • PIERRE PASQUARELLI • JEAN-PIERRE PASQUARELLI • JAGDISH PATEL • PARSOT PATEL • AMRITLAL PATEL • JITENDRA PATEL • JEAN PATENAUDE • HENRI PATENAUDE • BRYAN PATERSON • THOMAS PATERSON • JEAN PATRIE • GILLES PATRY • RICHARD PATRY • SHIRLEY PATRY • ANTHONY PATTINSON • FRANCE
SYLVAIN PAUL • REJEAN PAUL • STANLEY PAUL • RACHEL PAUL • JEAN PAUL HUS • FREDERIC PAUL HUS • ROLAND PAUZE • ANTONIO PAVONE • SYLVAIN PAYANT • LOUIS PAYANT • ROBERT PAYETTE • PAUL PAYETTE • RICHARD PAYETTE • ROGER PEARSON • JEFFREY PEDERSEN • JOSE PEDRO • GUY PELCHAT • DANIEL PELCHAT • M
CHRISTIAN PELCHAT • JACQUES PELCHAT • MARIA CARMEN PELETEIRO • PAOLO PELLE • GILLES PELLERIN • MARC PELLERIN • GISELE PELLERIN • ERIC PELLERIN • YVES PELLERIN • STEPHANE PELLETIER • DANIEL PELLETIER • PAUL PELLETIER • CHRISTIAN PELLETIER • MARIE PELLETIER • FRANCOIS PELLETIER • GEORGE
SYLVAIN PELLETIER • NORMAND PELLETIER • SYLVAIN PELLETIER • GAETAN PELLETIER • MICHEL PELLETIER • FRANCOIS PELLETIER • JEAN SEBASTI PELLETIER • CHRISTIAN PELLETIER • JACQUES PELLETIER • JEAN YVES PELLETIER • JEAN PELLETIER • MARC ANDRE PELLETIER • JEAN GUY PELLETIER • JEAN RENE PELLETIER •
NORMAND PELLETIER • FRANCOIS PELLETIER • GILLES PELLETIER • STEPHANE PELLETIER • LOUISA PELLICCIA • DAVID PELLING • DEREK PELLING • JACQUES PELOQUIN • MARTIN PELOQUIN • ROBERT PELTZER • GINETTE PELUSO • FRANCOIS PENAULT • GLORIA PENFOLD • DON PENNELL • FRANCOIS PEPIN • SERGE PEPIN • PIERRE PEPIN •
• DANIEL PEPIN • FRANCOIS PEPIN • LINDA PEPIN-INGRAM • MANUEL PEREIRA • NEANDO PERESA • CARLOS PEREYRA • ALAIN PERIARD • MARIETTE PERIGNY • JOHN PERKINS • JOE PERNA • RAPHAEL PERNA • LUC PERRAS • MICHEL PERRAS • ALAIN PERREAULT • MARC PERREAULT • RENE PERREAULT • DANIEL PERREAULT • PIERR
PHILIPPE PERREAULT • JEAN PERREAULT • YVON PERREAULT • ERIC PERREAULT • ALAIN PERREAULT • DANY PERREAULT • CLAUDE PERREAULT • JEAN REAULT • REJEAN PERREAULT • MARCO PERRELLA • DANIEL PERRON • SERGE PERRON • JEAN-CLAUDE PERRON • SYLVIE PERRON • YVES PERRON • SYLVAIN PERRON • MA
CLAUDE PERRON • CARL PERRY • MARIE PESCE • CLAUDE PESANT • JOAN PETERS • MARK PETERS • LISETTE PETERSON • RICHARD PETIT • NORMAND PETIT • MICHEL PETIT • PATRICK PETITPAS • CLAUDE JR PETROFF • BRANKO PETROVIC • LJUBKO PETROVIC • KARL PETRUCH • XUAN HUNG PHAM • VIET BANG PHAM • THANH PHAM • C
PHONG NHA PHAM • DANG LONG PHAM • CHI-TAM PHAM • THE-HAU PHAM • LIEM PHAM • DOMINIQUE PHANEUF • FRANCOIS PHARAND • ROBERT PHENIX • SERGE PHENIX • JEAN PHENIX • GILLES PHILIBERT • PAUL PHILIBERT • JOHN PHILLIPS • STEPHEN PHILLIPS • VINH THAI PHUNG • SEBASTIANO PIANCIAMORE •
ALBERT PICARD • MICHELINE PICARD • ANDRE PICARD • LUC PICARD • ISABELLE PICARD • SERGE PICARD • ROLAND PICARD • STEPHANE PICARD • YVES PICHE • ALAIN PICHE • CAROLE PICHE • STEPHANE PICHE • CLAUDE ANDRE PICHE • LUC PICHE • STAN PICKERING • JOHANNE PIECKEN • DANIEL PIERCE • JEAN PI
JOHN PIGGOTT • THOM PILGRIM • ANNIE PILLA • MICHEL PILLIERE • GAETAN PILON • MICHEL PILON • STEPHANE PILON • YVES PILON • JEAN CLAUDE PILON • ROBERT PILON • LOYOLA PILOTTE • SYLVAIN PINARD • ROGER PINARD • BENOIT PINARD • GARY PINE • MARC PINEAU • GILLES PINEAULT • JEAN LUC PINEAULT • MARC PINEL •
ANDRE PINET • YVON PINHEIRO • CATENA PINO • PIERRE PION • PASQUALE PIPERNI • ANTONIETTA PIPERNI • OTTAVIO PIRAS • VINCENZA PIRRO • JOHN PIRSCH • GIULIA PISARZEWSKI • VITO PISCIOTTA • MARIO PITRE • GILBAIN PITRE • JEAN PIERRE PIVETEAU • ARMAND PLAISANCE • MICHEL PLAMONDON • SYLVAIN PLANTE • F
• DALE PLANTE • JEAN PIERRE PLANTE • ROBERT PLANTE • CHRISTIAN PLANTE • REJEAN PLANTE • MICHEL PLANTE • SEBASTIEN PLANTE • RICHARD PLANTE • PAUL PLANTE • DIANE PLANTE BRODIE • VIOLINE PLANTE NADEAU • BETTY PLANTIN • ALEXIS PLATONOW • TED PLISZEWSKI • YVON PLOUFFE • MARC ANDRE PLOUFFE • SERGE P
FRANCOI PLOUFFE • LOUISE PLOUFFE PASSARELLI • RINO PLOURDE • GUY PLOURDE • CARL POIRE • JEAN LOUIS POIRIER • ANDRE POIRIER • MARC POIRIER • LYNN POIRIER • MICHEL POIRIER • NELSON POIRIER • DANNY POIRIER • DANIEL POIRIER • ROGER POIRIER • ROGER POIRIER • ROLLANDE POIRIER • N
PATRIC POIRIER • GEORGES POIRIER • SERGE POIRIER • STEPHANE POIRIER • DANIEL POIRIER • JOCELYN POISSANT • MICHEL POISSANT • MANON POISSANT • ROBERT POISSANT • CAROLE POITRAS • LOUIS POITRAS • DANIEL POITRAS • STEPHANE POITRAS • DENIS POITRAS • BERNARD POLACK • HAGOP-JACK POLADIAN • MAUREEN P
• DENIS POLIQUIN • DANIEL POLIQUIN • WALTER POLUCHOWICZ • CHRIS POLYKANDRIOTIS • MARIE POMERLEAU • ALYSON POND • MICHEL PONTBRIAND • JEAN FRANCOI PONTON • MAURICE PONTON • HALINA POPIELARZ • VALENTIN POPP • LOUIS POPLIER • SAVERIO PORTARI • DIDIER PORTELA • DANIEL PORTELA • JASON POSPISIL • FER
• MARIA POTH • FRANCOIS POTHIER • MICHELINE POTHIER • FABIEN POTHIER • ROBERT POTHIER • DENIS POTHIER • LORRAINE POTVIN • RENE POTVIN • JOCELYN POTVIN • STEPHAN POTVIN • LYNE POTVIN • SYLVAIN POUDRIER • NICOLE POUDRIER • LAURIAN POULETTE • DANIEL POULIN • ERIC POULIN • SYLVAIN POULIN • C
• DANIEL POULIN • MARTIAL POULIN • ANDRE POULIN • SUZANNE POULIOT • BERTRAND POULIOT • CLAUDE POULIOT • KENNETH POWELL • ARTHUR POWELL • MONIQUE POWELL • KEVIN POWER • BERNARD POWNALL • FILIPPO POZZOLO • ALBERT PRADERES • NIDHI PRASHAR • CORINA PREDOIU • NICOLE PREFONTAINE • JEAN PREGENT • TH
UMBERTO PREGNOLATO • ANDRE PRENOVOST • FRANE PRESCOTT • MARIO PRESSEAULT • MARC PREVOST • YVON PREVILLE • JULIE PREVOST • VIOLET PREVOST • ANDRE PREVOST • ROBERT PREVOST • JOCELYNE PREVOST • MARC PREVOST • FRANCE PREVOST • ALAIN PREVOST • YVES PREVOST • JACQ
DEAN PRICE • NORMAN PRICE • BRENDA PRICE • GARTH PRIEST • MICHEL PRIEUR • LUC PRIEUR • MARC ANDRE PRIEUR • BRENT PRIEUR • JOHN PRIEUR • BENOIT PRIEUR • MICHEL PRIMEAU • BENOIT PRIMEAU • ERIC PRIMEAU • GILBERT PRIMEAU • ERIC PRIMEAU • DOMENIC PRIMIANI • CHRISTIAN PRINCE • JEAN PRINCE • C
CARMELINA PRIOLETTA • ROY PRITCHARD • PHILIP PRITCHARD • CLAUDE PRIVE • VINCENZO PROCOPIO • LILIANE PROLON • LOUISE PRONOVOST • DOMINIQUE PRONOVOST • RONALD PRONOVOST • RACHEL PRONOVOST • ROGER PRONOVOST • CHANTAL PRONOVOST • CLAUDE PRONOVOST • JOCELYN PRONOVOST • NICOLE PROTEAU • J
• FRANCOIS PROULX • NICOLE PROULX • SYLVAIN PROULX • RICHARD PROULX • DANIEL PROULX • JASMIN PROULX • DENIS PROULX • SIMON PROULX • LUC PROULX • SYLVAIN PROULX • CHANTALE PROULX • PIERRE PROULX • BRUCE PROULX • MARC PROULX • RONALD PROULX • PIERRE PROVENCAL • MONIQUE PROVENCAL • ALAIN P
ALAIN PROVENCHER • RICHARD PROVENCHER • BRUNO PROVENCHER • GUY PROVOST • MARCEL PROVOST • ROBERT PROVOST • ROGER PROVOST • JEAN MARIE CLAUDE PROVOST • PATRICK PRUCHA • PAUL PRUD'HOMME • JEAN PRUD'HOMME • MAXIME PRUD'HOMME • ALAIN PRUNEAU • ROBE
PAUL PRYSKY • NICOLAS PSYCHARIS • SYLVAIN PULFORD • PING YI PUN • ALAN JAMES PURDY • RICHARD PURDY • RAJINDER SIN PURI • AMRIK SINGH PURI • LESLAW PURKHARDT • JASMINE QUALMANN • ERIC QUEENTON • GREGORY QUENNEVILLE • CHARLES R QUENNEVILLE • KEN QUENNEVILLE • LAURENT QUENNEVILLE • GIANFRA
PIERRE QUESNEL • YVES QUESNEL • GHISLAINE QUEVILLON-LEPAGE • PAUL QUIDOZ • RICHARD QUIGLEY • ANDRE QUILLIAN • MICHAEL QUINN • EDWARD QUINN • RICHARD QUINTAL • REAL QUIRION • PIERRE RACETTE • STEPHANE RACETTE VILLENEUVE • SYLVIE RACETTE • SERGE RACICOT • MICHELLE RACINE • A
RICHARD RAINVILLE • CHANTAL RAJOTTE • JEAN MARIE RAKOTOMANANY • HAROLD RAMDIAL • ARGIMIRO RAMIREZ • ANIL RANADE • VIJAYA RANADE • ORAGOLJUB RANCIC • ALAIN RANCOURT • CAROLE RANDOLL • LUCIE RANGER • TIMOTHY JOHN RAPLEY • ILDA RAPOSO • ABDI RASHIDI • MARCO RASPA • COSTA
DENISE RATELLE • JEANNINE RATELLE • CLAUDE RATELLE • PATRICE RAVARY • PETER JOHN RAWLINGS • PETER RAWLINSON • NANCY RAYMOND • PAULINE RAYMOND • JEAN CLAUDE RAYMOND • JEAN CLAUDE RAYMOND • MICHEL RAYMOND • ALAIN RAYMOND • NELSON RAYMOND • DANIEL RAYMOND • LY
JOHANNE RAYMOND • FRANCOIS RAYNAULT • ANTHONY READ • MOHAMED READ • ALFONSO REDA • VINTHA REDDY • SURJIT REEHAL • AHMED REGAGUI • JACQUES REGIMBALD • HUBERT REGIS • PATRICK REGNIER • FRANCES REHEL • GARY REHEL • MOHAMMAD REHMAN • JOSEF REICH • JOHN REID • ROBERT REID • JOHN REID •
LAWRENCE REID • HANS REILING • MICHELINE REIMBOLD • DAVID REIST • JACQUES REMILLARD • FRANCOIS REMILLARD • WALTER REMINGTON • YVES REMY • GILLES RENAUD • MARIO RENAUD • NORMA RENAUD • MARC ANTOINE RENAUD • GUY RENAUD • MARTIN RENAUD • STEPHANE RENAUD • FRANCOIS RENAUD • DOMIN
FRANCOIS RENAUD • DENIS RENE • DAVID RENQUINHA • ANDRE RENZO • ANTONIO RESTIERI • LEONARDO RESTIERI • CHERYL REY • SERGE REZJUKOW • CHRISTIAN RHEAULT • MARC RHEAUME • DENIS RHEAUME • BENOIT RHEAUME • PATRICK RHEAUME • KEITH JAMES RHODES • JOSE ANTONIO RIBEIRO • FERNANDO RIBIERO • RO
EDWARD RICARD • ANTONIO RICCIARDI • REMO RICCIARDI • ANTONIO RICCIARDI • JEAN PIERRE RICHARD • MAURICE RICHARD • JOSEPH ANDRE RICHARD • YVON RICHARD • SYLVAIN RICHARD • YVES RICHARD • STEPHANE RICHARD • GAETAN RICHARD • YANICK RICHARD • DOMINIQUE RICHARD • JEAN RICHARD • RO
• MICHELINE RICHARD • DALE RICHARDSON • GUY RICHARDSON • PIERRE RICHELIEU • ALAIN RICHER • FERNAND J RICHER • SYLVAIN RICHER • PATRICK RICHER • MANON RICHER • DANIEL RICHER • ALAIN RICHER • SERGE RICHER • PIERRE RICHARD RIDYARD • KONRAD JR RIECK • LARRY GORDON RIEGERT • MAF
• DENIS RIENDEAU • STEPHEN RIGARLSFORD • GAETANO RIGATUSO • ROBERT RIGLER • MENNATO RINALDI • MARC RINFRET • MARCELIN RINGUETTE • MICHELLE RIOPEL • LUCIE RIOPEL • ANTONIO RIOS • STEPHANE RIOUX • ISABELLE RIOUX • JEAN GUY RIOUX • REJEAN RIOUX • BERNARD RIOUX • GILLES RIOUX • FE
• DANIEL RIOUX • JEAN PAUL RIOUX • MAURICE RIOUX • ANDRE RIOUX • GYSLAINE RIOUX • YVES RIOUX • SOPHIE RIOUX • DANIEL RIOUX • JEAN ALLAIN RIOUX • MICHEL RITCHIE • GORDON RITCHIE • BERND RITTER • INGEBORG RITTWEILER • BENOIT RIVARD • ISABELLE RIVARD • C
DOMINIQUE RIVEST • SYLVAIN RIVEST • ROGER RIVET • GILBERTE RIVIERE LAURENDEAU • DOUGLAS RIXEN • STEFANOS RIZAKIS • JAMES ROBB • ANDREW ROBB • JEAN PIERRE ROBERGE • FERNAND ROBERGE • MICHELINE ROBERGE • YVES ROBERGE • SERGE ROBERGE • CLAUDE ROBERGE • DANIEL ROBERGE • SYLVAIN ROBERT • S
• RICHARD ROBERT • MARCEL ROBERT • RICHARD ROBERT • SERGE ROBERT • STEPHANE ROBERT • NORMAND ROBERT • CLAUDETTE ROBERT • PHILIPPE ROBERT • RENALD ROBERT • LUCIE ROBERT • LYNE ROBERT • BENOIT ROBERT • MICHEL ROBERTS • MADELEINE ROBERTS • DIANE ROBERTSON • DANIEL ROBERTSON • DAN'T
LOUISE ROBICHAUD • CHRISTIAN ROBICHAUD • LEON ROBICHAUD • DENIS ROBICHAUD • DANIEL ROBICHAUD • MICHEL ROBICHAUD • ALAIN ROBICHAUD • REAL ROBIDAS • SERGE ROBIDOUX • CLAUDE ROBILLARD • MICHEL ROBILLARD • SERGE ROBILLARD • JEAN CLAUDE ROBIN • SYLVIE ROBIN • JEAN ROBINEAU • ALAN ROBINS • PADI
JEFFREY ROBINSON • DAVID ROBINSON • BRUCE ROBINSON • DENNIS ROBINSON • REJEAN ROBITAILLE • GASTON ROBITAILLE • CAROL ROBITAILLE • PIERRE ROBITAILLE • ANDRE ROBITAILLE • LUC ROBITAILLE • NANCY ROBITAILLE • JEAN GUY ROBITAILLE • ETIENNE ROBY • CLAUDE ROCH • CHARLI
NADIA ROCHEFORT • GILLES ROCHEFORT • CLAUDE ROCHELEAU • PATRICK ROCHELEAU • CHRISTOPHER ROCHFORT • NORMAND ROCHON • GILLES ROCHON • MICHEL ROCHON • JEAN MARC ROCHON • JAMES ROCKS • ROY RODD • MIRIAM RODGERS • DANNY RODIER • DANIEL RODRIGUE • MICHEL
JEAN RODRIGUE • ANDRE RODRIGUE • EDDY RODRIGUE • LINDA RODRIGUES • JOHN RODRIGUES • PEDRO RODRIGUES • CARLOS RODRIGUES • DEBBIE RODRIGUES • HUMBERTO RODRIGUEZ • WILLIAM MARK ROE • RONALD ROEBUCK • MARC ROEGIERS • GILLES ROGER • MARC ROGER • FRANK ROGERS • SONIA ROIREAU • NATH
JEAN ROLLAND • RAYMOND ROLLAND • VALERIE ROMAGNINO • FRED ROMANAVSKAS • JOHN ROMANOWSKI • ANGELA ROMBERGDESLAURIERS • STEPHEN ROMPALA • JEAN JACQUES RONDEAU • ALAIN RONDEAU • SYLVAIN RONDEAU • DANIEL RONDEAU • NANCY ROONEY • SARWAN SINGH ROOPRAI • RAYMOND ROOSE
• ROBERTO ROSAURI • ALAIN ROSE • STANLEY ROSE • CASSANDRA ROSE • BRIAN ROSE • RONALD ROSE • LORI ROSS • JAMES ROSS • LOUISE ROSS • STEVE ROSS • ANDRE ROSSELIT • DAVID ROSSI • JACKIE ROSSIGNOL • HELEN ROSSY • BILL ROTH • JOCELYN ROUILLARD • ALAIN ROULEAU • GUY ROULEAU • GISELE ROULEAU • NATH
PIERRE ROULIER • RICHARD ROUSSEAU • DANIEL ROUSSEAU • ALAIN ROUSSEAU • MARTIN ROUSSEAU • LOUISE ROUSSEAU • SEBASTIEN ROUSSEAU • MARTIN ROUSSEAU • CLAUDE ROUSSEAU • GINETTE ROUSSEAU • CLEMENT ROUSSEAU • MICHELE ROUSSEAU MACELLLAN • JEAN ROUSSEL • SE
ROGER ROUSSY • YVES ROUTHIER • IAN ROWAN • JOHANNE ROWAN • MARC ROWAN • ROBERT ROWDEN • INGRID ROWLAND • FRANK ROY • CLAUDE ROY • ERIC ROY • CARMEN ROY • BRUNO ROY • ANDRE ROY • LYNDA ROY • LOUIS ROY • ADRIEN ROY • RENE ROY • JACQUES ROY • DANIEL ROY • MICHELYNE ROY • REJEAN ROY •
CHRISTIAN ROY • JEAN MARC ROY • ANDREW ROY • RONALD ROY • DENIS ROY • DENIS ROY • CHRISTIAN ROY • MAURICE ROY • PRIYA ROY • FRANCOIS ROY • MICHEL ROY • RENE ROY • STEPHANE ROY • RAYMOND ROY • ROBERT ROY • NYNON ROY • NICOLE ROY • SUZANNE ROY • MARC ANDRE ROY •
SYLVAIN ROY • PIERRE ROY • AURELLE ROY • ANDRE ROY • ANDRE ROY • MARC ANDRE ROY • CLAUDE ROY • MARTINE ROY • MARC PATRICK ROY • ALAIN ROY • MONIQUE ROY • MARC ANDRE ROY • PETER ROY • PIERRE ROY • MARIO ROY • CLAUDE ROY • STEPHANE ROY • DANIEL ROYAL • RICHARD ROYER • INGRI
JEFFREY RUCK • PATRICE RUDOLPH • JACQUES RUDOLPH • SERGE RUEST • MICHEL RUEST • JACQUES RUEST • WILLIAM RUSSELL • GEORGE RUSTINSKY • MARTIN RUTA • ROY RUTLEDGE • SERGE RYAN • MICHEL SAAD • SALIM SAATI • BASSAM SABBAGH • REAL SABOURIN • YVAN SABOURIN • JEAN SABOURIN • JEANNINE SABOURIN • LY
• STEPHANE SABOURIN • SERGE SABOURIN • RENE SABOURIN • DOMINIC SABOURIN • HANY SADEK • GURDIAL SADERA • HAITHAM SAFADI • PAUL SAGALA • SYLVIE SAGALA • ALDO SAGRAFENA • PATRICK SAINDON • J FRANCOIS SAINDON • CHARALBOS SAINIS • GILLES SAINTONGE • ANDREW SAKAMOTO • STEVE SAKOULAS • ELIE SALAME •
• GINO SALERNO • LUIS ANTONIO SALGUEIRO • CAMELIA SALOMON • MOHAMMAD SAMI MALICK • PHILIP SAMOSZEWSKI • MARTINE SAMRAY • RICHARD SAMSON • GILLES SAMSON • ALAIN SAMSON • DANIELLE SAMUEL • SAMUEL SAMVELIAN • BETTY-ANN SANCASTER • IVY SANCASTER CLAYTON • GREGORIO SANCHEZ • MICHAEL
MARKHAM SANDULAK • STEPHANE SANGLADE • JEFF SANSOME • FRANCIS SANSOUCY • ANTHONY SANTAGATA • STEPHANE SANTERRE • SYLVAIN SANTERRE • LEONARDO SANTILLAN • DOMINIC SANTINI • FRANCOISE SANTINI • MARCO SANTORO • ANTONINO SANTOS • NICOLAS SARDANO • JOHN SARIK • JEAN FRANCOI SARRAZIN • PAL
PAUL SARRAZIN • CHANTAL SARRAZIN • EDOUARD SARRIA • MARGARETA SASARMAN • ANDRE JR SASSEVILLE • VIRAPHANH SATTARATN • CLAUDE SAULAIS • SYLVAIN SAUVAGEAU • DOMINIQUE SAUVE • ANDRE SAUVE • MARC SAUVE • MICHEL SAULT • SANTANAH • SAUVE LEDOUX • SERGE SAVAGE • SOPHIE SAVARD • GA
JACQUES SAVARD • MICHEL SAVARD • JEAN SAVARD • DIANE SAVARD BRASSARD • GUY SAVIGNAC • GEORGES SAVIGNAC • RENE SAVIGNAC • VINCENZO SAVOIA • ANDRE SAVOIE • LEOPOLD SAVOIE • JOCELYN SAVOIE • HARRY HAMID SAYAN • KHAMMY SAYASEN • FRANCINE SAYEGH • VINCENT SCARAPICCHIA • ALEXANDER SCARLAT • FRAN
GIULIO SCAVELLA • CONCETTA SCERBO • PANAYOTIS SCORDAS • CLIVE SCOTT • JOHN SCOTT • RICARDO SCOTT • SHEENA SCOTT • PIERRE SCOTTI • KEVIN SCULLY • JOSEPH SDRAULIG • JEAN FRANCOI SEGUIN • SERGE SEGUIN • GERALD SEGUIN • ANDRE SEGUIN • DONALD SEGUIN • JEAN PIERRE SEGUIN • MARC SEGUIN •
JEAN SEGUIN • GUYLAINE SEGUIN • RONALD-JACK SELF • YAOVI SEMEGLO • LUIGI SEMENTILLI • MARINA SEMENTILLI • TONY SENAY • VALERIE SENAY • FRANCINE SENECAL • STEPHANE SENECAL • DENIS SENECAL • NORMAND SENECAL • ALAIN SENES • MEHRZAD SEPASI • KHALID SEPAHI • SE
• JEAN SERVAIS • SYLVAIN SERVANT • ROBERT SETO • BERNARD SEVIGNY • PIERRE SEVIGNY • NICOLE SEVIGNY • DANIEL SEYER • SALIM SFEIR • ANNE SHAHBAZIAN • MUSTAFA SHAIKH • AMANATULLAH SHAIKH • NICHOLAS SHARBER • RAM-KRISHAN SHARMA • DEAN SHARP • GRANT SHAW • RICHARD SHAW • ZAHIR SHEIKH • RANDALL G
WEI SHEN • HALIM SHENOUDA • HERZEL SHLOMO • IAN SHOONER • LARRY SHORKEY • RIMAN SHUKAYR • SISALEUM SIBOUNHEUANG • PETER SIBSTRIS • VLADIMIR SIDORENKO • RYSZARD SIERADZAN • MEE LEEN SIEW YAN YU • ANDREA SIGOUIN • JACQUES SIGOUIN • RUI LAUREANO SILVA • NANCY SILVERWOOD • GUY SIMARD •
BERTRAND SIMARD • SYLVIE SIMARD • ANDRE SIMARD • J FRANCOIS SIMARD • MICHEL SIMARD • PIERRE SIMEONE • GOJKO SIMIC • DIANE SIMON • GERARD SIMON • WOLFGANG SIMON • GUYLAINE SIMONEAU • YVES SIMONEAU • MICHAEL SIMONS • HERMANN SIMONS • PETER SIMPSON • NICOLE SINCLAIR ROY • S
BHUPINDER SINGH • BALBIR SINGH • ANGELO SINICROPI • RICHARD SIOUFI • PIERRE SIROIS • PIERRE SIROIS • DENIS SIROIS • ROGER SIRY • PETER SISLIAN • ANNETTE SIVAK • UMA SIVASWAMY • GIOVANNI SIVILLA • BERNARD SIXDENIER • BOHDAN SKARZYNSKI • JEFF SKLAR • JOHN SKOKOS • DANIEL SKORUPINSKI • LYNNE
MICHAEL SKULSKYJ • CHRISTOPHER SLATER • ROBERT SLINGER • MICHEL SLIVA • ROBERT C SLOVICK • YANNIC SMALLWOOD • PAUL EMILE SMALLWOOD • ANDRE SMITH • STEVE SMITH • LAWRENCE SMITH • J ALFRED SMITH • JOHN KENNETH SMITH • MARTYN SMITH • JAMES H SMITH • WILLIAM SMITH • DAVID J D SMITH • LYNN B
• JAMES SMITH • MICHAEL SMITH • WAYNE SAMUEL SMITH • RANDY SMITH • ELIZABETH SMITH BORDELEAU • LAURIE SMITHERS • WILLIAM SMYTH • CHARLES SOBEY • VINCENT SOCCIO • CHRISTOS SOFIANOS • NICOLAS SOKOLOFF • JOANNE SOLARI • DEMETRIO SOLE • RICARDO SOLE • VINCE SOLLAZZO • CORNELIA SOLOMON • MIG
DANIEL SOREL • MICHEL SORETTE • ANDRE SOTO • JUAN PABLO SOTO • EDUARDO SOTO • ROBERT SOUBYRAN • HERBERT SOUKUP • FRANCOIS SOULIERES • AMINE SOUNDARDJEE • JEAN LOUIS SOURIAC • VICTORIA SOUROUZIAN • PAUL SOUSA • ARAM SOUVADJIAN • LEON JERZY SOWA • MARIA SPADA • ANTHONY
AARON SPECTOR • JEAN PIERRE SPINELLI • VINCENZO SPOSATO • EUGENIO SPOSATO • KELLY SPRULES • EDWARD SQUATCH • EDWARD SQUIRES • JACQUES ST AMAND • LUC ST AMANT • SOPHIE ST AMOUR • SYLVAIN ST AMOUR • FERNAND ST ARNAULD • CHRISTIAN ST AUBIN • MICHEL ST CYR • RENE ST CYR • SYLVAIN ST CYR • NA
MICHEL ST DENIS • GILLES ST DENIS • CLAUDE ST DENIS • MICHELE ST GELAIS • GAETAN ST GELAIS • CHRISTIAN ST GELAIS • DANIEL ST GELAIS • JEAN ST GEORGES • BRUNO ST GEORGES • CLAUDE ST GERMAIN • NORMAND ST GERMAIN • CARL ST HILAIRE • CHANTAL ST HILAIRE • PIERRE ST HILAIRE • MADELE
GERARD ST HILAIRE • GILLES ST JACQUES • DANIEL ST JACQUES • BENOIT ST JAMES • ROBERT ST JEAN • MARCEL ST JEAN • ROGER ST JEAN • PHILIPPE ST JEAN • FRANCOIS ST JEAN • ROUVIO ST JEAN • SYLVAIN ST LAURENT • ANDRE ST LAURENT • SERGE ST LAURENT • MICHEL ST LAURENT • ROBERT ST LAURENT • A
REMY ST MARTIN • STEPHANE ST MICHEL • MARC ST ONGE • STEPHANY ST ONGE • PIERRE ST ONGE • JEAN ST ONGE • BERTRAND ST ONGE • JEAN-MARIE ST PIERRE • PIERRE ST PIERRE • LISANE ST PIERRE • ROBERT ST PIERRE • SYLVAIN ST PIERRE •
NORBERT ST PIERRE • ALAIN ST PIERRE • ALAIN ST PIERRE • ROBERT ST PIERRE • STEEVE ST PIERRE • MARIO ST JEAN • JEAN-MARTIN • CAROLE STABILE • LEONID STACHTCHENKO • JERZY STADNIK • PAUL STAFIEJ • JOHN STAMATELOS • DONALD L STANIFORTH • MICH
PIERRE STANKEVIC • ANTHONY STANTON • TREVOR STANTON • FRANK STARKIE • MICHAEL STASKOW • ALAN STATHAM • ROSAIRE STE MARIE • PIERRE STE MARIE • GUY STE MARIE • KENNETH STEEN • PETER STEFAS • KRZYSZTOF STELMASZCZYK • DONALD STEPHEN • GAIL STEPHEN • CAROL STEPHENS • ALLAN
WILSON STEVENSON • DAWSON STEVENSON • FRANK STEWART • CHANTAL STEWART • KEVIN STEWART • TODD STEWART • JOHN STEWART • CATHERINE STOCK • HAROLD STOCKER • ANTHONY CHAR STOCKS • WILLIAM STOKER • KEVIN STOKOE • GEORGE STOLZENBACH • PETER STOYEL • MARTIN STROTMANN • ROBERT STRUBEL • H
• FRASER STUART • ANDREW STUBBS • ANA STULZ • MARTIN STUTZ • PHILIP STUTZ • TOM SUDIA • MICHEL SULLIVAN • FERNAND SUPPA • JULES SUPPA • NIGEL SWETTENHAM • SUSAN SWOROWSKI • ALAIN SYLVESTRE • STEPHANE SYMONS • CLIFTON SYMONS • JOSEPH SZABO • SANDIE SZANISZLO • F
ROMAN SZYDLOWSKI • QUANG NHUT TA • ANITA TABCHARANI • ROMULO TABING • GEORGE TACHDJIAN • LUCIO TADDEO • ERIC TADDEO • BRIAN TAGG • RODNEY TAGGART • ABDULLAH TAIBI • SERGE TAILLEFER • JACQUES TAILLEFER • PAUL TAILLEFER • CAROL TAIT • GEORGE TAIT • BERTRAND TAIT • DEBRA LORI TAIT • RAFIK TAKVORIAN • ANDREW TALBO
• RITA TALBOT • DAVE TALBOT • MICHEL TAMBEAU • GEORGES J-P TAMBLINI • MOURAD TAMIMOUNT • BRIAN-PAUL TANG • JOHN TANGREDI • PAUL TANGUAY • VINCENT TANGUAY • LEOPOLD TANGUAY • MICHEL TANGUAY • CLINTON TANNER • RICHARD TAPIN • MARK TARCZYNSKI •
ANNE MARIE TARDIF • JEAN ROBERT TARDIF • DIANE TARDIF • RAYMOND TARDIF • DENISE TARDIF • SYLVAIN TARDIF • JACQUES TARDY • MARY TARTAGLIA • STEPHANE TARTE • GILLES TASSE • YVON TASSE • FERNAND TASSE • MARC TASSONE • VISWANATH TATA • DAVID TAUNTON • EMILIO TAUNISI • RA
RODNEY TAYLOR • JOHN TAYLOR • DAWN TAYLOR • DEREK TAYLOR • DAVID TAYLOR • ANDREW TAYLOR • JEAN TCHAMOURIAN • KEVOR TCHOLKAYAN • YI TEA • CHARLES TEAL • MARIO TEASDALE • THOMAS TELHEIRO • PAUL TELLIER • CATHERINE TELLIER • LINA TELLIER • MICHEL TELLIER • BORIS TEMCHENKO • JACQUES TENDLAND • BF
RICHARD TEODORI • JEAN TEODORO • NORMAN TERRAULT • PIERRE JR TERRAULT • VICTOR TERREROS AGUILAR • JOSEPH TERRIGNO • DANIEL TESSIER • JOHANNE TESSIER • PIERRE TESSIER • JEAN CLAUDE TESSIER • FRANCIS TESSIER • BRUNO TESSIER • VIATEUR TESSIER • CHARLES TESSIER • G
RICHARD TETRAULT • MARTIN TETRAULT • LISE TETREAULT • GINETTE TETREAULT • ALBERT TEULERY • FATIH TEZOK • RICHARD THEBERGE • ROSAIRE THEBERGE • CLAUDE THEBERGE • MIKE PHIDEAS THEMELIS • MIKE THEOPHANIDES • WAYNE THEORET • DANIEL THEORET • JACQUES THEORET • STE
SUZANNE THEORET • GILLES THEORET • SERGE THERIAULT • JEFFREY THERIAULT • CAROL THERIAULT • JEAN FRANCOI THERIAULT • SYLVAIN THERIAULT • LUCIE THERIAULT • YVES THERIAULT • ALAIN THERIAULT • PAUL THERIAULT • JEAN THERIAULT • ANDRE THERIAULT • MARTIN THERIAULT • MICHEL THERIEN • G
PIERRE THERRIAULT • NORMAND THERRIEN • LEOPOLD THERRIEN • CLAUDE THERRIEN • SYVE THERRIEN • GUY THERRIEN • FRANCOIS THERRIEN • CRAIG THIBADEAU • JEAN-PAUL THIBAULT • FRANCOIS THIBAULT • WILLIAM THIBAULT • FERNAND THIBAULT • LAURENT THIBAULT • L
MARC THIBAULT • PIERRE THIBAULT • MARC THIBAULT • JEAN FRANCOI THIBAULT • ALAIN THIBODEAU • JEAN FRANCOI THIBODEAU • JEAN GUY THIBODEAU • RONALD THIBODEAU • GILLES THIBODEAU • BENOIT THIBODEAU • RIO THIBODEAU • JENNIFER THIELE • SUZANNE THIFAULT • BRIGITTE THIFAULT • DANIE
ROGER THION MING • SAMYONG THIRAKUL • CLAUDE THIVIERGE • JOEL THIVIERGE • DANIEL THIVIERGE • BRUCE THOMAS • KEITH THOMAS • JEAN CHRISTO THOMAS • DON THOMPSON • WILLIAM THOMPSON • KIMBERLY THOMSON • GABRIEL THOUIN • MARTIN THUOT • STEPHEN THURSTON • TERRY TIBBERT • ROBERT TILLIN • GEOR
GIOVANNI TIMEO • DAVID TIMMIS • TROY TIMPERLEY • PETER TO • CAN THAM TO • CAN VY TO • PATRICK TOBIN • OLIVERA TODOROVIC • MOHAMED ALI TOHAMY • FLAVIO TOICH • BRIAN TOKAI • ANDY TOM • MONICA TOM • RAYMOND TOM • PETER TOMCHISHEN • GAETAN CLAUDE TOMPKINS • SARBJIT SING TOOR • RICHARD TOPHAM • LOU
VIKEN TORIKIAN • HENRY TOROSSIAN • NICOLA TOTARELLA • GORDON TOTTLE • DEBORAH TOTTLE • RENE TOUCHETTE • YVES TOUCHETTE • WILBUR GUY TOUCHIE • MADELEINE TOUGAS • GAETAN TOUPIN • JEAN TOURANGEAU • MARYSE TOURIGNY • DENIS TOUSSAINT • JEAN TOUSSIGNANT • MARC TOUSIGNANT • GAETA
GILLES TOUSSAINT • JEAN CLAUDE TRACEY • CLAUDE TRACHY • MARIO TRACHY • STEPHANE TRAHAN • MICHEL TRAINOR • CHAU TRAN • HUU CHI TRAN • CHAN MINH TRAN • VAN TRAN • YEN TRAN • DAO VAN TRAN • LIEM TRAN • KHAI TRAN DINH • TUYEN HAO TRAN THI • MARC TRAVERS • VICTOR TREGEAR • M
ERIC TREMBLAY • YVES TREMBLAY • LUC TREMBLAY • ANGELE TREMBLAY • REJEAN TREMBLAY • JEAN FRANCOI TREMBLAY • DANIEL TREMBLAY • RONALD TREMBLAY • BRUNO TREMBLAY • PAUL TREMBLAY • MARTIN TREMBLAY • PIERRE TREMBLAY • RICHARD TREMBLAY • LOUISE TREMBLAY • D
PIERRE TREMBLAY • RICHARD TREMBLAY • FRANCOIS TREMBLAY • ARTHUR TREMBLAY • PIERRE TREMBLAY • GRATIEN TREMBLAY • ROBERT TREMBLAY • JEAN TREMBLAY • NATHALIE TREMBLAY • ANDRE TREMBLAY • GILLES TREMBLAY • MARIO TREMBLAY • CLAUDE TREMBLAY • JULIE TREMBLAY CLOUTIER • JOCELYNE TREMBLAY TURGEON • MARTIN TREMPE • VI
• GILLES TREPANIER • FRANCIS TREPANIER • LORRAINE TREPANIER • FRANK TREVIS • BENOIT TREVISAN • CATHERINE TRICKEY • CARLOS GUY TRUDEAU • MY TRUNG TRINH • NGHIA PHUONG TRINH • JEAN CLAUDE TRITTEN • ANTHONY TRIVISONNO • STEVEN TROCH • CLAUDINE TROTTIER • DANIEL TROTTIER • JACQUE
STEPHANE TRUDEL • TUAN HUNG TRUONG • CONG DUONG TRUONG • GEORGE TSANTRIZOS • NICHOLAS TSANTRIZOS • PETER TSANTRIZOS • TAI GI TSE • CARMINE TUCCERI LIMITO • KEVIN TUCKER • ANDRE TUNE • J ROBERSON TUNON • SYLVAIN TURCOTTE • JEAN GUY TURGEON • SYLVAIN TURGEON • JULIEN TURCOTTE • CLAUDE TURCOTTE • SYLV
GILLES TURCOTTE • PAUL TURCOTTE • GEORGES TURCOTTE • FERNAND TURCOTTE • PIERRE TURCOTTE • SIMON TURCOTTE • ALAIN TURCOTTE • MARTIN TURCOTTE • E FAUBLE TURGEON • JACQUES TURGEON • SYLVAIN TURGEON • GUY TURGEON • MARC TURGY DESTUL • FRED TURMEL • ERIC TURMEL • EDDY TURNER •
• CAROLYNE TURNER • GILLES TURNER • BENOIT TURNER • GREGOIRE TURSKI • LOUIS TYE • LUCIE TYE • RICHARD TYRRELL • JOSEPHINE TYRRELL • NICK TZAFERIS • DANTEL UBALDI • BRION UGOLINI • ROMAN UNZ JR • GORDON UNSWORTH • WILLIAM UPTON • GINETTE URBAIN • ADRIAN VACANT • VICTOR VACANCIU • V
MAXIME VACHON • GERARD VACHON • ALAIN VACHON • ANDRE VACHON • CLAUDE VACHON • GERMAIN VACHON • CAMIL VACHON • RICHARD VACHON • MONIK VADEBONCOEUR • GIUSEPPE VAIANA • JEAN VAILLANCOURT • MARIE JOSEE VAILLANCOURT • JEAN VAILLANCOURT • V